Adventure Guide
to

THE HIGH SOUTHWEST

Adventure Guide
to

THE HIGH
SOUTHWEST

Steve Cohen

HUNTER
PUBLISHING INC

Hunter Publishing, Inc.
300 Raritan Center Parkway
Edison NJ 08818
(908) 225 1900   Fax (908) 417 0482

ISBN 1-55650-633-3

Maps by Joyce Huber, *Photographics*
Cover Photo: Kane Spring Canyon UT
Jenny Hager, *Adventure Photo*

Contents

Introduction

There may be no greater concentration of adventurous things to do on a year-round basis than in the nearly mythic region we are calling the High Southwest. This enormous area stretches over the borders of four western states and includes eight National Parks, numerous National Monuments, tribal and state parks, national forests, wilderness areas, and millions of additional acres of public lands accessible for hiking, biking, skiing, rafting, fishing, and much more.

We call it the High Southwest for several reasons. The region encompasses much of an expansive elevated tableland known as the Colorado Plateau as well as portions of the western slope of the Rocky Mountains, all situated far above sea level. The preponderance of rugged, virtually primeval terrain lends itself naturally to high adventure. And furthermore, the territory has long been pre-eminent in the pantheon of spiritual places to the native peoples who were the first to settle here, and whose ancient mysteries and modern presence are keenly felt today. The High Southwest shelters many secrets yet to be explored.

If you want to experience the special nature of this exceptional area, to learn new things about unusual places, and to get out and do things, this book is for you. It provides all the nuts and bolts information you need to plan and accomplish an informed trip, as well as specific, concise information on a variety of adventurous things to do, of which there are many.

Ride a horse for a day, raft through rapids the next. Climb mountains for a week and know all the best fishing spots in advance. Ski at world-class resorts or to backcountry huts. Climb through ancient Indian ruins. Steer a jeep or a mountain bike over the Continental Divide. Steer a steer over hill and dale on a modern-day cattle drive. Soar above it all in a glider, a balloon, or take a scenic motorized flight. Trek through labyrinthine canyon country with a llama to carry your gear. Snuggle under a blanket of stars while a draft horse pulls your sleigh through the snow. Dip a toe into thermal hot springs. Bargain at a trading post. Bid at an Indian rug auction. Paddle a canoe or cruise on a houseboat.

There's plenty to do, from easy ventures to more challenging fare. It's enough to fill vacations for years, and no surprise that many people return again and again.

This adventurous conception of the High Southwest bypasses large metropolitan areas. There is no big city in the High Southwest. The area encompasses the fabled Four Corners–where **New Mexico, Colorado, Utah,** and **Arizona** meet. Beyond, it extends westward across unparalleled natural lands in Utah's Canyon Country to the Grand Canyon, Flagstaff, the largest city along this route, and little Sedona, an area packing a powerful combination punch of extraordinary red rock scenery and visitor services to match.

Throughout, the epic workings of nature's geology, flora, and fauna are far more likely to be on display than the work of man, although you will encounter both on the ski slopes and bike trails in the 14,000-foot peaks of Colorado's **San Juan Mountains,** through Indian country around Colorado's **Mesa Verde National Park,** New Mexico's **Chaco Canyon National Historic Park,** Arizona's **Canyon de Chelly National Monument,** and Utah's **Monument Valley Navajo Tribal Park.** The area includes the entire **Navajo Nation**– 17,000,000 acres sprawling over three states and home to the largest American Indian tribe, as well as the tiny, indomitable **Hopi Reservation.** Hopiland fills only 631,000 acres and is surrounded on all sides by the vastly larger Navajo reservation, yet it retains its own distinctive cultural identity.

The High Southwest contains the modern mountain biking meccas of **Durango,** Colorado, and **Moab,** Utah. It also contains the lumbering century-old **Durango-Silverton Narrow Gauge Railroad.** Trendy, celebrity-studded, and stunningly situated **Telluride,** Colorado is included, an old mining town gone uptown and expected to become the state's next glittery Aspen. Its lower key neighbor, **Ouray,** known for its Victorian character, scenic locale, challenging jeep trails, and abundant hot springs is also found here. And there is much, much more, encompassing Utah's **Arches** and **Canyonlands National Parks,** little-known **Capitol Reef National Park,** better-known **Bryce** and **Zion National Parks,** the **San Juan** and **Colorado Rivers** flowing into **Lake Powell,** the world's second largest man-made body of water, and–best known of all–the **Grand Canyon** itself.

This is to say nothing about the expansive spaces between these landmarks, slickrock trails, beautiful multi-colored tiered sandstone formations, snow peaks above pristine alpine lakes, and cactus-studded deserts. There are volcano fields you can scale, a petrified wood forest (it's a National Park), and towering natural arches and bridges formed over millions of years by the effects of wind and water on stone. Some of the rocks you can see at the bottom of the Grand Canyon are a billion years old and you can touch them from a raft that is floating on waters powered by last season's melting snow.

It's a lot of ground to cover, so you need careful plans to manage the great distances involved and still have time to do the adventurous things you want to do. This adventure guide gets right down to the logistics of having fun by showing you how to connect with a multitude of pleasures in this wondrous part of the world. There's a lot of varied terrain to choose from and little doubt that any part of the High Southwest will easily justify itself to you.

Geography & History

The long-isolated Southwest has become incredibly popular in the last few years. It evokes visions of Indians and cowboys, snow-capped peaks, buttes and mesas stalked by howling coyotes, cattle drives, wild rivers, and long sunsets, all design elements in current fashion, and the list goes on. The secret is that the Southwest has always been in fashion to those in the know about wide open spaces beneath skies so clear they lend a brightness to the air.

The earliest nomads probably wandered down from Canada and the Bering Land Bridge, settling over time into the first stable populations. Their descendants were the ancient and now extinct Anasazi Indians whose skillfully constructed and mysteriously abandoned communities are the source of many of today's ruins. Other descendants were the Hopi Indians, whose oldest inhabited dwellings look a lot like ruins.

The Spanish came upon Navajos and other modern tribes when they explored the Southwest in the 16th century searching for gold. Only in the last 150 years has the area experienced modern civilization. First came gold-, silver-, or copper-miners, then ranchers, cowboys, and business people who created small towns–many of which stayed small or became smaller.

Most of the mines are closed but ranching and the cowboy arts are still widely practiced on vast, open rangelands. The rugged contours of Southwestern geography haven't changed much. The High Southwest still resists massive development although once-inhospitable places are today's pleasure spots. Towns are still few and far between but they're here. Confronting modern realities, these towns have survived by mining a mother lode of tourism dollars out of a hard land that has not been dominated by man.

The enormity of the High Southwest gives you the space that cannot be found in many urban lives. And even if you are accustomed to the outdoors, there's no place else where you can find so many diverse geological, historical, cultural, and just plain drop-dead beautiful features. It's a vast canvas on which to paint your own adventure.

In today's Southwest the pickup truck is the vehicle of choice for ranchers. Horses continue to serve cowboys who really do wear pointy-toed boots, broad-brimmed hats or, increasingly, baseball caps advertising farm equipment. Dusty jeans and shirts with pearl snaps identify the cowboy-style, a pervasive presence here. Except for ceremonial occasions most Indians wear clothing that looks a lot like cowboy duds.

The unlikely blending of three cultures–Indian, Hispanic, and Anglo–in a still remote, long-isolated environment far from any urban population centers, has combined with various natural attributes of mountains, rivers, and deserts, to produce a unique status quo.

Accommodations range from campgrounds and dude ranches–which offer as much time on horseback as you can handle–to deluxe resorts.

Dining out in the boonies here is mostly unsophisticated–not the chi-chi grilled avocado and mango salsa one finds in competitive Santa Fe–but corn dogs and chile, sloppy Joe's and salad bars. There are several better restaurants widely spaced over the High Southwest's 100,000 or so square miles.

As for entertainment you may be content to gaze at night skies filled with stars. But there are stomping cowboy bars with free two-step lessons or Indian dances. Some of these are ceremonial and restricted to tribal members only while others are open for all to enjoy.

There is no shortage of ever-popular Indian jewelry offered by roadside vendors, trading posts, and galleries. What you'll find on sale ranges from cheap stuff to high-priced objects. Blankets, rugs, baskets, and pottery were once offered as simple trade goods but even they are pricey these days, reflecting their recent return to eminence in the halls of fashion.

Activities related to the epic, hard terrain and seasons draw the ski crowd in winter, bikers and river runners in spring. Campers and hikers arrive in summer, leaf peepers and hunters in fall. The High Southwest has been claimed by a young, dynamic, fun-loving crowd. You will see sun-tanned hikers and kayakers cruising along in expensive four-wheel-drives with bike or boat racks. Alongside will be cowboys and Indians riding the range on horseback or in battered pickups with gun racks.

Personal values aside, the land remains the dominant force here. Everybody needs to pay close attention to nature's power. Arid and expansive desertscapes characterize Arizona and New Mexico. Broad, arroyo-tracked flats stretch to a far horizon broken only by cacti, a rare mesquite tree, or prehistoric sea-bed rocks rising in wind and water-carved majesty, seeming to defy gravity itself. From Utah's canyon country through the Grand Canyon, the earth reveals deep cracks, dropping precariously to distant rivers. Buttes and mesas are nearby, striped in iron-tinged red and orange colors painted by geological epochs, with mountains, usually snow-capped, looming beyond.

Sometimes, at a quiet moment in a place far from the ordinary, ghosts of those long departed may even pay a visit.

You can go a long way out here without seeing another human being but you probably won't get far without finding evidence of deer, elk, rattlers, coyotes, eagles, ravens, turkey vultures, or hawks. Less frequently spotted are black bears, mountain lions, pronghorn antelope, and bighorn sheep.

The High Southwest was created over eons by the geological forces of volcanoes, wind, erosion, flowing water, and movements of geological plates inside the earth's crust. The result is sometimes phantasmagoric, as displayed by improbably-shaped sandstone towers, serpentine canyons, or brooding mountains crowned by massive thunderheads. Water, though sometimes scarce, remains a fashion power as it flows from the snowmelt of high mountains. The streams it forms nourish forests and the giant Colorado River system, which drains the 130,000-square-mile Colorado Plateau. Even in the driest deserts a turbulent, impetuous downpour can fill thirsty stream beds in a frightening instant. Sudden flash floods can carry away homes, trees, and cars, then subside as rapidly as they appeared, leaving only damp testimony to nature's dominance of the land.

Of course, many have tried to tame these elemental forces. The Southwest has managed to attract a long line of explorers and settlers. Indians constructed primitive cities and cultures 1,000 years ago with a sharp eye to the vagaries of nature, yet even this devout respect could not protect them from its omnipotent energy. Deserted structures—once dwellings and now ruins—pepper the area and attest to ancient conflicts with drought, crop failures, and ensuing famine. Dusty trails may be all that remain of once-productive grassland that was thoughtlessly overgrazed and is now reclaimed by the desert. Crumbling mine structures recall expended mineral resources and dreams.

Humans are neophytes here in the long view of geologic eras that have created the High Southwest. Artifacts discovered in southern New Mexico suggest prehistoric human habitation as far back as 10,000 years ago; the date would position these primitive New Mexicans among the earliest known residents of North America. Modern researchers believe that these nomadic hunter-gatherers were predecessors of the Anasazi, presumed to be the area's first settlers 1,500 years ago–coincident with the advent of agriculture and the farming of beans and corn (which became dietary staples). Around 500 years later, another nomadic strain of Athabascan Indians of Asian descent began its migration south through Canada. The earliest of these arrivals began filtering in 600 years ago–at just about the same time the Anasazi were abandoning their cities and disappearing into the sands of time. They are thought to be the ancestors of today's Navajos and Apaches, as well as several other tribes. The term Anasazi actually comes from the Navajo language. Various interpretations give the meaning as "the ancient enemies" or simply "the old ones." From these differing beginnings a variety of cultural conventions emerged, lending distinctive spice to today's Navajo, Hopi and other Native American communities.

Over a span of some 1,000 years the Anasazi constructed an elaborate, multi-storied city at Chaco Canyon, incredible, unassailable cliff dwellings at Mesa Verde, sophisticated square and circular towers at Hovenweep, named ruins at numerous other sites and innumerable hidden monuments. The tiny ruins tucked away at the bottom of 1,000-foot-tall cliffs at Canyon de Chelly are especially telling; Navajos farm the fertile bottomlands to this day. Their ruins infuse a sense of history and a little dose of mystery. The complexity of these ruins and their extraordinary durability in this rugged environment suggests collaborative living standards and a sophisticated sense of organization. Yet these cultures disappeared and no one is quite sure whether their demise was the result of drought and subsequent famine, warfare, or perhaps something else altogether. Archaeologists do believe that modern Pueblo Indian tribes are somehow descended from the Anasazi but the links are less than crystal clear and who begot whom is still pretty much anyone's guess. Chacoans probably drifted to the south and east, evolving into New Mexico's Pueblo cultures. Many believe the Hopi are directly related to the Mesa Verde Anasazi. But nobody knows for sure and the puzzle is a large part of the historic appeal of the High Southwest.

Around 40 miles from the Four Corners, at Mesa Verde National Park, are the most popular Anasazi ruins. Lesser-known but compelling ruins are found at New Mexico's Chaco Canyon National Historic Park, Hovenweep National Monument, which straddles the Colorado-Utah Border, Canyon de Chelly National Monument and Navajo National Monument, both in Arizona. Hundreds of other settings are included throughout this text.

In the mid-1500s Spanish conquistadors, flushed with success after the plundering of Mexico, moved north through Texas, Arizona, and New Mexico. Failing to find treasure, they still managed to sow the seeds of religious conversion, building fortified churches which grew into settlements. Ultimately they established administrative bureaucracies in concert with the Catholic church. These alliances continue to exert powerful cultural influences to this day.

The earliest Anglos were ambitious, mostly hunters or traders exploring the territory of Nuevo Mexico–made up of Arizona and New Mexico–after the Mexican War of Independence in 1825. A scant 23 years later the United States government purchased 530,000 acres of the High Southwest from Mexico, including to-day's New Mexico, Arizona, Utah, and part of Colorado. Twenty or so years later, after the Civil War, Anglo migration began in earnest. News of gold, silver, and copper discoveries encouraged prospectors. Shop keepers followed and word of the vast new region spread. By the 1880s the railroads had begun to lay tracks, signaling the beginning of the end of centuries of isolation in the High Southwest.

With the rise of Anglo culture, once the U.S. government recognized the value of this epic wilderness, Indian interests were ignored or violated, igniting conflicts that would be resolved after much strife and bloodshed. Eventually–around the same time the railroads chugged into towns like Durango and Telluride–ancestral territories that belonged to the Indians in the first place (or in some cases less desirable land substitutions) were returned to various tribes in the form of reservations. These enforced real estate selections cover a good deal of the physical and spiritual geography of the High Southwest today.

Centrally located as one of the major communities of the Four Corners is Durango, Colorado. It has a range of accommodations, 50 or so restaurants, and the famous, coal-fired, steam-powered, narrow gauge railroad that once carried miners to remote mines. Today it serves tourists, transporting riders through a mountain wilderness to the tiny, tenacious old mining town of Silverton. Silverton's mines are closed now, and it too caters mainly to tourists. Either town offers easy access to surrounding National Forests that provide attractive environments if you're looking to backpack, ride a bike or a horse, rock climb, or photograph wildlife in these mountainous natural lands.

To the south and west of Durango, the environment changes completely. Northwest New Mexico is mostly high desert, ranging into pine forested mountains along the Arizona border. To the west, convoluted canyons and river networks of Utah and northern Arizona rest atop the parched Colorado Plateau.

High Southwest

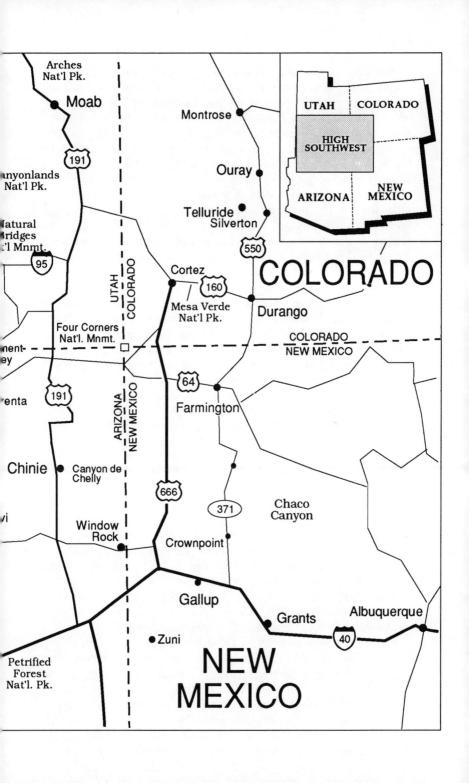

In southwest Colorado, pinyons and junipers yield to spruce and aspen as elevations increase north of Durango in the San Juan Range. Surprisingly to many people, the weather here is remarkably mild year-round, despite copious snowfall at high elevations. The mountains are always cooler than the deserts, but usually comfortably so, especially in summer when days are shirt-sleeve warm, while the heat leaves with the sun and a blanket is de rigueur for sleeping at night. As is common throughout the High Southwest, summer is the main tourist season in southwest Colorado, followed by the ski crowd in winter. Caution: Skiing through waist-deep soft powder in the high, dry air on a typical sunny winter day may be addictive. The sun always comes out after a storm, so skiers sans jackets by noon are another common sight.

Approaching the heart of the Four Corners near Mesa Verde, a new uniformity of sorts begins. Mountains fade into swells which yield to flats broken by monumental buttes and mesas. To the northwest the terrain varies further. Mountains reassert themselves in Utah's Abajo (Blue) and La Sal Mountains, rimmed by more tortured topography slotted by abrupt canyons. Here unfettered winds and raging waters of the Colorado River have created sculpted sandstone arches, towers, mesas, and scorched canyons on the Colorado Plateau. In late spring and summer temperatures seldom dip below the upper nineties. Winters can be vicious, wind-raked, and cold. They can also be less severe with more mud than snowpack.

Other parts of the Four Corners are also much the same as they were a century or a millennium ago. Monument Valley, which stretches across the Utah-Arizona border on the Navajo Reservation, is actually a Navajo Tribal Park with a lot of restrictions to access. Its famous buttes rising from the desert are certainly among the most photographed landscapes in all the High Southwest. A string of John Wayne movies in the 1940s and 1950s such as *Fort Apache* and *Stagecoach* made these vistas widely famous. It was director John Ford's favorite location and an overlook within the park has been named after the Hollywood legend. For more contemporary references just click on your TV. You're bound to see a commercial for a car or a soda that was filmed here.

Nature displays some of its most stunning sculpture in Utah's Canyon Country. At Lake Powell you can rent a houseboat for a day or a week of unhurried cruising through Glen Canyon and to the enormous stone span at Rainbow Bridge. West of Lake Powell and north of the Grand Canyon the multicolored turrets and stone monoliths of Bryce and Zion National Parks are as close to out-of-this-world as you are likely to find this side of the moon. If Bryce and Zion seem lunar then the red-hot and bone-dry canyons, along with the delicate, fascinating, and unlikely stone arches of Canyon-lands and Arches National Parks flanking the Colorado River, must resemble Mars. To give you an idea of the scale of this region there are three unconnected dead-end roads that lead to different parts of Canyonlands. The entrance to each route is separated by more than 100 miles.

Across southern Utah and Northern Arizona foliage becomes scarce as canyons deepen below desertscapes. Summer temperatures are fiercely hot all across the Navajo Nation and Hopiland to the Grand Canyon. They often top the century mark with brief respite in the high country around Flagstaff and Sedona's partly shaded Oak Creek Canyon. Famous for its red rocks, this canyon seems to hold a particular appeal to seekers of New-Age wisdom, crystal-gazers, vortex-hunters, and the like.

For these and others Northern Arizona offers impressive physical reality. Beyond Flagstaff the desert is not simply a flat expanse of sand but contains a variety of deep canyons, cliffs, and rock towers looming over 1,000 feet high. The Painted Desert and Petrified Forest National Park are virtual laboratories of prehistory. This amazing part of the state includes six life zones, ranging from lower desert to arctic/alpine, from saguaro cactus flats to the world's largest ponderosa pine forest. It also includes the Grand Canyon, deservedly considered one of the wonders of the world.

The Grand Canyon will always be a primary destination when visiting the High Southwest. It draws more people than any other Southwestern locale and few are disappointed by the mile-deep abyss. The scale of this extreme geography is both humbling and challenging. The commercially developed South Rim is really a small city with airfields and fast food restaurants. It can be reached most directly from Flagstaff or Williams, Arizona. Although it is only 10 miles as the crow flies across the canyon to the North Rim, driving is actually a 200-mile adventure. Far less developed, and closed in winter, travelers will generally find more privacy on the North Rim. Below either rim there's plenty of solitude to be found no matter where you start from.

The High Southwest has never really been fully explored. There are areas that are as close to primal wilderness as you are likely to find in the lower 48 states. Turbulent white-water rivers still churn from snow peaks in springtime. After an average winter with more than 300 inches of snow in the high country, the Colorado River may run 40 feet above normal. Rafters float over rocks they would normally be floating under. Of course the river comes back down and hardens into blistered, parched lowlands under the unforgiving summer sun. Yes, there are towns and dammed rivers, roads, airports, convenience stores on the reservations, satellite dishes everywhere, some crowning home lots featuring Navajo hogans made of mud, sticks, and straw. You can even book a scheduled flight directly to the Grand Canyon.

The roads are better than in the old mining days but rugged mountainous areas continue to defy all but idiosyncratic development, as evidenced by abandoned mines and ghost towns. Wildlife, wildflowers, and man all benefit as much from what's not here as what is.

Regarding fashion, the vagaries of style that are in today and laughable tomorrow, the High Southwest may be experiencing its Warholian 15-minutes of fame right now. For those who come in search of adventure, the mountains, rivers, canyons and mesas are very much the same as they were before they were stylish. They change at a glacial pace. They will be here tomorrow. Exploits await.

As always, the luxurious essence of the Southwest is discovered in the way being here makes you feel about yourself on the turf of cowboys, Indians, mountain men, and desert rats, amid historic geology that is testing and undeniably attractive. It's a hard country open to all comers but resistant to easy change. That is exactly what makes it irresistibly challenging.

The Nature of Adventure

In the 1990s, adventure travel has come into its own. It is no longer considered the province only of daredevils seeking the classic hang-by-your-teeth-over-the-jaws-of-death-type adventure, although that sort of trip is surely available in abundance out here. You probably won't have to cheat death unless you choose to, but if you partake in a sampling of this book's suggested activities, you will certainly raise your chances for having a life-affirming experience, without necessarily having a life-threatening one. Adventure doesn't need to be a death march expedition but it does need to get the juices flowing. At the least it should provide attainable challenges that any reasonably fit and active participant with an open mind can enjoy.

Inside this book you'll find extensive information on a range of activities, many of which will provide challenges relating to climate, altitude, remoteness, and physical fitness. Others may be less physically stressful while confronting your cultural perceptions. From easy-to-accomplish soft adventures, family and senior's trips, to daredevil ones that will really get your adrenalin pumping, you can find them here. There are activities you can pursue for an hour, a day, a week, or a month. Whatever your inclination may be the pay-off is in the remarkable generative power of a classic river trip, a cattle drive, an Indian ceremony, or an archeological dig. The High Southwest offers thousands of miles of maintained trails for you to hike, bike, and ride on horseback. If you're a water-lover, river trips will lure you into canoes, kayaks, and white water rafts. There are evocative back roads for you to explore by jeep and mammoth vistas to gaze upon from the gondola of a hot-air balloon. You can visit historic and modern Indian and cowboy sites. You can travel by dogsled in winter, raft wild rivers in springtime, climb cool mountains in summer, and explore canyons and high desert in fall, when mornings and evenings are cool, days warm, and changing leaves enhance the countryside with a special, multi-dimensional, glow.

How to Use This Book

This book divides the High Southwest into regions, Northwest New Mexico, Southwest Colorado, Southern Utah, Northern Arizona, and the Navajo Nation & Hopiland. The order of these chapters essentially describes a large circle, presuming that you will begin your journey through the major gateway of Albuquerque. It is unlikely that you will try to cover the entire region on one trip and just about anywhere that you dive into the High Southwest is going to offer high rewards.

Each chapter starts with an introduction to the region. This covers information on climate, history, and culture, along with the main sites and activities. It is followed by a short section called Getting Around which outlines the main roads and transportation options as well as the general route the chapter will follow. Each region is then broken down into touring sections listed in the same order as they appear on the selected route. These sections provide information and useful contact numbers such as chambers of commerce, regional United States Department of Agriculture Forest Service offices, Bureau of Land Management offices, National Park Service offices, and airline and rental car services.

After the general touring sections within each chapter, a separate section detailing specific Adventures within each region follows. These include options for independent travellers or those seeking guided tours. There are many activities to choose from and many more limited only by your imagination. For example, you can generally experience an enjoyable hike on a listed bike trail, or bike on a jeep road.

The following is a brief description of the range and nature of activities covered under Adventures categories.

On Foot
(Hiking/Backpacking/Rock Climbing)

Whether you want to go it on your own or with a guided tour, this category will show you where to go and how to do it. There are hundreds and hundreds of miles of hiking trails in the High Southwest. Some are strenuous, requiring specialized rock climbing skills and equipment, others are more like a walk in the park. It is impossible to list them all, but you will find a cross section of the hikes for all levels of ability, from short walks over easy trails to multi-day routes through maze-like canyon networks.

When hiking in backcountry, the more popular short trails are usually well worn and marked, but it's still remarkably easy to get lost. Don't head out into the wilds on your own without some preparation. Figure out where you want to go, then consult the Forest Service, BLM, or Park Service for up-to-date topographical maps and information. Discuss with them the difficulty of various trails and technical climbing skills or specialized equipment that may be required. Some adventures in this area can be accomplished easily alone, while others require special gear, permits, and expertise. If you're short on equipment or in doubt about your skills, seek help from the professionals before attempting a demanding adventure. This is serious country, often short on absolution. If you question going it alone in the High Southwest then you probably should not. Even if you know what you're doing there's no substitute for direct contact with people whose business is understanding the areas and activities you're pursuing. Numerous local contacts are provided in this book. The USDA Forest Service suggests that all users of the backcountry remember the following:

- Take no chances. Assistance can take hours or days.
- Be aware of conditions. Varied terrain exposes you to hypothermia, dehydration, and lightning hazards on exposed ridges. There can be snow fields in early summer.
- Start hiking early in the day–mornings are generally clear. Later in the afternoon you may encounter storms of varying intensity. An early start gives you time to get to your destination and set up your camp in comfort, not while fighting the elements.
- Travel with a companion. File a hiking plan with someone who is staying behind and check in with revisions so you can be found if something goes wrong.

- Be in shape. Don't push past your limits. Allow time to acclimate to altitude.
- Always take fresh water with you, especially in the desert where heat can be deceiving and water may not be available. A gallon of water per person, per day, is recommended for summertime desert travel.
- Pack extra food just in case something goes wrong and you're out there longer than you planned.

Travel with Llamas or Horses

You want to get out there on your own two feet but you don't want to lug heavy gear. An alternative if you prefer not to be burdened with packs but want to travel into some of the most improbable terrain imaginable is hiking with packstock. Llamas are employed by several operators. They're not strong enough to carry the weight of an adult human but they are prodigious hikers and can easily tote 100 pounds or so of food and equipment in specially designed packs. Other hiking trips are run with horses or mules to carry the gear. Without weight restrictions imposed by the strength of your own back, you can experience deep backcountry with a case of beer or a few bottles of wine, an extra pair of dry shoes, and other heavy and awkward items that will make your trip more enjoyable.

Harder on your bottom than your feet is the venerable primary mode of transportation, horseback riding. Horses are still common out here and trips on well-trained, tractable mounts or high-spirited animals are easily arranged for an hour, a day, or overnight pack trips of varying lengths. A number of guest ranches and resorts also offer horseback riding. These are listed under accommodations.

If you want to be a cowhand, working ranches often accommodate guests who can participate in all ranch activities, such as herding and branding, or actual cattle drives, moving a herd from one place to another over several days or longer. Ten to 12 hours a day in the saddle, moving at a slow pace, is hard work, but it is, for some, the ultimate adventure the west offers.

On Wheels
(Railroads/Jeeps/Stagecoaches & Wagons/Bicycles)

There are several short train trips offered in the High Southwest on some of the most scenically compelling and historic rail lines in the world. We're not talking about subways here, nor even about Amtrak, though one of its trains does make several stops along the I-40 corridor.

A jeep or other four-wheel-drive may sometimes be the only motorized vehicle able to negotiate the hundreds of miles of remote, minimal roads that are among the most scenic and historical in the High Southwest. Please stay on established roads and don't chew up the backcountry by carving your own route.

It's not unusual to see an old-fashioned horse-drawn wagon lumbering down a road in the High Southwest. What is unusual is that some of these operators will take you along for the ride. One fellow even builds authentic old-fashioned stagecoaches. He offers a variety of trips when the equipment isn't being used for a movie or commercial shoot.

Mountain biking has really blossomed as a mainstream activity throughout the High Southwest. New high-tech bikes with 18, 21, or more speeds, make it possible for just about anyone who can ride to negotiate at least some of the terrain. Mountain bikers move faster than hikers, and knobby tires can transport you into certain regions where motorized vehicles cannot go.

Throughout the region, the topography for biking is testing and picturesque. The assortment of logging roads, jeep routes, and single-track trails on public lands is immense, offering something for everyone, from easy paved bike ways to world-class backcountry excursions.

Again, it's impossible to include all the great biking routes here. The selection offered in this book are to suit varying skills and abilities, along with information sources for further exploration. Guided bike tours suggested here will generally handle logistical arrangements an independent rider would usually have to manage alone. Most guided tours provide a sag wagon if you really can't make it those last few miles. On a tour or on your own, every rider needs to carry extra food and water, a head lamp, maps, and rain gear. Of course a helmet is essential.

Local bike rental operators, repair shops, and tour resources are included throughout the text. An excellent single source of detailed information on bike routes throughout this region is *Mountain Bike Adventures in the Four Corners Region*, by Michael McCoy, The Mountaineers, 1990. Other valuable sources of information are the experts in local bike shops who know the terrain.

Although bike riding is generally supported in these states, continuing access to backcountry trails is partly dependent on the goodwill of you and other outdoors-folk. The International Mountain Biking Association has established rules of the trail to help preserve mountain bikers trail rights:

- Ride on open trails only. Respect trail and road closures, private property, and requirements for permits and authorization. Federal and state wilderness areas are closed to cyclists and some park and forest trails are off limits.
- Leave no trace. Don't ride on certain soils after a rain, when the ground will be marred. Never ride off the trail, skid your tires, or discard any object. Strive to pack out more than you pack in.
- Control your bicycle. Inattention for even a second can cause disaster. Excessive speed frightens and injures people, gives mountain biking a bad name, and results in trail closures.
- Always yield. Make your approach known well in advance to others using the trail. A friendly greeting is considerate and appreciated. Show respect when passing by slowing to walking speed or even stopping, especially in the presence of horses. Anticipate that other trail users may be around corners or in blind spots.
- Never spook animals. Give them extra room and time to adjust to you. Running livestock and disturbing wild animals is a serious offense. Leave ranch and farm gates as you find them, or as marked.
- Plan ahead. Know your equipment, your ability, and the area in which you are riding and prepare accordingly. Be self-sufficient at all times, keep your bike in good condition, carry repair kits, and supplies for changes in weather. Keep trails open by setting an example of responsible cycling for all to see.

As for the terrain, even routes classified as easy by locals may be strenuous for a flat-lander. Most downhill routes will include some uphill stretches. Pay particular attention to your personal limits if you're on your own.

On Water
(Whitewater Rafting/Canoeing/Kayaking/Boating/Fishing)

From around mid-May to mid-June rivers rise dramatically and the flows are at their highest, fastest, and coldest. Sometimes by August things are pretty sluggish. It all depends on the winter's snowfall, spring rains, and summer thunderstorms.

In general, at high or low water levels, it takes an experienced hand to negotiate the rivers of the High Southwest. Unless you really know what you are doing, it is highly recommended that you consider a river tour, rather than an independent river trip. Tour operators also handle the permits that are necessary for certain popular stretches, permits that may only be offered through lottery drawings and are therefore hard to come by. Some stretches of whitewater, such as Colorado's Upper Animas River, with continual Class V rapids for two days, can be deadly to all but highly experienced kayakers. Participants are required to take a pre-trip physical fitness test by all tour operators running this stretch. Down below, on the Lower Animas through Durango, half a dozen tour operators sell one- and two-hour raft trips through town to anyone who comes along. There is a river trip for just about everyone, but your enjoyment may be marred if you try to take on more adventure than you can handle.

For any river trip, the smaller the vessel, the bigger the ride. Be sure to inquire about the size of a raft and how many people it holds. Ask if you'll need to paddle or simply ride along while guides do the work. Listings that mention paddle boats mean you will have to paddle. Oar boats mean a guide does the work. Kayaks accommodate one person who will obviously do all the paddling.

With these things in mind, floating gently through ancient gorges decorated with water-seep gardens and Anasazi rock carvings, called petroglyphs, or racing along rugged whitewater rivers pouring out of the high country, has become justifiably popular. Tours are available for an hour, two hours, half-day, full day, or overnight for up to several weeks.

Lakes and reservoirs throughout the High Southwest offer boat ramps for your vessel. Larger bodies of water feature marinas offering boat rentals where you can secure a rowboat, a canoe, a motorboat, a windsurfer, and other equipment. Houseboats affording all amenities for a self-contained vacation are available on Lake Powell.

If you're seeking fishing waters rather than rapids, lakes and reservoirs are suitable for canoe and boat excursions. In addition, there are innumerable places to fish from the shores of streams, rivers, and alpine lakes. Many waters are well-stocked with a variety of fish including several species of trout, kokanee salmon, northern pike, large and smallmouth bass, crappie, bluegill, and channel catfish.

On Snow

(Downhill & Cross Country Skiing/Snowmobiling/Dog Sledding/Ice Climbing)

You'll find the High Southwest's most reliable and sophisticated downhill skiing operations in southwestern Colorado, but there are other areas too, notably at Brian Head, Utah and the Flagstaff vicinity. When the snow is good, which is typical, the skiing is fantastic. Temperatures are often 10 to 15 degrees warmer than more northerly locales; hang up your ski jacket and go for a swim in the powder.

Cross country skiing areas are generally more peaceful and less crowded than developed downhill areas, but unless you plan to stick to the easiest groomed trails, it is wise to know what you are doing. You can ski the backcountry for an hour or for days, but snow conditions are often unstable and avalanches are frequent in certain areas or under certain conditions. To help match your abilities with appropriate terrain, it is highly recommended that you consult with ski shop personnel or regional information sources before approaching the backcountry.

The listings in each chapter are some of the safest cross-country routes. Remember that conditions are completely unpredictable and depend entirely on weather conditions that can and do change rapidly. For current snowpack and wind conditions, on-the-spot research is essential before any backcountry ski trip. Dress warmly and carry high energy foods. Though less physically demanding, the same rules apply if you're snowmobiling or dog sledding.

Ice climbing requires special equipment and skills, to mention nothing of appropriate terrain. You can find it all in the listings under this heading.

In Air
(Scenic Flights/Ballooning/Soaring)

If you think the High Southwest looks impressive from the ground, then you might want to consider seeing it from the air on a scenic flight. A range of options are available including fixed-wing aircraft, helicopters, gliders, and balloons.

Eco-Travel & Cultural Excursions

This catch-all category includes trips that don't fit elsewhere. Another way of looking at this heading might be to think of it as Southwest Exercises for the Mind.

Where to Stay & Eat

Although not expressly an adventure, finding good places to stay and eat in the Southwest can be a challenge.

In some remote areas, there may be only a campground with a fire grill, or a single, shabby motel for many miles. In other places you'll find a number of excellent establishments. All listings are subjective and are included for some good reason, whether for exceptional service, ambience, great food, or good value. Rates range from inexpensive to deluxe choices. Because these services may change rapidly, local information sources may come in handy for updates.

Camping

Public campgrounds and information sources are included in this section. You will also find details regarding camping on Indian reservations and remote backcountry camp sites.

Travel Strategies & Helpful Facts

The High Southwest is really spread out. Consider whether you will be travelling to one area, say for a week at a dude ranch or a five-day pack trip, or whether you plan to sample several areas, such as a Four Corners loop. If you've booked a multi-day outfitted trip the outfitter may be able to meet you at the closest airport. Otherwise you need a car. Rentals are available in many places.

Airlines offering service directly to the High Southwest are Continental Express, United Express-Mesa Airlines, and America West. Grand Canyon Airways flies from Phoenix to the South Rim in summer. Major airports in Albuquerque, Phoenix, Salt Lake City, and Denver are served by many carriers with connections on the smaller feeder airlines to airports in Farmington, NM, Durango or Telluride, CO, and Flagstaff, AZ. There is a private landing strip at Goulding's Lodge in Monument Valley, but for charters only; no scheduled service is available.

An increasingly important factor to consider when visiting the High Southwest is the area's burgeoning popularity. In many areas, visitations have doubled in the last five years and the effects on privacy and the wilderness environment have resulted in controls being placed on access to certain public lands at certain times. Consider travelling outside the traditional summer season or the peak winter months. It's uniformly busiest from the Fourth of July through Labor Day. If you're here for the skiing, you may want to schedule trips in December or March instead of January and February. Spring skiing is a particularly good idea; the snow is the deepest, the weather's warmest, and many skiers' thoughts are already turning to cycling and kayaking so there are fewer folks on the slopes.

Climate

The diverse topography in this area causes wide variations in climate. The season you visit will depend on what sort of activities you wish to pursue, but be aware that summer is not necessarily the most comfortable time. Summer weather is considerably milder the higher you go into the mountains, and certainly quite spectacular on an 80 degree, blue sky day in the San Juans. Down below, in the flatlands and arid deserts, it can get dangerously hotter, especially if you're hiking the Grand Canyon in July or biking around Moab in August. Just the reverse is true in winter. While skiers are snowbound in Telluride because mountain passes are closed by avalanches, you may want to head to Chaco Canyon, only 150 miles or so south. It may be not only warmer, but is likely to be devoid of tourists at that time. There are always trade-offs. Certain outfitting or adventure tour businesses are only open during particular seasons; certain lodgings even close during the winter. The road to the North Rim of the Grand Canyon is closed in winter while the South Rim is open year-round, but with curtailed services. Parts of Mesa Verde are closed in winter, although that needn't prevent you from snowmobiling or cross-country skiing on unplowed, snow-covered park roads, and having the few open ruins virtually to yourself (and the ghosts).

If you come in the spring to raft rivers, you need to be prepared to deal with mud in the lowlands, or dust storms in the deserts. Fall is considered by many to be the perfect season. The air is cooler, but not yet cold. Desert areas are once again tolerable after the scorching summer, while mountains boast colorful foliage and fewer crowds. Because of the great ranges in elevation, fall lasts several months (from September in the high mountains, to November in the deserts).

Count on daytime temperatures of well over 100 degrees in the deserts by July and August. At the same time, temperatures are likely to be 70-80 degrees in Flagstaff, Durango or Telluride. A temperature drop of 30-40 degrees after the sun goes down is common throughout the High Southwest. January through March may be cold throughout the region, below freezing in the high deserts of Utah.

Clothing & Gear

The High Southwest is a casual place. Shorts and t-shirts are fine for summer days but long pants and a sweater or jacket may be needed at night, particularly at higher elevations, where it has been known to snow in every month except July. Because conditions can change very quickly, layering your clothes is the best idea so you can remove or add clothing as it gets hotter or colder.

Sneakers may not be rugged enough footwear for back country hiking, so heavier, lug-soled boots are recommended. A broken-in pair of cowboy boots may be a good idea for extended horse travel. Hiking boots with heels to catch in your stirrups will probably do for short trips of a few hours to a day.

Find out in advance everything you can about your destination, such as water supplies, rest room facilities, fireplace availability, and restrictions on camping, group size, fires, and wood cutting. Plan your gear accordingly; bring shovels, cook stoves, water jugs, or saws as needed.

Outfitters and tour operators can usually supply any special gear that may be required for specific activities, so checking with them regarding rental equipment is an option before buying expensive items.

Always carry extra food and water on any back country excursions. You never know when these things may come in handy.

Depending on the activities you wish to pursue, special clothing and gear may be needed. Rafting in spring may call for a wetsuit. In winter, if you're cross-country skiing hut-to-hut, special touring skis with metal edges are highly recommended. Cross-country skiing produces a lot of heat so you can easily work up a sweat but when you stop moving you will feel how cold it really is out there. Again, layers are the answer. And even in mid-summer, on a back country bike ride you might start out in 80 degree weather then run into a thunderstorm that drops the temperature dramatically. If you always plan for the most severe conditions you will be able to weather these changes in fine form.

At any time of the year the sun can be quite strong. Wear a hat, sunscreen, and bring sunglasses which can prevent snow blindness in winter when the glare can be oppressive.

Insect repellent is a good idea in the summer, particularly at lower elevations.

Driving

To really get out and experience the deserts and mountains of the High Southwest you need a car, and some of the best places to go are not on main roads. Always inquire of locals about current road conditions. Some of these back roads may be marked for four-wheel-drive vehicles only. Do not test local wisdom or these signs in your Pontiac coupe. You will be in deep trouble if you travel several miles down an ultimately impassable dirt road and discover you cannot turn around. After rains, dirt roads can become dense, muddy tracks from which there is no easy escape. In the desert, sandy roads can swallow a car up to its hubcaps before you know what hit you. Snow frequently closes main highways (though generally for short periods) and unmaintained back roads may disappear until spring.

Those cowboys in their pickups know what they're doing. A truck or a four-wheel-drive with high ground clearance are clearly the recommended vehicles of choice, but with or without one, precautions are de rigueur. The farther out you plan to go, the more important it is to carry spare fuel and water for your radiator. Top up the gas tank wherever you can. The next gas station may be 100 miles away. Smart backcountry winter travel means good snow tires, windshield wipers that work, a couple of blankets, and a shovel in your car.

Local people understand the conditions and will probably help you out if you have trouble, but there may be nobody around for many miles or many hours. A cellular phone or CB radio could make a big difference in getting help. And don't forget to travel with the most up-to-date maps. Reliable maps are available from offices of the Forest Service or BLM. Outdoors stores are also good sources. An excellent driving map called *Indian Country* is published by the Automobile Club of America and is available for sale or for free to AAA members.

Weather & Road Conditions

Always check with local offices of the state patrol and the National Weather Service for current information. Don't be lazy about this. Just because it looks okay where you're standing does not mean it's going to be that way where you're going. Conditions can change fast. Anticipation is the key to success on any wilderness trip.

Special Concerns

The areas covered in this book are here for all to enjoy and special care should always be taken to insure their continued existence. Some remote areas are designated wilderness areas with seriously enforced rules of etiquette, including restricted access limited to those on foot or with pack animals only. Throughout the High Southwest fishing and hunting are subject to state or tribal law. Certain areas have restrictions on camp fires, and even where fires are allowed, dry weather may lead to prohibitions on open fires. It's always safest to cook on a camp stove. If you need to make a fire, do not cut standing trees but burn dead wood only. And do not be tempted to pocket an arrowhead or a pottery shard you may find on your travels. Think of the next person who'll be coming along, and remember that artifacts are protected by strictly enforced laws.

It's a sound policy to take only photographs and leave only footprints. Before leaving a camp site, replace rocks and scatter leaves and twigs to restore the area to a near-natural condition. Pack out all your garbage and any other trash you may find. Take care with human waste, it should be buried 100 feet or more from any water source and not near possible campsites. Use only biodegradable soap and, whenever possible, wash from a bucket of water far from running sources.

Do not travel into a fenced area as the Forest Service or BLM may be protecting it for re-vegetation or protecting you from dangerous conditions, such as extremely wet roads. Private landowners do not need a reason to keep you out; respect private property. Cross streams only at designated crossings.

Watch out for lightning. Especially avoid exposed areas above the treeline during thunderstorms. If you are in a thunderstorm, don't hide under a tree or in your tent. Get back into your car, if you can, or look for a cave or a deep protected overhang. If none of these things are possible, crouch down as low as you can and hope for the best. Avoid narrow canyons during rainy weather; check weather reports for thunderstorm predictions. Disastrous flash flooding is a real danger.

Drinking water in lakes, rivers, and streams is not exactly the same wilderness treat it once was. Now it's more likely to provide a nasty trick, *Giardia lamblia*, a tiny protozoa that can cause big problems. Animal waste found in many water sources can give you diarrhea and violent stomach cramps, symptoms which may require medical attention that could be far away. To avoid problems, make sure you always have adequate fresh water. On longer trips this usually means boiling all lake and stream water for 20 minutes or carrying effective water purification paraphernalia, which can be purchased from area sporting goods stores.

The water is fine for swimming, but relying on it as your primary water source without adequate treatment may be painful.

Information Sources

The Bureau of Land Management administers millions of acres of public lands in the High Southwest. For the good reason that these lands are enormously diverse, these extensive holdings are divided into various regions. Regional headquarters will refer you to local offices which are listed throughout the book, or check the index for specific offices.

Many of these information sources are included in the chapter texts that follow, but these general sources can be a big help in getting you started before you make up your mind about exactly what you want to do. Most provide free information.

Arizona Office Of Tourism, 1100 West Washington Street, Phoenix, AZ 85007, 602/542-8687.

Arizona State Parks, 800 West Washington Street, Phoenix, AZ 85007, 602/542-4174.

Arizona Game & Fish Commission, 2222 West Washington Street, Suite 415, Phoenix, AZ 85007, 602/542-4174.

Flagstaff Chamber of Commerce Visitor Center, 101 West Santa Fe Avenue, Flagstaff, AZ 86001, 602/774-9541.

Havasupai Tourist Enterprises, Supai, AZ 86435, 602/448-2121.

Hopi Tribal Headquarters, PO Box 123, Kykotsmovi, AZ 86039, 602/734-2415.

National Forest Service, Southwestern Region, 517 Gold Avenue SW, Albuquerque, NM 87102, 505/842-3292.

Navajo Cultural Resources Department, PO Box 308, Window Rock, AZ 86515, 602/871-4941.

Sedona Ranger District (National Forest Service), Box 300, Sedona, AZ 86336, 602/282-4119.

Sedona-Oak Creek Chamber of Commerce, Box 478, Sedona, AZ 86336, 602/282-7722 or 800/288-7336.

Colorado Parks & Outdoor Recreation, 1313 Sherman Street, Denver, CO 80216, 303/866-3437.

Cortez Area Chamber of Commerce, Box 968, Cortez, CO 81321, 303/565-3414, or 800/346-6526.

Durango Area Chamber Resort Association, PO Box 2587, Durango, CO 81302, 303/247-0312 or 800/525-8855.

National Forest Service, Rocky Mountain Region, 11177 West 8th Avenue, Lakewood, CO 80225, 303/236-9431.

Ouray Chamber of Commerce, PO Box 145, Ouray, CO 81427, 303/325-4746.
Silverton Chamber of Commerce, PO Box 565, Silverton, CO 81423, 303/387-5654.
Southwest Colorado Tourism Center, 800/933-4340.
Telluride Chamber Resort Association, PO Box 653, Telluride, CO 81435, 303/728-3041.

New Mexico, Tourism & Travel Division, Montoya Building, Room 106, 1100 St. Francis Dve., Santa Fe, NM 87503, 505/827-0291
Farmington Convention & Visitor Bureau, 203 West Main, Farmington, NM, 505/326-7602.
National Forest Service, same as for Arizona.
National Park Service, Southwest Regional Office, 1100 Old Santa Fe Trail, Santa Fe, NM 87501, 505/988-6340.

Utah Division Of Parks And Recreation, 1636 West North Temple, Salt Lake City, UT 84116, 801/538-7221.
Utah Travel Council, Council Hall, Capitol Hill, Salt Lake City, UT 84114, 801/538-1030.
Canyonlands North Travel Region, 805 North Main, Moab, UT 84532, 801/259-8825 or 800/635-6622.
Canyonlands South Travel Region, 117 South Main, PO Box 490, Monticello, UT 84535, 801/587-3235, fax 801/587-2425.
Color Country Travel Region, 906 North 1400 West, Box 1550, St. George, UT 84771-1550, 801/628-4171 or 800/233-8824, fax 801/673-3540.
National Forest Service, Intermountain Region, 324 25th Street, Ogden, UT 84401, 801/625-5347.

Northwest New Mexico

The extreme northwestern part of New Mexico at first appears to be nothing more than sandstone and scrub grass, mostly flat terrain, dry, rocky, and hot. Closer inspection reveals multi-colored rock formations sprouting from desert-like flats, gnarled juniper and pinyon trees, few people, and thousands of acres of rugged, undisturbed nature. The region encompasses part of the vast Navajo Reservation, which will be covered as a single entity in a later chapter. Part of this corner of the state is not Navajo land, but includes a rich mix of cultural influences and this is the region we are concerned with here. Modern and ancient Hispanic cultures are strong forces in this region and, although it is not strictly Navajo Indian land, many Navajo people and other Indians do continue to live here. The New Mexico state tourism office has dubbed the area "Indian Country." It includes reservation lands belonging to Zuni, **Acoma, Laguna,** and **Ramah Navajo** tribes. All share a land that has revealed incredible archaeological treasures and continues to add the seasoning of ancient history to a fine mix of sometimes subtle natural beauty and adventurous opportunities.

Four rivers flow into the **San Juan River** in this area. The **Pine** and **Piedra** flow into the San Juan at **Navajo Lake** and near Farmington the **La Plata** and **Animas** empty into it, all flowing toward Utah. Other thirsty streams and dry river beds fill only during storms, rising dramatically and suddenly in flashes of thunder and lightning, only to drain abruptly when the sun returns, which it does reliably. Then the cracked and parched earth returns to grassland, spiky tufts clinging to life under the harsh, purifying sun.

To the south, the remnants of an ancient volcano break the flat horizon with disquieting lava tubes and an improbable ice cave at the **El Malpais National Recreation Area.** The **Bisti Badlands,** south of Farmington, offer other-worldly forms, jagged towers and mushroom-shaped rock sentinels guarding the fossilized remains of dinosaurs and ancient sea-bed life.

Aside from the readily apparent Navajo influence here, Apache and Pueblo tribes continue to leave marks on the striated, multi-hued mesas and buttes. Many ancient dwellings are still buried under sands swept by time. Other ancient and modern structures are visible and can be visited. The Anasazi, in particular, have left their mark here, and the ruins of these community-centered people are among the very best preserved of the entire Southwest. Even today, modern Indians follow largely isolated rural lifestyles,

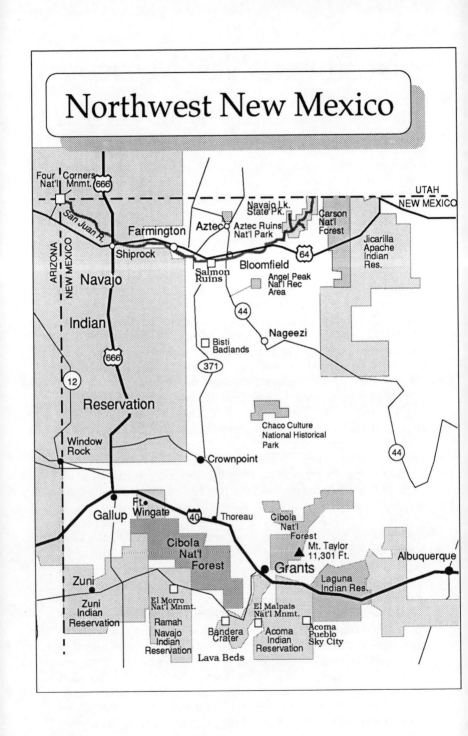

coming into the area's two major towns, Gallup and Farmington, only to do their business. They then return to their independent, family-centered, agrarian ways that have endured for centuries amidst the hot, deserted, dusty wind-swept prairies and box canyons.

The areas covered in this chapter range in elevation from 5,000 to 8,000 feet. If you're coming from lower elevations, expect to tire easily the first few days and exercise special caution when exploring the outdoors until your body adjusts to the lowered oxygen level in the air.

The arid climate makes dehydration a possibility. If you're going to partake in outdoor summer activities, particularly hiking or backpacking, make sure you have adequate water supplies. Winters can be rough, too, with occasional heavy snows and cold weather. You will need warm layered clothing.

Getting Around

The suggested route to follow through this part of the High Southwest begins west of Albuquerque, on Interstate 40, working westward to Gallup, and then north through Chaco Canyon, Bisti Badlands, Farmington, and Aztec toward the Colorado state line. As for exploring modern Indian pueblos, not federally regulated ruin sites, remember that these are private properties and you are a guest who is expected to act accordingly. Many pueblos consider it sacrilegious to record a religious dance on film, or even to photograph parts of the village. Always ask at the tribal office before taking photographs or video recordings. You may be asked to pay a fee for the privilege, or your request may be refused. Pay special attention to intruding on pueblo residents' privacy. If a site is marked as being off limits, don't test the system. Exploring a kiva in any pueblo village is also forbidden.

Touring

Laguna Pueblo

This small, mostly nondescript, modern pueblo community, which is comprised of several small villages, is approximately 25 miles east of Grants, close to exit 114 on I-40. There's not much to see here except for the San Jose de Laguna Church, which was built in 1699 by the Spanish. Inside the church are some elaborate decorative touches including a hand-carved pine altar and large religious murals.

For information contact **Laguna Pueblo**, PO Box 194, Laguna NM 87026, 505/552-6654.

Acoma Pueblo

One of the most unusual and telling Indian sites in all the Southwest is the **Acoma Pueblo**. According to Acoma legend, this unusual cliff-top community, called the **Sky City**, which is still occupied at least part-time by a dozen families, has been here for 1400 years. This would make it older than many Anasazi ruins, although other experts estimate the age of the original mortar and adobe structures to be only 900-1000 years old. Regardless of the actual dates, the Acoma community is one of the oldest in North America and functions to this day without running water or electricity. The initial effect produced by the absence of modern touches is one of distance from trivial cares, although your blissful reverie atop the prominent cliffs may be interrupted by a resident cranking up a noisy generator so the family can watch *Beavis and Butthead* on TV.

The pueblo's distinctive location, high on a steep, rocky outcrop, suggests a fear of invasion that these early settlers lived with, lending veracity to one school of thought that believes warfare, not drought and famine, was a primary cause for the dispersion of the Anasazi.

The only way to see the pueblo today is on a guided tour led by a tribal member. You are driven up the only road to the site, at the top of the 357-foot mesa, a narrow track built by a movie company in the 1960s. For thousands of years before the road was built, the only access to the city was by precipitous foot paths carved into the soft sandstone cliffs.

In the Sky City narrow streets are lined with crooked rows of multi-story adobe houses. There is an ancient cemetery and the impressive **San Esteban del Rey Mission**. The church was built with walls nine feet thick, according to the instructions of the Spanish governor of New Mexico in 1640, and is still in use today. Outside, potters and jewelers offer their wares on folding tables, while below, the panoramic view of the valley unfolds. Mount Taylor, capped in snow, is to the far north. Enchanted Mesa, another large rock outcrop rising vertically from the flat, sandy ground and the original site of the pueblo, is closer, to the northeast. Surrounded by corn and bean fields, it offers a view little changed from the earliest days of occupation. After an hour or so at Acoma, you can ride back to the small museum and Visitor Center at the base of the mesa, or walk down a steep, cramped, well-worn track, with steps and hand holds chiseled out of the vertical rock walls.

The Acoma Pueblo is located 12 miles south of I-40, off Exit 102. Signs lead to the site. For information contact **Acoma Tourist Visitor Center**, PO Box 309, Acoma, NM 87034, 505/252-1139.

El Malpais National Monument

This 114,000-acre valley, covered in black lava rock, was declared a National Monument in 1988. The entrance to the park is 18 miles southeast of Grants on NM 117. The National Monument includes the area to the south and west of Grants.

The name of this place means "badlands" in Spanish, and the lava rock that characterizes the landscape today is the result of several thousand years of geological activity generated by live volcanoes. The molten lava hardened into the sharp rocks you see today, among which are all sorts of geological oddities, including natural bridges, arches, sandstone cliffs, and lava caves. Also found throughout the region are numerous Anasazi ruins.

Places of interest here include the **Sandstone Bluffs** overlook, 10 miles south of I-40 on NM 17, and seven miles farther south on NM 17 is **La Ventana**, a graceful sandstone arch that is the largest such formation in New Mexico.

The **West Malpais Wilderness** and the **Chain of Craters** area are remote parts of the park where you can see giant lava tubes, including one 17 miles long, and wildlife such as mule deer and wild turkeys.

For information contact the Visitor Center at **Bureau of Land Management/National Park Service El Malpais Information Center**, 620 East Santa Fe Street, Grants, NM 87020, 505/285-5406, or the Grants Chamber of Commerce (see below, under Grants).

Grants

Grants was a big uranium boom town not so long ago, but today it's just another stop on the interstate, featuring chain motels and fast food. The **New Mexico Museum of Mining** is located here, at 100 Iron Street, Grants, NM 87020, 505/287-4802, in the same building as the Chamber of Commerce. You can take an elevator down into the mine shaft that once provided uranium ore for atomic weapons and power plants. After the tour of the mine, there are dioramas and interpretive exhibits outlining the geological and mining history of the region, as well as the economic base of the community from the time of the Anasazi, through the time Grants was known as the "Carrot Capital of the World," and the brief uranium mining boom days. When you're finished touring the museum you can get area-wide information from the Chamber of Commerce.

For information contact **Grants Chamber of Commerce**, PO Box 297, Grants, NM 87020, 505/287-4802, or the **Cibola Convention Authority**, PO Box 1210, Grants, NM 87021, 505/285-4625.

El Morro National Monument

El Morro was America's first National Monument, dedicated in 1906 by President Theodore Roosevelt. It is 43 miles southwest of Grants, via NM 53, or 56 miles southeast of Gallup via NM 32 and NM 53. Carved into the 1,278-acre monument's centerpiece, a 200-foot-tall **Inscription Rock**, are centuries-old petroglyphs and the names and messages of travellers who passed this way between 1605 and 1904. The oldest rock carvings are attributed to ancestors of today's Zunis, possibly from the time when the mesa top was inhabited by as many as 1,500 people. The village here was abandoned around 1400, but the etched carvings of animals, hand prints, and abstract designs remain, although their meanings are not known. Spanish explorers were the next known visitors to the area, and one of the names carved is that of Don Juan de Onate, the first Spanish colonizer of New Mexico, dated 1605. As late as 1774, Spanish friars, soldiers, and travellers scratched their names into the rock, probably when they stopped here to enjoy the rare, precious water they found in a rock pool kept filled with run-off from the mesa above. The last set of names are those of US soldiers who surveyed this area in the mid-nineteenth century after it was acquired from Mexico.

Atop the bluff are the ruins of two Zuni pueblos and, at its base, accessed by an easy half-mile trail, are the inscribed names and artwork, as well as the natural water hole that attracted Indians, Spanish explorers, and Anglo soldiers so long ago. A Visitor Center includes a small museum featuring artifacts from pueblo history, and there are picnic areas and a campground close by.

For information contact **El Morro National Monument**, Ramah, NM 87321, 505/783-4226.

Bandera Crater & Ice Cave

This site, 25 miles south of Grants on NM 53, contains a privately owned volcano. You can hike to the top of the cone and peek inside, then visit a refreshingly cool volcanic sink where water flowing through collapsed lava tubes has remained frozen for hundreds of thousands of years, thanks to the insulation of lava rock.

The early ranchers who discovered the ice cave were able to store food in it and, because of the constant 31 degree temperature, the collapsed lava tube also provided a cool place to escape the parching heat of the surrounding desert badlands.

You can walk into the cave and see the translucent green ice that survives year-round, even during oppressively hot summers.

Next to the ice cave is an extinct volcano known as the Bandera Crater, a 1,000-foot-deep cone that is believed to have blown its top more than 5,000 years ago. A maintained trail to the crater rim provides a panoramic view of the immense lava fields that remain from the volcano's active days. Also at the site is a trading post, snack bar, and picnic area.

For information phone **Bandera Crater and Ice Cave**, 505/783-4303.

Zuni Pueblo

Nearly 8,000 Zunis live here, in the largest pueblo community in New Mexico. The town of Zuni, situated 35 miles south of Gallup on NM 53, looks like many small towns in these parts. Its dusty, dirt streets and simple frame houses belie the ancient traditions that continue to exist in the revered presence of a Sun Priest, who runs sacred solstice ceremonies, a rainmaker, and various war gods.

At the same time, Catholicism is a significant influence woven into this world view that combines old and new. In the 360-year-old mission church here, **Our Lady of Guadalupe**, there is an altar, a statue of Our Lady of Guadalupe, and a crucifix. But these are flanked by huge, shaggy, mounted bison heads. On the inside of the six-foot-thick walls of the church are 50-foot murals depicting the Zuni religious cycle. These include 24 life-size, masked kachinas, representing ancestral spirits who bring rain, ripen corn, make hunting successful, and bestow happiness and prosperity, among other desirable circumstances.

The church had been abandoned in the mid-1800s. Renovations began in 1966 and were completed in 1972. That same year, the murals were started by Zuni artist Alex Seowtewa. The artist, who now works with his sons Kenneth and Edward, hopes the ongoing, part-federally sponsored project to return the church to its original 19th-century condition, will be completed around 1995. The goal is to preserve the vibrant Zuni culture that traces its roots to the ancient Anasazi and even farther back in time. Visitors who have stopped here to admire the work have included Mother Teresa and Jacqueline Onassis. The church is open to the public 2 PM to 3 PM, Monday through Friday, and mass is held every Sunday at 10 AM.

Outside the church, in the streets of Zuni, the scent of fresh baked bread wafts from traditional clay ovens called hornos. Many of the foundations below modest-looking homes have been here for 500 years or longer.

Zuni crafts are highly regarded. Artisans are known for silver inlay jewelry and intricate animal fetishes, which represent animals and birds thought to bring numerous varieties of good luck. Arts and crafts are available from local shops.

Permission from tribal authorities is needed to visit two local historic sites: the ancient ruins at the village of **Hawikuh**, the original townsite, 12 miles south of present-day Zuni, and the **Village of the Great Kivas**, which contains three unexcavated pueblos 19 miles north of town.

For information contact **Zuni Pueblo**, PO Box 369, Zuni, NM 87327, 505/728-4481.

Gallup

Gallup is a big city (population 20,000) to the rural Navajos and other Indians who do business here, but it is not, shall we say, the jewel of the Southwest. It does have nearly 2,000 motel rooms, many of them left over from the days when Route 66, which passes through here, was the main route connecting Chicago with the Southwest and ultimately the Pacific Ocean. It also has close to 50 restaurants, though probably few that you would travel out of your way to reach. Gallup's primary appeal is to Navajos who come here to drink (alcohol consumption is prohibited on the reservation, although changes in this policy are under consideration) and to travellers passing by on the interstate. Because so many Indians do come through here, it's a good place to shop for Indian jewelry and crafts. It is also close to a lot of beautiful and interesting places, including El Morro National Monument and Bandera Volcano and Ice Caves. An outdoor Indian market, held downtown on Saturdays, is a good place to buy authentic crafts directly from Navajo and Zuni artisans.

For additional information contact **Gallup Chamber of Commerce**, PO Box 1395, Gallup, NM 87305, 505/722-2228 or 800/242-4282.

Chaco Canyon National Historical Park

Chaco Canyon was once the center of a far-flung trading universe that stretched throughout the Southwest and all the way to Mexico. Situated between two long, dusty, rutted dirt roads, it was at one time, perhaps, the primary Anasazi community. Today it is a federally-protected site that offers some of the most sophisticated ruins and least compromised ancient environments anywhere in the Southwest.

Chaco is still remote and inaccessible, 72 miles southeast of Farmington, 95 miles south of Durango, and 115 miles northwest of Santa Fe. The nearest town is tiny Bloomfield, 60 miles north, where you can find gas and food and not much else.

There are no food, gas, lodging or repair services at the park. The closest services are 24 miles north, on NM 44, at Blanco or Nageezi, or 20 miles south at Seven Lakes, where you can find gas, tire repairs, and a telephone.

The northerly entry road to Chaco Canyon veers south for 24 miles from Blanco or Nageezi, southeast of Farmington. The southerly road connects with Grants. Both entries are over rugged dirt tracks that turn to impassable mud in wet weather, and even under the best conditions, the roads will test the springs and shocks in your car as you bounce over ruts and washboard tracks. The difficult condition of these roads is probably the main reason why Chaco is not completely overrun with tourists. In addition, park facilities are modest, consisting of a small museum, a water spigot, cold water bathrooms, and a shadeless campground nestled among sandstone outcrops complete with petroglyphs. It takes a few hours just to drive here off the main roads. The following are the only routes into Chaco Canyon.

• Travel north from Crownpoint (north of I-40) on NM 371 for 4.5 miles to Tribal Route 9. Go east 13.5 miles to NM 57 and 20 miles north on a very bad road to the park.

- Travel south for 16 miles from Blanco on NM 57 to the intersection with NM 45, and then another eight miles or so to Chaco.
- Travel 24 miles south on NM 45 from NM 44 at Nageezi.

In good weather these roads are not beyond the capability of most passenger cars, but it is always wise to phone the park, 505/786-7014, for updated reports. Do not attempt these roads in wet weather, nor without a full tank of gas, food, and water. You will probably want to spend at least a full day wandering around the short trails to the exceptional ruins or, if you want to stay for longer hikes, you will need to be prepared to camp out. Bring your own firewood; none is available at the park. Wood gathering is prohibited, and it does tend to get cold at 6,200 feet. It is often below freezing in winter and in the fifties during summer.

At all times in the park, remember that it was established to preserve and protect outstanding archaeological sites for everyone to enjoy. Stay on designated trails and follow the signs. Do not walk on, across or climb any walls. Do not enter rooms off the trail. Park only in developed lots. Leave all artifacts, including even the smallest pottery shards, where you found them. The Archaeological Resources Protection Act of 1979 is strictly enforced. Federal penalties can be as severe as a $5,000 fine and five years in jail for disturbing archaeological remains.

Chaco culture flourished between 900 and 1200 AD, and remains of 13 major ruins comprised of more than 2,000 sites have been found in this stark, high desert. The known sites provide evidence of Indian architecture and artifacts, clay pots bearing distinctive black and white geometric designs, and jewelry fashioned of turquoise and obsidian, suggesting the history of a complex community system more evolved than the Mesa Verde cliff dwellers of neighboring Colorado.

With only simple visitor services available, the big tourist hordes stay away, which means there is a far more personal experience of the ancient Anasazi available. This is an acknowledged World Heritage Site, certifying Chaco's cultural and historic significance.

The Visitor Center runs a short film about the lives of the area's ancient inhabitants, along with exhibits of pots, ornamental turquoise objects, and tools recovered from the ruins. Trail maps are available, along with required back-country permits, which are free. A 10-mile loop road leads to various ruin sites around the mile-wide canyon, now a rocky, dusty desert, but once an urban hub for the Anasazi.

Evidence of religious beliefs is found in numerous petroglyphs and fading, colorfully tinted drawings, called pictographs, emblazoned on stones believed to mark ceremonial spots. Atop the **Penasco Blanco Ruins**, a pictograph of a star, a crescent moon, and a hand print was discovered in 1972 beneath a 20-foot-high precipice. Scientists think the long-concealed painting illustrates a super nova that occurred in 1054 A.D., which was also chronicled by Chinese astronomers who reported its visibility in daylight for two years. At **Fajada Butte**, a sizable spiral is carved into the sandstone, 400 feet over the bottom of the canyon. Three giant rocks rest against the engraved surface and for approximately 1,000 years, until the stone slabs recently moved almost imperceptibly, a thin beacon of sunshine entered the space between the rocks and illuminated the petroglyph exactly at noon on the summer solstice.

Archaeologists are not in complete agreement about the fate of these skilled people. Some say vegetation was used to excess to construct roof beams and rafters for elaborate, multi-story dwellings and without root systems to hold water and replenish the soil, they lost their ability to grow life-sustaining vegetation. This could have led to the swift degeneration of Chaco culture and other nearby, related Indian communities. Scrub grass that may have remained was probably eaten by domestic livestock, brought into the area by white men who began to settle here in late 1870s, decimating the remnants of ground cover. Others believe that warfare led to their disappearance. Now, the ancient voices are stilled and only occasional breezes sing above parched desert.

Chacoan culture was at its most highly evolved levels around 1,000 years ago with the development of complex, two- and three-story buildings. During the following 100 years the burgeoning canyon community expanded to include upwards of 400 settlements, supporting a population of 5,000-10,000 people, and fourth and fifth stories were added to existing dwellings. Yet, within only another 200 years, during the 1300s, Chaco Canyon had been abandoned.

Europeans were building stained-glass basilicas while these primitive Indians in yucca-fiber sandals were living in remote Chaco Canyon, but no other North American clan left analogously detailed masonry construction, sophisticated irrigation schemes, or complicated networks of trade highways. Seventy-five neighborhoods have been conclusively linked to Chaco Canyon, extending over approximately 1,200 miles of precisely arranged trade routes fanning out like spokes of a wheel, each separated by no more than a day's travel.

In the ruins, seeds buried in pots and preserved in the bone dry climate are identical to types of beans, corn, and squash that originated in Mexico. Characteristic black and white pottery, turquoise, chalcedony, obsidian, shell artifacts, and yucca fiber clothing and baskets strongly imply connections with far away populations in Mexico and Central America.

Pueblo Bonito, dating from 900-1200 A.D., is the biggest and most impressive ruin in Chaco Canyon. It comprises some 800 rooms layered four stories high and surrounding 37 kivas, which are circular pits that were probably the sites of gatherings or religious observances. This single ruin could have accommodated several hundred people at one time. Most structures here were remodeled at various times and increasingly sophisticated layers were added to previous crude designs. These techniques may be observed at **Casa Rinconada, Chetro Ketl, Pueblo del Arroyo** and **Pueblo Alto**, which are smaller ruins around the perimeter of the loop road. Even smaller ruin sites may be reached by following easy hiking trails of one-half to five miles.

Chacoans mastered construction of free-standing masonry walls. They had no metal tools nor draft animals, not even wheels for transporting building materials. They had no written language, so only the carvings and drawings remain to tell their story. Yet for 300 years this was the nucleus of an expansive economic, spiritual, and cultural community spread over 30,000 square miles. Then Chacoans vanished.

For information contact **Bloomfield Chamber of Commerce**, 224 West Broadway, Bloomfield, NM 87413, 505/632-0880, or **Chaco Canyon Park Superintendent**, Star Route 4, Box 6500, Bloomfield, NM 87413, 505/786-7014.

Farmington

Farmington is the biggest town in the Four Corners with a population of 34,000. It is one of the main trade centers for the Navajo Nation, and serves as a regional center for oil, gas, and coal exploration. Though it is not the most scenic or unusual place, it does have a number of motels, fast-food restaurants, and gas stations, which makes it a possibility for a pit stop or an overnight stay. There are a few interesting places to visit here.

Farmington Museum, 302 North Orchard, Farmington, 505/599-1174, has exhibits detailing the area's various cultures, history, and environment.

B-Square Ranch, 3901 Bloomfield Highway, Farmington, 505/325-7873, is a 12,000-acre ranch, wildlife preserve, and experimental farm owned by the family of a former Governor of New Mexico. Tours by appointment only.

Angel Peak Recreational Area, 35 miles south of Bloomfield on NM 44, offers a 40-million-year-old geological formation surrounded by silent, pastel-shaded, eroded badlands. Angel Peak is the dwelling place of "sacred ones" to the Navajo people, and facilities include camping and picnic sites. No water or other services are available.

Bisti Wilderness, 36 miles south of Farmington on NM 371, is accessed by seven miles of dirt roads on the east side of the highway. This is one of the weirdest landscapes in the Southwest. The mushroom-shaped rocks, spires, petrified wood, and plant and animal fossils create an otherworldly, remote backcountry. There are hardly ever any people here, just you and the rocks. Wonderful photo possibilities are early in the morning or late in the afternoon, but probably best avoided in mid-day heat. The harsh desert climate has eroded shale and sandstone into bizarre hoodoos that look something like toadstools. The hoodoos occupy a 4,000-acre area of dry, deep arroyos that were once home to dinosaurs. There are no maintained trails through this sandy wilderness and it's easy to get lost in here. Make sure you have plenty of drinking water and pay attention to where you're going so you can find your way out; no one else is likely to be anywhere nearby to offer help.

Farmington's **Four Corners Regional Airport** is served by **United Express**, 505/326-4495 or 800/241-6522, with connections to Durango, Denver or Grand Junction, CO; **Mesa Airlines**, 505/326-3330 or 800/637-2247, with connections to major New Mexico cities, Durango, Telluride, Denver, Phoenix, or Dallas; **America West Express**, 505/326-4494 or 800/247-5692, with connections to major New Mexico cities, Phoenix, Flagstaff, Bullhead City, or Kingman, AZ, Durango, or Grand Junction, CO, or Palm Springs, CA.

Car rentals are available at the airport from **Avis**, 505/327-9864, or 800/331-1212; **Budget**, 505/327-7304 or 800/748-2540; **Hertz**, 505/327-6093 or 800/654-3131; **National**, 505/327-0215 or 800/227-7368. Also: in town, **Ugly Duckling Rent-A-Car**, 2307 East Main, Farmington, 505/325-4313.

For information on weather and road conditions, phone 505/325-7547 or 800/432-4269. Additional tourist information is available by tuning to 530 on AM radio, or by contacting the **Farmington Convention & Visitor Bureau**, 203 West Main, Farmington, NM 87401, 505/326-7602 or 800/448-1240.

Salmon Ruins/San Juan Archaeological Research Center

Salmon Ruins, 505/632-2013, is between Farmington and Chaco Canyon, just west of Bloomfield on US 64. A museum here displays artifacts from Chacoan settlements of the 11th century and there are ruins of an 11th- to 13th-century apartment complex here. At the center's **Heritage Park** you can learn how to fling a dart-like weapon called an "atlatl," used for hunting by the Anasazi before the bow and arrow was introduced. Other displays which you can enjoy include life-size replicas of a pit house complex, a Navajo forked-stick hogan, and sweat lodge, as well as Native American structures representing thousands of years of human occupation of the San Juan Valley. There is also an ice-age pond, an archaic sand dunes campsite, Ute and Jicarilla Apache "wickiups" and teepees.

Aztec Ruins National Monument

Travelling east on US 64 to Bloomfield, then eight miles north on NM 44 to the town of Aztec–named an All America City in 1963 and still proudly boasting of that quaint fact–is the Aztec Ruins National Monument and Museum, 505/334-6174, on US 550, north of Farmington. The ruins here have absolutely nothing to do with the Aztecs from Mexico. This was an Anasazi village at one time, connected by road to Chaco Canyon, and today it is the site of the world's largest reconstructed kiva and a small, easily toured cluster of pueblo ruins. The nice thing about these ruins is their manageable size and their proximity to the highway. Rather than mounting an expedition, you can drive right up to this sight, wander around for an hour or two, and be on your way. Some people enjoy a short visit to the **Aztec Museum & Pioneer Village**, 125 North Main, Aztec, NM 87410, 505/334-9829. Eleven permanent displays include historic items from San Juan County, and there is an oil and gas exhibit. The Pioneer Village consists of ten replicas of late 1800s structures, including a jail, school, church and general store.

For additional information contact **Aztec Chamber of Commerce**, 203 North Main Avenue, Aztec, NM 87410, 505/334-9551.

Trading Posts

An interesting aspect of this area if you're seeking souvenirs and art is the various trading posts. These have traditionally provided commercial goods to isolated Indian residents from the reservation, often in trade for a rug or a piece of jewelry, which would then be offered for sale. Among the most popular items available are collector's pieces, one-of-a-kind items, Navajo folk art, antique carvings, sand paintings, gourd rattles, prayer fans, herbs and sweet grass used in traditional ceremonies, jewelry, pottery, and rugs.

Trading posts are found virtually all over this region and, of course, the big spot for this sort of stuff is trendy Santa Fe; smart shoppers browse through this area too, often finding the same items offered at a fraction of the price. Of course, it is also easy to get ripped-off at one of these places. Unless you know exactly what you're looking for, the best insurance is to shop with reputable dealers.

The following are some of northwestern New Mexico's better local trading posts.

Tanner's Indian Arts, 1000 West US 66, Grants, NM 87020 505/863-6017.
Navajo Trading Company, 232 West US 66, Gallup, NM 87305, 505/863-6131.
Richardson's Cash Pawn, 222 West US 66, Gallup, NM 87503, 505/722-4762.
Tobe Turpin's Indian Trading Company, 1710 West 2nd, Gallup, NM 87305, 505/722-3806.
Indian America, 3310-30 East US 66, Gallup, NM 87301, 505/722-4431 or 800/748-1912.
Zuni Craftsmen Cooperative (located on West NM 53 in Zuni Pueblo), PO Box 426, Zuni, NM 87327, 505/782-4425.
Jewel Box Pawn Shop, 2400 West Main, Farmington, NM 87401, 505/325-5693.
The Outpost, 505/325-4044, on US 550, in Kirtland, NM.
Bob French's Navajo Rugs (15 miles west of Farmington on US 64), PO Box 815, Waterflow, NM 87421, 505/598-5621.
Hogback Trading Company (20 miles west of Farmington), 3221 US 64, Waterflow, NM 87421, 505/598-5154.
Thomas Harley Trading Company, 103 South Main Avenue, Aztec, NM, 505/334-8738.

Aside from trading posts, there are many pawn shops in the area that play a special role in the region's jewelry-driven economy. Here you'll find something other than the usual array of pawn shop goods such as stereos, musical instruments, and guns. Instead, these shops are filled with jewelry, sculpture, and sometimes even intricate silver horse gear. Items taken in pawn are generally authentic and of unusual value, including squash blossom necklaces, belts, and wide cuff bracelets with large turquoise stones.

Information Sources

For specialized maps and brochures contact these sources:

BLM Maps: Intermediate Scale Maps, PO Box 1449, Santa Fe, NM 87504, 505/988-6000.
City Maps, County Maps, and **State Highway Maps**: New Mexico State Highway and Transportation Department, 1120 Cerrillos Road, Santa Fe, NM 87501, 505/827-5412.
National Forest Wilderness Maps: USDA Forest Service Office, 517 Gold SW, Albuquerque, NM 87102, 505/842-3292.
State Parks Brochure: State Parks & Recreation Division, NM Natural Resources Department, PO Box 1147, Santa Fe, NM 87504, 505/827-7465.
Topographic Maps: US Geological Survey Distribution Center, Federal Center, Building 41, Denver, CO 80225, 303/234-3832.

Adventures

On Foot

This area is not particularly known for its hiking trails, but there are a few good ones. Numerous hiking trails can be found in the vicinity of **Mount Taylor**, an extinct volcano northeast of Grants, off NM 547. **Gooseberry Springs Trail** leads to the top of the 11,300-foot mountain. In the same area, south of Grants, you can hike across the lava fields in **El Malpais National Monument** or along the length of the **Big Lava Tube**. Bring water and probably forget about these hikes in summer. It's way too hot then. The best times are spring and fall.

Trail conditions in general are often uneven and steep. Make all necessary preparations before starting out. Extended exposure during extreme weather can be dangerous. Carry first aid gear. Brief, violent summer thunderstorms, or sudden winter snowstorms are always a possibility. Plan ahead for all contingencies. Help is likely to be far away.

An interesting hike is a 7.5-mile trail once used as a thoroughfare between Zuni and Acoma pueblos. The trailhead is 18 miles south of I-40 on NM 53. Before you set out, it's a good idea to get a trail map from the BLM/Park Service office in Grants (see above, under Grants). Extremely sharp lava rocks can cut your feet right through your shoes, and the high iron content of the rocks makes compass readings unreliable. Leave word with the ranger station about your intended route, just in case something goes wrong, or you might end up another fossil before you're found.

El Morro National Monument includes a steep two-mile, one-way trail to the mesa top and ruins. The trail is only open from April to December.

McGaffey Recreation Area, 15 miles east of Gallup on I-40, then 10 miles south on NM 400, offers several hiking trails through ponderosa pines and around the mesa. **Strawberry Patch Trail** starts at the base of the campground, south of McGaffey Lake, and leads to a fire tower that provides panoramic views of the area. For information contact the Cibola National Forest Office (see below, under Northwest New Mexico In Snow).

Chaco Canyon National Historical Park has eight self-guiding trails to major ruins on the canyon floor. Four backcountry trails lead from the canyon to more remote sites. Registration at the backcountry trailheads is required. Camping and fires are not permitted. All trails and ruins are closed from sunset to sunrise.

Extremely rugged hiking trails are found in the **De-Na-Zin Wilderess**, south of Farmington on NM 371 to the intersection of County Road 7500 East. This is BLM land so you can camp here for free, but there are no services, no trees, and there is no water. For information contact the local office of the **BLM**, 1235 La Plata Highway, Farmington, NM 87401, 505/327-5344.

On Wheels

El Malpais National Conservation Area offers good terrain for biking, but bikes are prohibited from El Malpais National Monument, which the conservation area surrounds. A rather lengthy 35-mile tour, that can be very hot in the summer, is a one-way ride around the border of the **West Malpais Wilderness**. It starts off of NM 53, 25 miles south of Grants, at the intersection of County Road 42. You ride south on the county road, within sight of Bandera Crater, and past immense, solidified lava flows. Approaching the Continental Divide, you can see the cinder cones that comprise the Chain of Craters. It's a smart idea to have shuttled a vehicle to the intersection with NM 117, approximately 45 miles southeast of Grants, in advance. Otherwise you have to ride back across the lava beds. For further details contact the BLM/NPS Information Center in Grants (see above, under Grants).

The **Mount Taylor** area offers superb trails for the highly skilled mountain biker. Trails in the **Zuni Mountains** are also good for biking, but you need to exercise care not to violate private property. For information contact **Cibola National Forest, Mount Taylor Ranger District**, 1800 Lobo Canyon Road, Grants, NM 87020, 505/287-8833. The office can also provide information on **McGaffey Recreation Area**. Many of these trails are suitable for biking and hiking. Also: Try jeep trails through areas of **Cibola National Forest.**

Six-Mile Canyon is 20 miles east of Gallup. Start riding at the Giant rest stop, 14 miles east of Gallup, and ride six miles parallelling the interstate. Follow the signs north into Six Mile Canyon, a steep climb, followed by an exhilarating downhill run back to the interstate.

Chaco Canyon is great for biking around the canyon floor. Most trails are open to hikers only but the **Wijiji Backcountry Trail** is open to bicyclists.

San Juan College, 505/326-3311, off 30th Street in Farmington, has a marked mountain bike trail offering sandy washes, arroyos, hilly jumps, steep climbs, and many side trails, including one connecting to Farmington Lake, which has its own trail network.

The Glade Run Trail System, north of Farmington, offers 40 miles of rolling desert roads and trails reserved for mountain bikes and small off-road vehicles. Motor vehicles seem to be more popular with local residents so weekends can be a bit noisy and crowded. Try this on a weekday. Contact Farmington Convention and Visitor Bureau for information. **Pinon Mesa**, three miles north of Farmington's 30th Street, on the La Plata Highway (NM 170), has many unmarked trails.

For a real adventure, ride into **Bisti Wilderness** or **Angel Peak Recreational Area**. There are dirt and gravel roads through each area, though fewer in the Bisti than around Angel Peak, which is traversed by numerous oil and gas roads winding through the scenic badlands.

On Water

Bluewater Lake State Park, 20 miles west of Grants on I-40, then six miles south on NM 412, contains a 2,000-acre lake stocked with catfish and rainbow trout. The lake is used for swimming, water-skiing, and boating, and there is a marina, cafe, and store. It's a popular spot for ice fishing in winter.

Zuni Lakes, on the Zuni Reservation, offer fishing on nine lakes, all reportedly well-stocked. A tribal permit is required, along with a state fishing license. The lakes include **Ojo Caliente Lake**, 20 miles southwest of Zuni, **Black Rock Reservoir** and **Eustace Lake**, two miles north of Zuni, and a string of three **Nutria Lakes**, 18 miles northeast of Zuni.

McGaffey Recreation Area (see above, under Adventures On Foot), offers picnicking, camping, and fishing at **McGaffey Lake**. **Ramah Lake**, another fishing spot, is 20 miles farther south on a gravel and dirt road. For information contact the Cibola National Forest, Mount Taylor Ranger District, (see below, under In Snow).

Thirty-eight miles east of Farmington, via Highway 64 and NM 511, is New Mexico's largest reservoir, **Navajo Lake**. The 150 miles of shoreline fed by three rivers (San Juan, Piedra, and Pine) provide fine lake fishing for German or rainbow trout, salmon, bass, bluegill, crappie, and catfish. Also boating, swimming, waterski-ing, windsurfing, camping, and picnicking attract 250,000 recrea-tional users annually to the 15,000-acre reservoir and adjacent **Navajo Lake State Park** (1448 NM 511 #1, Navajo Dam, NM 87419, 505/632-2278, or Navajo Dam Enterprises, Star Route INBU #6, Navajo Dam, NM 87419, 505/632-3245). There are three marinas with docks.

Just below the Navajo Dam is what many believe to be the best trophy stream fishing in the state. Catch-and-release waters are located 1/4-mile downstream from the dam. The four mile stretch known as the **Quality Waters** is carefully regulated to protect the large rainbow, cutthroat, and brown trout that swim in this stretch of the San Juan River and make it one of the top 10 trout streams in the country. Only barbless hooks and artificial lures are permitted and you are only allowed to remove one trout (of at least 20 inches) from this special catch section per day. Year-round fishing is avail-able in an additional 12 miles of open water.

Jackson Lake, off the La Plata Highway, north of Farmington, has good trout fishing year-round.

Morgan Lake, 15 miles west of Farmington, on US 64, on the Navajo Reservation, is open year-round for bass, crappie, and catfish. A special fishing license is required from the Navajo Tribe, 602/871-6451. The lake is also known for windsurfing in the ever-warm 83 degree water. Listed below are some of the best local fishing guides and outfitters.

Born-n-Raised on the San Juan River, Inc., PO Box 6428, Highway 173, Navajo Dam, NM 87419, 505/632-2194.

Duranglers, at Navajo Dam, 505/632-5952.

Four Corners Guide Service, PO Box 6399, Navajo Dam, NM 87419, 505/632-3569.

Heath Guide Service, 6209 Doe Street, Farmington, NM 87401, 505/325-1635.

Anthony Lee, Navajo Fishing Guide, PO Box 124, Bloomfield, NM 87413, 505/326-0664, specializes in location scouting for fishing expeditions.

Rizuto's Hackle Shop, 4251 East Main, Farmington, NM 87401, 505/326-0664.

Rizuto's Fly Shop, 1796 Highway 173, Navajo Dam, NM 87419, 505/632-1411.

Rocky Mountain Anglers, at Navajo Dam, 505/632-0445.

San Juan Troutfitters, PO Box 243, Farmington, NM 87401-0243, 505/327-9550 or 800/848-6899.

Sportsman Inn, at Navajo Dam, 505/632-3271.

State fishing licenses are available from these outfitters or from local sporting shops, for one day, five days, or the whole fishing season. For information and rates phone 505/827-7880.

On Snow

Compared with other areas of the High Southwest, there's not much snow in this area, except on **Mount Taylor**, where you can snowmobile or cross-country ski on the area's primitive roads. For information contact **Cibola National Forest**, Mount Taylor Ranger District, 201 Roosevelt Street, Grants, NM 87020, 505/287-8833.

In Air

Farmington International Balloon Festival, held in late May features races and rides in hot air balloons.

Four Corners Aviation, 1260 West Navajo, Farmington, NM 87401. 505/325-2867, offers charter flights.

Southwest Safaris–Flightseeing, PO Box 945, Santa Fe, NM 87504, 505/988-4246 or 800/842-4246, actually offers FAA approved natural history tours of the entire Southwest, based in New Mexico. The trips range from one-day to overnight expeditions and you may arrange to visit many major sites. After you land, you can continue exploring the backcountry in a ground vehicle or by raft.

Eco-Travel & Cultural Excursions

Gallup Inter-Tribal Ceremonial. This yearly gathering is one of the largest Indian events in the world, representing 50 or more tribes from all over North and Central America. Held for a week in mid-August at Red Rock State Park. The park is one mile north of I-40, four miles east of Gallup.

Activities include indoor and outdoor marketplaces featuring the work of more than 1,000 artists. You can buy directly from them at wholesale prices. The market is considered to include the best selections of Indian art, produced by the most accomplished artists, and at the best prices. A special ceremonial showroom offers sales displays of traditional and contemporary Indian fine arts. In all, more than $12 million worth of Indian arts are on display, while nearby, Indian artists will demonstrate various techniques.

Ceremonial activities include two nights of competitive drumming and dancing, including the top 400 Indian dancers in the United States, Canada, Mexico, and Central America. There are three nights of ceremonial Indian dancing, non-competitive traditional dancing, and three afternoons of all-Indian professional rodeo, featuring 500 participants competing in nine different events. Indian foods, such as barbecued mutton, Navajo tacos, and frybread, a greasy, doughy item that can only be described as a donut with no hole and no sugar, are all here for you to experience. A big event is a Saturday morning parade through Gallup, America's only All-Indian, non-mechanized event. Participants wear elaborate traditional clothing, heavy on beads, bones, and feathers, as they dance to the beat of rhythmic drumming, wending their ways through Gallup's streets. Make reservations early if you want to stay in Gallup for this event as motel rooms in town sell out far in advance.

For information contact **Inter-Tribal Indian Ceremonial Association**, PO Box 1, Church Rock, NM 87311, 505/863-3896, or 800/233-4528.

From Memorial Day to Labor Day, except for the days of the ceremonial, Indian dances are performed each night at 7:30 PM at Red Rocks State Park.

In addition, all of the Indian pueblos have feast and festival celebrations scheduled throughout the year. Contact pueblo offices for dates, or **Indian Country Tourism Council**, PO Box 1, Church Rock, NM 87311, 505/863-3896 or 800/233-4528.

Another Indian event is the monthly **Crownpoint Weavers Association Rug Auction**, PO Box 1630, Crownpoint, NM 87313, 505/786-5302, held in Crownpoint, on NM 371, 30 miles north of

Thoreau, at Exit 53 on I-40. Crownpoint is technically across from the southeastern corner of the Navajo Nation, but it is very much part of the reservation in spirit and style. Rug sales are more of a festival than a simple auction. The community of 1,000 residents increases by 50% or so on auction nights, as casually dressed travellers hob-nob in the Crownpoint Elementary School gymnasium with traditionally clothed Navajo women wearing velveteen shirts and elaborate turquoise jewelry. Outside the gym, vendors from nearby Acoma and Zuni pueblos sell pottery, jewelry, and kachina dolls representing various spirit gods.

On any auction night you can see cars in the parking lot bearing license plates from far-away. People come for the rugs, which are among the most beautiful you can find in Indian country. Bright geometric designs in shades of deep red and blue stand out against backgrounds of white, brown, gray, and black, combining traditional patterns with modern touches. A three-by-five-foot rug takes an average of 160 hours to produce. Prices vary between $10 for the smallest rug, and more than $3,000 for elaborate tapestries covering 60 square feet. Part of the fun is the reaction of the standing-room-only crowd to high-priced bidding duels between aggressive buyers.

The first auction here was in 1964 and the events have grown in popularity since then. Initially, if 50 rugs were sold, the night was considered a success. Today, it is not unusual for 400 rugs to change hands on a single night. The system works because weavers and buyers get a better deal here than they would at a trading post or gallery. You can preview the rugs on the afternoon of the auction, from 3 PM to 6 PM. Auctions are held from 7 PM to 11 PM. Don't forget to pick up a free auction card at the door if you think you might be bidding.

Farmington's **Lion's Wilderness Park** is the site of an outdoor summer musical drama, *Anasazi, the Ancient Ones*, 505/326-7602 or 800/448-1240, performed Wednesday through Saturday nights.

Indian Land Adventure Tours are arranged by Global Travel and Tours, 1400 South Second, Gallup, NM 87301, 505/722-2264 or 800/748-1600. These include customized scenic and historical itineraries visiting trading posts, pueblos, shopping areas, historical downtown Gallup, or other far-flung sites such as Canyon de Chelly, the Grand Canyon, the Petrified Forest, and the Painted Desert. Also: Special charters and transportation to and from Albuquerque.

The Culture of the Southwest is the name of a 10-day, nine-night tour that includes visits to Grants, Acoma Pueblo, Chaco Canyon, and Aztec Ruins, as well as Santa Fe and Taos. The focus of the trip is wildlife and native cultures, enlisting expert guides, lecturers in wildlife biology, anthropology, archaeology, and Southwest art. For information contact **Abercrombie & Kent**, 1520 Kensington Road, Oak Brook, IL 60521, 708/954-2944 or 800/323-7308.

Where to Stay & Eat

This was once a booming travel area when Route 66 was popular, but nowadays many travellers just zip right through on the interstate. There are many chains represented along the interstate corridor, and independent businesses are sometimes just bare-bones operations. There are, however, some special places a little off the beaten track, if you know where to go.

Grants Accommodations & Restaurants

Here you'll find mostly chain motels and Mom & Pop operations. The best one in town is probably a Best Western, **The Inn**, 1501 East Santa Fe Avenue, Grants, NM 87020, 505/287-7901. It has an indoor pool and a sauna.

For the most part, local cuisine will probably not win awards here, but it won't break the bank either. If you're hungry, try the **Iron Skillet**, I-40 at Horizon Boulevard exit, west of Grants, 505/285-6621. It's open 24 hours. Add the experience here to your ongoing saga of "salad bars of the Southwest."

For Mexican food try **Monte Carlo Restaurant and Lounge**, 721 West Santa Fe Avenue, Grants, 505/287-9250.

A step above average and out of time is the **Dinner Bell Cafe**, 505/287-5100, on old Route 66 in Milan, three miles north of Grants, off I-40. It's the oldest cafe in town, complete with booths and tables dating to the 1950s. Although the menu is not exotic, featuring burgers and sandwiches, you can get a solid, square breakfast or lunch for under $6. Homemade soups and pies fill out the bill.

Gallup Accommodations

Plenty of chains are represented here and a couple of independent hotels are definitely worth a try.

Holiday Inn, 2915 West US 66, Gallup, NM 87301, 505/722-2201.

The Inn Best Western, 3009 West US 66, Gallup, NM 87301, 505/722-2221 or 800/528-1234.

Rodeway Inn, 2003 West US 66, Gallup, NM 87301, 505/863-9385 or 800/228-2000.

El Rancho Hotel, 1000 East 66th Avenue, Gallup, NM 87301, 505/863-9311. George Washington did not sleep here, but Ronald Reagan did. And so did lots of other movie stars, including Burt Lancaster and Betty Grable, though not necessarily together. The place was built by the brother of director D.W. Griffith in 1937 to accommodate just these very stars while shooting films on location in the area. There is an excellent collection of Indian crafts on display in the lobby, including fine, old Navajo rugs, and there's less artful stuff, such as mounted deer and elk heads, a wooden Indian and, of course, autographed photos of the stars, including John Wayne, Humphrey Bogart, and Katherine Hepburn.

Gallup Restaurants

For the most part there's more of the same uninspiring food in Gallup. For standard fare, take your pick among **Peewee's**, 2206 East US 66, 505/722-5159, or **Roadrunner Cafe**, 3014 East US 66, 505/722-7309. A new gallery area is starting to transform the neighborhood of old houses around West Hill Street. **Desert Dreams**, 106 West Hill Street, Gallup, 505/863-4616, combines a coffee shop serving decent Mexican food, sandwiches, and pastries, as well as good coffee from Guatemala, Costa Rica, Mexico, and Ethiopia, with a new-age bookstore and gift shop. It's a comfortable place to sit down and relax with no pressure.

Shush Yaz Trading Co. and **A-OK Cafe**, 214 West Aztec, Gallup, NM 87301, 505/722-7027, fax 505/722-2005, combines six generations of Indian trading, dating to 1875, with a small cafe serving breakfast and lunch. Try blue corn pancakes for breakfast. They serve some of the best Navajo food around, including Navajo tacos, or A-OK tacos combining chicken, poblano and avocado, guacamole and beans, or squash, corn, potato, onion, and beans, all served with rice and jicama. The lamb sandwiches are tasty, there's a special soup daily, and, of course, frybread. There's also a small bakery attached serving fresh fruit and berry cobbler, gingerbread or chocolate cake daily and sometimes cardamon coffee cake.

As for the trading post, there's a large selection of art, as well as Pendleton blankets and Navajo squaw skirts at the lowest prices around.

La Barraca, 1303 East 66 Avenue, Gallup, 505/722-5083, serves homemade Mexican food that is extremely popular with locals but a well-kept secret. Specialties include a superlative mild green chile sauce, seedless chile rellenos stuffed with cheddar cheese and dipped in egg batter, enchiladas, tacos, and burritos.

For the hot stuff, try Genaro's, 600 West Hill, Gallup, 505/863-6761. It serves the hottest salsa in town and huge servings of smothered burritos, and sopapillas stuffed with beef, beans, cheese, and tangy guacamole, chile rellenos, and posole, which is chunks of pork cooked with hominy. Take sauces on the side if you're sensitive to hot, hot food.

Fifteen miles east of Gallup on I-40, then three miles south on NM 400, is another real find, The Lost Oasis Cafe, Bear Springs Plaza, Fort Wingate, 505/488-6640. The sunny, flower-decked dining room, with large windows and central fountain occupied by a salamander and goldfish, is truly a sanctuary of Nouveau Southwestern cuisine. Offerings include elk medallions, buffalo steaks, and seafood jambalaya, with a focus on traditional New Mexican flavorings added to unusual foods. This translates into elk marinated in green chile cilantro and lime, or charbroiled swordfish topped with salsa and pineapple. Mexican food specialities are also excellent. The cafe serves breakfast, lunch, and dinner, as well as Sunday brunch, and occasionally offers weekend dinner shows with live music.

Zuni Accommodations

This area is generally not known for its dining and accommodations, but things are changing. Although this is far off the beaten track, there are some hidden gems out here.

The Historic Vogt Ranch Bed & Breakfast, PO Box 716, Ramah, NM 87321, 505/783-4362, may be the most interesting place to stay in all of northwestern New Mexico, of particular appeal to those seeking a cultural lodging experience, rather than an antiseptic, undistinguished chain motel episode. This cozy, antique-filled, two-bedroom house was built in 1915 by the present owner's grandparents, who ran a sheep ranch here. Grandpa was also a photographer, newspaper editor, publisher, and the first superintendent of nearby El Morro National Monument, a position he held for 26 years.

He built his house out of stone extracted from nearby Anasazi Indian ruins in the days before this variety of recycling was discouraged by the federal government. Experts claim the ruins contained 26 rooms, and one of the things they found there, along with corn cobs and pottery, was a skeleton, which was reburied elsewhere. The property was originally used as a guest house starting after World War II and operating until 1965. It was reopened as a B&B in 1986.

The stone house today contains a collection of Anasazi artifacts, a 1915 upright piano, and a substantial collection of Southwestern books. The wood plank floors are covered in Navajo rugs, and the kitchen has a wood-burning stove. One of the bedrooms has a Zuni fireplace and the other has a wood stove. Both rooms have private baths. The owner does not live in the house, but comes in the morning to prepare your breakfast of blue corn pancakes, muffins, bacon, eggs, and fruit. Otherwise you're on your own out here.

The privacy and serenity are exquisite; there's no TV, and Gallup is 40 miles north. Grants is 54 miles east. The location is ideal for exploring the area, with nearby hiking, biking, bird watching, and Anasazi sites, as well as Ramah Lake. It's probably a good idea to bring some food if you're planning to stay a few nights, but there's a good Mexican restaurant a mile away in Ramah. You can get a pizza 21 miles west in Zuni. El Morro is 11 miles east of the ranch on NM 53, and El Malpais is 20 miles farther east on the same road.

Vogt Ranch is one mile southeast of Ramah, on NM 53, between mile markers 34 and 35. The ranch generally closes between January and March. Reservations are highly recommended.

Zuni Restaurants

Blue Corn Restaurant, in Ramah, in the Cowboy Stopover, on NM 53, 40 miles southeast of Gallup, or 20 miles east of Zuni, may be worth the drive for lunch or dinner. You can smell roasting red peppers as you walk in, and meals start with a big basket of red and blue corn chips with homemade salsa. Dishes include red pepper enchiladas covered in a cilantro cream sauce, beef Normandy, apricot stuffed chicken breast, blue corn crab enchiladas, and chile-lime chicken. For dessert try the kiwi-strawberry tarts in a puff pastry.

There are only a couple of restaurants in Zuni and the best one is **Chu Chu's Pizzeria**, on NM 53, 505/782-2100. The gent who runs the place learned how to make pizza in New York City.

Farmington Accommodations

Chains and small Mom & Pop motels are available here. The safest bets are the chains.

Comfort Inn, 555 Scott Avenue, Farmington, NM 87401, 505/325-2626 or 800/221-2222. Free continental breakfast, outdoor pool.

Farmington Anasazi Inn, 903 West Main, Farmington, NM 87401, 505/325-4564, is unimpressive from the outside, but comfortable inside, with Southwestern furnishings enlivening the typical Farmington motel experience. It also has a passable restaurant.

Holiday Inn of Farmington, 600 East Broadway, Farmington, NM 87401, 505/326-9811, has a fitness room, heated outdoor pool, and free airport courtesy van.

The Inn Best Western, 700 Scott Avenue, Farmington, NM 87401, 505/327-5221, has rooms with refrigerators, indoor pool, jacuzzi, saunas, fitness center, and courtesy airport transportation.

La Quinta Inn, 675 Scott Avenue, Farmington, NM 87401, 505/327-4706 or 800/531-5900, offers free local phone calls.

Twelve miles west of Farmington on US 64, then 35 miles south on NM 44 to Nageezi, is the location of the only accommodations anywhere near Chaco Canyon. **Chaco Inn at the Post**, PO Box 40, Nageezi, NM 87037, 505/632-3646, is a modest and friendly Navajo-run B&B.

Farmington Restaurants

As for dining, from the visible glut of franchise operations along Farmington's main drag, it appears that local tastes run to fast food. There are a few decent places to eat, though. **The Trough**, 505/334-6176, behind the Country Palace Bar, two miles east of Farmington on US 550, serves enormous western-size steaks, pork chops, and seafood. The ambience is casual, the portions are filling, and the food is edible, which is more than can be said for many dining options in these parts.

For Mexican food try **Senor Pepper's**, 505/327-0436, located at Farmington's Four Corners Regional Airport. There's not all that much air traffic here, so this place is mainly supported by locals. One popular dish, Steak Mazatlan, was once featured in an issue of *Bon Apetit*. This place also offers Sunday brunch.

Coyote's, at the Anasazi Inn (see above), serves three meals a day. It offers acceptable Mexican food and an all-you-can-eat catfish special on Friday nights.

Something Special Bakery & Tea Room, 116 North Auburn Avenue, Farmington, 505/325-8183, is hidden away several blocks off Main, serving good home-cooked lunches and baked goods. Dinners are served on Friday only.

The Farmington Convention and Visitor Bureau (see above, under Touring-Farmington) can give you the complete roster of places to stay and dine in town.

Aztec Accommodations

Accommodations in this small town are pretty basic motels, but one is nicer than the others. **Enchantment Lodge,** US 550 West, 1800 West Aztec Boulevard, Aztec, NM 87410, 505/334-6143, has a heated pool, morning coffee, and a picnic area. It is within walking distance of Aztec Ruins.

Navajo Lake Area Accommodations

The only motel at Navajo Lake is **Abe's Motel & Fly Shop,** 3391 NM 173, Navajo Dam, NM 87419, 505/632-2194.

Camping

There are numerous commercial campgrounds throughout this region, but for anything close to adventure, the public camping areas are more likely to deliver the goods. Listed below are some of the most scenic.

Two campgrounds are in the **Mount Taylor Recreation Area,** close to I-40. These are the primitive **Lobo Canyon Camp** and the **Coal Mine Campground,** which can accommodate large recreational vehicles. Both are off NM 547, north of Grants.

Bluewater Lake State Park (see above under Adventures On Water) has RV hookups and tent sites, a dump station, and showers.

There is a small, primitive campground at **El Morro National Monument.** Water is available, but not RV hookups.

Red Rock State Park is four miles east of Gallup on NM 566. The campground has 130 spaces, some for tents, some with hookups. It also has a dump station, showers, laundry, general store, and a post office.

The Zuni tribe operates several primitive campgrounds down rugged dirt roads in the hilly park lands near the Zuni Lakes.

McGaffey Recreation Area, in the Zuni Mountains, 15 miles east of Gallup on I-40, then south 10 miles on NM 400, has two campgrounds, **Quaking Aspen** and **McGaffey**, a few miles farther south on NM 400.

Chaco Canyon's **Gallo Campground** has 64 sites with picnic tables, fireplaces, cold water bathrooms, but no showers. Drinking water is available at the Visitor Center, one mile away.

Angel Peak Recreation Area, in the Naciemento Badlands, offers 16 paved campsites, with fireplaces, tables, and porta-potties, but no water or other services.

Pine River Site, Sims Mesa Site, or **San Juan River Recreation Area**, all at Navajo Lake State Park, offer 200 spaces, eight full hook-ups, 50 electrical hook-ups, picnic tables, rest rooms, and a dump station. The **Cottonwood Campground**, also at the park, has elaborate facilities for the handicapped, including elevated fishing platforms and paved trails.

Southwest Colorado

Colorado's southwestern corner encompasses a blending of cultures derived from at least two easily discernible sources. This much is known: Indians controlled the land for a very long time before white settlers arrived seeking gold and silver, or trailing herds of livestock, shortly after the Civil War. Descendants of these groups are still here, doing things their own way and offering a rare chance in this modern world for you to experience a place where Indians and cowboys are not only common folk today, but evoked in earlier incarnations virtually everywhere you choose to look.

Geography & History

The area revels in its historic roots. The ancient Anasazi Indians left behind their cliff dwellings and mysteries 700 years ago at **Mesa Verde National Park**, **Ute Mountain Tribal Park**, and **Hovenweep National Monument**, among other sites. The white men who came seeking riches eventually built ornate Victorian structures, as well as railroads to haul their precious ore, at the end of the last century. Fine examples of this architecture can be seen today in **Durango, Silverton, Ouray** and **Telluride**. And 200,000 tourists ride the famous Durango and Silverton Narrow Gauge Railroad every year between these two cities, the only line left out of all the rail routes that once serviced many of the remote mountain communities.

The historically accurate train belches black smoke, and airborne cinders are likely to become tangled in your hair as you look out at spectacular forest views from open-air gondola cars. It follows exactly the same route that it did in 1891. The first 10 miles or so through Durango has probably changed alot in the last century, but outside town the forests and wilderness are not much different than they were 100 or 1,000 years ago.

Durango's population of 14,000 makes it the big city in these parts. Cortez has a population of around 7,000, while Telluride boasts 1,300. Silverton, Ouray, Ridgway, Dolores, and Mancos measure populations in the hundreds only.

These small, scattered communities are in an area of exceptional beauty and resonate with history, while offering everything you need in the way of hospitality. You can find all sorts of services here, from campsites to ultra-modern, top-notch resorts, from fast foods to fine dining. And these tenacious communities, far off the beaten path, are separated by epic hiking trails, mountain bike routes and ski slopes. There are rugged rivers to run or to fish for trout. Spruces, aspens, gambel oaks, and cottonwoods offer forest cover for deer, elk, and the occasional black bear; grizzlies are all gone, or so experts say. The howling of coyotes echoes through rocky, pastel-shaded canyons. Shimmering deserts are dappled with yucca, cacti, and pinyon. Ruins evoke mysteries, a clarion call for explorers.

The humbling geography bridges two discrete terrains. The year-round snow caps of the **San Juan Mountains** reach cloud heights surpassing 14,000 feet near Silverton, Ouray, and Telluride. Evergreen and aspen thickets extend from the barren tree line, cloaking the angular grades and packing the valleys of the craggy Lizard Head Wilderness near Telluride, and the enormous **Weminuche Wilderness** near Silverton, as well as the adjacent **Uncompaghre** and **San Juan National Forests**.

The San Juan forest is immense, covering nearly two million acres. It stretches from peak to peak across southwest Colorado, butting up against high desert in the south and west, near Indian land, which displays a differing vitality.

Beyond the mountains the land is predominantly dry, dominated by sandstone, apparently inhospitable, yet with its own distinctive geological features. To the south lies New Mexico. Along the western edge of the forest the **Dolores River** slices through this borderland, pouring out of the most rugged range in the Rockies. The San Juans seem to plunge abruptly rather than blend into the 130,000 square miles of the Colorado Plateau, a region distinguished by sensational natural forms, sage-scented bluffs, deep, vertical-walled canyons, and the wind whistling through elegantly sculpted sandstone created over millions of years. It's a powerful landscape and one in which man has always had to face challenges. Change is visible in epochal time. Adventure materializes routinely.

Southwest Colorado receives abundant sunshine, averaging 300 days of it each year. In the high country, snows average around 300 inches yearly, which means that in a typical year water will gush from the mountains each spring as their snows melt.

No doubt this beneficence of nature attracted the nomadic Indian tribes who found this place around 1,500 years ago, evolving into the community-centered Anasazi, who were probably the earliest settlers here. They first lived in caves and holes dug in the ground, eventually mastering irrigation techniques for farming beans, corn, and squash. Agriculture preceeded the building of

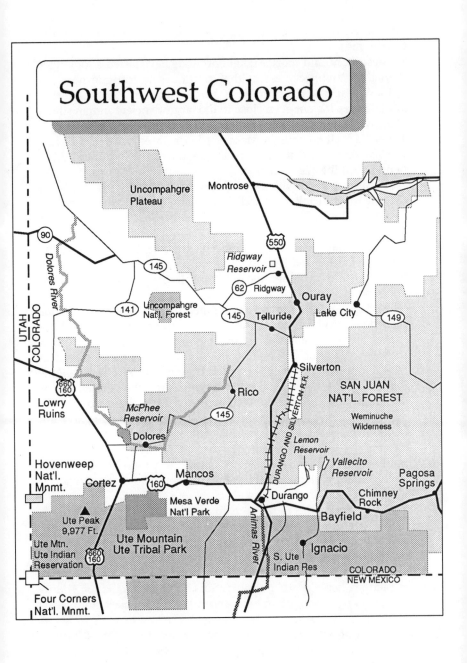

primitive cities in protected canyons that feathered off from the fruitful mesas.

These stone and mortar neighborhoods have lasted a lot longer than their architects, a fact that continues to intrigue nearly a million yearly visitors to Mesa Verde National Park. Covering 52,000 acres, it's not even close to the largest ancient Indian site in southwest Colorado. That distinction belongs to the Ute Mountain Tribal Park. It surrounds Mesa Verde on three sides and covers 125,000 acres. And it's practically unknown. Only around 3,000 people visit the site each year.

Spanish settlers, who came through here briefly in the 1600s looking for gold, left mainly Hispanic names in and around today's San Juan Mountains. Durango was built on the banks of *El Rio de las Animas Perdidas*, "The River of Lost Souls," known today simply as the Animas. *Mesa Verde* means the green table. Nearby are the towns of Cortez and Dolores. The names have lasted longer than the Spanish, who missed the gold and silver riches that were here to be found.

Gold strikes in the 1870s precipitated the development that has extended to today. Miners and related fortune seekers settled the snowy San Juans and the remote region was poised to soon rival Denver as the hub of the Rockies. Silverton was incorporated in 1874. Durango was founded by the Denver and Rio Grande Railroad in 1880. Cattle ranchers built Mancos in 1881. As millions of dollars in gold and silver were extracted from the region, boom towns attracted gunslingers employed to protect the haul, hookers intent on extracting their share, gamblers, and many others. Boisterous saloons prospered, along with business services catering to miners and cowhands. Silverton, Ouray, and Telluride were built to serve hard rock miners. Indians were never far away. It was the wild west. In many ways it still is.

The western spirit remains. Add staggering natural beauty and, despite these busy times, liberty to play, and you can see how southwest Colorado has prevailed through boom and bust with an expansive sense of optimism.

Scenic splendor and a sense of history are the most obvious attractions here. There are hundreds of miles of trails for you to hike, backpack, mountain bike, and ride on horseback, with more miles of rivers to raft, canoe, or kayak. There are hot springs to soothe your weary bones, and the fish are biting in lakes and streams. You can ski the steeps in Telluride, or more moderate terrain at Purgatory, or explore the snowy backcountry. You can wander through ruins or soar above it all on a scenic glider flight. Under a night sky brimming with stars you can conjure visions of Indians and cowboys who knew a good place when they found it.

Getting Around

Southwestern Colorado is a long way from any major highways. There are only a few main roads, which essentially loop though forests, mountains, and deserts punctuated by towns every 20 to 50 miles.

Durango offers the greatest variety of services, including the largest regional airport. It makes a good base for day trips in all directions. And since the Durango-Silverton narrow gauge train is the biggest visitor attraction in town, our suggested route heads north to Silverton, tracing the route of the San Juan Skyway, starting on US 550, one of America's premier scenic drives. In order, the 232-mile loop road passes through Ouray, Ridgway, Telluride, Dolores, Cortez, Mancos, and Hesperus before heading back to Durango.

Of course, we'll take a few detours along the way, tarrying at mountains, rivers, and canyon lands of the Southwest, which are clearly the major sightseeing attractions. But the hand of man has also created a number of sights that may enhance your knowledge and enjoyment of the surrounding natural environment, and perhaps help define the spirit of this place. We'll hit those special places, too, tracing roots that reach from the ancient Anasazi, through the wild west and mining eras, and are lovingly nourished to this day.

Information Sources

Colorado Road Conditions: 303/639-1111.
Colorado Division of Wildlife, Central Regional Office, 606 Broadway, Denver, CO 80216, 303/296-1192, provides information regarding fishing licenses and regulations throughout the state.
US Forest Service, PO Box 25127, 11177 West 8th Avenue, Lakewood, CO 80225, 303/236-9431, provides information on travel, camping, hiking, and other activities in NationalForests.
US Bureau of Land Management, 2850 Youngfield Street, Lakewood, CO 80215, 303/236-2100, provides information regarding recreation on BLM land.
National Park Service, PO Box 25287, Denver, CO 80225, 303/969-2000, provides information on all aspects of travel within National Parks, National Monuments, and recreation areas.
Colorado Division of Parks and Outdoor Recreation, 1313 Sherman Street, Denver, CO 80203, 303/866-3437, offers information regarding State Parks and recreation areas.

US Geological Survey, 1961 Stout Street, Denver, CO 80294, 303/844-4196, provides topographical maps.
Colorado Outfitters Association, PO Box 32438, Aurora, CO 80041, 303/751-9274, offers listings of backcountry outfitters.
Colorado Campground Association, 5101 Pennsylvania Avenue, Boulder, CO 80303, 303/499-9343, offers information on private campgrounds.

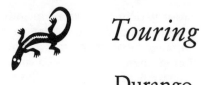

Touring

Durango

Rural philosopher Will Rogers once characterized Durango as being "out of the way and glad of it." This is still the case today, to some extent, although no place is that far out of it anymore. And while tourism has breathed life into the community, there are still plenty of folks around here who would like to close the gate behind themselves and keep Durango a secret.

If you try to find a parking space in July on historic Main Avenue –still the center of commerce in this small city–you'll see that the secret is out.

Summer has always been the busiest time of year for Durango. The winters can be harsh, with plenty of snow and cold weather, though always leavened by plenty of sunshine. It's great if you ski, even though the local ski area is actually 25 miles north of town, unlike Telluride with a ski hill right in town. The distinction makes Durango less of a resort community than a bastion of real life, a town for families and homey values, including inexpensive places to eat and stay, shady city parks, even a local drive-in movie where kids under 12 usually get in free.

In recent years, Indians, miners, ranchers, and cowboys have been joined by others who appreciate the diverse natural endowments of the area. You are equally likely to see fancy all-terrain vehicles toting bike racks or kayaks as you are to see ranchers in battered pickups hauling bales of hay, horses, or cattle. What they all share is an appreciation of the outdoors.

Durango is a friendly, laid-back town. The setting, nestled among red sandstone cliffs that frame the Animas River, which flows through town, is impressive. There are many turn-of-the-century Victorian structures, including complete National Historic Districts on commercial Main Avenue and residential Third Avenue. Both areas can be walked in an hour or so, or you can ride in a horse-drawn carriage.

The **Durango & Silverton Narrow Gauge Railroad** still chugs right through town from May to October, as well as for a month or so in mid-winter, tooting its horn and billowing smoke. Its authentically restored cars add to the sense of the old west that lingers here and is carefully maintained by several historic hotels, honky-tonk saloons, western melodrama performances, modern and traditional Indian and western art galleries, and even an in-town rodeo. Specifics on these attractions and many more are listed in detail throughout the rest of this chapter.

For the most part, simply wandering around the historic downtown business district on Main Avenue, from Fifth to Twelfth streets, will lead you to most of the best local architecture, shopping, and dining. The area has all the elements of a real main street, including the train station, and is not not just a touristy western Disneyland.

For history buffs, the **Animas School Museum**, 31st Street and West 2nd Avenue, Durango, CO 81301, 303/259-2402, offers a concise selection of Anasazi artifacts, other man-made items from the early mining and ranching eras, and displays explaining the area's natural history. The building is a restored turn-of-the-century schoolhouse and one exhibit features the pioneer "Joy" cabin.

For a more academic appraisal of the area's charms, the **Center of Southwest Studies**, Fort Lewis College, College Heights, Durango, CO 81301, 303/247-7456, is connected to the **Fort Lewis College Museum and Archive**. It offers one of the best collections of writings, charts, and rare documents all relating to the history of the Four Corners region. In addition, the four-year college hosts special events, lectures, and concerts throughout the school year.

Durango Arts Center, 835 Main Avenue, Durango, CO 81301, 303/259-2606, is upstairs in the Main Mall. Gallery shows change every three weeks and include national travelling shows, local artists, juried shows, educational exhibits, and children's shows. The Arts Center also coordinates summer concerts in city parks and is a ticket outlet for cultural events.

A **Municipal Pool** is located at 2400 Main Avenue, 303/247-9999.

Getting There

Durango is served by the modern little **La Plata County Airport**, 16 miles east of town and served by several airlines.

America West Express, 303/259-5178 or 800/247-5692, serves Durango with connections through Phoenix. **Continental Express**,

303/259-3466 or 800/525-0280, offers connections through Denver. **Mesa Airlines,** 303/259-5178 or 800/933-MESA, offers connections through Albuquerque. **United Express,** 303/259-5178 or 800/241-6522, serves Durango with connections through Farmington, NM or Denver.

Rental cars are available at the airport from, **Avis,** 303/247-9761; **Budget,** 303/259-1841; **Dollar,** 303/259-3012; **Hertz,** 303/247-5288; **National,** 303/259-0068 or 800/227-7368; or **Sears,** 303/259-1842. Other car rental agencies are located in the area. **Rent-A-Wreck of Durango,** 21698 US 160 West, Durango, CO 81301, 303/259-5858 or 800/421-7253, fax 303/247-2111; **Sunshine Motors,** 20909 US 160 West, Durango, CO 81301, 303/259-2980; or **Thrifty Car Rental,** 20541 US 160 West, Durango, CO 81301, 303/259-3504 or 800/367-2277.

For additional information, the **Durango Area Chamber Resort Association** maintains an office at Gateway Park, 111 South Camino del Rio, Durango, CO 81302, 303/247-0312 or 800/525-8855. Their mailing address is PO Box 2587, Durango, CO 81302. The office maintains considerable files and brochures relating to activities and services throughout the entire region and far beyond the city limits.

Southeast of Durango

About 10 miles south of La Plata Field on CO 172 is the small town of Ignacio, the tribal headquarters of the Southern Ute tribe. These modern Indians have long operated a small motel, the Sky Ute Lodge, 303/563-4531, a restaurant, tourist center, and a **Cultural Center Museum and Gallery,** all at the same phone number. They also have one of the few radio stations in the area, KSUT, 89.9 FM, with something besides country music or top 40. It's the local National Public Radio station, so scheduling includes nationally syndicated news and features, as well as creative programming.

The tribe used to run bingo tournaments on Friday nights, but that has been replaced by the newest enterprise on the reservation—a 40,000-square-foot limited stakes casino that opened in the fall of 1993 in the remodeled **Sky Ute Lodge & Casino.** A mega-bingo purse totalling a million dollars is possible 5 days a week, Wednesday through Sunday. Various poker and blackjack tables, as well as more than 100 slot machines are open daily from 8 AM to 4 AM.

The **Sky Ute Downs Equestrian Center,** 303/563-4502, offers riding instruction and seasonal rodeo events. And the tribe hosts a four-day-long spring Bear Dance, a Sun Dance in July, and an early

September Pow-Wow with members of tribes from around the country. On Wednesdays, June through August, the tribe's Southern Ute Heritage Dancers perform along with drummers and storytellers. The shows include a tour of the Cultural Center and Museum, and a barbecue dinner. For information contact **Southern Ute Tourist Center**, 303/565-4531 or 800/876-7017.

There's not really much happening in Ignacio, although casino gambling is changing that. One thing you can do here is order a custom-fitted, hand-made pair of cowboy boots. Stop in for a fitting and to select from a variety of leathers at **Custom Boots by Larry Smith**, 655 Browning Avenue, Ignacio, CO 81137, 303/563-9510. They're guaranteed to fit.

North of Ignacio and 42 miles east of Durango is the **Chimney Rock Archaeological Area**. The site is situated on CO 151, three miles south of US 160 East. It contains 16 excavated ruins of an Anasazi village, presumed to be related to Chaco Canyon. The ruins are perched atop a high mesa overlooking the Piedra River and are only accessible if you take a two-hour guided walking tour, offered four times daily, May 15 to September 15. There are two trails leading to excavated ruins and an estimated 200 undisturbed sites. One trail is a third of a mile over a smooth surface. The other trail is rougher, over loose rock, and is a half-mile. The tour includes a visit to a Forest Service lookout tower offering views of the Pueblo ruins and the **Piedra Valley**. For information phone 303/883-2442 or 303/264-2268.

Northeast of Durango

Vallecito Reservoir is 23 miles northeast of Durango at the end of Florida Road. It offers 22 miles of forested shoreline, surrounded by peaks of the San Juans, motels, a guest ranch, and campgrounds. Several operators have boat rentals and at times the fishing is pretty good for trout, kokanee salmon, bluegill, or crappies. Additional information can be found under accommodations and various adventure categories below, or you can contact **Vallecito Chamber of Commerce**, PO Box 804, Bayfield, CO 81122, 303/884-9782.

The smaller **Lemon Reservoir** is just a little up the road from Vallecito and is also covered later under adventures on water.

San Juan National Forest

The **San Juan National Forest** extends in all directions from Durango, east to west from Pagosa Springs to Dove Creek, and from Silverton in the north to the New Mexico state line. The forest includes a federally designated scenic byway, the San Juan Skyway, which links the major towns covered in this chapter and is considered one of the top scenic drives in the nation.

The forest is laced with miles and miles of maintained hiking trails, many of which you can enjoy on mountain bikes or horseback. There are numerous lakes, rivers, and streams which offer opportunities for trout fishing, canoeing, rafting, windsurfing, and boating. Ski areas lease forest land in the vicinity of mountains ranging to more than 14,000 feet.

Cold, crystalline alpine lakes are fed by snowmelt, and waterfalls tumble into rugged, remote canyons. Improbable geological formations stand guard over abandoned gold and silver mines, all taking on a special glow in the fall when aspen and cottonwood leaves turn golden yellow among reddening oaks and a dense, dark backdrop of evergreens. At extreme elevations the only month of the year when it is unlikely to snow is July.

The Forest Service provides numerous recreational facilities that are covered in more detail later in this chapter. For information contact **San Juan National Forest**, 701 Camino del Rio, Durango, CO 81302, 303/247-4874.

Weminuche Wilderness

Within the San Juan National Forest, the **Weminuche Wilderness** encompasses one of the most sizable wilderness areas in the United States, covering 459,000 acres, including 80 miles along the continental divide, preserved by law in a primitive state. Fixed improvements and human residency are prohibited. The mountainous Weminuche boasts elevations averaging 10,000 feet and includes more than 400 miles of trails for hikers or horseback riders. Mountain bikes, motorized vehicles, chain saws, helicopters, and all other mechanized reminders of civilization are prohibited.

The wilderness area offers no permanent facilities, not even ready-made campsites, picnic tables or latrines, although primitive camping and licensed fishing are allowed. The Weminuche is accessible by hiking trails beginning at Vallecito Lake, 26 miles northwest of Durango, Silverton, or via a lengthy overland route from Purgatory-Durango Ski Area. The closest access to the wilderness area is from the Durango-Silverton Narrow Gauge Railroad, which will drop you at Needleton, south of Silverton. You can then flag the train down at the same spot when you want transportation back to civilization.

High country travel in the Weminuche can be demanding or even treacherous before mid-June. Unless it's been an unusually dry winter, above 10,000 feet you will usually see snow on the ground into July. Melting snow means muddy trails and fast-moving, hazardous streams you may have to ford on foot if no log bridge is available.

Once the snow is gone, colorful carpets of wildflowers begin to appear in direct proportion to how wet the previous winter has been. Wild berries appear in mid- to late August, and last through the first tentative freezes in early September, when the leaves start to change.

Visitor services may be found on the periphery of the Weminuche, in Silverton, Vallecito, or more commonly, in Durango. Information is available from the San Juan National Forest office in Durango (see above, under San Juan National Forest).

Silverton

Silverton, situated at a lofty elevation of 9,032 feet and, 50 miles north of Durango on US 550 North, calls itself "the mining town that never quit." This was once a prosperous boom town in the heyday of the gold and silver mines from which millions of dollars in ore were extracted. Today, Silverton retains something of the feel of a frontier town, if only because it's a little too down at the heels to qualify as a trendy, restored exhibit. Durango is Yuppiesville compared to Silverton, which is more remote and occasionally inaccessible. During the hard winter of 1993 Silverton was isolated by avalanches and road closures for six days during a heavy snowstorm. Food had to be airlifted in.

Most of the time, though, you can get here from Durango or Ouray via US 550 or, during the summer, on the Durango-Silverton Narrow Gauge Railroad. The town exists largely on train passengers tourist dollars and, when the railroad stops running in October, many of the local shops and services close for the season. The town is not unlike a step back in time. Practically every structure on Greene Street, the short main drag, has historic significance dating to the dawn of the 20th century or before, and the whole town has been certified a National Historic Landmark. Depending on how interested you are in these rather dusty and authentic-feeling structures and the plethora of gift shops and tourist-oriented businesses that now occupy them, you can spend anywhere from an hour to a day of sightseeing (you get two hours if you take the train and are waiting for the soonest return departure for Durango).

In many of the old buildings business is still conducted on a daily basis, such as at 1129 Greene, which was the town's first butcher shop, built in 1893. The present occupant, the **San Juan Cafe & Saloon**, boasts an original hardwood floor, 13-foot pressed tin ceiling, unique antique bar and backbar, and Victorian decor. Other buildings have been preserved by the county, such as the one-time County Jail, circa 1902, now housing the **San Juan County Historical Museum**, 1567 Greene Street, Silverton, CO 81433, 303/387-5838. Modest displays recount pioneering life in the community, mining lore, and natural history of the San Juan Mountains.

The Silverton Standard & Miner, 1257 Greene Street, Silverton, Colorado, 81433, 303/387-5477, claims to be the longest running newspaper, as well as the oldest business, on the western slope of the Colorado Rockies. The wooden structure where it resides was originally a general store in 1875 and is one of the oldest buildings in town. Today you can buy books, videos, maps, or the quirky, enduring newspaper. The building next door, now occupied by Silverton Liquors, was built in 1883 as a combined furniture store and undertaker's. And Blair Street, often referred to as Notorious Blair Street, was where most of the raunchiest saloons, boarding houses, and bordellos were located during the prosperous early mining years when there was "silver by the ton" being removed from the nearby mountains to be spent in town. The building at 1161 Blair was built in 1883 and was the location of Mattie's Place, also known from a sign in the window as the Welcome Saloon.

Other long-lasting structures with a more temperate historic background include the one that housed Silverton's Congregational Church, soon after its cornerstone was laid in 1880. It's now the **United Church of Silverton**, 1060 Reese Street, 303/387-5325. The **Carnegie Library**, 1111 Reese Street, 303/387-5770, was constructed in 1906 and is still the town's public library.

Much of Silverton's current appeal resides in the surrounding mountains that dwarf the town. The Weminuche Wilderness (see above) is nearby, as is the **Million Dollar Highway**, actually US 550 North, connecting to Ouray over Red Mountain Pass. Depending on what story you want to believe, the highway got its name from a million dollars worth of gold chips mixed-in with the pavement, or from the initial cost of building the road in the 1880s. Some claim the name has to do with the million-dollar views you get from a roadbed clinging to steep, hairpin switchbacks, carved out of solid rock, in the shadows cast by mountain peaks.

For a big step into the past, the **One Hundred Gold Mine Tour**, PO Box 430, Silverton, CO 81433, 800/872-3009, offers a one-hour underground adventure, five miles east of town, on CO 110 (Greene Street). The tour includes a ride down into the mine shaft via train. Open June through September, tours depart every half-hour in July and August, every hour during June and September.

If you continue past the One Hundred Gold Mine, in another eight miles you will come to **Animas Forks**, another ex-boom town circa 1880, now a well-preserved ghost town. Numerous decrepit, photogenic buildings remain, along with an old mill, boarded-up mine shafts, and unrecognizable structures or crumbling foundations. The road is passable in a passenger car if the weather is dry, but a four-wheel-drive will provide a more secure ride, particularly if you plan to explore beyond Animas Forks. Adjacent to the ghost town is a steep and dangerous road popular for jeeping, leading to 12,800-foot **Engineer Pass** and the **Alpine Loop Backcountry Byway**. The Alpine Loop is an exceptional, challenging, 63-mile drive in the ultra high country, beyond a doubt one of the most spectacular scenic drives in the west.

The Chamber of Commerce maintains a year-round Visitor Center at the Y on Highway 550, at the western edge of town. An in-town branch at 12th and Blair, near the train stop, is open during the summer. For additional information contact **Silverton Chamber of Commerce**, PO Box 565, Silverton, CO 81433, 303/387-5654 or 800/752-4494.

Ouray

Ouray is another one-time mining town that has managed to cling to life in the challenging mountains of southwestern Colorado, thanks largely to a vast network of underground thermal hot springs. Nestled within a deep box canyon beneath snow-topped mountains, the serene, Alpine setting and therapeutic waters have brought the town the nickname "The Switzerland of America."

Regrettably, there are more than a few ersatz chalet-type homes and motels throughout the town, but for the most part you'll see more mining era Victorian homes lining unusually broad, tree-lined streets.

Situated 25 miles north of Silverton and over the north side of Red Mountain Pass on US 550, the earliest permanent structure here, in 1875, was a saloon. Church services were first held in a different saloon. Worshippers sat on whiskey kegs.

Not too long ago, Ouray was only a summer destination, with much of the town shuttered during reliably harsh winters. But the ever-increasing popularity of nearby Telluride changed that. Little Telluride is located up and over on the other side of 14,150-foot Mount Sneffels, or 50 road miles from here. It attracts more skiers than it has rooms for, so a deal was worked out where skiers could stay in Ouray, or other nearby communities, and receive a half-price lift ticket. Then, some of the refugees from Telluride discovered the terrific cross-country and backcountry skiing, along with great ice climbing on frozen waterfalls nearby. A winter season was born. Now some, though not all, motels, restaurants, and other town businesses stay open year-round.

It's still plenty quiet in winter when Red Mountain Pass is closed by an avalanche and today, rather than making outdated comparisons with Switzerland, sporty locals claim that "Ouray is like Telluride used to be."

Bigger crowds come to town in the summer, which is still the high season here, primarily for camping, hiking and jeeping, then taking a soak in the hot springs. The latter is something reportedly enjoyed by the town's namesake, Chief Ouray, a Ute Indian leader who is said to have bathed in the steaming waters. The town is very small, with only around 800 residents, which is many fewer than were here in 1900, when local gold mines were in full swing. The legendary, hugely profitable, Camp Bird Mine was producing $3 million in gold yearly. Camp Bird's owner, Tom Walsh, eventually spent some of his $20 million fortune to buy the Hope Diamond.

You can easily walk the few main streets to have a look around or, if you've had it with Victoriana in Silverton, drive directly to the north end of town and jump into the largest thermal pool in town, the one-million-gallon **Hot Springs Pool**, 303/325-4638. The facility includes two outdoor thermal pools maintained at 104 degrees F year-round, picnic tables, a playground, an indoor gym, and locker rooms.

Back in the center of town, the one indoor attraction that merits an hour or two of time, the **Ouray Historical Museum**, is on the corner of Fifth Street and 6th Avenue, 303/325-4576, in a building that was originally a hospital built in 1887. It has an interesting collection of Victorian-era goodies, hotel logs, guns, saloon memorabilia, mining tools and equipment, and so forth, as well as a recreated hospital room, general store, and law office. For a different experience of what gold mining was like, try the **Bachelor-**

Syracuse Mine Tour, 1222 County Road 14, PO Box 380W, Ouray, CO 81427, 303/325-4500, a mile north of town, then right on County Road 14. Between May 20 and September 15 you can ride 3,350 feet horizontally on a tram car into Gold Hill. Inside, a guide describes the hard rock mining that was conducted here until the 1980s. Emerging from the shaft, you can pan for gold, dine at an outdoor cafe, or visit the gift shop and buy a gold nugget. The only day the mine tour is closed during its season is the Fourth of July. That's because the whole town usually turns out for the biggest event of the year, water fights on Main Street. Participants wearing defensive gear, including motorcycle helmets and chest protectors, spray each other with fire hoses with three-inch nozzles. Whoever hits the pavement first is the loser.

Speaking of water, you can walk from town to the 285-foot **Box Canyon Falls and Park**, 303/325-4464. There's a picnic area in the park, open from May to mid-October, and there are two bridges, one wooden, near the base of the falls, and one made of steel at the top of them.

There's a Visitor Center next to the Hot Springs Pool. For additional information contact **Ouray Chamber of Commerce and Ouray Tourism Board**, Box 145, Ouray, CO 81427, 303/325-4746.

Ridgway

There's not a whole lot going in the town of Ridgway, other than that it is fast becoming a bedroom community for Telluride (designer Ralph Lauren has an enormous ranch near here as does the actor, Dennis Weaver). The town offers the same lodging/half-price lift ticket deal with the ski area as Ouray.

A new, big attraction here is the **Ridgway State Recreation Area**, 15 miles north of Ridgway, off US 550. Opened in 1989, the state park encompasses a large reservoir, complete with a marina, boat ramp, fish cleaning station, beach, and several campgrounds. Winter sports available include ice-fishing, snowmobiling, and cross-country skiing. An information center is near the entrance to the park. Phone 303/626-5822 or 800/678-2267.

A Visitor Center is set in a large, modern, Victorian-style structure at the intersection of US 550 and CO 62. For additional information contact **Ridgeway USA Visitor Center**, 102 Village Square West, Ridgeway, CO 81432, 303/626-5805.

Telluride

Trendy, fashionable Telluride was not always thus. It's really only in the last few years that people who pay attention to such things started calling it the next Aspen.

Well, it's got all the natural attributes and a pretty, savvy, and increasingly wealthy population of 1,300 and counting, to make that threat come true. Real estate prices are astronomical. Hollywood stars have started to buy property. Tom Cruise was married here. Mr. and Mrs. Donald Trump honeymooned here. Can the *National Enquirer* be far behind?

This is basically another wild mining town that recognized the need to encourage tourism to insure its survival. Continued conflict between forces for and against development demonstrate that the community has not embraced the concept wholeheartedly, yet, for its size, Telluride offers some of the greatest variety and highest quality of attractions, events, services, and activities of anywhere in southwestern Colorado.

Situated at 8,745 feet, on CO 145, Telluride occupies a scenic and memorable site. The town, which is a Registered National Historic Landmark, sits nestled in a deep and narrow canyon near the headwaters of the **San Miguel River**, at the base of a waterfall, **Ingram Falls**.

Surrounded by the peaks of the **San Juan Mountains** and the **Uncompaghre National Forest**, Telluride was established in 1878, incorporated from humble beginnings as an incorrigible tent city and mining camp called Columbia. In 1891, the town's population topped out at 4,000. Tents and lean-tos were replaced by large, elegant Victorian homes, public buildings constructed of cut stone, fancy hotels, including the **New Sheridan House**, a hotel built in 1895 and still operating today, 26 saloons and a dozen brothels.

Future outlaw Butch Cassidy was a mule skinner for one of the mines here. He practiced fast getaways on horseback on Main Street. Then he held up his first bank, the San Miguel Valley Bank, right here in Telluride, on June 24, 1889.

In 1896, shortly after a collapse in silver prices, William Jennings Bryan, a perennial presidential candidate, stood in front of the New Sheridan House and delivered his legendary "Cross of Gold" speech, decrying the new gold standard which had decimated the silver mining operations overnight in 1893.

Within 30 years the bottom had completely dropped out of the gold and silver markets and, combined with labor union riots over plummeting wages that plagued the town and the closing of the Bank of Telluride, the population dropped to around 500 residents in 1930. The last bordello closed in 1959. The town languished through the 1960s when you could have bought a house for as little as $3,000. It would have been a good investment. Today there's nary a property in town you can touch for under $200,000.

The creation that turned things around for Telluride was the ski area which opened in 1972, the same year the town cancelled the annual Fourth of July celebration after motorcycle gangs effectively closed down Main Street for their own private party. In the spirit of the good old days, firemen had to hose them down.

Over time, as skiers discovered the exceptional terrain here, the town gradually put itself back together. Homes and buildings were restored and the Telluride Mountain Village, a modern upscale enclave designed to take pressure off the small downtown, was built. It includes a hotel/spa, bed and breakfast lodge, condominiums, restaurants, golf course, tennis courts, ski company offices, and a convenience store. It is situated seven miles south of Telluride on the other side of the ski hill, off CO 145. You can access it by skiing directly from town.

Aside from turn-of-the century buildings and supposedly compatible modern architecture, Telluride is surrounded by ghost towns and abandoned mining camps, hiking and jeep trails, horseback and mountain bike trails, fishing holes and, of course, the estimable skiing and winter sports. These are all detailed below, under Adventures.

As for the old buildings and houses in town, many are spruced up with multi-color paint jobs, and the compact downtown is perfect for the obligatory walk-around of an hour or two, longer if you dip into shops and galleries or the **Sheridan Bar**. It's downstairs in the hotel at 225 Colorado Avenue, 303/728-3626, an historic monument in its own right, complete with tin ceiling, tiered wooden floor, and an ornate cherry wood backbar.

Among the more interesting sites is the **San Miguel County Historical Museum**, 317 North Fir Street, Telluride, CO 81435, 303/728-3344, occupying the old Miner's Hospital Building, circa 1895. The collection features such eclectic memorabilia as an 800-year-old Anasazi blanket, a silver nitrate film of Leo Tolstoy's life brought to town by an immigrant, a lightweight wicker casket used to transport the bodies of miners who died in high country mines, dance hall garments from the bordello district, mining artifacts, and lots of old photos. Open late May to mid-October.

East of town on CO 145 is the longest waterfall in the state, 365-feet **Bridal Veil Falls**. At the top of the falls is an old hydro-electric mill that is a registered historic landmark. It is being refurbished to produce electricity again for the first time since 1954.

And if you want to get to the mountaintop without breaking a summer sweat or putting on skis in winter, chairlift rides are offered from town to a 10,500-foot overlook via the **Coonskin Chairlift**. You can ride or walk down. Open Thursday to Monday, mid-June through September.

Telluride's **Town Park** is where the largest outdoor summer festivals (see below, under Eco-Tours & Cultural Excursions) are held. It is also the site of a playground, children's fishing pond, baseball, soccer, basketball and volleyball facilities, two free tennis courts, and a covered picnic area with barbecue pits. In winter the town operates a skating rink and a groomed cross-country ski trail that circles the large park. Camping is available.

Getting There

Telluride Regional Airport, 303/728-3436, is the highest commercial airport in the United States, situated at 9,080 feet, five miles west of town. Service is currently provided by **Continental Express**, 303/728-3194 or 800/525-0280, which offers the most flights from Denver, or in winter only by **Delta Connection**, from Salt Lake City, **Mesa Airlines/America West Express**, from Phoenix or Albuquerque, or **United Express** from Denver. Contact the airport or central reservations (see below) for airline information.

Rental cars are available from **Budget** or **Thrifty**.

For additional information contact **Telluride Chamber Resort Association**, PO Box 653, 666 West Colorado Avenue, Telluride, CO 81435, 303/728-3041, fax 303/728-6475, or **Telluride Central Reservations**, PO Box 1009, Telluride, CO 81435, 303/728-4431 or 800/525-3455, fax 303/728-6475.

Lizard Head Wilderness

This 42,000-acre wilderness is located, west of CO 145, 10 miles southwest of Telluride and 40 miles northeast of Cortez. Within the wilderness are **Mount Wilson, Wilson Peak**, and **El Diente Peak**, all higher than 14,000 feet, as well as other summits above 13,000 feet. Hiking, horseback riding, backpacking, and mountain climbing are popular in the area. Weather is always unpredictable here and the terrain is challenging, including many exposed ridges, loose rock, and permanent snow fields. There are practically no trail signs. Maps are necessary. For information contact the **Dolores Ranger District**, San Juan National Forest (see below, under McPhee Reservoir), or **Norwood Ranger District**, Uncompaghre

National Forest, 1760 East Grand Avenue, PO Box 388, Norwood, CO 81423, 303/327-4261.

Dolores

Dolores occupies a position along CO 145, on the border of the Rockies and the Colorado Plateau. It's more of a base station for area explorations than a destination in itself – a place to buy gas, a fishing license, and maybe a meal if you're really hungry and not too particular. It does have a few old buildings, a fine museum, and a prominently displayed example of a strange rail car known as the **Galloping Goose**. Part bus, car, and rail car, the Goose was at one time the vehicle of choice on the frequently snow-clogged tracks of the old Rio Grande Southern Railroad which ran through here.

The main attractions are out of town. **McPhee Reservoir** (see below) is nearby, and rafting certain stretches of the **Dolores River** may provide legendary adventure during the high water season.

The **Anasazi Heritage Center**, 27501 CO 184, Dolores, CO 81323, 303-882-4811, was created to preserve Anasazi artifacts removed from 1,600 Anasazi sites located in the Dolores River Canyon when it was flooded to create McPhee Reservoir. Operated by the BLM, it actually contains a collection of Indian tools and artifacts from the entire Four Corners region. Inside the museum are interactive exhibits employing high tech equipment, alongside an ancient stone used for grinding corn, called a *metate*, a loom, and a recreated pit house typical of the Anasazi era. There's a "please touch" section for children and a hologram display showing what the Anasazi looked like based on a human skull. Up a hill from the museum, overlooking the reservoir, are the 12th-century **Dominguez and Escalante Ruins**.

West of the Anasazi Center on CO 184, then north on US 666 to the south edge of Dove Creek, the "Pinto Bean Capital of the World," and east on a signed dirt road for 11 miles, is the **Dolores Canyon Overlook**. From this 2,500-foot-high perch set above the Dolores River, you can see the twisting, red-walled canyon as well as the mountain ranges of southwestern Colorado and southeastern Utah.

For information about the Dolores area contact **Dolores River Valley Chamber of Commerce**, PO Box 602, Dolores, CO 81323, 303/882-4018.

McPhee Reservoir

Situated northwest of Dolores, off CO 145, this is a 4,500-acre man-made lake snuggled into a timbered shoreline. It opened in 1988 and is just starting to hit its stride with good fishing for trout, smallmouth bass, crappies, and kokanee. In addition, a range of watersports is available, including swimming, water skiing, jet skiing, and a no-wake canoeing area. There are hiking trails, campgrounds, and picnic areas, most in and around two full-service recreation complexes.

The **McPhee Recreation Area** is on the west side of the reservoir and includes the full-service **Beaver Creek Marina**. **House Creek Recreation Area** is on the east side of the reservoir, 15 miles north of Dolores, off the Dolores/Norwood Road (Forest Road 506). There are also five other fishing access points spaced at intervals around the lake.

For information contact the **Dolores Ranger District,** San Juan National Forest, 521 Central Avenue, PO Box 210, Dolores, CO 81323, 303/882-7296.

Cortez

Eight miles south of Dolores on CO 145, at US 160, where the mountains meet the desert, Cortez calls itself "The Gateway To Indian Country." The promotional terminology is actually true in this case, mainly because of the number of ancient and modern Indian sites that are within day-trip distance of this small, western agricultural town. It is estimated that 40,000 Anasazi lived in and around the site of modern day Cortez, in the Montezuma Valley, from 900 to 1300 A.D. Today, around 7,000 residents call Cortez home.

To the east of town are the **La Plata Range** of the San Juans, reaching over 13,000 feet high. To the west, the vast high **Sonoran Desert** of the Colorado Plateau stretches to an almost unimaginably distant horizon.

One of the most useful places to go in town is the **Welcome Center,** 928 East Main, Cortez, CO 81321, 303/565-4048 or 800/346-6528. The center is operated by the Cortez Chamber of Commerce. It offers free maps, brochures, coffee, and information about the Four Corners region. There are Indian dances or theatrical gunfights at 7 PM every night in the summer at the city park, next to the center. There is also a municipal pool with a highly regarded water slide.

A little-known but fascinating in-town site is just a block off Main, at the **Cortez Center-University of Colorado Museum**, 25 North Market Street, Cortez, CO 81321, 303/565-1151. The small, informative museum offers interpretive exhibits on the progression of Anasazi history, from the earliest Basketmakers, through the classic Pueblo period. The museum also has several videos describing various Anasazi sites in the area. Indian storytellers and artists give presentations during the summer at 8:15 PM.

Again, a small downtown area can be covered easily on foot in an hour or two. There are several interesting antique shops here, and on the east side of town, on US 160, several trading posts sporting huge, garish signs. You can't miss them--that is unless you prefer to keep going.

Hovenweep National Monument

The rugged red-walled canyons, scrubby desert lands, and mesas north of the San Juan River were occupied by numerous bands of pre-Columbian Pueblo Indians until their disappearance in the 1300s. The entire region, including private property holdings, is dotted with Indian ruins, including many, many more than are open to the public. One public site that is worth the lengthy trip on bad roads is **Hovenweep National Monument**, c/o Mesa Verde National Park, CO 81330, 303/529-4461.

The park is situated among slickrock and desert, 50 miles west of Cortez via McElmo Canyon Road (County Road G), which starts three miles south of Cortez, off US 160, or by the Pleasant View Road (County Road CC), 20 miles north of Cortez, off US 666, to County Road 10, which leads to the site. Some of these roads are poorly marked, or unmarked, so take a map with you.

Hovenweep was created in 1923 and straddles the Colorado-Utah border. It includes 784 acres and six major groups of unusual ruins indicating the prior residence of a large community, possibly Anasazi, who stopped here after leaving the cliff dwellings at Mesa Verde. The ruins here are further distinguished by their unusual designs of square, oval, circular, and D-shaped towers, indicative of refined masonry techniques. Today, there are walls standing 20 feet high, although any mortar that had been used to hold the rocks together 700 years ago has long since deteriorated.

Hovenweep is just one of the fantastic Anasazi sites in the Southwest. It's easy to imagine Indians living here in these haunting towers, surveying the expansive high desert, perhaps watching out for the approach of enemies through peepholes.

Sqaure Tower Ruin is the most famous and frequently photographed ruin site here. It is the best preserved and the only site accessible by car. Relatively easy hikes along well-marked, rocky trails lined with cacti and low-slung trees lead to all the other ruins. The two crumbling pueblos of the **Cajon Ruins**, across the stateline in Utah, are the least well preserved, having been heavily vandalized before the monument was established. On the Colorado side are the **Holly, Hackberry Canyon, Cutthroat Castle,** and **Goodman Point Ruins.**

There is a ranger station where you can pick up trail maps, and inside is a small display explaining the terrain and ruins here. There is a campground but no visitor services–save for a soda machine. There are trading posts at **Hatch,** 16 miles west, or **Ismay** 14 miles southeast, but they keep irregular hours. Bring provisions from Cortez and start out with a full tank of gas. Hiking is allowed, but only on maintained trails. This is also a good place for bike riding which is restricted to maintained roads. Make sure you have plenty of water, especially during summer months, when it gets extremely hot out here.

Lowry Ruins

Sixteen miles north of Hovenweep, on County Road 10, then one mile west on County Road CC (or nine miles west of US 666 at Pleasant View) lies a tiny National Historic Landmark–**Lowry Pueblo Ruins**. For information contact Bureau of Land Management, 701 Camino del Rio, Durango, CO 81302, 303/247-4082. The roads leading to Lowry are probably unmarked. The site is somewhat austere–no campground, no Visitor Center, and no park ranger. The gravel road from Pleasant View is a good one, but it is not maintained in winter. The site does have a picnic table.

Lowry is thought to have been occupied by only 100 or so farmers who grew the standard array of corn, beans, and squash for only 50 years, until 1140 A.D. Today, Lowry is visited by very few, and therein lies its special charm.

The Lowry site includes one of the largest circular *kivas*, which were communal gathering spots, yet discovered in the Southwest. The ruins also contain 40 rooms, some of which had three stories, and eight smaller kivas. There is also a rare painted kiva, which is protected by a modern roof to help preserve five layers of old, faint plaster paintings inside.

Ute Mountain Tribal Park

Twelve miles south of Cortez on US 160 is the entrance to an extraordinary ancient Indian site that dwarfs nearby Mesa Verde National Park and surrounds it on three sides. It is regarded as sacred ground by the Ute Mountain Utes, whose arid reservation lands spread across the extreme southwestern corner of Colorado, and has been virtually untouched for hundreds of years. For information call the **Ute Mountain Tribal Park**, Towaoc, CO 81334, 303/565-3751 extension 282.

The park extends along the now dry **Mancos River Valley** and contains only a few excavated surface ruins and cliff dwellings decorated with petroglyphs and paintings. Hundreds of additional sites remain unexcavated. Long protected and now carefully operated by Indians, the area has maintained a completely different sensibility than other Anasazi sites administered by the federal government. If you are intrigued by the Anasazi and their ruins, this is the one site that should not be missed. Its evocative simplicity reverberates with an unequalled authenticity and the Indian guides add a resonance that is not generally provided by uniformed federal park rangers.

Visitors are not allowed into the tribal park on their own and are required to reserve space for guided half- or full-day tours. Your guide meets you outside the park and drives through the 125,000-acre site in his own vehicle. A small group of participants, limited to 20 per tour, follow in their own vehicles. A full-day tour takes six hours and crosses nearly 100 miles of sage-scented, rugged high desert. There are frequent stops to wander over an ancient Anasazi domain, blanketed with thousands of distinctive pottery shards, tool fragments, corn cobs, and other shattered remnants of a vanished race. The guide points out buried pit houses and burial mounds, leads short hikes to hidden petroglyph panels from 1200 A.D., rock paintings, and strategically placed guard towers. Towards the end of the tour, you visit the only excavated ruins in the park, walking single file along a narrow trail in a shady canyon. There are several short ladders you must climb to reach the trail leading to a handful of ruins. Those who wish to, may climb a 30-foot ladder leading to an incredible, unrestored Anasazi ruin that has been left intact by the Utes, exactly as it was when people lived here 800 years ago.

Carry water, food, and start with a full tank of gas. A day here may be physically demanding, especially in the summertime when temperatures commonly top 100 degrees, and the only water in the park is in a tank near the start of the road.

Aside from group tours, you may reserve an Indian guide for day-long or overnight backpacking, biking, or horseback trips through prehistory.

The newest addition to the Ute Mountain Ute Reservation is a limited stakes casino. The small, active casino is almost directly opposite to the entrance for the Ute Mountain Park, 11 miles south of Cortez on US 160/666. It's open 8 AM to 4 AM daily and offers slots, video poker, blackjack, poker, and bingo. Phone **Ute Mountain Casino**, 303/565-7000 or 800/258-8007 for information.

Due west of the Ute Mountain Tribal Park, directly behind the new casino, is a curious landmark visible for 50 miles from the east or west. **Sleeping Ute Mountain** rises almost 10,000 feet from the horizontal desert floor. Some people don't see the resemblance, but for others it really does look like a reclining Indian chief, a sleeping Ute on his back, his head to the north, his feet to the south, with strong arms folded across his proud chest. It can be seen clearly from Hovenweep, Ute Mountain Tribal Park, and Mesa Verde, but the best view is probably from the parking lot of the casino!

Mesa Verde National Park

Situated seven miles west of Cortez, off US 160, this is by far the most visited tourist attraction in the region. Mesa Verde National Park attracts nearly one million visitors yearly to its prominent, broad-topped mesa, haunting side canyons, expansive scenic vistas, and stabilized, maintained, ancient Indian ruins. Situated in the high canyon country between Cortez and Mancos, the park offers scenic paved roads and short trails leading to a large concentration of Indian ruins.

This site contains the most mysterious of all Anasazi structures–the puzzling and inaccessible cliff dwellings. These are literally holes cut into the vertical canyon walls and no one really knows how the Anasazi got to these sites–it is presumed they used very long ladders–or why they bothered. Were they seeking protection, or simply privacy? Only the strange, remote architecture remains, raising questions, providing no clear cut answers.

Utes and Navajos have known about these ruins for much longer than the archaeologists who have been studying them for only 100 years. But Indians don't like to hang around places where other Indians have died, so they left the site alone. Local cowboys tracking stray cattle discovered this place only in the late 1880s. It was declared the nation's first National Park reserved to protect man-made artifacts in 1906.

Mesa Verde National Park

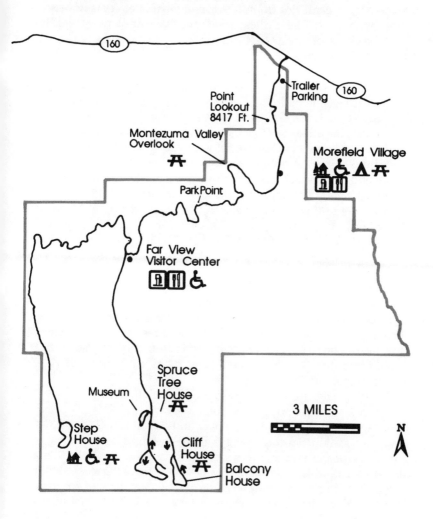

160

Trailer Parking

160

Point Lookout 8417 Ft.

Montezuma Valley Overlook

Morefield Village

Park Point

Far View Visitor Center

Spruce Tree House

Museum

Step House

Cliff House

Balcony House

3 MILES

N

Many of the cliff dwellings, and other canyon rim ruins of a more conventional nature, may be viewed from paved overlooks you can drive to on well-maintained roadways. Numerous other architectural remains are harder to see, requiring arduous hikes ranging in altitude from 6,000 feet to 8,600 feet. Trails to certain ruins involve clambering up and down narrow steps cut out of the rugged terrain. Still other sites are reached only by sturdy, but possibly scary-looking, ladders.

The park represents successive generations of Anasazi who progressed over centuries from living in elemental caverns or hand-dug pit houses. The earliest residents wove baskets of wildly prolific yucca or hemp that thrived here; archaeologists named them Basketmakers.

No evidence of a written language has ever been found, but some of their stories are told in cave paintings that have survived. Other artifacts, coiled clay pots and pottery shards, yucca fiber sandals, stone tools, skeletons, shriveled corn cobs, and irrigation courses on the mesa tops that have remained intact in the ultra-dry, high desert, have been dated to 550 A.D. Along with the impressive structural ruins, these things provide the clues to explain the lifestyles and behavior of these primitive residents. Only later did they master the complex stone and mortar construction that they abandoned here in this rarefied environment, presumably little worse for the wear from the days when this was a significant community.

The good stuff–the five major cliff dwellings and numerous mesa top villages–are 20 miles up the entrance road from US 160. It's at least a 45-minute ride to reach the major ruins, that is assuming there is no traffic, which means any time except the summer. At that peak time, the crowds can be daunting as the vast bulk of visitors make the switchback pilgrimage. Summer can be brutally hot, fall is ideal. Winter is the most deserted, some believe the most mysterious; it definitely affords a more personalized experience than August, though some ruins are closed and Park Services are reduced in winter.

It's four miles from the highway to **Morefield Village**, where a huge, full-service campground for tents, cars, and RVs is located. It's the only campground in the park and has all amenities including a gas station. Several hiking trails start around here. Nearby, at the peak of the winding entrance road, is **Point Lookout**. It's a one-mile round-trip hike to look out over the lip of the mesa at four states, ranging from the desert flats and slot canyons of Arizona, through New Mexico, Utah and the 13,000-foot La Plata Mountains in Colorado. Today the area is known as the **Four Corners**. To the Utes who adopted this land many years after the Anasazi had declined, the view from this spot revealed "the rim of the little world."

It's another nine miles to the **Far View Visitor Center**. Most of the numerous services available in this area are open only from April to October. These include a motel, restaurant, gas station, store, and informative displays.

Open in summer only, there's a turn off for **Wetherill Mesa** at Far View. From the turn, it's a serpentine 20 miles or so to the **Long House Ruins**, **Step House**, and **Badger House** sites spanning almost the entire range of Anasazi occupation. Visits to Long House are restricted to ranger-guided tours only.

A mini-tram takes visitors on a four-mile loop of the area, with numerous stops where you can get out and walk a half-mile to the various ruins. These include mesa-top pit houses, estimated to be nearly 1,400 years old, and structures from the Classic Pueblo period, circa 1,200 A.D.

If you keep going straight for seven miles on the main park road from Far View, you will reach **Chapin Mesa**–the site of an **Archaeology Museum** and the **Park Headquarters**. Both of these are open year-round. The museum has a variety of displays representing just about everything that has ever been recovered from the park. Artifacts, old photos, documents, and maps enumerate the known and presumed chronology of the Anasazi along with the history of the park.

A short trail from the museum leads to **Spruce Tree House**, a big ruin nestled under the rim of a canyon. You can climb around it, peek in the tiny windows and low doorways, go down into a kiva, or simply look at the site from an overlook. Spruce Tree House is open year-round.

It's a half-mile from the museum to the turn-offs for two separate six-mile loops of **Ruins Road**.

The easterly loop leads to the largest cliff dwelling in the world, **Cliff Palace**. It's a half-mile round-trip hike, climbing four 10-foot ladders and stone steps, to reach the site. **Balcony House Ruins**, on the same loop, is situated high in a cliff. You have to climb ladders and crawl through a little tunnel to get to it–the only way to do this is on a guided tour.

The westerly loop leads to **Square Tower House**, **Sun Point**, and **Sun Temple Ruins**.

Hour-long, ranger-guided tours start every 30 minutes to Long House and Balcony House. A ranger is on duty at Spruce Tree House and Cliff Palace during summer. In winter, guided tours are offered to Spruce Tree House only, weather permitting.

The park is open year-round, but campsites, motel accommodations, and gas are only available inside the park from May through October.

For information on tour schedules, other ranger-led programs, special activities, and weather conditions contact **Mesa Verde National Park** CO 81330 or phone 303/529-4461, 303/529-4475 or 303/529-4465.

Mancos

Mancos, seven miles east of Mesa Verde, doesn't look like much more than a couple of neon motels and gas stations from US 160, which bisects the town. But there are some unusual things going on here, including one of the best restaurants in the entire High Southwest, **Millwood Junction**, and several idiosyncratic shops. The **Mesa Verde Stage Line** makes authentic stagecoaches and offers horse-drawn stagecoach rides in the Mancos Valley. At **The Bounty Hunter**, 115 Grand Avenue, Mancos, CO 81328, 303/533-7215, you can order a high quality, customized cowboy hat. A few doors away, at **Buck's Saddlery** (120 West Grand Avenue, Mancos, CO 81328, 303/533-7958), you can order a custom-fitted saddle.

The commercial heart of Mancos, Grand Avenue, is where these and several other western-oriented shops are situated. It is all of two short blocks long and is two blocks south of US 160, off Railroad Avenue (CO 184).

For information contact the **Mancos Merchants Association**, PO Box 196, Mancos, CO 81328, 303/533-7434.

Hesperus

Fifteen miles east of Mancos on US 160 is the small town of Hesperus, consisting of a gas station/convenience store, post office, a low-slung cinder block motel, and a cafe. Little **Hespersus Ski Area** is located here along with a peaceful, little-known place to stay, **Blue Lake Ranch**. The modest little cafe, **Chip's Place**, attracts an eclectic clientele of locals and savvy travellers engaged in the quest for the ultimate burger.

It's 11 miles east from Hesperus on US 160 to Durango, the last link on the San Juan Skyway loop.

Adventures

On Foot

Some of the best Alpine hiking in the world is found in southwestern Colorado, including challenging ascents of 14,000-foot peaks. Easier routes offer their own rewards in beauty, seclusion, or historical appeal.

Colorado's Fourteeners, by Gerry Roach, Fulcrum Publishing, is an excellent book for serious Alpine backcountry hikes.

The following trail listings are by no means complete–you could easily spend many summers exploring and never follow the same tracks twice.

DURANGO/SILVERTON HIKING

The San Juan National Forest and Weminuche Wilderness **Area** offer some of the most rugged and rewarding hiking in the area, ranging from verdant riverside trails to barren alpine tundra. Hiking or backpacking excursions of one hour to several weeks duration are feasible. For information contact the **Animas Ranger District**, 303/247-4874.

The 469-mile **Colorado Trail** connects Durango with Denver. The southwest portion of it begins west of Durango, off Junction Creek (25th Street), west of Main Avenue. The terrain is tough, but you can hike smaller portions of the trail, which traverses alpine wilderness between 7,000 and 11,000 feet.

Perins Peak Trail is a five-mile loop starting at the end of 22nd Street in Durango. The short but arduously steep trail passes through evergreen glades and entails clambering up a ten-foot cliff for a picturesque panorama of Durango and the La Plata Mountains.

Red Creek Trail runs around six miles one-way to the top of **Missionary Ridge**, for spectacular views of the entire **Animas Valley**. Access is from Florida Road (East Third Avenue), 10 miles north of town, to the sign for Colvig Silver Camps, then turn left and continue two more miles to the trailhead.

Needleton Trail, elevation 8,200 feet, is 13 miles south of Silverton. The easiest way to reach the trailhead is by the Durango & Silverton Narrow Gauge Railroad to Silverton. An alternative is a subsidiary line, the Animas River Railway, which travels from the small town of **Rockwood**, 16 miles north of the train station in

Durango, to **Elk Park**, north of Needleton, at half the cost. **Elk Creek Trail** may be accessed from the train at Elk Park. It covers eight miles to the Continental Divide above **Elk Creek Valley**.

The **Needle Creek Trail** from Needleton is one of the more popular ones in the Weminuche Wilderness. The 14-mile trail leads to **Chicago Basin**. From there it is between two and five miles to **Mount Eolus**, 14,084 feet, **Sunlight Peak**, 14,059 feet, or **Windom Peak**, 14,087 feet. Hikers can flag the train down at Needleton for the return trip to Durango or Silverton. Topographic maps are required for most routes and are available from the Forest Service or sport shops in either town.

Two other trailheads also offer somewhat lengthier access to Eolus, Sunlight, and Windom, but bypass the train.

Purgatory Trail (elevation 8,000 feet) starts at Purgatory Campground across from Purgatory-Durango Ski Area, on the east side of US 550 and 26 miles north of Durango. The **Cascade Creek Trail** is four miles one-way, mostly down, to the Animas River, then up seven miles farther on the **Animas River Trail** to Needleton, the Weminuche, and the fourteeners.

Vallecito Trail is at 7,900 feet, at Vallecito Campground. To get here you drive 20 miles east of Durango on Florida Road (East Third Avenue) to Vallecito Reservoir. Drive five miles farther to the junction on the west side of the reservoir, bear left for three miles to the campground. The trails in this area are the longest and least used leading to the Weminuche. It's a 35-mile trek to reach the base of a 14,000-foot peak from here, making this a viable option only for those seeking an extended backpacking trip.

Little Molas Lake, off US 550 between Purgatory and Silverton, provides a passage to the Colorado Trail via the **Clear Creek Trail**. The trailhead is at South Mineral Creek Campground.

Many day-hikes start around Silverton, switch back through forests and meadows, then climb into high country or to alpine lakes. The **Ice Lake Trail** from South Mineral Campground is a good day-hike. Another possible day-trip is the hike to **Highland Mary Lakes**, starting at the end of Cunningham Gulch.

Access to the Weminuche from Silverton is possible on trails from **Cunningham Gulch Road**, the **Stony Pass** jeep road, and the **Kendall Mountain** jeep road.

Good sources for information on hiking trails, maps, books, and equipment are the following outdoor stores:

Backcountry Experience, 780 Main Street, Durango, CO 81302, 303/247-5830, features equipment and clothing sales, information, maps and books. Camping rental equipment is available.

Pine Needle Mountaineering, 835 Main Avenue, Durango, CO 81302, 303/247-8728 (in the Main Mall), features high quality outdoor gear and clothing, maps, and books.

Guided climbs, group and private rock and ice climbing classes for all levels of climbers are offered by **SouthWest Adventures** (see below, under Durango Mountain Biking). Rock classes are designed for a four-day progression beginning with Level I, an introduction to basic climbing techniques, then on to refined techniques and skills in Level II, followed by an advanced rock program, and finally an ascent of the 800-foot face of Snowdon Peak. This includes an introduction to multi-pitch climbing in an Alpine setting. Other scheduled climbing trips include a three-day seminar in the West Needles Mountains, focusing on basic rock climbing and rappelling techniques, and modern snow climbing techniques; a five-day seminar in Alpine rock and snow climbing in Ice Lake Basin north of Durango; three-day Vestal Basin ascents for those with a minimum of Level II rock climbing abilities; a five-day Chicago Basin ascent that includes transportation on the Durango-Silverton train; summit climbs of Mount Eolus (14,083 feet), North Eolus (14,039 feet), Windom Peak (14,082 feet), and Sunlight Peak (14,059 feet); customized climbing and hiking trips in the Needles mountains.

OURAY/TELLURIDE/DOLORES HIKING

Although these towns are far apart if you travel by road, they share the same mountains. There are many, many hiking trails to choose from. One of the most accessible is **Lower Cascade Falls Trail,** only a half-mile in length one way, beginning in the town of Ouray at the top of Eighth Avenue. You hike down over big rocks, with wet spots likely, to the bottom of the falls.

The **Portland Trail** is probably easier than Lower Cascade, though longer at five miles. It starts on the east side of Ouray, at Amphitheater Campground, gaining around 700 feet in elevation.

Also beginning at Ouray's Amphitheater Campground is the 2.5-mile **Upper Cascade Trail.** The 1,500-foot elevation gain affords fine views of the valley and the falls.

Mount Sneffels (14,150 feet) is seven miles west of Ouray, or five miles north of Telluride. Two area trailheads offer the best access.

The south side of Sneffels is accessed through **Yankee Boy Basin Trail.** It's situated at 10,700 feet and is not so easy to find. Turn south on CO 361, off US 550, .4 of a mile south of Ouray. From there it's 17 tricky miles to the trailhead. Inquire locally for specific directions and road conditions.

East Dallas Creek Trail (9,340 feet) provides access to the north side of Sneffels. To get here you go nearly five miles west on CO 62 from the intersection with Highway 550 in Ridgway, then south on CO 7 (East Dallas Creek Road) for another nine miles. Again, inquire locally for explicit directions and road conditions.

Telluride has many beautiful trails starting right in town, ranging from easy walks to strenuous backcountry excursions. The most popular route is probably the short trek to **Bridal Veil Falls**. The round trip from Pandora Mill at the east end of Telluride covers two miles, up a steep dirt road, gaining 1,000 feet in elevation. It should only take around two hours. At the top is an old hydro-electric power plant. The scenic falls are the largest in the state, tumbling 500 feet out of the hills.

If you want to keep going after you reach the power plant, **Blue Lake Trail**, starts a quarter-mile beyond it. It's the trail that forks to the left. Stay to the left at the next fork in the trail and it's a 90-minute hike to Blue Lake.

Another short trek to scenic views is the **Jud Weibe Trail**, a loop which covers 2.5 miles, starting at the north end of Telluride's Aspen Street, at Cornet Creek.

Bear Creek Trail is at the south end of Pine Street, where the road turns from pavement to dirt. The trail, which is at its worst near the bottom, leads to a waterfall. It's a 4.5-mile round-trip.

Liberty Bell Mine Ruins Trail, begins off Tomboy Road at the north end of Oak Street. Go up Tomboy Road and turn left at the first dirt road. Allow at least five hours for the round-trip.

Thirteen miles southwest of Telluride, in the Lizard Head Wilderness Area (see above), lie three more fourteeners: **Wilson Peak**, (14,017 feet), **Mount Wilson** (14,246 feet), and **El Diente Peak** (14,159 feet). These are serious mountains to climb, with some routes requiring technical equipment and maneuvering.

The best access to these mountain trails is through **Silver Pick Trail** (10,650 feet), approximately eight miles south of CO 145, midway between Telluride and Placerville, on Forest Road 622 along Big Bear Creek. Another option is **Kilpacker Basin Trail** (10,080 feet), located 5.5 miles west of CO 145, nine miles north of Rico. The trailhead is 2.5 miles north of Burro Bridge Campground and 3.5 miles north of Dunton on Forest Road 535.

Navajo Lake Trail (9,340 feet), a mile north of Burro Bridge Campground on Forest Road 535, also leads to the peaks of El Diente or the Wilsons. An easier alternative is climbing only to **Navajo Lake**, at 11,154 feet. The trailhead is 7.5 miles west on Dunton Road (Forest Road 535) from CO 145, north of Rico. Alternatively it's 12.5 miles east of Dolores on West Fork Road, and then 24 miles north on Forest Road 535 to the campground and trailhead. It's a 10-mile round-trip hike to the lake, sitting in the shadow of 14,159-foot El Diente.

An interesting yearly event that participants attempt on foot is the **Imogene Pass Run**, held in the second week of September. It is not meant to be a hike, but rather an 18-mile mountain foot race. It starts in Ouray and ascends a four-wheel-drive road to the top of Imogene Pass (elevation 13,100 feet).

Local information, maps, books, equipment for backpacking, climbing and camping are available from the following stores:

Outdoor World, 1234 Greene Street, Silverton, CO 81433, 303/387-5628.

Telluride Mountaineer, 219 East Colorado Avenue, Telluride, CO 81435, 303/728-6736, offers sales, rentals and service across the street from Town Park.

Skip's Taxi & Shuttle Service (129 West San Juan, Telluride, CO 81435, 303/728-6667) can provide trailhead drop-off and pick-ups for hikers.

CORTEZ HIKING

The best hiking around here is far outside town. The best hikes lead to Anasazi Indian ruins, while others offer an introduction to sloping slickrock and the canyon country, found in greater concentrations west of here in southern Utah. One of the nice things about this part of southwestern Colorado is that it borders mountains and desert. Hiking atop plateaus and mesas provides expansive, unobstructed views of up to 200 miles.

Hovenweep Trails are a network of well marked trails within the National Monument and offer hikes of varying lengths through rugged, but comparatively level terrain. It is very hot here during summer, the best times for hiking are spring and fall. Winter, if there's not too much snow on the ground, can also be rewarding. Trail maps are available from the ranger station at Square Tower Ruins. Hiking trails lead to the **Cajon Ruins** in Utah, or the **Holly Ruins**, **Hackberry Canyon Ruins**, **Cutthroat Castle Ruins** and **Goodman Point Ruins** of Colorado.

Ute Mountain Tribal Park also has a trail network with interesting backpacking possibilities. Access is restricted to those who hire a Ute guide to accompany them. Trails lead to the few excavated ruins in the park, as well as to numerous unexcavated sites buried along 25 miles of the Mancos River valley. One of the most popular trails starts at the park entrance and traverses 13 miles along the river. Aside from archaeological sites along the way, including modern Ute rock carvings, the little used park is a haven for wildlife, including deer and antelope.

Hiking in **Mesa Verde National Park** is carefully restricted to maintained trails and, despite the size of the park, no backcountry hiking is allowed. Hikers must stay on five trails and register at the park ranger's office. Nevertheless, the park trails can be rewarding as they offer the peaceful ambience of pinyon and juniper groves, striated canyons, towering mesas, and the largest concentration of excavated Indian ruins in the Southwest. It gets brutally hot in summer–don't think that because there are restaurants and services within the park you can get away without carrying water and a supply of high energy food.

Several short trails are detailed above under Mesa Verde National Park. Among others which tend to see slightly less usage because of their length are the following:

A 2.5-mile loop, **Petroglyph Point Trail** continues beyond the heavily traveled path to Spruce Tree House near the park headquarters. It crosses along the rim of Spruce Tree Canyon, hugging the top of the mesa. You will see Anasazi rock carvings at Petroglyph Point, the midway point of the loop.

The two-mile **Spruce Canyon Trail** veers off in the opposite direction from Spruce Tree House. It covers some steep terrain as it takes you down below the mesa top into the heavily foliated Spruce Tree Canyon, then back up again to the park headquarters.

Durango-Silverton Llama Treks

Let a llama lug your load. They're cuter than they are friendly, but they never complain that you brought too much stuff.

One-day hikes, customized backpacking trips, or llama leasing are offered by **Turnbull Llama Company**, 455 High Llama Lane, Durango, CO 81302, 303/259-3773.

Buckhorn Llama Company, 1834 County Road 207, Durango, CO 81301, 303/259-5965, offers a variety of guided, fully-outfitted llama treks, including excursions of four to eight days in the Chicago Basin area of the Weminuche Wilderness and trips of four days or longer into Anasazi/Canyon Country.

Horseback Riding/Pack Trips

Travel on the back of a well-trained horse for an hour or days on end. For some this is the ultimate way to experience the backcountry. Among the best local outfitters are the following:

DURANGO

Weminuche Wilderness Adventures, 17754 County Road 501, Bayfield, CO 81122, 303/884-2555 (May to November), or PO Box 1899 Wickenburg, AZ 85358, 602/684-7259 (December to April). Starting above Vallecito Reservoir, guided and fully-outfitted trips of five to 10 days pass through alpine meadows, up into ponderosa pine, blue spruce, and Douglas fir forests. These give way to alpine tundra above timber line. Deer, elk, coyotes, and big horn sheep frequent these trails. Custom trips can also be arranged.

Hermosa Creek Outfitters, PO Box 2295, Durango, CO 81302, 303/259-5393. Specializing in big game hunting, this outfitter also offers family horseback trips of one to five days in the San Juans, photo adventure tours focusing on wildlife, and high alpine scenery, including workshop sessions with a top local photographer, or fly fishing trips to remote streams that require the use of pack and saddle horses.

Over the Hill Outfitters, 3624 County Road 203, Durango, CO 81301, 303/247-9289, offers a variety of horseback trips, from 1.5-hour breakfast or supper rides to customized family pack trips along the Continental Divide in the San Juans. Summer fishing trips are also available.

Rapp Guide Service, 47 Electra Lake Durango, CO 81301, 303/247-8923, fax 303/259-2953. Customized trips of a half-day or longer, or scheduled pack trips of three to six days, are offered in the Upper Animas River Canyon, Silver Mesa, the Needles Mountains along the Continental Divide to Starvation Gulch, or the Ute Mountain Tribal Park.

Engine Creek Outfitters, PO Box 3803, Durango, CO 81302, 303/259-2556 or 303/259-3500, offers hourly, breakfast, lunch, and dinner rides, or summer pack trips of two to five days in the area of 12,000-foot peaks around Cascade Creek and Engineer Mountain. It is based out of Cascade Village (see below, under Durango Accommodations).

San Juan Outfitting, 186 County Road 228, Durango, CO 81301, 303/259-6259, offers big game hunting trips, high country pack trips in the Weminuche Wilderness, an eight-day Continental Divide ride covering 100 miles from Wolf Creek Pass to Silverton, or customized trips.

Mayday Livery (4317 County Road 124, Hesperus, CO 81326, 303/385-6772) offers horseback rides by the hour, half-day rides, and customized guided pack trips.

Buck's Livery, US 550 at Purgatory, Durango, CO 81301, 303/385-2110, offers one-hour, two-hour, half-day, or day-long trail rides, sunset steak or trout dinner rides, high country fishing trips, or three- to five-day pack and prospecting trips.

Outlaw West Livery, 180 Forest Lakes Drive, Bayfield, CO 81122, 303/884-9631 (summer), or 303/884-2074 (winter), specializes in shorter trips of one hour, two hours, half-day or a full day from Vallecito Reservoir. They also offer three-hour breakfast rides, guided fishing trips, or full-service pack trips of three, five or seven days duration.

Southfork Stables, 28481 Highway 160 East, Durango, CO 81302, 303/258-4871, offers hour-long rides scheduled fivetimes daily in summer, as well as breakfast rides, half-day rides, full-day rides, including lunch, an evening chuckwagon supper ride, or a moonlight champagne ride. Customized, guided, fully-outfitted pack trips and horse leasing are available.

SILVERTON

LK Outfitters, 1646 Cement Street, Silverton, CO 81433, 303/387-5861.

San Juan Outdoor Recreation Center, PO Box 45, Silverton, CO 81433, 303/387-5866 or 800/697-5672.

Silverado Outfitters, 1116 Mineral, Silverton, CO 81433, 303/387-5747 or 303/247-1869, offers hourly and half-day horse-back rides at Molas Lake, 10 miles south of Silverton on US 550. Also available are dinner or breakfast rides, and overnight trips, including a pack trip from Durango to Silverton, with the return on the narrow gauge train.

Silver Trails, 600 Cement Street, Silverton, CO 81433, 303/387-5869.

Sultan Mountain Livery, 4th Street, PO Box 33, Silverton, CO 81433, 303/387-5480, offers customized horseback trips.

George Pastor Mountain Guide, 830 Empire Street, Silverton, CO 81433, 303/387-5556.

OURAY

Ouray Livery Barn, 834 Main, Ouray, CO 81427, 303/325-4606 or 303/626-5695, offers horse rides of one hour, two hours, half-day, full day, and pack trips. Also offered are dinner rides on Deep Creek Mesa.

RIDGWAY

San Juan Mountain Outfitters, 2882 CO 23, Ridgway, CO 81432, 303/626-5360, offers half-day, full day, and overnight pack trips. You get a free Ouray Hot Springs swim pass with each ride.

TELLURIDE

D&E Outfitters, 805 West Pacific Avenue, Telluride, CO 81435, 303/728-3200. One-hour, full-day, and overnight pack trips. Also dinner rides and horse-drawn wagon trips.

Telluride Outside (666 West Colorado, Telluride, CO 81435, 303/728-3895) operates trail rides and pack trips.

DOLORES/CORTEZ/MANCOS

The Outfitter, 410 Railroad Avenue, Dolores, CO 81323, 303/882-7740, offers guided horseback rides and overnight pack trips into 18 miles of the Lower Dolores Canyon. The 2,000-foot deep canyon is accessible only by horseback or on foot, with colorful rock walls and Anasazi caves. The canyon bottom over-flows with ponderosa pine, sage, and wildflowers. It provides habitat for eagles, hawks, black bear, and mountain lions. The Dolores River flows through and the trout fishing is excellent. Tours include camping accommodations and meals.

Gene Story, Box 300, Dolores, CO 81323, 303/882-4990, is a guide and outfitter.

Triple Heart Ranch, Box 117, Dolores, CO 81323, 303/882-4155, offers guide and outfitting services.

The Trappers Den, 37101 US 160, Mancos, CO 81328, 303/533-7147, offers horseback riding in the Mancos Valley, a mile east of Mesa Verde.

Echo Basin Stable and Roping Arena (see below, under Mancos Accommodations) 2.5 miles east of Mancos on US160 and three miles north on Echo Basin Road, offers one- , two- or three-hour trail rides along the west fork of the Mancos River, four-hour lunch rides to higher elevations, all-day rides in high country, breakfast or dinner rides, and overnight extended pack trips in the La Plata and San Juan Mountains. They also offer riding lessons, team roping, barrel racing, team penning, and horse shows.

CATTLE DRIVES

Parts of the movie *City Slickers* were filmed in and around Durango, and some of the stars were local residents, namely the cattle. If you really want to experience the life of a cowboy, there's no better way than to hitch on to a real western cattle drive.

Southfork Riding Stables & Outfitters (see above, under Durango Horseback Trips), offers a spring cattle drive in conjunc-tion with Decker Ranch. Guests participate in gathering, herding, and driving 400 head of cattle across 50 miles of open territory.

Framed by the San Juan and La Plata Mountains, the terrain is hilly. After gathering the herd, you then drive it to a corral where you can help with the branding. A horse-drawn chuckwagon follows along the trail, packing your personal belongings, camping gear, and food.

On Wheels

RAIL TRIPS

Railroads used to be a lifeline for remote mountain communities. Most of them are long gone, but one remains–the **Durango & Silverton Narrow Gauge Railroad**, 479 Main Avenue, Durango, CO 81301, 303/247-2733.The carefully restored steam engines and train cars are a Registered National Historic Landmark, as well as a National Civil Engineering Landmark.

Nearly a quarter of a million travellers ride these rails through the San Juan National Forest yearly, covering 45 miles of track in a style very little changed from its inception in 1882. It first chugged into existence to transport an estimated $300 million in gold and silver during the mining era.

The trip is among the longest narrow gauge routes in the world, as well as one of the most picturesque rail trips anywhere. Passengers can travel in colorful, perfectly restored orange and black Victorian-style coaches, some dating to the 1880s or in open gondola cars. These are drawn by an immense coal-fired, steam-powered locomotive–an Iron Horse–built for the Denver & Rio Grande Railroad.

The restored engines that are used date from 1923 to 1925. You can't call a repair shop for parts so the rolling stock is maintained in tip-top running order at a 15-stall roundhouse in Durango. Parts are fabricated there and you can observe the various maintenance and restoration procedures on a Yard Tour. The 45-minute tour is available daily, May through October, behind the train station, at 479 Main Avenue in Durango. It includes the locomotive service and storage areas, turntable, machine shop, and car shop, replete with unusual tools and equipment for working on the uncommon coaches and locomotives.

The train route parallels the Animas River for most of the way, hugging the three-foot-wide rails through slim canyons and clean-scented evergreen forests, powering slowly through isolated stretches of the National Forest that are inaccessible by road. Other than the train, the only ways in to this land are by foot or on horseback. The sound of the train's forlorn whistle, its clanking steel, flying cinders, and swelling gray fog of coal smoke recall uncomplicated days when legendary wealth rode these rails.

The slow-moving rail tour is 3.5 hours one way, climbing around 3,000 feet from Durango to Silverton. After a two-hour layover in Silverton, the train returns to Durango.

There are as many as five departures daily from May 1 to October 31. An abbreviated trip is offered from April 17 to April 30, and again from Thanksgiving (late November) to January 1, from Durango to Cascade Canyon, a 52-mile round-trip. Fall, when the colors of foliage are spectacular, and winter, when the route is blanketed in snow, are particularly pretty times to travel.

The Cinco, Animas, and Nomad are private cars which are available for charter. The Alamosa Parlor Car, circa 1880, is a deluxe, refurbished bar car which is available daily, offering first-class service and alcoholic beverages.

You may purchase a round-trip ticket and lay over in Silverton for as many nights as you want. For those who find the one-way trip sufficient exposure to old-time railroads, a bus from Silverton to Durango is available June 7 through September 25.

During the summer, one departure daily is offered on the **Animas River Railway**, from Rockwood to Elk Park, in the Weminuche Wilderness. This trip is not heavily publicized, but it does eliminate the slow crawl through Durango and immediately plunges into the prettiest part of the Durango to Silverton route. It is favored by backpackers who hop off at Needleton or Elk Park for access to the Weminuche, and it is considerably less expensive than the full Durango-Silverton fare.

JEEPING/FOUR-WHEEL-DRIVE TRIPS

The Iron Horse, of course, takes you only where its tracks are laid–if you really want to cover some ground in a short time in the backcountry, travel by jeep or four-wheel-drive. Always check with local authorities about road conditions before you set out. Some high passes may not open at all, others could remain snow-clogged well into August after a severe winter. Normally, though, even the highest routes will be open by July.

Durango

Rocky Mountain High Tours, PO Box 3337, Durango, CO 81302, 303/247-0807 or 800/530/2022, offers a variety of jeep tours, or jeep rentals. Half-day guided tours go into the San Juans near Silverton, past pioneer cabins and abandoned mines, up to the ghost town at Animas Forks (elevation 11,300 feet). Two-hour tours are also available. Another option is to participate in a jeep safari. You rent a jeep and follow behind a guide in his jeep. You can go off on your own if you want or follow the leader, sort of like a modern-day wagon train. The safari is a day-long excursion that includes background information on history, wildlife, vegetation, and folklore of the area. Make your choice for lunch at an old, historic mountain inn, or a catered picnic lunch beside an alpine lake or in an old miner's cabin.

New West Adventures, PO Box 2744, Durango, CO 81302, 303/385-4940 or 800/748-1188, suggests reservations a day in advance for its guided tours. These include a four-hour wildlife safari at dawn or dusk (seeking out deer, elk, eagles, hawks, coyotes, foxes, bobcats, and bears) with breakfast or dinner included, or a day-long Silverton/Ghost Town Tour, covering the Alpine Loop (see below, under Silverton). Also available are special three- to four-hour photographic tours and seasonal photo seminars with professional instructors teaching field techniques for photographing summer wildflowers or fall colors. They will provide a guide and jeep to drive you to a remote trailhead, then lead you on a hike or backpacking trip, with or without llamas.

Rocky Mountain High Tours, PO Box 3337, Durango, CO 81302, 303/247-0807, offers jeep tours and rentals based out of Tamarron Resort, Purgatory-Durango Ski Resort, Needles store and Silverton. Fall foliage packages include jeep rental, accommodations at the Alma House or Wyman Hotel in Silverton, and meals at Silverton's Handlebars or Zhivago restaurants.

Silverton

Jeeping is popular around here, with more than 700 miles of accessible jeep roads in the area and several firms offering rentals.

The **Alpine Loop Backcountry Byway** is a 65-mile trip over gravel and dirt roads, some of which may be rocky, rutted or washed-out, necessitating a four-wheel-drive. The route, open July through October, connects the towns of Silverton, Ouray, and Lake City. It crosses Engineer Pass, at 12,800 feet, and Cinnamon Pass, at 12,620 feet. Highlights include many miles of road above tree line, amid alpine tundra, as well as numerous abandoned mining sites, including the ghost town at Animas Forks, and old mining camps, cabins, mines and tramlines.

Stony Pass is another jeep route from Silverton, which crosses the Continental Divide at 12,000 feet, then follows the headwaters of the Rio Grande River to the mountain town of Creede. It's located east of town, on County Road 110 to Howardsville, then turn right on Cunningham Gulch Road. After two miles you will come across Stony Pass Road on the left.

Black Bear Pass, connecting the top of Red Mountain Pass with Telluride, one-way only, is extremely challenging, beautiful, and dangerous in a jeep. The road is narrow, with long, steep drops. Some switchbacks require three-point turns. Some people do it on a bicycle. If your vehicle doesn't make it you may find yourself doing it on foot. Approach with respect and caution.

Ophir Pass, 11,740 feet, connects Silverton and Ophir, nine miles south of Telluride. It starts approximately five miles north of Silverton, off US 550, on an unmarked turn-off across from a sign that says Red Mountain Summit Five Miles. It's 45 miles to Ophir, but the road's not too bad as far as jeep roads go. This is one of the more popular backcountry jeep roads.

Jeep rentals, maps, and road condition information are available from the following sources:

Triangle Jeep Rentals, 864 Greene Street, Silverton, CO 81433, 303/887-9990 or 303/387-5498.
Silverton Lakes Jeep Rentals, PO Box 126, Silverton, CO 81433, 303/387-5721, open May 1 to October 15.

Ouray

This area considers itself the jeeping capital of the world and the number and variety of routes in the area bear out the claim. You can take trips to old gold mines and ghost towns, hugging narrow ledges over sheer drop-offs on harrowing roads that seem more appropriate for mountain goats than motor vehicles. In short, just the sort of terrain that four-wheel enthusiasts dream about.

One of the easiest routes is through **Yankee Boy Basin**, beginning at Camp Bird Road, south of town, off US 550. It takes you along Canyon Creek to the legendary Camp Bird Mine, then through a series of meadows along the base of looming mountains.

Imogene Pass offers a more challenging tour over a 13,509-foot pass to Telluride. It starts at the Camp Bird Mine and is not for the inexperienced.

Jeep rentals, maps and information, or guided tours are available from the following sources:

San Juan Scenic Jeep Tours, PO Box 143, Ouray, CO 81427, 303/325-4444 or 303/325-4154, is a possibility for those who prefer an experienced driver behind the wheel. They offer half-day and full-day tours on pre-set or customized itineraries. They also offer jeep rentals.

Switzerland of America, PO Box 184, Ouray, CO 81427, 303/325-4484 offers jeep rentals.

Colorado West, PO Box 1850, 322 Fifth Avenue, Ouray, CO 81427, 303/325-4014, offers tours or jeep rentals.

Polly's Jeep Rentals, 1805 Main Street, Ouray, CO 81427, 303/325-4061, rents jeeps.

Budget Rent-A-Car, PO Box 290, Ouray, CO 81427, 303/325-4154 or 800/221-2419, rents four-wheel-drive vehicles.

Timber Ridge Jeep Rentals, PO Box 606, Ouray, CO 81427, 303/325-4523, rents jeeps.

Telluride

There are hundreds of jeep roads in the Telluride vicinity. Some connect with Silverton or Ouray routes listed above. The Chamber Resort Association (see above, under Touring Telluride) or jeep tour operators can provide complete information.

A challenging and popular jeep route is **Imogene Pass** (13,059 feet) from Telluride to Ouray. It is accessed on the Telluride side by going north on Oak Street to the Imogene Pass Road. The road passes the Tomboy Mine ruins and then gets serious. This is a difficult and dangerous road and, although the scenery is rewarding, do not take this drive lightly.

Jeep rentals and tours are available from the following sources:

Budget Rent-A-Car, 657 West Colorado, Telluride, CO 81435, 303/728-4642 or 800/221-2419, rents four-wheel-drives for jeeping.

Telluride Outside, 666 West Colorado, Telluride, CO 81435, 303/728-3895 rents four-wheel-drives and operates half-day, full-day, customized and private guided tours. Also offering backpacker drop-offs and four-wheel-drive, sit-down dinner tours to the Alta Lakes Observatory, or sunset, cowboy and barbecue dinner tours to Deep Creek Mesa.

Thrifty Car Rental, 129 West San Juan, Telluride, CO 81435, 303/728-3266, or 800/367-2277 offers jeep rentals, all-wheel-drive mini vans, four-wheel-drive Cherokees and guided four-wheel-drive tours.

Skip's Taxi & Shuttle Service, 129 West San Juan, Telluride, CO 81435, 303/728-6667, offers four-wheel-drive tours in a convertible, visiting ghost towns, hidden lakes, and mining ruins.

Mountain Limo, PO Box 1662, Telluride, CO 81435, 303/728-9606, offers four-wheel-drive tour services for the Telluride region.

STAGECOACH RIDES

The Mesa Verde Stage Line, 122 West Grand Avenue, PO Box 346, Mancos, CO 81328, 303/533-7264, offers tours in old fashioned, horse-drawn stagecoaches from Mancos into Weber Canyon, below Mesa Verde. Three-day advance reservations are required, along with a 50% deposit. Minimum eight passengers per trip, so call as far in advance as possible to get your choice of dates from May 1 to October 31. Trips of a half-day, full day (21-mile round trip, seven hours, includes lunch), or a three-day adventure on a 72-mile loop onto the Ute Mountain Ute Indian Reservation are available. They will also customize trips to suit you.

WAGON RIDES

Mayday Livery, 4317 County Road 124, Hesperus, CO 81326, 303/385-6772. Spend a few days on the seat of a real chuckwagon, rolling through the San Juans, Canyon de Chelly, or Monument Valley. Each trip is custom designed for your group.

Deep Creek Sleigh & Wagon Rides of Telluride, 130 West Colorado, Telluride, CO 81435, 303/728-3565, operates horse-drawn wagon rides at sunset, into the San Juans, where a bonfire is built and a western dinner is served.

MOUNTAIN BIKING/BICYCLING

Durango likes to call itself the mountain biking capital of America. Because of the abundance of steep forest roads and backcountry trails, a number of professional bike riders live and train in the area. The town has hosted the **Iron Horse Bicycle Classic** every Memorial Day (late May) weekend for more than 20 years. It started with about a dozen riders racing the narrow gauge train to Silverton, and has now grown into an internationally recognized event that attracts several thousand professional and amateur bike riders. They still race the train, still climb tenaciously over two 10,000-foot passes and, just like that first race, the best bike riders always win. Many other participants compete only with themselves and are happy enough just to finish the race—even if they arrive in Silverton hours after the train. In addition, Durango hosted the first unified World Mountain Biking Championship in 1990. The championship track at Purgatory Ski Area is open to bike riders in the summer.

Durango

The **Animas Valley Loop** is rated as easy, but that doesn't mean you should attempt it on your first day at 6,500 feet coming from sea level. People who live here and ride at this elevation all the time consider it easy. You stay on county roads all the way, over essentially level terrain, with rolling hills. Total elevation gain is 280 feet on the full 30-mile loop. There is an alternative 15-mile loop.

The 30-mile route goes north on County Road 250 from Durango on the east side of the Animas Valley. You cross US 550 at Baker's Bridge (where parts of the movie *Butch Cassidy and the Sundance Kid* were filmed). On the west side of US 550, you take County Road 203 south to Durango, down the west side of the scenic, red-rock valley.

Also starting right in town, the **Animas City Mountain Loop** is a short but steep trail for advanced riders. Follow the signs off East 4th Avenue, north of 32nd Street. The 5.5-mile trail gains 1,250 feet in elevation, but your sweat is rewarded with a bird's-eye panorama encompassing Falls Creek, the Animas Valley, and the West Needle Mountains.

Old Lime Creek Road is considered intermediate terrain. It's an old stagecoach road parallel to US 550 at Coal Bank Pass (10,630 feet) north of Purgatory and south of Silverton. It's eleven miles one-way, with the Silverton side 2,000 feet higher than the Purgatory side. Most riders start eleven miles south of Silverton, at the turn-off from US 550 on the east side of the road. The shady route drops from over 10,000 feet to just under 9,000 feet, past forested hillsides, streams, and the brick remains of the low Chines Wall. The wall was once all that prevented horse-drawn wagons and carriages from a tumbling drop down hundreds of feet of sheer hillside.

Purgatory-Durango Ski Area (26 miles north of Durango on US 550, 303/247-9000 or 800/525-0892) offers an entire network of well-marked mountain bike trails during the summer. You can tackle the world championship course, or ride a chairlift up with your bike and ride down. Purgatory supplies maps of such routes as the **Championship Trail** (an advanced eight-mile loop), **Hermosa Cliff Overlook** (a nine-mile intermediate trail that takes you to a stunning view point atop the Hermosa Cliffs), **Harris Park Loop** (a four-mile intermediate trail down the north face of the ski mountain and into the Hermosa Valley), and several beginner trails. They also offer guided tours.

Bike rentals are available at Purgatory from **Mountain Bike Specialists** from June 15 to September 6 (303/247-9000, extension

5102). They also operate a full-service bike shop year-round in Durango (949 Main Avenue, Durango, CO 81301, 303/247-4066). Guided tours include bikes, helmets, lunch, trail-side snacks, rain gear, and sag wagon. In addition to half-day and full-day tours they offer the following itineraries (these include accommodations and most meals):

Ute Mountain Tribal Park Tour is a fully outfitted day-long trip from Durango to the park. You drive to the park, then ride 26 miles round-trip up and down the river valley, stopping to view Anasazi archaeology and wildlife. Trip comes complete with an Indian guide.

The **Iron Horse Tour** is a three-day trip, including accommodations in Silverton and Purgatory. The first day you ride the narrow gauge train to Silverton with your bike. You can ride to a ghost town, a mountaintop, or just around town that afternoon. The second day you ride the Old Lime Creek Road (see above) to Purgatory. You can bike around the area, fish, or ride a horse that afternoon. The third morning you ride the chairlift with your bike to the top of the ski mountain and then bike your way south toward Durango, ending five miles north of town at Trimble Hot Springs for a well-earned soak in a natural hot springs pool.

A five-day bike tour encompasses the entire 232-mile **San Juan Skyway Loop**. You ride the train to Silverton, then bike to Ouray. Day two ends in Telluride. Day three ends in Mancos. On day four you visit Mesa Verde National Park, then return to Mancos. On the last day you return to Durango. Some gung-ho bike riders attempt to cover this five-day route in one day, in which case it is affectionately called the death ride.

Custom tours are also available, to such sites as wildflower meadows in July and August, mining camps, or special photo tours.

A six-day bike tour encompassing the San Juan Skyway, beginning and ending in Durango is offered by **Backroads Bicycle Touring** (1516 5th Street, Berkeley, CA 94710-1713, 415/527-1555 or 800/245-3874, fax 415/527-1444). It includes a ride on the narrow gauge train, accommodations at local inns, and two nights at Mesa Verde National Park.

Other local sources for bike rentals, repairs, sales, and expert biking information are the following:

Hassle Free Sports, 2615 Main Avenue, Durango, CO 81301, 303/259-3874 or 800/835-3800.

Durango Cyclery, 143 East 13th Street, Durango, CO 81301, 303/247-0747.

SouthWest Adventures (780 Main Avenue, Durango, CO 81302, 303/259-0370 or 800/642-5389) offers mountain bike rentals for an hour, a half-day or full day. Also available are guided tours of a half-day or full day.

Silverton

There are many, many miles of trails and jeep roads around Silverton, but the most diverse is probably the **Alpine Loop Scenic Byway**. You can ride over two 12,000-foot passes, visit ghost towns, wildflower meadows, and alpine lakes. See above for details on the Alpine Loop and other Silverton area jeep routes good for mountain biking.

In Silverton, contact **San Juan Outdoor Recreation Center** (PO Box 45, Silverton, CO 81433, 303/387-5866 or 800/697-5672) for mountain bike tours and rentals.

Ouray

All the jeep roads around Ouray are also good for bike riding. You can veer off the Alpine Loop near Engineer Pass and ride down around 5,000 feet in 10 miles to Ouray.

Downhill Biking, 722 Main Street, Ouray, CO 81427, 303/325-4284, rents mountain bikes for a half-day, full day or weekly. Also available are tours in which riders are driven up a mountain for a downhill-only ride back to town.

Telluride

Telluride is loaded with incredible bike routes many of which are strenuous.

One of the easier ones is to **Bear Creek Falls**. It's two miles up a road to the falls from the south end of Pine Street.

The steep dirt road that leads to **Alta Lakes** passes through a ghost town. The road is five miles south of Telluride, off CO 145, at the Alta sign.

Black Bear Pass is a longer, more difficult ride. You follow the jeep road leading to Bridal Veil Falls. It's at the end of Colorado Avenue, past the Idarado Mine. You can stop at the top of the falls and at the power plant, then, on your way back down, follow the switchback to the right at the one-way sign just below the power plant. The road gets very steep going over Ingram Falls, then passes through an immense alpine basin before reaching US 550, at the top of Red Mountain Pass, midway between Silverton and Ouray.

Ophir Pass is less difficult than Black Bear Pass, but still challenging. Follow CO 145 south. Turn left at Ophir and keep going until you reach US 550 in Silverton.

Tomboy Road and **Imogene Pass** starts at the north end of Oak Street, continues past ghost town ruins at Tomboy, and then up Imogene Pass. At the top you rapidly descend into Ouray.

> **Free Wheelin' Bike & Board Shop**, 101 East Colorado, Telluride, CO 81435, 303/728-4734, specializes in mountain bike sales, service, rentals, and tours.
> **Olympic Sports** (150 West Colorado, Telluride, CO 81435, 303/728-4477 or 800/828-7547) offers mountain bike rentals and repairs.
> **Telluride Outside** (666 West Colorado, Telluride, CO 81435, 303/728-3895) offers mountain bike rentals and tours, including a 17-mile downhill mountain bike tour from the top of Lizard Head Pass featuring a 2,000-foot descent along an old railroad line.
> **Paragon Ski And Sport**, 213 West Colorado, Telluride, CO 81435, 303/728-4525, sells, services, and rents mountain bikes

A unique, night-night, seven-day mountain bike tour is offered by **San Juan Hut Systems**, Box 1663, 117 North Willow Street, Telluride, CO 81435, 303/728-6935. It's a 205-mile trip from Telluride to Moab, Utah, with nightly accommodations in a series of five wooden huts and one 20-foot, fabric frame, octagon shelter on a platform. The tour stays mainly on Forest Service or BLM dirt roads. The modest huts are 35 miles apart along a route designed for intermediate riders in good shape.

Advanced technical single track is found in the vicinity of each hut for highly skilled cyclists. There is no vehicle support, and riders should be knowledgeable in maintenance and repair. Participants are required to carry their own pump, patch, and repair kit, as well as warm clothes, rain gear, and three quarts of water.

You can bring your own food, or the complete package tour includes three meals a day, hut facilities, sleeping bag, trail map and descriptions. It does not include a guide, although one is available for an additional fee.

There are a lot of climbs involved in getting out of Telluride, then the route levels somewhat into slickrock canyon country, high red rock deserts of sage, juniper, and pinyon. It's a memorable and challenging ride. You can also rent a bike and all the necessary equipment for the whole hut tour, or rent bikes by the hour, half-day or day.

Dolores/Cortez/Mancos

Cortez-Mancos-Dolores Half Century, is a 43-mile intermediate road ride, for road or mountain bikers. If you start in Cortez, on US 160, you travel east past the entrance to Mesa Verde, and continue on through rolling meadows and ranch land into Mancos. In Mancos you head north on CO 184 to Dolores. The return to Cortez is south, and mostly downhill for around 10 miles into Cortez on CO 145.

The 17-mile **Cutthroat Castle Ruins & Negro Canyon Loop** starts 17.5 miles south of US 666 at Pleasant View, off County Road BB, on the way to Hovenweep National Monument. The route is marked with bicycle emblem signs. You pass Cutthroat Castle Ruins on the way into Hovenweep Canyon, cross rolling hills, and the same stream several times. Then you climb out of the Canyon and back down into the cottonwood groves and stream beds of Negro Canyon, before climbing several hills and returning to County Road BB.

Ute Mountain Tribal Park has rides that are similar to those offered by Mountain Bike Specialists, minus the outfitting services. These are run by the Ute Tribe, 303/565-3751.

Dolores River Canyon offers an easy 22-mile ride along the river, with opportunities to play in the water or picnic. The route is well-marked with bicycle emblem signs. Park your car at the Dolores Canyon river access. It's 34 miles north of Cortez on US 666, then east at the sign that reads Public Lands Access, Dolores River Canyon, and Overlook.

There are several bike trails at **McPhee Reservoir** and **House Creek Recreation Area**, but they're not well marked. It's a good idea to have topographic maps. Contact the **San Juan National Forest** office in Dolores, 303/882-7296, for details.

Two six-mile loops on **Ruins Road** offer easy biking to various Indian ruins at the top of Mesa Verde. It is, however, 21 miles of steep, advanced terrain from the turn-off on US 160 to the area around Chapin Mesa, where the loop roads are located. It's really crowded in the summer and not much fun to be sharing the narrow roads with cars, trucks, and motor homes. Try spring or fall–the weather's more comfortable, and there's much less traffic. No bicycles are allowed on the Wetherill Mesa Road, and no off-road bike travel is permitted within the National Park.

For information, bike rentals, service, or sales try **Southwest Bicycle**, 450 East Main, Cortez, CO 81321, 303/565-3717, or the **Bike Hiker**, 402 South Park, Cortez, CO 81321, 303/565-9342.

On Water

Floating slowly through ancient gorges decorated with Anasazi art or racing along a whitewater river pouring out of the high country have become justifiably popular. Tours are available for an hour, two hours, half-day, full day, or overnight for up to a week.

Durango/Silverton

The **Upper Animas**, from Silverton to Rockwood, is considered by experts to be the most exciting and advanced whitewater run available commercially in the Rockies. The stretch offers two days of expert kayaking over numerous Class V rapids, covering 28 miles of isolated, difficult, and hazardous terrain through exquisite wilderness. The next three miles after Rockwood are not navigable.

The **Animas River** is called the "River of Lost Souls" out of respect. About six miles north of Durango, from Trimble Lane south for 10 miles, the much slower Animas can be canoed.

The **Lower Animas**, passing through Durango, is milder still, suitable for rafts, kayaks, or canoes, although a small section south of the US 160 Bridge is not to be taken lightly. It drops through several rapids and is used for professional kayak races each spring. Even smooth spans of river can be stimulating and risky during spring run-off (mid-May to mid-June).

The following Durango area tour companies offer river trips.

SouthWest Adventures, 780 Main Avenue, Durango, CO 81302, 303/259-0370 or 800/642-5389, offers two-hour or half-day river trips on the Lower Animas, rated Class III, in oar or paddle rafts. Also available is a one-day guided voyage in self-bailing rafts on the Upper Animas, rated Class IV and V, covering 12 miles of extreme, continuous whitewater. The trip includes shuttle via the narrow gauge railroad. Also: One- , two- , or three-day kayak schools for beginners or experienced kayakers seeking technical proficiency.

Durango Rivertrippers, 720 Main Avenue, Durango, CO 81302, 303/259-0289, offers two-hour or half-day trips on the Lower Animas in oar or paddle rafts.

Mountain Waters Rafting, 108 West 6th Street, Durango, CO 81302, 303/259-4191 or 800/748-2507, offers two-hour, half-day, full-day, and dinner trips on the Lower Animas. A two-day, Class V whitewater trip on the Upper Animas is also available, depending on water levels, from late June to mid-July. In Silverton contact Mountain Waters Rafting, 1314 Greene Street.

Flexible Flyers, 2344 County Road 255, Durango, CO 81302, 303/247-4628, offers one- or two-hour trips on the Lower Animas.

American Adventure Expeditions, 701 Main Avenue, Durango, CO 81302, 303/247-4789 or 800/288-0675, offers two-hour or half-day raft trips, or two-hour trips in inflatable kayaks, on the Lower Animas. Also available are one- or two-day trips on the Upper Animas. Customized multi-day trips are also offered.

RiversWest, 520 Main Avenue, Durango, CO 81302, 303/259-5077, offers one-hour, two-hour, or half-day raft trips on the Lower Animas.

Among out-of-town tour operators, **Wilderness Aware Rafting**, PO Box 1550A, Buena Vista, CO 81211, 719/395-2112 or 800/462-7238, runs Upper Animas and Dolores River (see below) trips for four to 18 participants.

Several other outfitters offer trips on the Animas and southwest Colorado's rivers, though not as their primary focus. A number of these are included under River Trips in following chapters.

For those determined to go it alone, **Four Corners River Sports**, 360 South Camino del Rio, Durango, CO 81301, 303/259-3893 or 800/426-7637, offers novice, intermediate, and advanced whitewater kayak and canoe classes.

Telluride/Dolores

The **San Miguel River** starts near Telluride and flows 70 miles to Naturita, with some whitewater and waves in May and June. Most trips are an hour or two long.

The **Dolores River** flows through steep sandstone canyons, past Anasazi ruins and petroglyphs. It is reminiscent of the desert Southwest, as opposed to the Alpine flavor of other rivers in southwest Colorado. The Dolores loses its punch quickly, though, so its well-known and dramatic whitewater rapids that are treacherous in May and June can be mild in July.

The **Upper Dolores** flows 37 miles from Rico to Dolores, through some of the regions' prettiest mountains, into desert canyons. It's usually a two- to three-day trip. There are, however, an additional 171 miles of the river that can be floated through incredible canyon country, with some of the biggest rapids, such as the infamous Snaggletooth. The entire stretch can be done in around a week.

For area rafting tours and information contact the following sources:

Olympic Sports (150 West Colorado, Telluride, CO 81435, 303/728-4477 or 800/828-7547) offers whitewater rafting trips.
Telluride Outside (666 West Colorado, Telluride, CO 81435, 303/728-3895) operates whitewater rafting trips.
Telluride Whitewater, 224 East Colorado Avenue, Box 685, Telluride, CO 81435, 303/728-3985, runs guided one- to six-night river trips on the San Miguel, Dolores or Upper Animas rivers.
Humpback Chub River Tours, 202 South 4th Street, Dolores, CO 81323, 800/882-7940, offers river trips on the Dolores.

Peregrine River Outfitters, 447 Grand Avenue, PO Box 808, Mancos, CO 81328, 303/533-7235, runs Dolores River trips.

Dvorak's Kayak and Rafting Expeditions, 17921 Highway 285, Nathrop, CO 81236, 719/539-6851 or 800/824-3795, fax 719/539-3378, operates a number of river trips in the Four Corners that will be listed in upcoming chapters. Dolores River trips are offered for five, eight, 10, or 12 days, from mid-April to mid-June. A special eight-day "Classical Music Journey" is offered in early June, featuring daily concerts.

Echo Canyon River Expeditions, 45000 US Highway 50 West, Canon City, CO 81212, 719/275-3154 or 800/748-2953, runs early season (spring) two-day river trips on the San Miguel River, out of Telluride.

BOATING/FISHING/FLY FISHING

Everyone over 14 years old needs a Colorado fishing license. These are available from most sporting goods stores and many convenience stores.

Durango/Silverton

Always consult local fishermen where the fish are biting. There's generally some good fishing in the following waters:

Animas River Drainage Fishing

The **Animas River** offers the best fishing for rainbow and brook trout right in Durango or south of town. Fishing in the **Animas River Canyon** (north of Durango), accessed by Forest Service trails or the narrow gauge railroad, is not as good due to heavy mineralization in the water.

Cascade Creek, 26 miles north of Durango, off US 550, is stocked with rainbow, brook, and cutthroat trout. Access is by Forest Service trails near Purgatory.

Florida River, northeast of Durango, above Lemon Reservoir, has good fishing for rainbow, brook, and cutthroat trout adjacent to the national forest campground.

Hermosa Creek Drainage, west of Purgatory Ski Area, has many small trout streams off various Forest Service Roads and trails.

Lime Creek, accessed north of Purgatory or south of Silverton, from Old Lime Creek Road is usually worthwhile for trout fishing.

Mineral Creek, five miles west of Silverton on US 550 and County Road 585 to South Mineral Creek Campground, has good trout fishing, but lots of fisher-folk angling for rainbows and brookies.

Molas Creek, accessed via Forest Service trails from US 550 at Molas Pass, is good for brook trout fishing.

Lake and Reservoir Fishing

Andrews Lake (set at 10,774 feet) is seven miles south of Silverton on US 550, then south on a gravel access road, is a 14-acre lake stocked with rainbow and brook trout.

Clear Lake (at 12,000 feet) west of Silverton on US 550, and west on Forest Service Road 585, is a 42-acre lake stocked with rainbow and brook trout. You need a four-wheel-drive to get to the lake.

Electra Lake, is a private, 816-acre lake at an elevation of 8,320 feet. A fee is charged for fishing for rainbow, brook, and cutthroat trout. It's located 20 miles north of Durango on US 550.

Haviland Lake (at 8,100 feet) is a 65-acre lake stocked with rainbow and brook trout. Head 19 miles north of Durango on US 550, then east on a gravel access road.

Ice Lakes (at 12,260 feet) is a 15-acre lake. It's stocked with brook trout and located west of Silverton on US 550, then west on Forest Service Road 585 and up a steep Forest Service trail.

Lemon Reservoir, is a 662-acre lake at an elevation of 8,145 feet. It's popular for rainbow and brown trout, or kokanee salmon. It is 17 miles northeast of Durango on County Road 240 to County Road 243.

Big & Little Molas Lakes are 10 miles south of Silverton on US 550. Big Molas (at 10,905 feet) is a 20-acre lake. Little Molas covers 10 acres at an elevation of 10,500 feet. Catch-and-release trout fishing is encouraged.

Vallecito Reservoir, covering 2,723 acres at 7,662 feet, is home to rainbow and brown trout, kokanee salmon, and northern pike. It's 22 miles northeast of Durango on County Road 501. There are boat ramps around the lake, as well as several commercial marinas, including the following:

Angler's Wharf, 17250, County Road 501, Bayfield, CO 81122, 303/884-9477. Located at the north end of Vallecito Reservoir, services include boat rentals for fishing, pleasure, pontoon boats, canoes, and paddle boats, information on daily fishing conditions, free fishing instructions, guide services, as well as equipment sales and rentals, licenses and bait.

Shorty's Vallecito Marina, 14518 County Road 501, Bayfield, CO 81122, 303/884-2768 or 303/884-4161. Services offered include fishing licenses, public boat ramp, docking facilities and mooring, free fishing lessons, equipment rental, tackle and bait sales, and fishing or pontoon boat rentals.

Mountain Marina, 14810 County Road 501, Bayfield, CO 81122, 303/884-9450 or 303/884-9389. Services offered include rentals of fishing boats, pontoon boats, pleasure boats, canoes, fishing gear, tackle and bait sales, licenses and guides.

Pine River Drainage Fishing

The **Pine River**, south of Vallecito Reservoir, is accessed via paved and gravel roads. North of the reservoir, access is via Forest Service trails. Catch-and-release trout fishing is encouraged.

East Creek, east of Vallecito Reservoir, contains brook trout. It is accessed via Forest Service trails.

Vallecito Creek is accessed via Forest Service trails north of the reservoir. Catch-and-release trout fishing is encouraged.

Ouray/Ridgway Fishing

A number of stocked lakes include the following:

Ptarmigan Lake, below Imogene Pass.
East Dallas Lake, at the Willow Swamps campground, is four miles west of Ridgway, then seven miles south on East Dallas Divide Road.
Silver Jack Reservoir is 12 miles north of Ouray on US 550, then east on Forest Service Road 858.
Ridgway Reservoir, 15 miles north of Ridgway on US 550, has a full-service marina and boat ramp.

Telluride Fishing

The **San Miguel River**, west of Telluride to Placerville, is stocked in July. Fly fishing for rainbow, brown, cutthroat, and brook trout is good between Telluride and Norwood.

Other potentially trout-filled waters include the following:

Leopard Creek, west of Dallas Divide, toward Placerville, to the San Miguel River.
Alta Lakes, southwest of Telluride off CO 145.
Trout Lake, set at 10,000 feet, south of Telluride, allows boats.

Dolores/Rico Fishing

Dolores River Drainage Fishing

Bear Creek, northeast of Dolores and Mancos is accessed via Forest Service trails. Catch-and-release trout fishing is encouraged.

Coal Creek, between Rico and Lizard Head Pass, contains rainbow trout and is accessed through Dunton.

Roaring Forks, northeast of Priest Gulch on CO 145, contains cutthroat trout and is accessed via Forest Service Road 435.

The **Dolores River**, which starts high in the mountains, near Lizard Head Pass, travels through Rico, along CO 145 to Dolores and McPhee Reservoir. It is considered one of the best 100 trout streams in America for rainbows, snakeriver cutthroats, and German browns, many in the three- to four-pound range. It offers Gold Medal trophy fly fishing for trout on the 12-mile stretch of river from McPhee Dam to the bridge on County Road 505, known as Bradfield Bridge.

Fisherman may use flies and artificial lures only, and everything you catch here must be thrown back in. Westward from Bradfield Bridge you may keep your limit of browns or rainbows, without limitation on the type of tackle used.

Among the major Dolores River tributaries offering good fishing are the following:

West Fork of the Dolores, between Dolores and Dunton along Forest Service Road 536, is stocked with rainbow, brown, and cutthroat trout. Camping is available.
Barlow Creek, northeast of Rico, off CO 145, contains native trout.
Stoner Creek, north of Dolores on CO 145 contains rainbow and brook trout and is accessed by Forest Service trails.
Taylor Creek, also north of Dolores on CO 145, and also containing rainbow and brook trout, is accessed by a gravel road, Forest Service Road 545.

Lake and Reservoir Fishing

Ground Hog Reservoir, 32 miles north of Dolores on paved Forest Service Road 526 to gravel Forest Service Road 533, contains rainbow and cutthroat trout in 668 acres and is set at 8,718 feet. There is a boat ramp, marina (motors are permitted), and there are campsites. The area may be closed in early spring or late fall if there has been heavy snow.

Jackson Gulch Reservoir, a 216-acre lake set at 7,822 feet, is six miles northeast of Mancos on County Road 42, at Mancos State Recreation Area. There is a boat ramp for access to rainbow trout and small yellow perch. Camping is available.

Joe Moore Reservoir, five miles north of Mancos on CO 184 and County Road 40, is 45 acres, set at 7,688 feet. Best fishing is in early summer for rainbow trout, largemouth bass, perch, crappie, bluegill, and green sunfish.

McPhee Reservoir is northwest of Dolores on CO 184. It features cold- and warm-water fishing and it's stocked with trout, kokanee salmon, largemouth and smallmouth bass, perch, bluegill and catfish. Boat and equipment rentals and guide services are available from **Beaver Creek Marina**, 303/882-2258, and there is a no-wake zone exclusively for canoeists. Bass 15 inches and under must be released.

Puett Reservoir, is 14 miles northwest of Mancos on CO 184. It's a 145-acre lake at 7,260 feet elevation. A rough road keeps many away from fishing for walleye, yellow perch and northern pike. There is a boat ramp and camping is available.

Summit Reservoir is 11 miles northwest of Mancos on CO 184. It's 350 acres and is at 7,386 feet elevation. Restrictions apply to fishing for rainbow trout, smallmouth bass, channel catfish, and crappie. There is a boat ramp and camping is available.

Toten Reservoir is two miles east of Cortez on US 160, then north on County Road 29. It's a 220-acre lake at 6,156 feet elevation, meaning warmer water than high mountain lakes, so it can be stocked with walleye, bluegill, yellow perch, crappie, and largemouth bass. There is a boat ramp.

For additional information, rental equipment, licenses and guide services contact the following sources:

Duranglers, 801 B Main Avenue, Durango, CO 81301, 303/385-4081. This is a full-service fly-fishing store, offering equipment sales and rentals, custom fly-tying, up-to-the-minute stream reports, and guided trips.

Olympic Sports, 150 West Colorado, Telluride, CO 81435, 303/728-4477 or 800/828-7547, offers guide services and fly-fishing schools, rental equipment, licenses, and expert advice on local fishing.

Telluride Outside (666 West Colorado, Telluride, CO 81435, 303/728-3895) offers guided trophy fly-fishing trips on the San Miguel, Dolores and San Juan rivers, or mountain lakes. Also offered are one- , two- , or three-day fly-fishing schools, featuring instruction in casting, entomology, reading the water, fly-tying, vernacular of fly-fishing, presenting the fly, equipment, and knot-tying. After your lessons you practice techniques on the San Miguel River and mountain lakes. Also: Licenses, supplies, flies and gear rentals, as well as winter fly-fishing trips on the San Juan River below Navajo Lake.

Tellair Inc., PO Box 2130, Telluride, CO 81435, 303/728-5358, offers customized, guided fly-in fishing trips on the San Juan River in New Mexico, the Green River in Utah, and other sites.

The Outfitter (410 Railroad Avenue, Dolores, CO 81323, 303/882-7740) offers guided fly-fishing trips on the Quality Waters of the Dolores River.

HOT SPRINGS

Mineral-laden hot water flowing from underground springs soothes the body and the mind–especially after a tiring day in the mountains.

Trimble Hot Springs, 6475 County Road 203, Durango, CO 81301, 303/247-0111, fax 303/247-4493, offers modern services at an historic mineral hot springs. It is a National Historic Site and was reputedly frequented by Ute Chief Ouray. The facilities include an Olympic-size natural hot springs pool, a therapy pool, private hot tubs, massage therapy, body and skin treatments, physical therapy, and a fitness program including yoga instruction.

Wiesbaden Lodge, PO Box 349 (6th Avenue and 5th Street), Ouray, CO 81427, 303/325-4347, is a motel situated directly over a geothermal spring. The facility includes a steamy, shallow, underground vapor cave and an outdoor swimming pool heated by the hot springs. The pool's warm enough for swimming outdoors year-round, even in mid-winter with snow piled high all around.

Orvis Hot Springs, (one mile south of Ridgway on US 550), 303/626-5324, offers four private tubs, a sauna, an indoor soaking pool, and an outdoor hot mineral pool. There are also a few guest rooms.

On Snow

There's usually more than enough snow for several months of winter sports in southwestern Colorado, with many areas averaging more than 300 inches yearly. Of course it doesn't fall at one time, but it does tend to accumulate, rather than melt, until spring. Planning a winter trip between January and March would give you excellent odds of encountering prodigious white stuff for all your snow time pursuits.

Downhill ski areas are well-maintained and carefully patrolled. Cross-country skiing is becoming increasingly popular, but be warned that backcountry routes can be both spectacular and dangerous. Careful preparation and extra caution are highly recommended. A variety of other snow sports are also available through outfitters or on your own. Equipment rentals are available at the ski areas or from numerous shops in Durango, Ouray, Telluride, or other communities.

DOWNHILL SKIING

Some people consider the powder terrain in these parts to be the best you can find anywhere.

Purgatory-Durango Ski Resort, PO Box 166, Durango, CO 81302 303/247-9000 or 800/525-0892. Located 26 miles north of Durango on US 550, Purgatory seems to always be in the throes of management problems. There's never enough money to upgrade facilities and the area has not always offered the highest levels of service to skiers. But it is the only game in town for legitimate, easily accessed alpine terrain and Purgatory does provide reliable intermediate powder skiing, four triple chairlifts and five double chairlifts to 70 trails spread over 640 acres of ski terrain. Vertical drop is 2,029 feet, and the terrain is 20% beginner, 50% intermediate, 30% advanced. Facilities include a ski school, equipment rentals, nursery, and slope-side condominiums. Also: snowmobiling, sleigh rides, and groomed cross-country ski trails.

Hesperus Ski Area, 9848 US 160, Hesperus, CO 81326, 303/259-3711. This little ski hill, located 12 miles west of Durango on US 160, has a vertical drop of only 900 feet, but it's steep. Lift tickets are about half the cost of those at Purgatory or Telluride, and there are lights for night skiing until 9:30 PM. The area is mostly used by local kids and frequently you feel as if this is your private mountain. Also: cross-country trails are nearby.

Telluride Ski Resort, PO Box 307, Telluride, CO 81435, 303/728-3856 (for snow reports call 303/728-3614). Telluride offers one high-speed quad-lift, two triple chairs, six double chairs, and one poma lift to 62 trails spread over 1,050 acres. Close access to the mountain is available from the center of town or from the Telluride Mountain Village.

The area contains 21% beginner, 47% intermediate, and 32% advanced terrain, including some of the steepest terrain in the Colorado Rockies. The vertical drop is 3,165 feet and the longest run is nearly three miles. Facilities include a ski school, equipment rentals, and a nursery. The area sponsors weekly NASTAR races, maintains groomed cross-country trails, and offers helicopter skiing, snowmobiling, hockey, ice skating, and sleigh rides.

Telluride offers skiing on three mountain faces for different levels of ability. This includes 400 acres on Gold Hill for expert skiers, providing a virtual backcountry ski experience, complete with glades and chutes. The ski area is well-run and the scenery here is incomparable.

CROSS-COUNTRY SKIING

The following listings include some of the most scenic and safest cross-country ski routes in southwestern Colorado. Groomed trails are generally perfectly safe, but always remember that backcountry conditions are unpredictable and dependent on factors that are more likely than not to change rapidly; on the spot research is essential before any backcountry ski trip.

Foremost, consider the weather. It can turn from clear to stormy before you know it, obliterating a trail and an unprepared skier's sense of direction in minutes. Sunny, warm days may provide glorious ski conditions but can also increase avalanche dangers after heavy snowfall.

The current snowpack needs to be considered, particularly in relation to wind conditions, which may have a profound effect on your pleasure and safety.

On any cross-country ski trip, dress warmly with layered clothing. Carry high energy foods, and be prepared for the worst so you can have the best time.

Durango/Silverton

Hillcrest Golf Course, 2300 Rim Drive, Durango, CO 81301, 303/247-149, is up College Drive (6th Street) in Durango. The undulating hills and flats are great for cross-country skiing and overlook the fairy-tale, snow-covered town.

Bear Ranch, 42570 US 550, Durango, CO 81301, 303/247-0111, is practically across the street from Purgatory Resort. Groomed cross-country trails are available, along with sleigh rides.

The **San Juan National Forest** contains numerous backcountry ski trails, but knowledge of snow and avalanche conditions is essential. The trails around **Haviland Lake**, 17 miles north of Durango on US 550, are good for beginners who can ski near the campground area. Check out some of the hiking and jeep trails listed above for other ideas, or consult with Forest Service personnell (303/247-4874) for area updates and ski conditions.

Tamarron Resort 40252 US 550, Durango, CO 81301, 303/259-2000 or 800/678-1000, has a hilly, championship golf course used for cross-country skiing in winter.

The Silverton area offers many more miles of diverse and challenging cross-country ski terrain. Avalanche dangers are usually high, but there are certain areas known to be safer to ski. There are numerous trails fanning out from **Molas Pass**, six miles south of Silverton on US 550. One fairly easy trail leads to **Little Molas**

Lake, on the west side of the highway and a half-mile up a snow-covered road.

South Mineral Creek Road (near Silverton), from US 550 to the Forest Service campground, offers five miles of easy terrain.

Ouray

Red Mountain Pass is a serious cross-country skiers' haven. You can usually see ski tracks all over the place, but these are left by knowledgeable backcountry skiers. **St. Paul Lodge** (see below under Accommodations) offers rustic backcountry accommodations and challenging cross-country ski terrain, but not for rank beginners.

There are hundreds more miles of cross-country ski trails around Ouray and Ridgway. Ouray has formed the Ouray County Nordic Council to coordinate a system of trails in the **Ironton/Red Mountain Pass** area south of town. Easy to challenging terrain is available. Get information from local sport shops or the Ouray Visitor Center (Box 145, Ouray, CO 81427, 303/325-4746).

Ridgway/Telluride/Rico/Dolores

East Dallas Creek Trail is five miles west of Ridgway, off CO 62, to County Road 7. You can drive up the county road for a few miles, then ski farther up it for another five miles. It is fairly steep, but lacking in the extreme avalanche danger found on other routes. It's a lot easier coming down than going up.

San Juan Hut Systems (Box 1663, 117 North Willow Street, Telluride, CO 81435, 303/728-6935) maintains an extensive, demanding cross-country, telemark and nordic trail system between Telluride and Ouray. They operate five rustic ski huts placed strategically between the towns, approximately a one-day ski apart, or huts may be accessed individually via Forest Service Roads or hiking trails. Huts have padded bunks, propane cook stove, propane lamp, wood stove, firewood, and all necessary kitchen implements. You melt snow for water. Sleeping bags can be rented and food can be provided, along with guide services.

The hut system is designed to accommodate skiers of all abilities, but you should have intermediate skiing skills at the least. Above each hut is terrain for advanced-intermediate, expert, and extreme powder skiing, or telemark skiing.

All skiers must be aware of changing weather conditions, as well as snow and avalanche conditions. This is not light touring terrain, but requires nordic skis with metal edges. You need to pack in extra clothing, sufficient food, and any gear you might need for unexpected weather conditions or an emergency bivouac. A full line of rental equipment is available, including avalanche transceivers and shovels.

There are 15 kilometers of groomed cross-country trails at the top of the Telluride Ski Area's **Sunshine Express Lift**, as well as another 15 kilometers of groomed trails at the **Telluride Mountain Village Golf Course**.

Cross-country skiing around **Lizard Head Pass**, can also be splendid but hazardous along backcountry trails. Avalanche danger is low if you stick to the huge open meadows on either side of CO 145. **Cross Mountain Trail** starts on the west side of the highway, two miles south of Lizard Head Pass, and is a mostly uphill trail for 1,200 feet. It is four miles to the recommended turn-around point at a level clearing. Avalanche danger increases beyond this point, but the eight-mile round-trip is a good intermediate/advanced route.

There's good intermediate terrain around **Dunton**. A four-wheel-drive is required to reach areas north of Dunton on West Fork Road, 33 miles north of Dolores, or via CO 145 to Dunton Road (Forest Service Road 535), and 20 miles west to Dunton. Park at the end of the plowed road. You can ski on **Forest Service Road 535**, past the intersection with Forest Service Road 611, bearing right after two miles to head toward Burro Bridge Campground. An alternative route for novice skiers starts the same way but bears left on **Forest Service Road 611**. The first mile of skiing is through aspen glades and into open meadows, and beyond is hilly telemark skiing terrain in sight of Dolores Peak.

Scotch Creek, 2.5 miles south of Rico off CO 145, on the east side of the highway, is an historic toll road once used to carry supplies to the Rico mining district. The novice/beginner trail follows the left side of the creek for three miles, passing between high canyon walls. Turn around where the trail crosses the creek.

Taylor Mesa is 15 miles south of Scotch Creek, north of CO 145. A seven-mile beginner/intermediate trail climbs gradually through evergreens, aspen, and cottonwoods for 3.5 miles to **Little Taylor Trail**, on the right. It gets steeper beyond this point, so beginners may want to turn around. Stronger skiers can continue up Taylor Creek.

Boggy Draw/Norwood Road, north of Dolores, offers up to 20 miles of gently rolling terrain along unplowed roads and open fields suitable for family outings. Follow Forest Service Road 526 north from Dolores to the intersection with Forest Service Road 527. Ski north on the Norwood Road or east on 527.

Mesa Verde National Park/Mancos

The entrance road to **Mesa Verde National Park** is plowed in winter but other park roads are not. You can drive up to the empty **Morefield Campground** and ski around there on a mile or so of easy terrain. Alternatively, continue up the main road for 20 miles to Chapin Mesa. Atop the mesa you can ski around the park's Ruins Road on the six-mile **Balcony House Loop**. Snowfall is generally not too heavy here and may not remain on the ground terribly long. Call the park (303/529-4461, 303/529-4475 or 303/529-4465) for snow conditions and required permission to ski.

Chicken Creek Canyon, 1.5 miles north of Mancos on CO 184, then three miles farther on Chicken Creek Road, offers 20 miles of maintained trails for all levels of skiers. These include six miles of double-track and skate lanes, as well as five miles of single-track in various loops and spurs. These are the only groomed trails in the area. Detailed maps are available from stores in the town of Mancos.

Railroad Trail is 5.5 miles east of Mancos on US 160, at the summit of Mancos Hill. Drive north a quarter-mile to the end of the plowed road and park there. You can ski on Forest Service Road 316 for a mile, then turn east (right) onto Forest Service Road 568 which is eightmiles one-way. The trail follows an old railroad grade through an oak brush plateau and aspen groves, dropping 480 feet in the last mile to the Cherry Creek Picnic Area. An alternative is to ski uphill for six to eight miles on Forest Service Road 316, but this route is only recommended for advanced or strong skiers.

SNOWMOBILING/DOGSLEDDING/ICE CLIMBING

There are hundreds of miles of snowmobile trails in southwestern Colorado. Snowmobile tours are available from **Purgatory-Durango Ski Resort** and **Telluride Ski Resort.**

Telluride Outside (666 West Colorado, Telluride, CO 81435, 303/728-3895) also offers snowmobile tours, including one- or three-hour dinner tours to Skyline Ranch and full evening dinner tours to the Alta Lakes Observatory. They will customize tours to suit your needs.

Customized dog sled trips are offered by Durango's **Black Feather Mushers** (303/247-8281).

Telluride Sledog Touring Co. (c/o Telluride Outside, above) runs one-hour, half-day, and full-day dog sled tours. It also offers private dogsledding lessons.

SouthWest Adventures (780 Main Avenue, Durango, CO 81302, 303/259-0370 or 800/642-5389) teaches scheduled two- to five-day classes in Alpine ice climbing and waterfall ice climbing. Other ice courses and private guiding are available.

Ouray is known around the world for its ice climbing on **Box Canyon Fallls** and more than a dozen other accessible areas for ice climbing. This is quite serious stuff, requiring ropes and harnesses. Contact the Visitor Center (Box 145, Ouray, CO 81427, 303/325-4746) for information.

One- to five-day courses in technical ice climbing, winter peak ascents, and guided Alpine tour services are offered by **Fantasy Ridge Mountain Guides**, PO Box 1679, Telluride, CO 81435, 303/728-3546. Also available: technical summer rock climbing instruction and non-technical ascents to 14,000-foot peaks.

Horse-drawn sleigh rides are offered by **Mayday Livery** (4317 County Road 124, Hesperus, CO 81326, 303/385-6772) and **Buck's Livery** (US 550 at Purgatory, Durango, CO 81301, 303/385-2110).

Deep Creek Sleigh Rides of Telluride (130 West Colorado, Telluride, CO 81435, 303/728-3565) offers sleigh rides twice each evening. A steak dinner served in a heated tent is included.

In Air

Val-Air Soaring, 27290 Highway 550, Durango, CO 81301, 303/247-9037, offers glider rides over the Animas Valley from an airfield three miles north of Durango. Thirty- or 60-minute flights are available seven days a week, May 15 to October 15.

Gregg Flying Service, Animas Air Park, Durango, CO 81302, 303/247-4632, offers scenic flights or airplane charters to locations throughout the Four Corners and as far as the Grand Canyon from a small airfield a few miles south of town. Also: flight instruction and aircraft maintenance services.

Durango Air Service, La Plata Field, Durango, CO 81301, 303/247-5535, offers scenic flights for a minimum of two people from an airport 15 miles southeast of town. Also: charters and airplane rentals, flight instruction, and aircraft maintenance services are available.

New Air Helicopters, PO Box 3268, Flight Line Road, Animas Air Park, Durango, CO 81302, 303/259-6247, has helicopters for charter and offers scenic tours of 15 or 30 minutes in speedy jet helicopters that cover a lot of ground in a short time. A novel idea is to ride the narrow gauge train to Silverton and arrange for a helicopter flight back to Durango–the best of both worlds. Other services include photo tours and remote site transportation.

Air Durango, PO Box 2138, Durango, CO 81302, 303/385-1749, offers year-round hot-air balloon flights every day (weather permitting). To take advantage of the calmest weather of the day, launches take place at 6:30 AM from the Durango High School parking lot on Main Avenue. Typical one- to 1.5-hour flights float over Durango and the train station, revealing the mountainous terrain that surrounds the city and the Animas Valley, landing south of town. A traditional champagne toast is included.

Mariah Balloon Company, PO Box 2744, Durango, CO 81302, 303/385-4940 or 303/259-0746, offers traditional champagne flights, usually over Durango's Animas Valley or where the wind blows. The whole excursion takes around three hours and includes a hotel pick-up at sunrise.

New West Adventures (PO Box 2744, Durango, CO 81302, 303/385-4940 or 800/748-1188) also offers balloon flights.

San Juan Balloon Adventures, PO Box 66, Ridgway, CO 81432, 303/626-5495, or 303/728-3895 (in Telluride), or 800/831-6230, offers hot-air balloon flights of a half-hour, one-hour, or a deluxe Balloon 'n Brunch flight, over the Ridgway Valley.

Telluride Soaring, Telluride Regional Airport, 303/728-5424, offers glider rides over what they claim to be "the most spectacular scenery in the country." They may be right.

Mesa Verde Soaring, 303/565-6164, at Cortez Airport, three miles south of Cortez on US 160, offers sailplane rides over the world of the Anasazi Indians.

Cortez Flying Service, PO Box 997, Cortez, CO 81321, 303/565-3721, offers scenic flights and charter services in fixed-wing aircraft.

Eco-Travel & Cultural Excursions

DURANGO

American Southwest Adventures, PO Box 3471, Durango, CO 81302, 303/247-5274 (or contact Durango Travel, 563 Main Avenue, Durango, CO 81301, 303/259-0090 or 800/748-2021), offers customized educational and photographic tours of one-day or longer throughout the Four Corners region. Itineraries include sites such as Mesa Verde, Ute Mountain Tribal Park, Chaco Canyon, Monument Valley, Canyon de Chelly, canyons of southeastern Utah and numerous ghost towns. Their focus is on photography, ecology, wildlife, and Native American cultural history. The trips, which include transportation in an air-conditioned four-wheel-drive, lunch, entrance fees, and photographic assistance, are led by an environmental education specialist who is also a professional photographer. Reservations are required.

Durango Pro Rodeo, PO Box 299, Durango, CO 81302, 303/247-1666. A pro rodeo takes place Tuesday and Wednesday nights, from early June to late September, at the La Plata County Fairgrounds, 25th Street and Main Avenue, Durango. The competition features all seven rodeo events, calf roping, saddle bronc riding, bareback riding, bull riding, bull dogging, team roping, and barrel racing.

Hiss the villain at the **Diamond Circle Theatre**, 699 Main Avenue, Durango, CO 81302, 303/247-4431, which features live turn-of-the-century melodramas, from early June to late September.

Bar D Chuckwagon, 8080 County Road 250, Durango, CO 81301, 303/247-5753, offers a popular chuckwagon supper of barbecue beef, beans, and biscuits, and a western show that's been running every summer for more than 25 years. The show includes original songs, western classics, yodeling, and comedy skits. There's also a miniature train ride, art gallery, leather shop, t-shirt store, blacksmith shop, and a record shop selling Bar-D Wrangler records. **Durango Jamboree**, 5800 Main Avenue (at the Iron Horse Inn), Durango, CO 81301, 303/259-1290, offers "downhome" music (western, bluegrass, folk, and gospel), and corny comedy, along with a barbecue dinner. It's sort of a *Hee-Haw*-type show and runs from early June to late September, Monday through Saturday.

There is not a great deal of night life in the Durango area, but one of the most popular spots on summer evenings is a throwback to simpler times, the **Rocket Drive-In Theatre**, 26126 US Highway 160, Durango, 303/247-0833. The sound from small, clip-on speakers is tinny, but where else can you see a double feature these days? Basically the whole town comes out for these shows, so the audience is a show in itself. Children under 12 usually get in for free, and the intermission snack bar trailers, exhorting viewers to extricate themselves from their cars for hot dogs, popcorn and soft drinks, appear to be authentic 1950s vintage.

There are quite a number of western bars in Durango, making bar-hopping a cultural experience of its own. The classic **Diamond Belle Saloon**, 699 Main Avenue, Durango, CO 81301, 303/247-4431, makes you feel as if you are entering Dodge City when you pass through its swinging doors. Inside, a honky-tonk pianist is pounding the ivories. Bar girls are dressed in scanty 1880s costumes. Even the male bartenders wear garters on their sleeves. **Sundowner Saloon**, 3777 North Main Avenue, Durango, CO 81301, 303/385-4410, offers live country western dance music Monday through Saturday nights.

SILVERTON

A Theatre Group, 1069 Greene Street (upstairs in the American Legion Building), Silverton, CO 81433, 303/387-5337 or 800/752-4494, is one of Colorado's few year-round mountain town theatre companies, comprised of local, university, and professional talent.

OURAY

San Juan Odyssey, Main Street at 5th Avenue (the Old Opera House), Ouray, CO 81427, 303/325-4607, uses five screens, 15 projectors, and surround-sound stereo to bring the San Juans to you.

TELLURIDE

Skiing is the winter activity that revived the prosperity of Telluride, but in summer, a weekly roster of festivals lures thousands of people to town. During the biggest events, such as the Bluegrass, Jazz or Film festivals, every room in town is booked months in advance, so plan early if you want to participate, or be prepared to camp out or stay somewhere out of town. Contact the **Telluride Chamber Resort Association** (PO Box 653, 666 West Colorado Avenue, Telluride, CO 81435, 303/728-3041, fax 303/728-6475) for updated information. Festivals vary from the wildly popular to the obscure, and schedules change each summer, but the following is a sampling of what you might expect in a typical year.

- Native American Writer's Forum features workshops, discussions, and readings.
- Steps to Awareness incudes 30 workshops related to self-generated healing, including topics ranging from native herbal remedies, to shamanism, to birthing.
- Mountainfilm offers movies and discussions devoted to mountain adventure and the environment.
- A Balloon Festival features hot air balloons over the valley.
- Talking Gourds is a cross-cultural gathering of poets, story-tellers, and performance artists, offering three days of discussions, workshops, and presentations.
- The Telluride Theatre Festival includes theatrical seminars and presentations in acting, playwriting, direction, and design.
- The Telluride Bicycle Classic features pro-am races.
- The Telluride Bluegrass Festival is always one of the biggest local events of the year; attendance is limited to 10,000, and it's always a sell-out. Outdoor performances in Town Park are by

well-known and aspiring banjo-pickers, mandolin-manipulators, and other sympathetic performers. There are also workshops for adults and children.

- Deep West Arts Circuit offers modern dance performances.
- A Telluride Mountain Bike Festival features organized group bike rides, bike polo, bike rodeo, and pro races.
- Telluride Wine Festival includes tastings, matching wines with foods, and a champagne brunch.
- KOTO Community Concert Series features outdoor concerts sponsored by a local radio station.
- Fireman's Fourth of July is just an excuse for a traditional small town celebration, including a parade, children's games, rides on an antique fire truck, a barbecue, and after dark, fireworks.
- Lunar Cup Ski Race features pros and amateurs competing at 12,500 feet in dual slalom, telemark, and snowboard events–in July!
- Shakespeare on the Shellman Stage is performed by the Telluride Repertory Theatre in Town Park.
- The Superwinch/Rotary Club 4x4 Tour includes guided off-road driving.
- A Telluride Ideas Festival has featured workshops on creating a sustainable rural community.
- The Telluride Jazz Celebration features a weekend of music, with some big names, performed outdoors in an incomparable setting.
- A Chamber Music Festival features intimate concerts.
- Jimmy Huega's Mountain Bike Express features three-person teams competing in a four-hour relay marathon.
- The Telluride Mushroom Festival is actually one of the longer-running festivals, now featuring a parade, a cook-and-taste feast, mushroom hunting expeditions, and workshops on edible, poisonous, and psychoactive mushrooms.
- Magic Arts Festival closes the streets downtown for western arts displays, street performers, and magicians.
- The Telluride Film Festival is internationally renowned. Screenings include national and international premieres, world archive treasures, experimental films, retrospectives, and three yearly tributes. Screenings and accommodations are booked solid far in advance by a mix of Hollywood and international filmdom celebrities, critics, and hard-core film-goers.
- The Imogene Pass Run covers 18 miles over 13,000-foot pass.

- A Living in Harmony Concert was organized by Peter, of Peter, Paul & Mary.
- A Hang Gliding Festival features the world's top pilots. They come year after year for this week of high flying which includes the World Aerobatic Hang Gliding Championships.
- A Behind Closed Doors Home Tour visits historic and contemporary houses, which are opened to the public for a weekend during the prime foliage season.
- A Telluride One-World Festival offers international music by top stars from all over the world in Town Park and local clubs.
- As much fun as all this is, at the insistence of vociferous local residents, one weekend each summer is set aside for a Nothing Festival. Nothing special is planned.

Telluride Outside (666 West Colorado, Telluride, CO 81435, 303/728-3895) offers two-hour, geologist-guided expeditions for stream-side gold panning and special geology tours to explain the processes which formed the region.

Telluride Institute, PO Box 1770, 283 South Fir Street, Telluride, CO 81435, 303/728-4402, fax 303/728-4919, is a non-profit think-tank which sponsors the **Deep West Arts Circuit**, presenting performing, composing and other creative arts programs. Also: regional studies and education programs are offered.

The Ah Haa School For the Arts, PO Box 1590, 135 South Spruce, Telluride, CO 81435, 303/728-3886, offers classes for adults and children in painting, ceramics, photography, bookmaking, drawing, print making, silver casting, basket making, creative writing, and other subjects.

Herb Walker Tours, PO Box 399, Telluride, CO 81435, 303/728-4538 or 303/728-4559, runs educational herb/nature hikes. Participants learn to identify and use wild plants and mushrooms while exploring the many trails in the Telluride area. These hikes range from leisurely walks in town, to climbing in the high country. Topics include how to differentiate between poisonous and beneficial plants, medicinal/culinary uses, folklore, and preparation.

CORTEZ/MESA VERDE

The Crow Canyon Archaeological Center, 23390 County Road K, Cortez, CO 81321, 303/565-8975 or 800/422-8975, is an innovative archaeological research and education center focusing on the prehistoric Anasazi Indians. One-day programs include examining 700-year-old artifacts and archaeological site visits. These are offered Tuesday, Wednesday, and Thursday, from the first week in

June to the last week of October. Week-long programs include hands-on work at an actual excavation site, one of which is Sand Canyon Pueblo, the largest ruin ever found in the Southwest. Also: workshops on Native American crafts, including pottery, weaving, basketry, and jewelry. Cultural explorations, led by archaeologists and Native Americans, are also offered. Reservations are required at least a day in advance for day programs.

Mesa Verde National Park offers several guided tours and multi-media shows from mid-April to mid-October. Information is available at Far View Lodge (see below under Accommodations).

Where to Stay & Eat

Southwest Colorado counts on tourism to pay the bills, and therefore provides all levels of accommodations, from free and primitive wilderness campgrounds to luxury resorts charging hundreds of dollars a day. Most accommodations fall somewhere in the middle of these limits. There are many independent or chain motels, most quite ordinary, as well as historic hotels, bed & breakfasts, condominiums, cabin rentals, and dude ranches. Many of the ranches offer a western variant of the all-inclusive vacation, with meals, horseback riding, backcountry excursions, and other activities for a flat price.

Summer is considered high season throughout southwestern Colorado except for accommodations at or near ski areas, where rates increase when the snow flies. Some bargains can be found in winter and accommodations are considerably less expensive in Durango than slope-side at Purgatory. The Durango Lift offers round-trip bus service from town to the ski area or you can drive the 26 miles; US 550 is kept well-plowed.

Depending on what you want to do in southwestern Colorado, you could probably stay in one or two places and drive from these bases to anywhere suggested in this chapter. The widest range of accommodations is in Durango which boasts around 6,000 beds. In Silverton prices are deservedly inexpensive and dining can be a challenge. Ouray has a few interesting places to stay and Telluride offers numerous well-equipped condos and some ultra-deluxe accommodations.

Cortez is closest to Indian Country. Mesa Verde National Park has a motel that fills up far in advance in summer. In April-May or September-October, you're more likely to get a room on the spur of the moment.

Restaurants in southwest Colorado include many no better than adequate or worse, but there are some good ones to be found. Prices tend to be within reason, although some of the better restaurants are raising the ante.

There are many, many more accommodations and restaurants in this area than what follows. At some of these hotels you can stay for as little as $25 nightly in low-season (though close to double that in high-season) or receive change from a 10 dollar bill for dinner. Contact local Visitor Centers or Chambers of Commerce for complete listings.

In-Town Durango Accommodations

The classiest historic hotel in southwestern Colorado is the **Strater Hotel**, 699 Main Avenue, Durango, CO 81302, 303/247-4431, 800/247-4431 (in Colorado) or 800/227-4431. It's been a Durango landmark since 1881 and has recently been designated a museum. Each of the 93 rooms is different and all are furnished with antiques comprising one of the largest collections of Victorian walnut furnishings in the world. Rooms have modern bathrooms and cable TV. No pool, but there is a spa room with jacuzzi. There is a disappointing, hotel-quality restaurant here. **Henry's** serves three meals a day, the **Diamond Belle Saloon** and the **Diamond Circle Theatre** (699 Main Avenue, Durango, CO 81302, 303/247-4431) are also on the premises. Reserve early during summer.

The General Palmer Hotel, 567 Main Avenue, Durango, CO 81302, 303/247-4747 or 800/523-3358, is also a Victorian-style hotel a block south of the Strater. It's got a cozy, antique-filled lobby right on Main Avenue, a block from the Silverton train, but its 39 rooms contain reproductions, not antiques. Certain "inside rooms" lack windows.

Jarvis Suite Hotel, 125 West 10th Avenue, Durango, CO 81302 303/259-6190 or 800/824-1024, has studios, one- and two-bedroom suites with small rooms, homey living rooms, and full kitchens. Situated downtown just five blocks from the train station.

The **Durango Hostel**, 543 East 2nd Avenue, Durango, CO 81301, 303/247-9905, is cheaper than many campgrounds, though not much more deluxe. Dorms, or private rooms, with a shared kitchen are available.

Leland House, 721 East Second Avenue, Durango, CO 81301, 303/385-1920, is a friendly B&B in a remodeled 1927 building. It has antique-furnished rooms with kitchenettes, or suites with full kitchens.

In addition there is a virtual motel strip of one after another modest motel on North Main Avenue, some with pools. Contact the chamber of commerce for complete listings.

Out-of-Town Durango Accommodations

Tamarron Resort, 40252 US 550, Durango, CO 81301, 303/259-2000 or 800/678-1000, is a large, luxurious, contemporary, western golf resort hotel, with 350 large rooms and multi-bedroom condo units. All have kitchens or kitchenettes. Scenically situated 16 miles north of Durango, facilities include an indoor-outdoor pool, saunas, whirlpool, children's program, golf, tennis, cross-country ski trails, horseback riding, ski shuttle to nearby Purgatory, airport transportation, and two dining rooms.

Tall Timber, SSR Box 90A, Durango, CO 81302, 303/259-4813, is completely secluded on the banks of the Animas River, north of Durango. Most people ride the narrow gauge railroad or a helicopter to get here. The alternatives are to hike or ride a horse–the closest road is five miles away.

When you finally get here, you discover a top-rated, luxurious hideaway for a maximum of 30 guests. With only 10 modern multi-bedroom units, each with fireplace and deck, five-star dining, indoor-outdoor pool, sauna, whirlpool, putting green, executive nine-hole golf course, tennis court, exercise room, skiing and hiking trails, horseback riding, fishing, heli-picnics, and heli-hiking, it certainly offers plenty to keep you busy. Rates include meals and transportation to the resort. There is a four-day minimum stay.

Steward Ranch Cabins, 4385 County Road 207, Durango, CO 81301, 303/247-8396 or 303/247-8962, offers 40 acres of privacy, a one- or two-bedroom log cabin with fireplace, kitchen, barbecue, and picnic table. Parts of the movie *City Slickers* were filmed here, just west of Durango, off US 160.

Diamond Lodge Guest Ranch, 2038 Sierra Verde Drive, Durango, CO 81301, 303/259-9393 or 812/332-3342, or 317/842-1994. Located 17 miles northwest of Durango at 9,200 feet elevation, this modern guest house contains 24 bedrooms with private baths. The ranch offers Sunday to Sunday lodging from late May to mid-September, including horseback riding, cookouts, trout fishing, and hiking.

Colorado Trails, 1261 County Road 240, Durango, CO 81301, 800/323-3833, fax 303/385-7372, is 12 miles northeast of Durango, and has operated as a well-regarded family guest ranch since 1960. Facilities accommodate 75 guests per one-week minimum stay, and include cabins with single rooms or two-room suites, all meals, horse riding program, water skiing and tubing, heated pool and spa, archery, riflery, trapshooting, fishing, tennis, square dancing, hayrides, camp-outs for kids, music shows, dancing, chuckwagon dinners, children's and teens' programs.

Wit's End Guest Ranch, 254 County Road 500, Bayfield, CO 81122, 303/884-4113. Located at Vallecito Reservoir, this year-round resort features luxuriously furnished log cabins with stone fireplaces, decks, brass beds, and kitchens. There's a good dining room, a hot tub/jacuzzi, fishing, evening entertainment, horseback riding, pool, tennis, and water skiing. Cross-country skiing is available in winter.

Wilderness Trails Ranch, 776 County Road 300, Durango, CO 81301, 303/247-0722, has been a guest ranch since 1950. Located on the edge of the Weminuche Wilderness Area, the ranch accommodates 50 guests per minimum week-long stay in two- , three- , or five-bedroom log cabins, or duplexes. Activities include special children's and teens' programs, horseback riding, square dancing, staff shows, campfire sing-alongs, an overnight camp-out, volleyball, fishing, water skiing, and four-wheel-drive trips. There is a heated pool and all meals are included. Guests may participate in a cattle round-up the last week in September.

D'Mara Resort, 1213 County Road 500, Bayfield, CO 81122, 303/884-9806, offers several modern cabins with kitchens. These accommodate two to eight people and are set on the edge of Vallecito Reservoir. There is a three-night minimum stay in summer.

Purgatory Village Hotel, PO Box 2082, Durango, CO 81302, 303/247-9000 or 800/879-7874, at the ski area, offers luxurious one- , two-, or three-bedroom suites with balconies, wood- burning fireplaces, kitchens, in-room saunas, and whirlpool baths.

Cascade Village, 50827 US 550, Durango, CO 81301, 303/259-3500 or 800/525-0896, offers a range from large studios to three-bedroom luxury condos, with a full kitchen, cable TV, stereo, fireplace, balcony, and private jacuzzi tubs. There is a heated pool, a steam room, and an exercise room. Guests have easy access to **Cafe Cascade** (see below, under Durango Restaurants), a strong contender for the best restaurant in these parts.

In-Town Durango Restaurants

The Red Snapper, 144 East 9th Street, Durango, 303/259-3417, serves Durango's freshest seafood (flown in several times a week), along with Durango's best salad bar and epic desserts.

Griego's Taco House, 1400 East 2nd Avenue, Durango, 303/247-3127, is a tiny, evocative drive-in serving tasty tacos, burritos, and burgers. Open only during the summer. **Griego's North**, 2603 North Main, Durango, 303/259-3558, has similar food, but less atmosphere in a sit-down dining room open year-round.

Durango Diner, 957 Main Avenue, Durango, 303/247-9889, serves classic diner fare, huge servings of hash browns with your breakfast eggs, lunch specials, burgers, sandwiches, homemade pies, and so forth. Sit at the counter if you want to find out what's really going on around town.

Carver's Bakery and Brew Pub, 1022 Main Avenue, Durango, 303/259-2545, serves good coffee, baked goods, big salads, sandwiches, and several varieties of beer brewed slowly in a back room. Service is, shall we say, casual.

The Old Tymer's Cafe, 1000 Main Avenue, Durango, 303/259-2990, serves good nachos grande, burgers, and booze in an old historic building.

Durango Coffee Company, 730 Main Avenue, Durango, 303/259-2059, serves the best cup of coffee in town. They're getting a run for their money from the **Steaming Bean**, 915 Main Avenue, Durango, a casual, take-off-your-shoes-and-read-a-magazine-style coffee house with classic garage-sale-style decor.

Durango Bagel, 106 East 5th Street, Durango, is just a few doors east of the train station at the south end of Main Avenue, and serves the best fresh bagels in the Four Corners. Unfortunately they don't serve lox, but muffins, pastries, sandwiches, and good coffee are available.

Durango Country Creamery, 600 Main Avenue, Durango, 303/247-8111, serves the best ice cream in town.

Red Lion Inn, 501 Camino del Rio, Durango, 303/259-6580, has the best Sunday brunch buffet.

Out-of-Town Durango Restaurants

Edelweiss Restaurant, 689 Animas View Drive, Durango, 303/247-5685 or 800/964-5564, is a mile north of Main Avenue and serves excellent German, Italian, and American cuisine, including hasenpfeffer, scampi marinara, and prime rib. Wash it all down with one of the many imported beers on offer.

Mama's Boy, 32225 US 550, Hermosa, 303/247-9053, serves the best pizza in town, even though this tiny restaurant is located five miles north of Durango. A new second location at 3690 North Main

Avenue, Durango, across the street from the Pizza Hut, is larger, but the food suffers in comparison with the original.

Cafe Cascade, 50827 US 550, Durango, 303/259-3500, offers the most exotic menu in the Durango area–it's also one of the most expensive. It's definitely worth it; the food and service are first-class, and nowhere else nearby can you find an appetizer of fried Louisiana alligator, or entrees of wild boar, stuffed marlin, Muscovy duck, antelope, or quail, along with steaks and fresh seafood. Save your appetite for dinner here; the servings are huge. The dining room is casual, spacious, and comfortable. After an active day in the mountains this is a great place to relax and dine, not just eat. The drive here from any direction is beautiful and the setting amidst soaring peaks is stunning. Located a mile north of Purgatory.

Silverton Accommodations

Alma House, 220 East 10th Street, Silverton, CO 81433, 303/387-5336, is a cozy, restored Victorian hotel in a 1908 building. It's largely done in antiques and upholds the old custom that it's okay for some rooms to share a bathroom. Open mid-May to late September. Room service is available and pets are welcome.

The Grand Imperial Hotel, 1219 Greene Street, Silverton, CO 81433, 303/387-5527, is a more ornate Victorian restoration than the Alma House. It has 40 rooms with private baths, some with oak pull-chain toilets. There is a restaurant and a saloon with a bullet-hole in the bar. Open mid-March to October 1.

Wingate House Bed & Breakfast, 1045 Snowdon Street, Silverton, CO 81433, 303/387-5713, is an antique-filled B&B in a century-old home, with breakfast included at the **French Bakery** (see below, under Silverton Restaurants), or you can use the kitchen to prepare your own meals.

The Wyman Hotel, 1371 Greene Street, Silverton, CO 81433, 303/387-5372, off-season 303/249-5423, is Silverton's only AAA-rated lodging. Rooms in the 1902 building have private baths, something of a novelty around here, and VCRs, with free tapes. Open mid-May to mid-October.

Teller House Hotel, 1250 Greene Street, Silverton, CO 81433, 303/387-5423 or 800/342-4338, is above the French Bakery, where breakfast is included with a room. Bathrooms are down the hall and dorm rooms are available. The 800# also represents **Wingate House** and **Smedley's**, 1314 Greene Street, Silverton, CO 81433,

303/387-5423, another antique building offering suites with private baths and kitchens.

St. Paul Ski Lodge, PO Box 463, Silverton, CO 81433, 303/387-5367, offers rustic backcountry lodging set at 11,440 feet, above Red Mountain Pass and accessible only by hiking or cross-country skiing. This is an historic mining structure, cunningly remodeled with second-hand materials to accommodate 22 guests in dorm rooms, with an indoor-outhouse, sauna, hot showers, and kerosene lamps. Also: The lodge provides excellent access to challenging cross-country skiing in the heart of the San Juans and hosts periodic avalanche and medical seminars.

Silverton Restaurants

It's hard to recommend one over any other of Silverton's dozen or so restaurants. The last time I ate in town, at a restaurant that shall remain nameless, there was a hair in my food. When I mentioned this to the waitress she asked what color it was and tried to pick it off the plate, presumably so I could finish eating.

You might consider a picnic, driving south on US 550 to Cafe Cascade, or try your luck at the following:

The French Bakery Restaurant, 1250 Greene Street, Silverton, 303/387-5423, is a restaurant and bakery, which converts in winter to a restaurant and ski rental shop.

Romero's, 1151 Greene Street, Silverton, 303/387-9934, serves tolerable Mexican food, which tastes better after a few margaritas.

Ouray/Ridgway Accommodations

St. Elmo Hotel, 426 Main Street, Ouray, CO 81427, 303/325-4951, is a beautifully restored, well-run, nine-bedroom, 1898 Victorian Bed & Breakfast that's open year-round.

Wiesbaden Lodge and Spa, Box 349, Ouray, CO 81427, 303/325-4347, has a wonderful underground vapor cave fed by the hot springs that run below this hillside property. There's also a good-size outdoor mineral hot pool. The motel rooms are standard, but several lodge rooms are interesting, including one with a rock wall made out of the mountainside that has rivulets of steaming mineral water running down it.

Alpenglow Condominiums, 215 5th Avenue, Ouray, CO 81427, 303/325-4664 or 303/325-4972. Open year-round, it offers modern one- , two- or three-bedroom condos, with kitchens, private decks, fireplaces, and cable TV.

Box Canyon Lodge & Hot Springs, 45 Third Avenue, Ouray, CO 81427, 303/325-4981 or 800/327-5080, is most notable for its outdoor mineral hot springs and hot tubs. It's open year-round.

Damn Yankee Bed & Breakfast, PO Box 709, 100 6th Avenue, Ouray, CO 81427, 303/325-4219, offers eight deluxe rooms in a modern chalet with queen beds, down comforters, and private baths.

San Juan Guest Ranch, 2282 CO 23, Ridgway, CO 81432, 303/626-5360, is a classic, small guest ranch, not fancy, but modernized and comfortable. Activities include horseback riding in the remote San Juans, ballooning, jeep tours, and swimming in Ouray's Hot Springs Pool.

Orvis Hot Springs, in Ridgway, has a few rooms for guests.

For a clean, modern, standard motel room, the **Ridgway-Telluride Super 8 Lodge**, 303/626-5444 or 800/800-8000, is well-situated on US 550 in Ridgway, just south of the turn to Telluride on CO 62. Facilities include an indoor pool, jacuzzi and sauna, and a free continental breakfast is included with a room. Half-price Telluride lift tickets are available every day in winter (in conjunction with accommodations).

Ouray/Ridgway Restaurants

The Outlaw, 610 Main Street, Ouray, 303/325-4366, serves aged Colorado beef, prime rib, or seafood, and also offers a High Mountain Cookout, May through October. This includes a jeep ride to a mountain stream for a steak, seafood, or chicken barbecue.

Bon Ton Restaurant, 426 Main Street, Ouray, 303/325-4951, is downstairs from the St. Elmo Hotel and, like the hotel, is impeccably restored in the Victorian style. It serves good Italian food.

The Catamount, 220 South Lena Avenue, Ridgway, 303/626-5044, is one of the few places to eat in Ridgway, serving prime rib, curry chicken, raspberry pork chops, and seafood pasta. Breakfast is available daily and there is a weekly Sunday brunch.

Telluride Accommodations

Skyline Guest Ranch, Box 67, Telluride, CO 81435, 303/728-3757 or 303/728-6728, is the prettiest and classiest guest ranch in southwestern Colorado. The beauty comes from its serene location. Set at 9,600 feet, it is surrounded by broad meadows and lofty peaks eight miles south of Telluride, off CO 145. The class comes from a ranch that provides a rarefied, conscientious western experience with real intelligence, not Hee-Haw-style hokiness. The food is great, not just gray cowboy food.

It offers small but cozy lodge rooms or private cabins, with down comforters on the beds. There is a stocked trout-fishing lake on the property, and horseback riding, pack trips, hiking, mountaineering, jeep trips, a sauna and hot tub are available. The dining room is open to non-guests by reservation.

San Sophia, 330 West Pacific Avenue, Telluride, CO 81435, 303/728-301 or 800/537-4781, is a distinctive, elegant, modern B&B with 16 luxurious rooms. All rooms have private baths, brass beds, and a cable TV. There is a rooftop observatory, library, lounge, and a garden with a jacuzzi. A complimentary afternoon happy hour is offered.

New Sheridan House, 231 West Colorado Avenue, Telluride, CO 81435, 303/728-4351, is an old, historic hotel built in 1895. Some rooms have shared baths.

Telluride Lodge, 747 West Pacific Avenue, Telluride, CO 81435, 303/728-4446 or 303/728-4400, or 800/662-8747, offers rooms with full kitchens and cable TV. Some rooms have fireplaces. Hot tubs and a steam room are available.

The Peaks at Telluride, PO Box 2702, Telluride, CO 81435, 303/728-6800 or 800/789-2220 fax 303/728-6567, was formerly the Telluride Doral Resort & Spa. It remains an ultra-modern 177-room luxury hotel at the Mountain Village with a 42,000-square-foot spa, indoor/outdoor pool, jacuzzis, saunas, steam rooms, massage therapy, beauty treatments, racquetball, two restaurants, ski-in/out access, and all situated on the Mountain Village golf course. Some special "Ski Free" packages may be available, as well as other holiday, ski and vacation packages.

Telluride Mountain Village Resort Management Company, 550 Mountain Village Road, Telluride, CO 81435, 303/728-6727 or 800/544-0507, represents luxury properties in the Mountain Village. Offerings include studios, one-, two-, three-, or four-bedroom condos, and private homes.

Resort Rentals, 673 West Pacific Avenue, Telluride, CO 81435, 303/728-4405, manages rentals of luxury properties, from studio condos to four-bedroom homes.

Pennington's Mountain Village Inn, PO Box 2428, Telluride, CO 81435, 303/728-5357 or 800/545-1437, offers 12 large suites with private decks, stocked refrigerators, and a full breakfast every day. There is an indoor spa at this luxury property on the Mountain Village golf course.

Telluride Restaurants

Campagna, 433 West Pacific Avenue, Telluride, 303/728-6190, serves Italian food in an old, historic home.

Floradora, 103 West Colorado Avenue, Telluride, 303/728-3888, serves burgers, Southwestern dishes, sandwiches, soup, and a salad bar.

Baked in Telluride, 127 South Fir Street, Telluride, 303/728-4775, is a busy locals hang-out serving fresh baked goods, even decent bagels. Counter service for sandwiches and pizza.

Angel's Athenian Senate, 124 South Spruce Street, Telluride, 303/728-3018, serves Greek, Italian, and vegetarian food.

La Marmotte, 150 West San Juan Avenue, 303/728-6232, serves classical country and light nouvelle French cuisine in Telluride's old Ice House.

San Juan Brewing Company, 300 South Townsend, 303/728-0100, is a brew pub and restaurant.

Sofios, 110 East Colorado Avenue, Telluride, 303/728-4882, serves Mexican and Southwestern dishes, also fruit smoothies and espresso.

Swede Finn Hall, 427 West Pacific Avenue, Telluride, 303/728-2085, serves seafood, regional game, and vegetarian dishes. Nine beers are on tap, and pool tables are available for rent by the hour.

The Excelsior Cafe, 200 West Colorado Avenue, Telluride, 81435, 303/728-4250, serves cheap eats, a Telluride rarity, for breakfast and lunch.

T'Ride Country Club, 333 West Colorado Avenue, Telluride, 303/728-6344, serves cook-your-own steaks and seafood.

Rico/Dolores/Cortez Accommodations

Rico is a tiny old mining town, 25 miles south of Telluride on CO 145. There's fine Alpine scenery and adventurous territory nearby, but not much of a town. In winter, when half-price Telluride lift tickets are offered, it might not be such a bargain if Lizard Head Pass–the only way to reach Telluride–is closed by avalanches.

Rico Motel & Cabins, Silver Street, PO Box 303, Rico, CO 81332, 303/967-2444, has motel rooms with refrigerators, microwave ovens and coffee pots, or small self-contained cabins. The property is open year-round and offers half-price Telluride lift tickets.

Rico Hotel and Restaurant, 124 Glasgow Avenue, Rico, CO 81332, 303/967-3000, is a funky B & B in an old miner's boarding house. The restaurant serves lunch and dinner, and the hotel offers half-price Telluride lift tickets.

Rio Grande Southern, 101 Fifth Street, Dolores, CO 81323, 303/882-7527, is an old railroad hotel and the oldest building in town. The six little guest rooms come with full breakfast in the hotel's restaurant.

Lost Canyon Lake Lodge, PO Box 1289, Dolores, CO 81323, 303/882-4913, is a contemporary two-story log lodge with four guest rooms, all with private baths. It overlooks Lost Canyon Lake Reservoir at 7,300 feet elevation. Rates include breakfast and snacks.

Rag 'O Muffin Ranch, 26030 CO 145, Dolores, CO 81323, 303/562-3803, offers two housekeeping units, with kitchens, in a log cabin on 12 acres, on the Dolores River.

Kelly Place, 14663 County Road G, Cortez, CO 81321, 303/565-3125, is a most unusual, five-room bed & breakfast. It is set on 100 acres, west of Cortez, in red rock and slickrock country. You can help excavate Indian ruins on the remote property, study weaving, pottery-making, canning, quilting, tanning, farming with draft horses, or blacksmithing. Reservations are required.

Rico/Dolores/Cortez Restaurants

Old Germany Restaurant, 200 South 8th Street, Dolores, 303/882-7549, serves German dishes, and imported beers and wines.

Nero's Italian Restaurant, 303 West Main Street, Cortez, 303/565-7366, serves Italian food.

Stromsted's, 1020 South Broadway, Cortez, 303/565-1257, serves steaks, seafood, and barbecued ribs. In warm weather you can dine outdoors on a deck overlooking Mesa Verde and Sleeping Ute Mountain.

Francisca's, 125 East Main Street, Cortez, 303/565-4093, serves Mexican food, vegetarian plates, and renowned magaritas.

M&M Truckstop and Restaurant, 7006 Highway 160, Cortez, 303/565-6511, serves hearty truck-stop fare, eggs, pancakes, burgers, sandwiches, and steaks 24 hours-a-day.

Mesa Verde/Mancos/Hesperus Accommodations

Far View Lodge, PO Box 277, Mancos, CO 81328, 303/529-4421, is the only motel inside Mesa Verde National Park, open May to October. Ordinarily it wouldn't rate a second glance, but the spectacular mesa-top location does recommend it. There are 150 rooms and a restaurant.

Lake Mancos Ranch, 42688 County Road N, Mancos, CO 81328, 303/533-7900, accommodates 55 guests in private cabins or ranchhouse rooms, and offers fishing, jeeping, hiking, and cookouts. Meals are included in weekly rates, but horseback riding is extra. Also: pool, volleyball, horseshoes, and a children's program, including camp-outs, are available.

Echo Basin Dude Ranch, 43747 County Road M, Mancos, CO 81328, 303/533-7800 or 800/426-1870, offers lodge rooms, bunkhouse or cabin accommodations, and tent or RV sites on 600 acres north of Mancos. Activities available include fishing in a stocked lake, horseback riding, boating, hayrides, cookouts, snowmobiling, hiking and backpacking, and there is a swimming pool.

Jersey Jim Fire Lookout Tower, c/o U.S. Forest Service, Mancos Ranger District, PO Box 320, Mancos, CO 81328, 303/533-7716, is not very fancy, but it certainly offers a spectacular view. Located 20 miles north of Mancos in an old, obsolete, 55-foot-tall fire lookout, it's just a small room, with a stove, refrigerator, lanterns, and bird's eye views of four states. There is no running water, but you can hoist the water and supplies you bring along from the ground with the original pulley system. You bring your own sleeping bag and everything else you want. Make reservations far in advance for this ultimate retreat which is generally booked solid a year in advance, although there are occasional cancellations.

Blue Lake Ranch, 16919 CO 140, Hesperus, CO 81326, 303/385-4537, fax 303/385-4088, is a well-hidden B&B 20 miles west of Durango. Call for exact directions. To protect guests privacy, there's no sign on this luxurious 100-acre hide-away. It consists of a main house with four suites, a separate log cabin overlooking a small lake, and several other cottages scattered around exquisite flower and herb gardens. Breakfast usually includes eggs from ranch chickens, homemade jams, and jellies.

Mesa Verde/Mancos/Hesperus
Restaurants

There are three unexceptional restaurants inside Mesa Verde National Park, c/o ARA Mesa Verde, 303/529-4421. **Far View Terrace Cafe**, open May through October, and the **Spruce Tree Terrace**, open year-round, offer institutional cafeteria fare such as burgers, sandwiches, or tacos. The **Metate Room**, at Far View Lodge, serves Mexican and American food.

Millwood Junction, 101 West Railroad Avenue, Mancos, 303/533-7338, is worth the drive. Situated seven miles east of Mesa Verde, or 28 miles west of Durango, this is simply an excellent, unpretentious restaurant, serving inexpensive nightly specials, a gargantuan Friday night seafood buffet, and an eclectic menu of imaginative nouvelle entrees, as well as beef, chicken, or seafood standards. A fabulous, home-made salad bar is a meal in itself, and rich desserts include numerous flavors of home-made ice cream. Some nights there's live music in the bar.

Chip's Place, 4 County Road 124, Hesperus, 303/259-6277, is an unpretentious, friendly cafe attached to the modest, one-story Canyon Motel. Chip serves giant burgers, including an award-winning Super Chili Cheeseburger, sandwiches, tender steaks, and home-made fries, along with daily specials. You won't leave hungry, nor much poorer than when you walked in.

Camping

There are hundreds of public and private campgrounds throughout southwestern Colorado, ranging from free, primitive wilderness sites without water or rest rooms, to deluxe RV parks. For RV hookups, campers will most frequently have to rely on private campgrounds.

San Juan National Forest Camping

There are 38 developed campgrounds in the **San Juan National Forest** which are fully operational from late May to mid-September. The most popular campgrounds are near major lakes, highways, and communities. These include large campgrounds near

Lemon and Vallecito Reservoirs (nine campgrounds, 266 campsites), and small campgrounds at **Purgatory** (14 campsites), Silverton's **South Mineral Creek** (23 campsites), along the West Fork of the Dolores River at **Burro Bridge** (14 campsites), at **McPhee Reservoir** (see below) and north of Mancos at **Target Tree** (51 campsites), or **Transfer** (13 campsites).

Seventeen campgrounds subscribe to a reservation system. Phone 800/283-2267 for information. The rest of the campgrounds are available on a first-come first-served basis. Fee campgrounds include a table and fire grate, rest rooms, drinking water, and trash pick-up. There is a 14-day limit at all campgrounds.

For complete information contact the **Forest Supervisor**, San Juan National Forest, 701 Camino del Rio, Durango, CO 81301, 303/247-4874 and request a free copy of the *San Juan National Forest Campground Guide*.

The campgrounds at McPhee Reservoir in Dolores, offer a wide range of services. At the **McPhee Recreation Area** on the west side of the Reservoir, there are 80 campsites, rest rooms, showers, five sites with electrical hook-ups, a group camping area, picnic sites, and a trailer dump station. All are situated among pinyon, pine, and junipers on a bluff overlooking the 450,000-acre reservoir.

Another camping area is located at the **House Creek Recreation Area**, on the east side of the reservoir, 15 miles north of Dolores. It offers, tables, grills, water, toilets, and trash disposal.

For information phone the **Dolores District of the San Juan National Forest**, 303/882-7296.

BLM/Wilderness Camping

Camping is permitted in designated wilderness areas, although no formal campgrounds exist and no services are available. There are three campgrounds along the **Alpine Loop Backcountry Byway**, administered by the Bureau of Land Management.

Ouray/Ridgway/Telluride Camping

National Forest campgrounds are administered by the **Uncompaghre National Forest**, Norwood Ranger District Office, 1760 Grand Avenue, PO Box 388, Norwood, CO 81423, 303/327-4261, or the Ouray Ranger District Office, 2505 South Townsend Avenue, Montrose, CO 81401, 303/249-3711. These include Ouray's popular

Amphitheatre (33 campsites) and **Silver Jack** (60 campsites), north of Ridgway.

Ridgway State Recreation Area offers developed camping and access to water sports.

Telluride's **Town Park** has 42 campsites with showers and restrooms, but no RV hook-ups.

Cortez/Mesa Verde/Mancos Camping

Hovenweep National Monument has a small campground. There is a rest room, but no drinking water. In summer, make sure you have insect repellent–biting bugs can be pretty nasty out here.

The **Ute Mountain Tribal Park** has a primitive campground surrounded by one of the most evocative prehistoric Indian sites in the Southwest. Water is available, but all your other needs should be organized in Cortez before you head out here. Reservations are required. For information phone 303/565-3751, ext. 282.

Morefield Campground, at Mesa Verde National Park, has 477 campsites, including some with hookups. Facilities include rest rooms, showers, laundry, groceries, gas, and dump stations.

Lake Mancos Recreation Area, 303/883-2208, is six miles northeast of Mancos, on a lake set at 7,800 feet. It includes campgrounds, picnic sites, boat ramps, hiking and horseback trails.

Southern Utah

There may be more deer, antelope, bighorn sheep, lizards, and rattlesnakes than human residents in this epic sandstone wonderland that includes **Arches, Canyonlands, Capitol Reef, Bryce Canyon** and **Zion National Parks**, the **Glen Canyon Recreation Area, Lake Powell**, several National Monuments, remote primitive areas and state parks. Nearly 80% of Utah's land is administered by public agencies and just running through this list, it's easy to see that southern Utah's public lands are phenomenally extensive. Beside simple expansiveness, these lands include some of the most unusual and improbable landscapes in the world.

Lake Powell, the centerpiece of the Glen Canyon Recreation Area, is the second largest man-made reservoir in the United States.

Red sandstone buttes, blue mesas, purple rock pinnacles, narrow spires, and deep, plunging canyons line the muddy **Colorado River** and decorate the uplands of the **Colorado Plateau** as if it were a rock garden of the gods.

Lofty mountains with lakes, forested slopes, and a blessedly cooler climate than the lower desert-like plateaus, rise above 12,000 feet in the **Henry, Abajo (Blue)** and **La Sal Mountains**.

Mazes of slickrock trails that are easy to cross when dry, but slippery when wet, lead to deserted cliffs, towering vistas, and empty lands that provide a geology lesson in the forces of wind, water, and erosion.

Few people live here, and relatively few have trodden these mysteriously vacant grounds, among the last places in all the United States to be explored.

All of Southern Utah offers vast recreational opportunities. Just sightseeing is something of a quest amidst this mostly arid topography. There are few paved roads, but hundreds of miles of gravel and dirt tracks more suitable to pack animals than vehicles. Hiking and biking trails wind through stunted juniper and pinyon forests, over slickrock and down into shady cottonwood riversides. Since most of Southern Utah is public land, with small towns spaced far apart along scenic byways, adventurous possibilities are the norm, rather than the exception; limits for recreation are bounded only by imagination.

Float a lazy river or bounce through roaring rapids. Ride a horse into areas where the hand of man has had little impact. Travel by mountain bike or four-wheel-drive to secluded campsites affording views of unsurpassed, strange beauty that are reminiscent of another planet. Examine remote archaeological ruins. Fish your own vacant stretch of river. Hike for weeks on end without ever seeing another soul. Bask in flaming pastel sunsets.

Geography & History

Land, water, and sky are clearly the major attractions here, the ancient lure for settlers and travellers such as the Anasazi Indians, who left only ruins and petroglyph inscriptions behind nearly a thousand years ago. They were followed by Paiutes and Navajos, who began settling in for the long haul at the time the Anasazi were disappearing. Later, Spanish explorers scouted trade routes to California through the slickrock and canyons, and a one-armed Civil War veteran named John Wesley Powell paddled and mapped the Colorado River.

Among the most tenacious influences on the area were Mormon settlers branching off from the Great Salt Lake area to spread their religion. A Mormon wagon train travelling from Cedar City, in southwestern Utah, set out for southeastern Utah in 1875, anticipating a six-week trip. Instead, they had to blast through rock and build roads; it took six months of tortuous travel to reach Bluff.

Once they got there they stayed. The Mormon influence is still keenly felt today in just about all of southern Utah's small towns. Many of them are laid out around a central church in the grid pattern designed by Brigham Young. These square towns still impress as moral, one example being some rather arcane liquor laws. Most alcoholic beverages must still be purchased in state-operated shops. Mixed drinks are served in some licensed restaurants, but restaurants cannot offer you a cocktail or wine list unless you ask for it. Bars serve only 3.2 beer. Most people drink in private clubs. The good news is that you can buy a temporary membership to these clubs for about the cost of a mixed drink.

As for the grid system applied to city streets, which typically produces a confused-sounding address such as 100 East 200 North, you just need to remember a few things to find your way around. Streets run north-south and east-west from a mid-point somewhere in town. Blocks are numbered in increments of 100. Once you've located the mid-point, 100 East 200 North is one block east and two blocks north.

The grid system notwithstanding, travel through here is considerably easier, though not a whole lot less labyrinthine than the routes of the pioneers. You will put many miles on your car if you try to traverse the whole area covered in this chapter, but along the way you will see some of the most impressive scenery in the country, if not the world. You won't always find the most sophisticated concentration of services, but you can usually reach a motel and restaurant if you allow for it in your plans. Gas stations may be few and far between, but they're out there. Fill up whenever you can.

Adventure outfitters are plentiful in this region where the magnitude of possibilities for adventure can be daunting. A skilled outfitter will provide everything you need, including permits, specialized equipment, and food. A knowledgeable guide can provide perspective in this rugged, immense, and challenging land filled with delightful surprises around each curve in the road or bend in the river.

Getting Around

There are few air connections to this region. The closest major airports are in Salt Lake City or Grand Junction, Colorado. You really need to drive to get around, but those who want to fly can check with **Alpine Air**, 801/373-1508 or 800/253-5678. Alternatively, go through the airline's Moab representative, **Tag-A-Long Tours**, 801/259-8946. The airline offers daily service between Moab's Canyonlands Field and Grand Junction or Salt Lake City. **Sky West/Delta Connection** also offers service to Cedar City, St. George, and Page, Arizona. For information see below under area touring categories.

Driving in the region is particularly convoluted due to the unusual topography of canyon networks, the Colorado River, and the simple lack of roads across the central portion of southern Utah. The shortest distance between two points is rarely a straight line.

It is not even possible to travel by road through Canyonlands National Park to the three distinct sections of the enormous park; to explore each area requires a circuitous routing along widely spaced entrance roads. A fourth section of the park, the River District, including Cataract Canyon and the confluence of the Green and Colorado rivers, is accessible only by the river or by strenuous hiking trails. It creates the boundaries of the other three sections, **Island in the Sky** to the north, the **Needles** to the east, and the **Maze** to the west. The entire Canyonlands Park encompasses some 527 square miles, making it the largest park in the state.

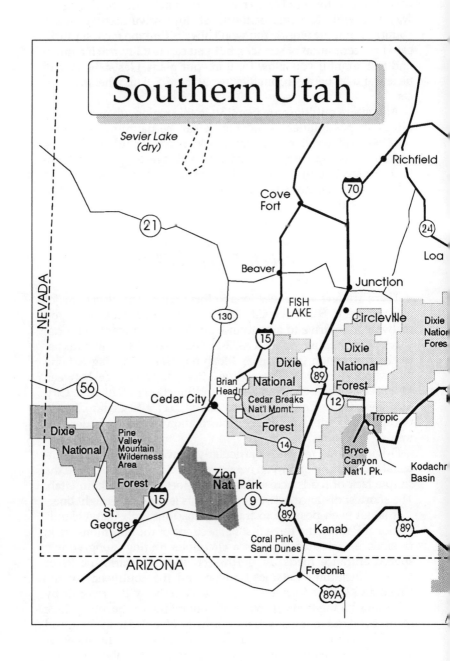

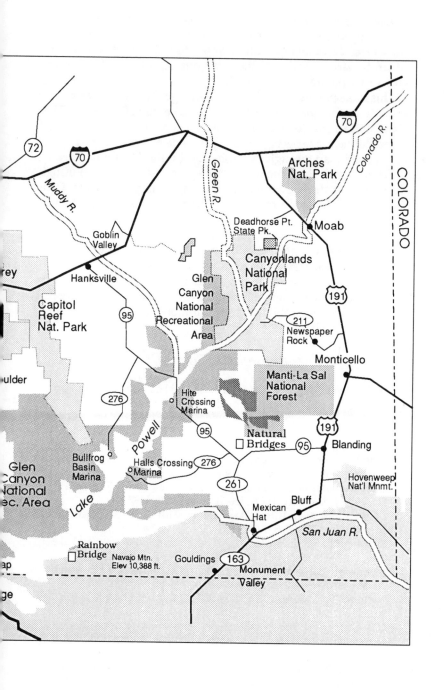

The suggested itinerary for this area follows a zig-zag course from the northeastern corner of southern Utah, starting in the **Moab** area and moving south through **Monticello, Blanding,** and **Bluff**. It skirts the edge of the Navajo Reservation (which is covered in a separate chapter) and heads in a northwesterly direction.

This route passes through **Natural Bridges National Monument** and across the northern extremity of **Lake Powell** and the **Glen Canyon National Recreation Area**. North of there is the only road access to the Maze Section of Canyonlands National Park and the only paved road through the large **Capitol Reef National Park**.

From Capitol Reef, the route dips southwesterly again, through the little-visited, fascinating, and challenging **Escalante River Canyons**. This is followed by stops in **Bryce Canyon National Park, Cedar Breaks National Monument** and **Zion National Park** before winding back eastward, finishing in **Page, Arizona**, on the lower stretches of Lake Powell, where the majority of visitor services based on the lake are located.

It is not recommended to cover this whole area on a single trip of a week or two. There's just too much to see and do. Choose selective adventures and leave some undone so you'll have a good reason to come back.

Information Sources

Utah Travel Council, Council Hall, Capitol Hill, Salt Lake City, UT 84114-1101, 808/538-1030, provides copious free information, including maps, accommodation guides, and lists of airlines, guides & outfitters, scenic flights, bike tours, river trips, four-wheel-drive routes, and boating.

Utah Division of Parks and Recreation, Southeast Region, 89 East Center, Moab, UT 84532-2330, 801/259-8151.

Utah Division of Parks and Recreation, Southwest Region, PO Box 1079, Cedar City, UT 84720-1079, 801/586-4497.

Utah Guides & Outfitters Association, 3131 South 500 East, Salt Lake City, UT 84106, 801/466-1912.

Bureau of Land Management, 324 South State, Suite 400, Salt Lake City, UT 84111-2303, 801/524-5030.

U.S. Forest Service, Intermountain Region Office, 324 5th Street, Ogden, UT 84401-2394, 801/625-5182.

National Park Service, PO Box 25287, Denver, CO 80225-0287, 303/969-2000.

U.S. Geological Survey, 125 South State Street, Room 8105, Salt Lake City, UT 84138, 801/524-5652, provides topographical and geological maps.

Camping Reservations, 800/284-2267. Most campgrounds are first-come, first-served, but if you know where you want to camp you can try the free number.

Utah Campground Owners Association, 1370 West North Temple, Salt Lake City, UT 84116, 801/521-2682. For private campground information, of special usefulness to those travelling in RVs.

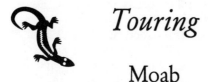

Touring

Moab

Moab is by far the biggest town in southeastern Utah, and its population of 5,000 includes entrepreneurs at the hub of virtually the entire adventure travel industry for an enormous region.

Moab is located on US 191, just south of Arches National Park and UT 128, a scenic road that meanders alongside the Colorado River past **Fisher Towers, Castle Rock**, and the **Priest and Nuns** formation. If the towers and Castle Rock look familiar, it's probably because they've been the settings for numerous TV commercials. The 1,500-foot-tall, slender red rock spires of Fisher Towers are distinctive, and you probably remember seeing cars photographed from above, improbably balanced atop Castle Rock. There is a picnic area and a three-mile hiking trail around the base of Fisher Towers. Other sites along the road afford contrasting views of the snow-capped **La Sal Mountains,** and turn-outs lead in a short distance to Colorado River beaches–good for picnics or fishing.

Moab, more so than other towns farther south, is the preferred base by many for exploring **Utah's Canyonlands,** which is a generic name for this whole region of dramatically sculpted landforms, high alpine mountains, and arid desert valleys, as well as the name of the National Park. The area has certainly been discovered by adventure seeking souls, as evidenced by a plethora of adventure outfitters based here. A staggering variety of trips by mountain bike, river raft, four-wheel-drive, hiking, horseback, and backcountry skiing are offered here.

The **Green** and **Colorado Rivers** are within easy access, as are the dramatic, dizzying vistas of **Dead Horse State Park** and the **Canyon Rims Recreation Area. Arches National Park** is just a few miles away, and the **Island in the Sky** and **Needles District** of **Canyonlands National Park** are close by.

The motels and restaurants are more plentiful around Moab than farther south, but the crowds bigger here too, especially from May to September. Motel rooms or even campsites may be hard to come by on the spur of the moment during those months.

This long-time ranching community was transformed into a uranium boom town in the 1950s, then, after the glow faded from uranium mining, re-invented as a Hollywood film location for numerous features and commercials, and finally as a vacation destination. Today it is in full flower as a recreation mecca.

In town is an interesting and unlikely attraction dealing with the movie history of the area–**Hollywood Stuntman's Hall of Fame**, 100 East 100 West, Moab, UT 84532, 801/259-6100. Exhibits recall the many films that have been shot in the area and include videos of amazing stunts, familiar-looking costumes worn by stunt doubles for *The Flying Nun,* and Paladin's black cowboy duds from the classic western series *Have Gun Will Travel.* You will also find items used in more recent Moab films, such as *Thelma and Louise.*

The **Dan O'Laurie Museum**, 118 East Center, Moab, UT 84532, 801/259-7430, displays prehistoric Indian pottery, sandals, baskets and tools, such as the elegantly simple corn-grinding *metate*, which is merely a rock. Other exhibits detail early Spanish explorers, the mining era, pioneer life in Moab, and mineral specimens from the area, including uranium ore and dinosaur fossils.

Understandably, Moab has a lot of rock shops. **Ottinger's Rock Shop**, 137 North Main, Moab, UT 84532, 801/259-7312, offers rocks for sale and also presents nightly slide shows highlighting area scenery.

South of town, **Arches Vineyard**, 2182 US 191, Moab, UT 84532, 801/259-5397, is Utah's only winery. Tours are offered, and there is a tasting room.

The best place to get a handle on all the things to do around here, both in-town and out-of-town, is at the office of the **Grand County Tourism Council**, PO Box 550, 805 North Main Street, Moab, UT 84532, 801/259-8825 or 800/635-6622. The staff can provide information and even a few videos on historic walking tours in Moab, car or four-wheel-drive trips, hiking trails, mountain bike routes, movie locations around the Moab area, winter recreation ideas, and accommodation and restaurant details.

Also in Moab are the main administrative offices for Arches and Canyonlands National Parks, as well as Natural Bridges National Monument. For information contact **National Park Service**, 125 West 200 South, Moab, UT 84532, 801/259-7155.

The Bureau of Land Management maintains two Moab offices. Contact **BLM District Office**, 82 East Dogwood, Box 970, Moab, UT 84532, 801/259-6111, or **BLM Grand Resource Area Office**, Sand Flats Road, Box M, Moab, UT 84532, 801/259-8193, which handles Colorado River and Westwater Canyon permits.

Arches
National Park

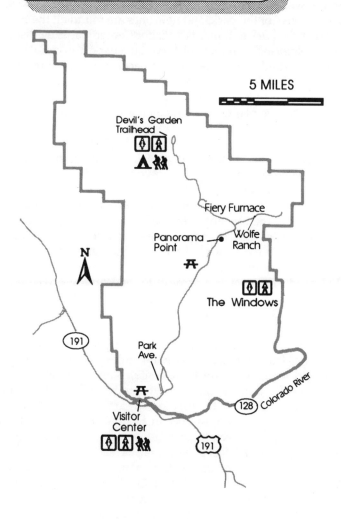

5 MILES

Devil's Garden
Trailhead

Fiery Furnace

Panorama
Point

Wolfe
Ranch

N

The Windows

191

Park
Ave.

Colorado River

128

Visitor
Center

191

Arches National Park

The entrance to Arches National Park is three miles north of Moab on US 191. The park contains some of the strangest-looking, implausible geography anywhere, ranging in elevation from 3,960 feet to 5,653 feet, and including enormous red rock pinnacles, fins and domes, plus the largest concentration of natural stone arches in the world. More than 1,600 arches have been found within the 73,368 acres of the park, and new ones are found all the time.

Near the park entrance is a Visitor Center featuring displays on the geological and human history of the park. You can also pick up brochures and maps here, the free backcountry permits which are required for hikers and backpackers, and additional free literature, including trail guides outlining hikes to some of the off-road arches. Native plants are marked on a short nature trail that starts here.

There is a paved road through the park that leads to the main sights of interest, a round-trip of 39 miles. Along the way, the road passes such sites as **South Park Avenue**, made of mammoth clusters of vertical sandstone slabs edging a dry wash, and resembling Manhattan skyscrapers lining a broad avenue. The site was the film location for the opening scenes of *Indiana Jones, The Last Crusade*. Other parts of the park provided locations for *Thelma and Louise*.

Farther up the park road there's a short trail around **Balanced Rock**, an enormous stone set precariously on a rocky pedestal. Past Balanced Rock there's a turn-off to the **Windows Section**, which includes four giant arches, the **North** and **South Windows**, **Turret Arch** and **Double Arch**, all of which may be easily viewed from short walks.

There are also unpaved roads in the park, including one that branches from the main road, a few miles past the Windows turn-off, and leads to **Wolfe Ranch**, site of an old homestead and a trailhead for a three-mile round-trip hike to **Delicate Arch**. Delicate Arch is perhaps the best-known arch in the park, if only by virtue of its recent appearance in a Burger King commercial. You have to cross a swinging footbridge and walk up a few steep slopes, gaining 500 feet in elevation, to reach it.

The **Fiery Furnace** area is farther up the main park road and includes unusual, tightly stacked, fin-shaped rocks 100-foot tall. A 2.5-hour ranger-led tour is recommended for covering a confusing two-mile trail through the narrow, maze-like canyons. **Devils Garden** lies at the end of the main road and is the site of a picnic area and campground, as well as the trailhead for the large and impressive **Landscape Arch**, plus many others.

Hiking trails off the main road lead to view sites, and there are remote backpacking areas as well as four-wheel-drive roads inside the park boundaries. For additional information contact **Arches National Park**, PO Box 907, Moab, UT 84532, 801/259-8161.

Deadhorse Point State Park

Located nine miles north of Moab on US 191, then 23 miles south on UT 313, the park sits on an isolated, island-like mesa atop sheer sandstone cliffs, towering 2,000 feet above the serpentine Colorado River as it winds through multi-colored rock pinnacles. Steeples and broad buttes take on constantly shifting hues according to the time of day and the angle of the sunlight.

From the impressive park overlook you can see 5,000 square miles of Colorado Plateau country, including the La Sal and Abajo Mountains. This site, with only one way on or off the mesa across a narrow strip of land, was used by early cowboys as a natural corral for horses, but one herd of steeds was left out in the sun too long and died of thirst, trapped high above the river, hence the name of the park.

The park includes a Visitor Center, campground and picnic area, as well as hiking trails. For information contact **Deadhorse Point State Park**, Box 609, Moab, UT 84532, 801/259-6511.

Canyonlands National Park (Island in the Sky District)

The Island in the Sky District of Canyonlands National Park is accessed via the same roads from Moab that lead to Deadhorse Point (see above). Signs indicate where to go. It is the most easily accessed portion of the vast Canyonlands Park, with paved roads that lead to imposing overlooks, numerous hiking trails, and four-wheel-drive roads.

This section of the park has its own Visitor Center where you may obtain the free backcountry permit required for any backpacking or camping along the **White Rim Four-Wheel-Drive Trail**. Beyond the Visitor Center, you cross the narrow neck of land that connects to the Island in the Sky, which is similar to Deadhorse Point, but larger (40 square miles). The Visitor Center offers no services beyond information about the park and has no water on tap. For information phone 801/259-6577.

Much of the hiking to secluded side canyons and arches is strenuous around here, and jeeping the White Rim Trail down to the Colorado River is only for well-experienced drivers. Short hikes are possible, though, and the one to **Mesa Arch** is only a half-mile round-trip. It leads to a staggering view from the edge of a 2,000-foot cliff. It starts 5.5 miles from the Visitor Center.

A good deal of the region can be viewed from **Grandview Point**, where you can see the Henry, La Sal and Abajo mountains, as well as miles of curling canyons rising above the Colorado River. Numerous named rock formations are also visible, including the Needles, Lizard Rock, the Maze, and the Golden Stairs.

To get to the trailhead, turn left past the Mesa Arch trailhead, at the road junction. Continue driving for 2.5 miles, then turn right and drive four miles to **Grandview Picnic Area**.

Two other trails start at the picnic area.

White Rim Overlook Trail covers a 1.5-mile round-trip to look out over Monument Basin.

Gooseberry Trail is only for more serious hikers. It covers 2.5 miles one-way and drops over 1,400 feet in elevation.

Grand View Point is another mile farther past the picnic area on the main road. You can view the Colorado River, side canyons, the Needles, and various mountains in the distance from this southernmost point of Island in the Sky.

View points for **Upheaval Dome**, a crater-like hole three miles long and 1,200 feet deep, are accessed via the short, one-mile round-trip, **Crater View Trail**. Go back down the road from Grandview Point and bear left at the main road junction. Continue to the end of the road to the trailhead. No one knows for sure what created the crater, although some geologists suspect it was formed by the crash of a giant meteorite. If you're really intrigued by this site you may want to tackle an 8-mile hike that encircles it.

South of Moab/Canyonlands
(Needles District)

On the way to the Needles District, on US 191, 15 miles south of Moab, there's a weird, kitschy tourist attraction called **Hole-in-the-Rock**. It's a 5,000-square-foot, 14-room house and gift shop built around rock pillars, all set within solid sandstone rock. The Flintstones-like edifice includes a bath tub built into rock and a 65-foot chimney drilled through solid rock.

Thirty-two miles south of Moab on US 191 is a marked turn-off to the west for the **Canyon Rims Recreation Area**. It's a 20-mile drive to the **Needles Overlook** which offers impressive views from 1,000 feet of the Island in the Sky, Deadhorse Point, the Needles District, and the Abajo, La Sal and Henry Mountains. It also shows the confluence of the Green and Colorado rivers, and Canyonlands' Maze District. Five or six miles before the Needles Overlook is a gravel road heading north for 17 miles to the **Anticline Overlook**, another ethereal cliff-top perch 1,600 feet above the Colorado River, which separates the overlook from Deadhorse Point. Wildlife is common throughout the Canyon Rims area. Look across the sagebrush flats for pronghorn antelope, muledeer, and coyotes, or up in the sky for swallows and swifts.

There are several campgrounds within the recreation area, as well as hiking and four-wheel-drive trails. For information contact the BLM office in Moab.

The **Needles District** of Canyonlands National Park is accessed 39 miles south of Moab by turning west from US 191 onto UT 211 and continuing for another 38 miles to the ranger station.

Twelve miles west of US 191 is **Newspaper Rock State Park**. Sandstone cliffs near the parking area are carved with an incredible assortment of petroglyphs ranging from the Anasazi era through modern Navajo times. They include Kokopelli figures (the ubiquitous Indian flautist whose image appears all over the Southwest), a large animal that may represent a mastodon, and animal fertility scenes. A short nature trail details regional flora. There is also a picnic area and campground, but no water.

The paved road (UT 211) continues past Newspaper Rock Park, through **Indian Creek Canyon**, to the Needles District.

A mile before the ranger station, just outside the park, is the **Needles Outpost**, Box 1107, Monticello, UT 84535, 801/259-2032. Open March to October, this is the last chance before entering the National Park to buy gas, food, and supplies. There is a general store, campground, and snack bar, as well as showers, firewood, maps, books, information and a 4,500-foot landing strip. The outpost also offers scenic flights, jeep tours, and jeep rentals.

The **Needles Ranger Station**, 801/259-6568, inside the National Park, is where you obtain required backcountry hiking and camping permits, as well as hiking and jeep trail guides. The paved road continues through the park to scenic overlooks and turn-offs for jeep roads and hiking trails.

About a half-mile past the ranger station is a quarter-mile hiking trail to **Roadside Ruin**, an Anasazi stone structure used to store grains.

About another quarter-mile on the main road is a turn-off to **Cave Spring Trail**. It's a mile drive to the trailhead for the half-mile loop trail. Nearby is a cave that was used as a campsite by cowboys for nearly 100 years until the area was declared a National Park in 1964.

Two and a half miles past the ranger station is a turn-off for **Squaw Flats Campground** and a picnic site at **Elephant Hill** (three miles past the campground). There are several trailheads at the campground and picnic site, and a rugged four-wheel-drive road continues beyond Elephant Hill.

Five miles past the ranger station is the **Pothole Point Nature Trail**, a half-mile loop. Another mile farther on the main road is the start of the **Slickrock Trail**, a 2.5-mile round-trip to scenic over-looks. The paved main road ends at the **Big Spring Canyon Over-look**, 6.5 miles past the ranger station.

San Juan County

Be grateful these small southeastern Utah towns have gas sta-tions, restaurants, and motels. There's not much in the way of visitor services available in this part of the state.

Monticello is on US 191, 54 miles south of Moab. It offers the closest town access to the **Abajo Mountains**, a rugged range reach-ing as high as 11,362 feet at **Abajo Peak**. There are no marked hiking trails in the Abajos and even backcountry four-wheel-drive roads may be difficult to follow.

One four-wheel-drive route, the **Blue Mountain Loop**, ascends to within a mile of Abajo Peak. It is possible to hike to the peak from there, but it is recommended that you stop first in Monticello to consult with the following useful information sources.

> **Manti-La Sal National Forest**, 496 East US 666, PO Box 820, Mon-ticello, UT 84535, 801/587-2041, can provide details about hiking, back roads, and camping in the Abajos.
> **BLM San Juan Resource Area**, 435 North Main, PO Box 7, Mon-ticello, UT 84535, 801/587-2141, administers the Grand Gulch, Dark Canyon, and several other primitive areas. It also covers the San Juan River.
> **National Park Service**, 32 South 100 East, PO Box 40, Monticello, UT, 84535, 801/587-2141, can provide information, books, and maps of Natural Bridges National Monument, Arches, and Can-yonlands National Parks.
> **Monticello/San Juan County Multi-Agency Visitor Center**, 117 South Main, PO Box 490, Monticello, UT 84535, 801/587-2231, fax 801/587-2425, can provide regional travel information, including

cross-country skiing and snowmobile trail guides and much of the information available from the Forest Service, BLM, and National Park Service.

San Juan County, of which Blanding is the largest town, population 4,000, is on the edge of the Navajo Reservation. There is a high percentage of Indian residents and some good shops selling Native American jewelry, pottery, rugs, and other arts and craft work. The best one is **Blue Mountain Trading Company,** PO Box 263, Blanding, UT 84511, 801/678-2570. **Huck's Museum and Trading Post,** US Highway 191 South, Blanding, UT 84511, 801/678-2329, contains a substantial private collection of Indian artifacts in a log building on the south end of Blanding.

Blanding's premier attraction is **Edge of the Cedars State Park,** 660 West 400 North, Blanding, UT, 84511, 801/678-2238. The park contains an excellent museum displaying Anasazi pottery and other Anasazi artifacts, as well as exhibits detailing later Indian occupation and pioneer life. Outside are restored ruins, including a kiva that you enter by climbing down a ladder.

Bluff is a community of only 250 or so. There are two small motels, a couple of restaurants and trading posts, including one with a very good restaurant, **Cow Canyon Restaurant.**

About three miles east of Bluff is the **San Juan Footbridge,** a swinging bridge across the San Juan River that leads to a cliff dwelling known as **17 Room Ruin.**

Mexican Hat is a small town 22 miles north of the Utah-Arizona border on US 163, separated from the Navajo Nation by the San Juan River. It's named after a large rock north of town that looks like an inverted sombrero. A popular put-in and take-out point, as well as a convenient spot to stop for supplies on a river run, the town is well-known to river rats. It is mainly distinguished by its surroundings, not by its in-town amenities which, although colorful, are modest.

The **Goosenecks of the San Juan River,** are nine miles northeast of Mexican Hat at the end of UT 316, west of UT 261. They comprise a series of tight switchbacks carved into a 1,500-foot-deep chasm, containing 380 million years of geological history. The phenomenon is called an entrenched meander, which means the river curves tightly back upon itself, spanning six miles of river frontage that are compressed within a distance of only 1.5 miles. There is a famous overlook at the end of UT 316, in **Goosenecks State Park,** where there is a picnic area. Camping is allowed, but there is no water.

Moki Dugway is 11 miles northeast of Mexican Hat on UT 261. It is a three-mile graded dirt section of road that rises a precipitous

1,200 feet up the side of a sandstone cliff. Once a uranium ore hauling route, it now is known for the panoramic views it offers. Just south of Moki Dugway, off UT 261, 10 miles northwest of Mexican Hat, is one end of the 18-mile-long **Valley of the Gods Loop Road** (see below, under Mexican Hat Mountain Biking). A deserted scenic road, it passes through desert lands decorated with stone outcrops that resemble a compressed Monument Valley. A four-wheel-drive vehicle is not strictly necessary for the Valley of the Gods road, except when the road is wet. Valley of the Gods returns to US 163 eight miles northeast of Mexican Hat.

Muley Point is at the end of a four-mile dirt road, southwest of the Moki Dugway. It provides an ethereal overlook of the canyons of the San Juan River and views south to Monument Valley.

Cedar Mesa is the name of the primitive area accessed from atop Moki Dugway. The mesa top contains numerous Anasazi and Pueblo Indian sites, and the canyons leading to the mesa contain cliff dwellings and granaries.

Natural Bridges National Monument

There are two roads leading to **Natural Bridges National Monument** from southeastern Utah: UT 95, west from Blanding, or UT 261, north from Mexican Hat.

Beyond the turn-off for Natural Bridges, UT 95 continues in a northwesterly direction to Hite Crossing at Lake Powell, and Hanksville. UT 276 branches off in a southwesterly direction from Utah 95 and goes to Halls Crossing Marina, where there is a ferry across Lake Powell to Bullfrog Basin Marina. It then continues north to re-connect with UT 95 northwest of Hite Crossing.

Sites of special interest north of Mexican Hat on UT 261 are listed above, under San Juan County touring.

Travelling west from Blanding, UT 95 passes close to numerous canyons and Indian ruins. **Butler Wash Overlook** is 15 miles west of Blanding. The site is reached by a half-mile trail marked with rock cairns and contains 23 Anasazi structures (including a square kiva) estimated to be more than 800 years old.

Two and a half miles west of Butler Wash on UT 95 is a parking area providing scenic overlooks at the top of **Comb Ridge**, an 80-mile-long ridge characterized by 800-foot-tall cliffs that drop into **Comb Wash**.

Northwest of Comb Wash is **Arch Canyon**, a site full of un-marked hiking trails that lead to several other scenic canyons, with scattered Anasazi ruins throughout the area. Four miles north of the junction with UT 95 on County Road 263, is an overlook into Arch Canyon.

Cave Canyon Towers are the ruins of seven unstabilized Anasazi towers built around a spring-fed pool. Other ruins and petroglyphs are nearby. The site is located off a rough, unmarked jeep road, a quarter-mile east of the junction of UT 95 and County Road 263, then a half-mile south.

The residents of **Mule Canyon Ruin** were probably associated with the Anasazi who lived at Cave Canyon Towers. The site is two miles northwest of the Cave Canyon ruins. It has been stabilized and includes a kiva, a circular tower, and a dozen rooms, all linked by tunnels. The site is accessed by a highway turn-out on UT 95, 26 miles west of Blanding.

The entrance to **Natural Bridges National Monument**, Box 1, Natural Bridges, Lake Powell, UT 84533, 801/259-5174, is three miles west of UT 261 on UT 95, then five miles farther northwest on UT 275. The site contains three enormous stone bridges created by flowing water.

A solar-powered Visitor Center and campground is near the entrance to the park. A slide show and exhibits in the center describe the geological pressures that produced the natural bridges and the surrounding canyon country, as well as Indian history of the area, and local plant and animal life. The rangers can provide information on the park, the local area, and the large solar electrical system.

Overlooks of the canyon country, bridges, and Indian ruins are situated along the eight-mile **Bridge View Drive** park road, which is open year-round. Short trails lead from parking areas to each bridge, or a nine-mile loop trail along the river connects all three of the Natural Bridges. No backcountry permits are required, but camping is only permitted in the campground near the Visitor Center.

The first viewing spot–for **Sipapu Bridge**–is two miles from the Visitor Center. The rock bridge spans 268 feet and is 220 feet high. A mile farther is another viewpoint half-way down a steep one-mile round-trip trail that leads to the bottom of Sipapu.

Horse Collar Ruins, an 800-year-old Anasazi site, may be seen from a viewpoint another quarter-mile up the road, or you can get to the ruins from the canyon-bottom trail.

The viewpoint and trailhead for **Kachina Bridge** are two miles farther up the road. This natural bridge is 210 feet tall and spans 204 feet. A trail to the canyon bottom is a mile and a half round-trip. Anasazi pictographs can be seen along the way.

Owachomo Bridge can be viewed from a stop another two miles farther on Bridge View Drive, where a trailhead to Owachomo is also located. It's a half-mile round-trip to the base of the natural bridge, which is 106 feet high and spans 180 feet.

Dark Canyon Primitive Area and the adjacent **Dark Canyon Wilderness** are accessed 15 miles north of Natural Bridges National Monument. No motorized vehicles are permitted in these areas, but there is a dirt road that branches north from UT 275 (about a mile past the junction with UT 95), and from there it's six miles to **Bears Ears Pass.** Two miles north of Bears Ears Pass the road branches left. From there it is another four miles to a trailhead for **Upper Woodenshoe Canyon**–part of the wilderness area.

Another access is south of Hite Marina, farther west on UT 95, where dirt roads lead to the **Sundance Trail.** An alternative way to reach Dark Canyon, 14 miles north of Hite Marina, is via boat on Lake Powell.

The lower wilderness area of the 45,000-acre preserve is administered by the **Manti-La Sal National Forest** office in Monticello. The upper primitive area portion is administered by the **BLM** office at Kane Gulch (see below) or the BLM's Monticello office (435 North Main, PO Box 7, Monticello, UT 84535, 801/587-2141).

The large canyon system, which can only be investigated by hikers or horseback riders, contains broad and narrow canyons. Diverse varieties of vegetation can be found at elevations ranging from more than 8,000 feet in the forested north, to 3,700 feet along the desert-like shore of Lake Powell. Wildlife, including bighorn sheep, deer, coyotes, and the occasional black bear or mountain lion, are drawn to flowing water at the south end of the canyon. Anasazi ruins are also found within the canyon system.

Grand Gulch Primitive Area is a 50-mile-long canyon system containing significant Anasazi ruins (including cliff dwellings), mesa-top structures, and numerous examples of rock art.

A ranger station is located at **Kane Gulch**, four miles south of UT 95, on UT 261–its hours are somewhat unpredictable. Information on the area is also available from the BLM office in Monticello.

There are numerous Anasazi ruins and rock art sites in the Grand Gulch area. It begins five miles south of Natural Bridges at 6,400 feet elevation. Fifty miles later the twisted canyons, cliffs as high as 600 feet, and spires reach the San Juan River, elevation 3,700 feet.

The area is filled with a greater variety of wildlife and vegetation than Dark Canyon. Combined with the Anasazi sites clustered in the upper reaches of the area, Grand Gulch is a gigantic outdoor natural and cultural history museum.

The area is popular with hikers and horseback riders, many of whom are content to visit short sections on three- to four-day excursions. It may be getting too popular. Restrictions to access may be in force by the time you read this, so check with the authorities as to current status of the area.

Glen Canyon National Recreation Area

HALL'S CROSSING/BULLFROG BASIN/HITE CROSSING/LAKE POWELL

Continuing westward from the area around Natural Bridges there are three choices at the southerly UT 95-UT 276 junction (eight miles west of UT 275, the Natural Bridges road).

UT 276 veers in a southwesterly direction for 45 miles to **Hall's Crossing Marina** where there is a ferry that crosses Lake Powell to **Bullfrog Basin Marina**. From there, it covers another 46 miles north, along the eastern side of the Henry Mountains, to rejoin UT 95, north of Hite Crossing.

For those travelling in a four-wheel-drive vehicle there is the option of a 65-mile-long dirt road from Bullfrog that follows the western flank of the Henry Mountains, along the Waterpocket Fold, to Capitol Reef National Park.

The other option is to continue on UT 95 for 60 miles, through **Hite Crossing**, crossing over three bridges at the northern end of Lake Powell, to the northerly junction of UT 95 and UT 276. From the junction it is 26 miles to Hanksville, an access point for the Maze District of Canyonlands National Park, Goblin Valley State Park, and Capitol Reef National Park.

Lake Powell, a 186-mile-long man-made lake, is the centerpiece of the Glen Canyon National Recreation Area, a 1.2-million-acre wilderness of untracked canyons and rugged terrain. Most of the lake is in Utah, but the greatest concentration of services is based out of the area around Page, Arizona, where the lower five miles of lake are located. These services are covered below, under Touring Page/Lake Powell.

The services available at Hall's Crossing are a couple of stores, private and public campgrounds, and a ranger station. You can rent trailers called housekeeping units, park an RV or camp in a tent, stock up on food and supplies, fill your tank with gas, get a shower and do your laundry. **Hall's Crossing Marina**, UT 276, Lake Powell, UT 84533, 801/684-2261 or 800/528-6154, includes a ranger station, and a store offering essential supplies, including boating equipment. The marina also offers fishing, waterskiing, houseboat rentals, fishing tours, and tours to Rainbow Bridge. For those with a boat, you can dock here or get gas.

The **John Atlantic Burr Ferry** can carry 15 passenger cars, two buses, and as many as 200 passengers on the 20-minute crossing to Bullfrog Marina. It departs hourly from 7 AM to 6 PM, mid-May to October, on even-numbered hours from Hall's Crossing and odd-numbered hours from Bullfrog. The rest of the year it operates on demand, between 9 AM and 4:30 PM only. Every so often the ferry is closed for repairs; a sign is supposed to be posted at the road junction of UT 276 and UT 95.

Bullfrog Resort & Marina, Box 4055-Bullfrog, Lake Powell, UT 84533, 801/684-2233 or 800/528-6154, offers more boating and tour services than Halls Crossing Marina. It is larger and includes full service gas stations offering repair service for cars or boats. There is also another public campground, a ranger station, and another marina and a Visitor Center. **Defiance House Lodge** is also here and includes the **Anasazi Restaurant**. The lodge runs boat tours (from April to October) to Rainbow Bridge and **Defiance House**, a restored Anasazi site 12 miles north. Several trailer and RV parks are also operating at Bullfrog, with shower and laundry facilities plus a variety of housekeeping units.

Twenty miles west of Natural Bridges on UT 95 is Fry Canyon, where there is a modest grocery store, gas station, motel, snack bar and campground which may or may not be open. Although these provide the only services until Hite Marina, which is another 25 miles farther up UT 95, it's probably best not to count on anyone being around here to help you out.

Hite Marina, Box 501, Lake Powell, UT 84533, 801/684-2278 or 800/528-6154, is below Cataract Canyon and the farthest north of all the Lake Powell marinas. Services include several primitive campgrounds, a few small grocery/convenience stores and gas stations for cars or boats. Docking space is available, as are boat rentals for fishing, waterskiing or houseboating. Trailer housekeeping units are also available.

Canyonlands (Maze District)/Goblin Valley/Hanksville

Little Hanksville, population 400, at the junction of UT 95 and UT 24, claims whatever fame it can from the area east of town known as **Robber's Roost**, which was once a hideout for Butch Cassidy and his outlaw gang. Today the town is most popular with visitors as a staging area for backcountry trips into the Maze District, Goblin Valley State Park, and Capitol Reef National Park.

The only certified attraction in Hanskville is probably the wooden paddle-wheel that was once used to crush ore at the nearby Woolverton Mill, at the regional office of the BLM, a half-mile south of UT 24 on 100 West (First Street). There are also several 19th century structures in town, including an old stone church. There is a motel, a bed & breakfast, a campground, plus several modest restaurants.

The remote and extremely rugged Henry Mountains are south of town. Running along the eastern slope of the Waterpocket Fold and Capitol Reef National Park, they are flanked by tortuous canyons and discouraging desert. Terrain ranges from desert plateaus to the 11,522-foot North Summit Ridge of **Mount Ellen**, complete with gnarled bristlecone pine and spruce forests. The range contains one of the only free-roaming buffalo herds in the United States, as well as mule deer, bighorn sheep, and mountain lions. Backcountry travel can be difficult, but there are several campgrounds and numerous hiking and four-wheel-drive roads which may or may not be passable at any given time.

For information contact the **BLM Hanksville District Office**, Box 99, Hanksville, Utah 84734, 801/542-3461.

The **Maze District** of Canyonlands National Park is accessed off UT 24, 21 miles north of Hanksville. A dirt road east from there covers nearly 60 miles, through the Glen Canyon National Recreation Area, to the park. The only bare bones services available in the entire area are found at the **Hans Flat Ranger Station**, 801/259-6513, outside the Maze in the Glen Canyon National Recreation Area (25 miles from the turn-off on UT 24). The ranger station is the only local information center for both the Glen Canyon National Recreation Area and the Maze District. Other details are available from the National Park Service (125 West 200 South, Moab, UT 84532, 801/259-7155).

This western district of Canyonlands is the most rugged and least crowded area of the 527-square-mile National Park, comprising 30 square miles of Anasazi ruins, Indian rock art, unlikely stone towers, slender, gravity-defying rock fins, sheer cliff walls, and other seemingly chaotic elements of strangely beautiful, challenging topography. Many hold perfectly descriptive names such as Golden Stairs, Doll House, and Land of Standing Rocks.

The area is only for serious outdoors people. Make sure you enter with a full tank of gas, sufficient water, food, and any other supplies you may need. There are no services available other than information and emergency water at the ranger station, and the soft sand or hard-packed clay roadbeds are virtually impassable in wet weather.

Within the Maze District trails through severe desert lands and confusing canyon networks are mostly unmarked; travellers need current topographic maps and confidence in their navigational skills. Backcountry permits are required for hikers and campers in the Maze. Primitive campgrounds are available, some near spring water or river water sources that need to be purified before consumption.

No permits are required for backcountry travel or camping in the Glen Canyon National Recreation Area.

It is highly recommended that you consult with the park ranger regarding road and trail conditions, as well as available water sources. Also, file your travel plans with the ranger; if something does go wrong, the likelihood of being found is slim if the authorities don't know where to look for you. There are good reasons why the Maze is probably the most under-used National Park–except possibly for remote sites in Alaska. It is extremely tricky in there, terribly hot in the summer, always isolated, and far from help. Use caution.

Horseshoe Canyon, a site filled with incredible, life-size, pre-Anasazi cave paintings, is only slightly more accessible than the Maze. A Four-wheel-drive is required. For details, see below under Hiking.

The turn-off to **Goblin Valley State Park**, PO Box 93, Green River, UT 84525, 801/564-8110, is a half-mile farther north on UT 24 from the road to the Maze District. From that turn to the west, it's another 12 miles to the bizarre sandstone goblins, of which there are hundreds. These rocks have been naturally sculpted into whimsical or spectral forms, depending on your perspective, complete with eroded eyes and other bodily orifices, among a delirious scramble of rock fins, pinnacles, and small arches.

There are several short hiking trails in the six-square-mile park that lead to particularly evocative areas and scenic overlooks. There are also jeeping, biking, and longer hiking trails that may be accessed from this area, including southeastern areas of the San Rafael Swell, 12 miles north of Goblin Valley. These are covered below, under Adventures.

The **San Rafael Swell**, administered by the BLM, is a colorfully layered rock dome, laced by canyons and craggy outcrops, 80 miles long and 30 miles wide. It protrudes 2,000 feet above the desert floor on its eastern flank, the **San Rafael Reef**. It is expected that this area will become Utah's next National Park. In the meantime, contact the **BLM San Rafael Resource Area Office**, Drawer AB, Price, Utah 84501, 801/637-4584, for information about backcountry driving, jeeping, biking, and hiking.

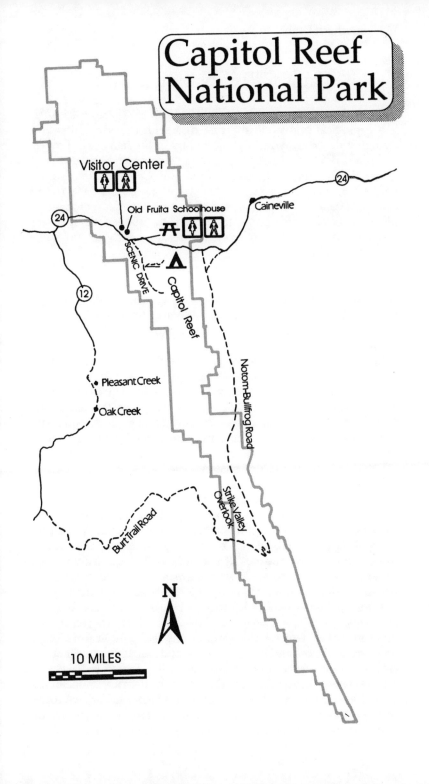

Capitol Reef National Park

Capitol Reef National Park, Torrey, Utah 84775, 801/425-3791, is a geological oddity of upthrust rock with towering cliffs and plunging desert canyons highlighted by improbably lush flower-laden meadows during spring and early summer. Second in size among Utah's National Parks, behind only Canyonlands, Capitol Reef's 378 square miles range from elevations around 3,800 feet to nearly 9,000 feet. The park stretches in a narrow band of layered, pinched rocks, water pools created by the slanted tiers, desert canyons, arches, and finely eroded spires, for nearly 100 miles–almost to Lake Powell.

The heart of the park is the **Waterpocket Fold**, a 100-mile-long uplift combining numerous layers of folded rock elevated high above the desert floor. The eccentric, compressed folds that catch water are the waterpockets, and these are surrounded by every variety of eroded rock sculpture found anywhere in Utah's Canyonlands.

Capitol Reef is the northern part of Waterpocket Fold, perhaps the area with the most intensely strange and evocative cliffs and rock forms. Some of the arched mounds as tall as 1,000 feet, eroded out of sandstone 1,000 feet thick, reminded pioneer travellers of the dome of the Capitol Building in Washington, DC. They had some time to think about the second part of the name-the massive stone reef impeded their progress and left them stranded like a sea vessel wallowing in coral-guarded shallows.

The most accessible attractions of the park are in this area, fairly close to the only paved road crossing the park. Then there is the immense backcountry, laced with rugged hiking, biking, horseback riding, and jeeping trails, remote campgrounds and statuesque, brightly multi-colored rock forms decorated with Indian ruins and primitive rock art. It is a little-visited and truly remote natural wonderland, with fertile areas along the rivers and streams, and stark but intriguing rocky deserts everywhere else.

A Visitor Center is 37 miles west of Hanksville, or 11 miles east of Torrey, on UT 24. The road follows the course carved by the **Fremont River**, which slices through the reef. The Visitor Center offers a slide show and interpretive exhibits related to the geological and cultural history of the area, including Indian artifacts and Mormon history displays, plus details on the flora and fauna of the park. Information about hiking trails and four-wheel-drive roads through the park may be obtained here, along with reports on current conditions and the required free camping permits.

There are no food services or accommodations available in the park, but there is a campground two miles south of the Visitor Center. It is surrounded by fruit orchards, which are maintained by the Park Service, and visitors are allowed to pick apricots, cherries, apples, pears, or peaches during the June to October harvest season. You can eat all you want for free while wandering around the orchards. If you want to take some fruit along for the ride, or back to your campsite or motel, a nominal fee is charged.

The old Mormon **Fruita Schoolhouse** is a mile east of the Visitor Center on UT 24, and a half-mile farther east are pre-Anasazi petroglyphs carved into a cliff on the north side of the road. An old settler's cabin, made of chiseled pieces of sandstone, is six miles east of the Visitor Center. A roadside waterfall is one mile farther east.

Two and a half miles west of the Visitor Center is a short gravel road leading a quarter-mile south to **Panorama Point**, offering a broad view of Capitol Reef and Boulder Mountain, actually a high plateau to the south.

A mile farther south are short, easy trails leading to the **Goosenecks Overlook**, elevation 6,400 feet, which looks down on Sulphur Creek, and Sunset Point, offering more expansive views of distant topography.

The park's Scenic Road heads south from UT 24 for 12.5 miles, below river-carved cliffs along the reef, and into the canyons of **Grand Wash**. More petroglyphs are found 10 miles south, in **Capitol Gorge**, another canyon.

Other roads into the northern depths of the park from UT 24 are recommended for four-wheel-drive although a few may be accessible to passenger vehicles–contact the ranger station for road condition reports. Also, inquire about portions of the Notom Road, which goes south for 60 miles along the east side of the reef, or the Burr Trail, which heads 40 miles west across the reef from Notom Road to Boulder, or see below under Four-Wheel-Drive Trips.

Torrey to Bryce Canyon National Park

Torrey, 11 miles west of Capitol Reef National Park on UT 24, is the closest town to the park offering accommodations and dining. There are several motels and modest restaurants. Other than that, there's not much happening here.

Bicknell and **Loa** are smaller towns northwest of Torrey on UT 24, also offering accommodations and dining possibilities. One reason for heading west on UT 24 from Torrey might be to stop in at the Teasdale Ranger Station, which administers the northern and eastern parts of the **Dixie National Forest**. The office is two miles west of Torrey, on UT 24, then one mile south.

For information contact **Teasdale Ranger Station**, Dixie National Forest, PO Box 99, Teasdale, Utah 84773, 801/425-3435.

Among the attractions in this area are the scenic drive possibilities along **Utah 12**, a paved two-lane road south from Torrey to Boulder. It's a pretty drive through aspen and evergreen forests, over a 9,200-foot-high pass on the **Aquarius Plateau**, also known as **Boulder Mountain**–the highest plateau in the United States. The route offers a variety of classic overlooks of Capitol Reef, the Waterpocket Fold, the Henry Mountains, and the Circle Cliffs. There are several tree-shaded campgrounds along this route and opportunities for mountain hiking and fishing on nearly 100 alpine lakes. The lake country offers a sharp contrast to the nearby desert lands, as well as the imposing rocks of Capitol Reef and the canyons of the Escalante River farther south.

For information and maps of trails and fishing spots contact the appropriate Forest Service office, Teasdale Ranger Station (see above) or, for the southern and western part of the Dixie National Forest, **Escalante Ranger District**, PO Box 246, Escalante, Utah 84726. The Escalante office is on West Main.

Boulder, population 150, is 35 miles south of Torrey on UT 12. It's another very small town and was the last town in the United States to have a road built to it. Until 1939 mail was delivered by pack train. Today it has a few stores and gas stations.

It's the western terminus of the 40-mile **Burr Trail Road**, which crosses the Waterpocket Fold, in the southern part of Capitol Reef National Park. The eastern end of the Burr Trail Road is at the junction with the Notom-Bullfrog Road, which runs north to south along the eastern boundary of the National Park. At the road junction the National Park lies 30 miles to the north, and Bullfrog Marina at Lake Powell lies 30 miles to the south. Only the first 20 or so miles of the Burr Trail Road are paved from Boulder. The rest, including sharp switchbacks crossing the fold, is dirt.

Anasazi Indian Village State Historical Monument, PO Box 393, Boulder, UT 84716, 801/335-7308, is three miles south of Boulder on UT 12. It contains the ruins of an Anasazi community, circa 1050-1200 A.D., thought to have housed as many as 200 residents. You can walk through the various Anasazi ruins, or take a look at a replica six-room Anasazi dwelling, which illustrates a variety of construction methods. A small museum features excavated artifacts from the site, a slide show, and other informative displays, including a small model of the village as it probably looked in its heyday, and a replica of a granary and petroglyph panel.

In the 30 miles from Boulder to Escalante, UT 12 descends into the **Escalante Canyon** system, featuring hundreds of miles of wilderness hiking trails through slender slot canyons, to the Escalante River, which drains into the Colorado River and was the last river to be found and surveyed in the contiguous 48 states.

Calf Creek Recreation Area, 801/826-4466, is nine miles south of Boulder, or 15 miles east of Escalante on UT 12. Calf Creek is a tributary of the Escalante River, which cuts a fertile swath through the surrounding layers of colorful sculpted rock. It has a small shaded campground and a picnic area.

A level 2.5-mile trail, along the canyon bottom from the campground, leads to a 126-foot waterfall–**Lower Calf Creek Falls**. The falls tumble into a crystalline pool, surrounded by oasis-like hanging gardens thriving amid the harsh, rocky splendor of the desert canyon. The trail closely follows the creek flowing through the box canyon, which was once used as corral for cattle and, before that, by the Anasazi and earlier Indians who may have lived in caves along the canyon and left behind rock art still visible today. Information about the area is available from the BLM office in Escalante (see below).

Escalante Petrified Forest State Park, PO Box 350, Escalante, UT 84726, 801/826-4466, is 1.5 miles northwest of the town of Escalante, off UT 12. It has a shaded campground and self-guiding trails past colorful, gem-like slabs of petrified wood, dinosaur bones, and the ruins of a pre-Anasazi Indian village. Wide Hollow Reservoir is next to the campground, offering fishing and boating.

The town of Escalante has only 600 residents, but it is nonetheless the largest town for 60 miles in any direction. Modest accommodations and dining are available, along with small grocery stores.

There is a **Dixie National Forest office** in Escalante at 270 West Main. Other helpful offices in town include one for the **BLM, Escalante Resource Area**, PO Box 246, Escalante, Utah 84726, 801/826-4291, and next door, a mile west of town on UT 12, one for the **National Park Service**, PO Box 511, Escalante, Utah 84726, 801/826-4315. The Forest Service can provide hiking, driving and fishing maps and information on current conditions in the forests north of town. The BLM or Park Service can provide information and hiking maps to the Escalante River drainage canyons and into the Glen Canyon National Recreation Area. Either office can provide the necessary backcountry permit required for primitive camping.

There is also an **Escalante Interagency Office**, 755 West Main, PO Box 246, Escalante, UT 84726, 801/826-5499, which provides information on travel throughout the region, including maps and details regarding backcountry hiking, biking, jeeping, fishing and camping areas administered by the several federal agencies in town.

Beyond Escalante, UT 12 winds through the undistinguished towns of Henrieville and Cannonville, where there is a turn-off to **Kodachrome Basin State Park**, PO Box 238, Cannonville, UT 84718, 801//679-8562. The park is seven miles south of UT 12 on a paved road. It is known for its colorful, photogenic cliffs, arches and petrified geyser holes, also known as sand pipes, which are standing shafts of rock left exposed by the erosion of surrounding rocks, some the size of a person, others nearly 200 feet tall. There is a picnic area and a campground.

Well-marked, easy hiking trails through the park, including a short nature trail, lead to brightly colored rocks and the protruding sand pipes.

Angel's Palace Trail covers an easy one-mile loop from the group campground. **Eagle's View Trail** offers great views, but you have to climb up 1,000 feet from the campground. It ends two miles later in Henrieville.

Two marginal dirt roads head south from the park to US 89, providing a short-cut to Kanab or the southern end of Lake Powell. For details see below, under Four-Wheel Drive Trips.

UT 12 winds north from Cannonville through Tropic, another small rural town featuring some old historic architecture, as well as a couple of motel/B&Bs, and two restaurants. One of the restaurants, at the **Bryce Pioneer Village**, is beside a log cabin built by Ebenezer Bryce, the namesake of Bryce Canyon. Also, you can hike from UT 12, north of town, on the three-mile round-trip **Mossy Cave Trail**, into Bryce Canyon National Park.

The trailhead is north of town, off UT 12, near the **Water Canyon Bridge**, four miles east of the turn-off to the park Visitor Center at the junction of UT 12 and UT 63. The trail leads to an alcove with hanging gardens and refreshing water seeps.

Driving north from Tropic on UT 12, through **Tropic Canyon**, UT 12 passes into the northern area of **Bryce Canyon National Park**, Bryce Canyon, Utah 84717, 801/834-5322, distinguished by evocative, multi-colored, pink, purple, red, blue, yellow and orange free-standing rock spires and towers beneath the rim of the **Paunsaugunt Plateau**.

The enchanting mazes of hoodoos, pinnacles, and crenelated cliffs have been formed over 60 million years into whimsical sculptural shapes that look like palaces and chess pieces, mythical beasts and humans, all of which range through a bursting, ever-changing palette of tones according to the time of day and the angle of the sun. The park is open year-round, but there may be snow in winter

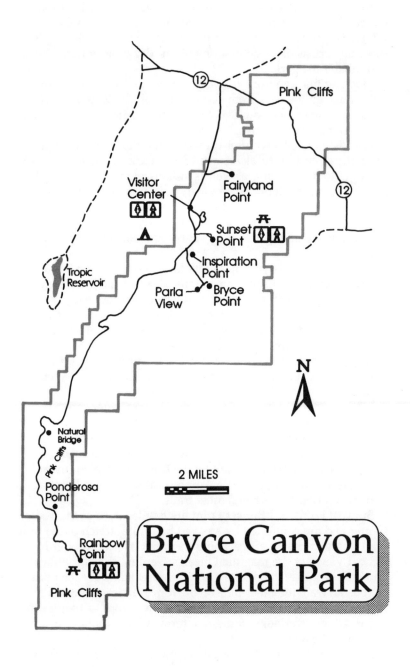

Pink Cliffs

Visitor Center

Fairyland Point

Sunset Point

Tropic Reservoir

Inspiration Point

Parla View

Bryce Point

N

Natural Bridge

Pink Cliffs

Ponderosa Point

2 MILES

Rainbow Point

Pink Cliffs

Bryce Canyon National Park

at the park's cool 6,600- to 9,100-foot elevations. Park roads are plowed but, unlike the crowded summers, few visitors show up. Winter is a special, extra-colorful time to visit, with clean bright snow and crusts of ice glimmering off the dazzling stone sentinels that inhabit the park.

Clocking mileage from Tropic, you have to drive a total of nine miles through the park from east to west on UT 12, and then turn south for three miles on UT 63 to reach the Visitor Center and the park's 17-mile scenic drive.

The Visitor Center features exhibits and a slide show explaining the natural and cultural history of the park, focusing on park geology, flora and fauna, as well as Indians and pioneering explorers and homesteaders. Park rangers lead numerous interpretive programs, campfire talks and hikes from May to September. Staff at the center can provide maps, handouts, and information on hiking and camping inside the park, and outside in the Dixie National Forest.

The park is small by Utah standards, covering only 35,000 acres, and you can take in some marvelous views of the area from the scenic drive. As with the rest of southern Utah, you really need to get out of the car and walk a bit to soak up the flavor of the place. Sixty miles of trails lead directly to many geological features that are barely visible from the scenic drive.

A number of trails are detailed below, under Bryce Canyon National Park Hiking. Overnight camping is only permitted on the **Under-the-Rim Trail** or **Riggs Spring Loop Trail**. Required backcountry permits are available from the Visitor Center.

The scenic drive actually begins two miles before the Visitor Center at **Fairyland Point**, overlooking hoodoos and contorted formations of Boat Mesa and the Chinese Wall in Fairyland Canyon. This is also a starting point for the **Rim Trail**, which covers 5.5 miles around the top of Bryce Amphitheater to Bryce Point. Rim Trail also connects to several other trails.

Sunrise Point and **Sunset Point** are a mile south of the Visitor Center and are connected by a paved half-mile stretch of the Rim Trail. In the morning and evening the point overlooks offer highlighted views of the majestic **Queen's Garden**, the amphitheater and far beyond. A trail into the amphitheater starts at each point.

You can walk for a half-mile on the Rim Trail from Sunset Point, or drive a mile farther south on the scenic drive to **Inspiration Point**, which overlooks statuesque forms with a military bearing known as the Silent City.

Four miles from the Visitor Center, off the scenic drive, is **Bryce Point**, with more overlooks to the north from the south end of Bryce Amphitheater. This is also one end of the Rim Trail, and the starting point for several others, including **Peekaboo Loop Trail,** which leads to views of Alley Oop, Three Wise Men, and Fairy Castle among other famous sites. It is the only park trail open to horseback riders.

Paria View, is off a side road to Bryce Point, offering rim views of the Pink Cliffs, Yellow Creek and beyond.

Farview Point is nine miles south of the Visitor Center on the scenic drive, offering extensive views spanning several hundred miles, including the layer-cake levels of surrounding plateaus, the distant Aquarius Plateau and the chalky White Cliffs.

Natural Bridge is close to the scenic road, two miles past Farview Point. Another mile farther is **Agua Canyon Overlook,** surveying the rosy Pink Cliffs and jumbled hoodoos, and two miles farther is **Ponderosa Canyon Overlook.**

The drive then passes through evergreen and aspen glades before the road ends at an elevation of more than 9,000 feet near **Yovimpa Point** and **Rainbow Point.** They are only a short distance apart, but offer very different perspectives of the Colorado Plateau and rock formations below.

Bristlecone Loop Trail follows a one-mile loop from Rainbow Point past ancient, gnarled pine trees that are thought to be among the oldest living things on earth. Other longer trails start around here, too.

Just west of Bryce Canyon on UT 12 is **Red Canyon,** essentially part of the same geological formations as the National Park, but with far fewer people wandering around. There is a campground, hiking trails, and four-wheel-drive roads through pine forests and erosional features that easily rival nearby Bryce Canyon.

A Visitor Center is on UT 12, 10 miles west of UT 63. For information contact **Powell Rangr District,** 225 East Center Street, PO Box 80, Panguitch, Utah 84726, 801/676-8815.

Cedar Breaks National Monument

From Bryce Canyon and Red Canyon there are two ways to reach Cedar Breaks National Monument, a rugged canyon filled with colorful cliffs and spires, along with aspen and evergreen forests. Either way, you have to drive 12 miles from the junction of UT 12 and UT 63 to US 89.

You can then turn south on US 89 and drive 20 miles to Long Valley Junction, and head west on UT 14 for 22 miles to UT 148, which is the southern entrance to the park. Alternatively, drive north for seven miles on US 89 from UT 12, to Panguitch, then 28 miles southwest on UT 143 to Cedar Breaks' north entrance.

There are a few motels in Hatch, north of Long Valley Junction on US 89. Eight miles west of the junction of US 89 and Utah 14 is a turn-off to **Strawberry Point**, which lies nine miles south of UT 14 on a dirt road. At the end of the road is a short trail to a scenic overlook at 9,000 feet, encompassing the **Markagunt Plateau** and **Zion National Park**.

Also on the way to Cedar Breaks National Monument, heading west from Long Valley Junction on UT 14, are recreational areas around Duck Creek Village, Duck Lake and Navajo Lake.

Panguitch is useful mainly for the services it provides in modest motels, restaurants, and gas stations. There are also some old, historic brick structures in town. Helpful information sources are also here. There's an information center in the city park. For area-wide information contact the **Garfield County Travel Council**, PO Box 200, Panguitch, UT 84759, 801/676-2311. There's also a Forest Service office in town.

Heading south from Panguitch on UT 143 is **Panguitch Lake**. Four miles south of Panguitch Lake on UT 143 is a turn-off to the east, leading in two miles onto a dirt road to **Mammoth Creek Springs**, a clear-flowing, lush, vegetated garden spot.

Ten miles past the springs turn-off on UT 143 is **Mammoth Cave**, the remnant of an ancient lava flow. You can walk and crawl through two levels of tunnels.

Cedar Breaks National Monument, PO Box 749, Cedar City, UT 84720, 801/586-9451, contains a massive amphitheater 2,500 feet deep and three miles wide, filled with whimsical rock forms, spires and pinnacles in a full artist's palette of bright colors. It looks a lot like Bryce Canyon but–at 2,000 feet higher, ranging from 8,000 feet to 10,600 feet–the feeling is one of more ethereal serenity.

The high altitude means a short season here. Due to snow closures, the five-mile scenic rim drive is generally open to cars only from mid-May to mid-October, although it is open to snowmobilers and cross-country skiers in winter.

A Visitor Center is also open only in the summer and is a mile north of the south entrance to the park on the scenic drive, with a few small exhibits describing flora and fauna, as well as rocks in the park and surrounding areas. Interpretive programs and hikes are led by park rangers. There are four overlooks on the scenic drive and several hiking trails along the rim, but no trails descend into the amphitheater from inside the park.

Brian Head, elevation 9,850 feet, is on UT 143, 2.5 miles north of Cedar Breaks National Monument, or 14 miles south of Parowan, a rock-ribbed Mormon community and the oldest town in this part of Utah. Since the Cedar Breaks road from the south is often closed in winter, the Parowan route from the north may be the only way to reach Brian Head at that time of year.

Brian Head is the site of a year-round resort complex, featuring downhill and cross-country skiing in winter, and mountain biking in summer.

In addition, the resort area has around 3,000 rooms in condos, hotels, and motels, so the level of amenities is somewhat more sophisticated and diverse than those found throughout most of the area covered in this chapter; you can find hot tubs and swimming pools, decent food, and even wine lists. Several choices for accommodations and dining are covered below, under Cedar Breaks National Monument Accommodations & Restaurants.

You can drive to the top of **Brian Head Peak**, elevation 11,307 feet, in a passenger car. Drive south two miles on UT 143, then three miles northeast on a dirt road to reach the mountain top for expansive scenic views.

For area information contact **Brian Head Chamber of Commerce**, Brian Head, Utah 84719, 801/677-2810.

Zion Overlook is 16 miles east of Cedar City, eight miles west of the south entrance to Cedar Breaks National Monument on UT 14. When you pull off the road you can see a big slice of southwestern Utah, all the way south to Zion National Park.

Cedar City/St. George

Cedar City really is a city, at least compared to everything else so far in southern Utah, with a population of around 11,000. It's even close to a real interstate highway, I-15, 50 miles northeast of St. George (southwestern Utah's other commercial metropolis). Cedar City is 18 miles west of Cedar Breaks National Monument on UT 14. There are plenty of places to stay and eat in town.

Cedar City is justifiably renowned for its **Utah Shakespearean Festival**, Cedar City, UT 84770, 801/586-7884. It includes six plays performed twice daily from late June to September, and other Shakespearean-related activities, such as jugglers and puppet shows, backstage tours, production seminars and a Renaissance Feaste. It all takes place at **Southern Utah University**, 351 West Center, Cedar City, UT 84720, 801/586-7700. There's a recreation of a Shakespearean-era theater at the school, as well as other special events scheduled periodically.

The **Iron Mission State Historical Park and Pioneer Museum**, 595 North Main, Cedar City, UT 84770, 801/586-9290, contains items relating to the history of the area, from ancient and modern Indian artifacts to pioneer-era farm equipment and horse-drawn vehicles. There's even a stagecoach complete with bullet holes supposedly deposited by Utah's most famous outlaw, Butch Cassidy.

Cedar City Chamber of Commerce, 286 North Main, PO Box 220, Cedar City, UT 84770, 801/586-5124, maintains a Visitor Center which can provide information about the city and surrounding areas. One of their free brochures details a 14-site historical tour of the town. The most interesting site of the tour is probably the Rock Church at Center and 100 East, 801/586-8475. It was made out of many different types of local rocks during the depression when local Mormons couldn't afford anything else.

The local office of the Dixie National Forest can help with information about backroad adventures on the Markagunt Plateau. Contact **Cedar City Ranger District**, 82 North 100 East, PO Box 627, Cedar City, UT 84720, 801/586-2421.

The airport in town is served by **Skywest/Delta Connection**, with service primarily to Salt Lake City, Las Vegas and St. George. For information phone 800/453-9417.

Rental car agencies at the airport include **Avis**, 801/586-3033, and **National**, 801/586-7059. In town car rental agencies include **Hertz**, 801/586-6096, and **Speedy**, 801/586-7368.

Travelling west of Cedar City on UT 56 leads quickly away from civilization and back into the sage-laden, sandy terrain of the **Escalante Desert**. After 19 miles, there's a turn-off to the south, which leads in three miles to the remains of **Old Iron Town**, a ghost town that once thrived on iron smelting. There's not much left today, but you can see some foundations and ovens and, if you want to stop for a picnic, there's a table.

Continuing west for another 20 miles, then turning south onto UT 18, leads back into the farthest western portion of the Dixie National Forest. After 12 miles you can turn west to go to **Enterprise Reservoirs** to fish, or continue south on UT 18, up the flank of **Big Mountain**.

Six miles south of the Enterprise exit on UT 18 is a turn-off to **Mountain Meadows Massacre Site and Memorial**. There's a small monument a mile west of the main road. In 1857, local Mormons and Indians killed 120 members of a wagon train that was passing through on the way to California. It took 20 years to bring one of the major culprits to justice, but eventually he was executed here, at the massacre site.

Seven miles farther south on UT 18 is the small town of Central, where a turn to the east leads in seven miles to **Pine Valley**, site of one of the oldest Mormon churches in the state. Pine Valley is high in the forested, cool mountains again, on the edge of the **Pine Valley Recreation Area** and **Pine Valley Mountain Wilderness Area**. There's not much happening in the way of business here, other than the **Pine Valley Lodge** (see below, under Cedar City Accommodations), which does offer cabin rentals and horseback riding. There are several campgrounds and many trails for hiking, as well as streams and a reservoir for trout fishing. You can also hire a backcountry guide at the lodge. The wilderness area is accessible only on foot or by horseback.

Back on UT 18, heading south for six miles will bring you to **Veyo**. This town is notable mainly for the **Veyo Pool Resort**, which features a natural hot springs swimming pool. Ten miles southwest of Veyo on UT 91 is **Gunlock State Park**, the centerpiece of which is **Gunlock Reservoir**, noted for boating and waterskiing, as well as bass fishing.

Fifteen miles farther southeast on UT 18, and east on UT 300, is **Snow Canyon State Park**, PO Box 140, Santa Clara, UT 84765, 801/628-2255. The park has crenelated red rock escarpments, contrasting black lava beds, volcanic cones, sand dunes, desert flora, rattlesnakes, lizards and three **Lava Caves** that can be explored on foot. There is a campground, hiking trails, and horseback riding.

The village of Santa Clara, four miles west of St. George on UT 91, is the site of the **Jacob Hamblin Home**, 801/673-2161, a pioneer homestead open to tours. Hamblin was sent to the area at the request of Brigham Young in 1856. With the cooperation of four wives he helped create 24 little Hamblins.

St. George is five miles southeast of Snow Canyon on UT 18, or 50 miles south of Cedar City on I-15. It's the largest city in southern Utah and the state's fastest growing one, with a population nearing 30,000. It's booming primarily from a migration of retirees and winter residents who come to "the other Palm Springs" for the salubrious, warm and sunny climate, not to mention a glut of golf courses.

One of the earliest snowbirds was Brigham Young, who built a house here in 1873, at 89 West 20 North, 801/673-2517. Guided tours of the house show the many original furnishings. It's part of a 23-site historic St. George Walking Tour sponsored by the **Daughters of the Utah Pioneers Museum**, 145 North 100 East, St. George, UT 84770, 801/628-7274. The museum contains pioneer portraits and artifacts, and is also part of the nine-block walking tour.

The most obvious landmark in town is the **St. George Temple** at 400 East 200 South. Built in 1877, it's Utah's oldest Mormon church, and you have to look at it from the outside only—unless you're a bonafide Mormon. Guided tours of the grounds are available and there is a small Visitor Center, 801/673-5181, with historical displays and background on the Mormon religion. You can also take a guided tour of the **Mormon Tabernacle**, at Main and Tabernacle, 801/628-4072.

Another interesting cultural attraction is the **St. George Art Museum**, 175 East 200 North, 801/634-5800, featuring unverified works said to have been painted by Degas, Rembrandt, and Van Gogh. Yet another cultural site is a 15-foot-high, 127-foot-long tiled mural depicting local history. The mosaic is on an outer wall at the **Dixie College Fine Arts Building**, 700 East 100 South.

For information about the area contact the following sources:

St. George Chamber of Commerce, 97 East St. George Boulevard, St. George, UT 84770, 801/628-0505. This 1876 building was once a county courthouse and is worth a stop even if you don't want any brochures.
Washington County Travel & Convention Bureau, 425 South 700 East, St. George, UT 84770, 801/634-5745.
Pine Valley Ranger District Office, 196 East Tabernacle, St. George, UT 84770, 801/673-3431, can provide information on outdoor activities for the areas north of St. George in the Dixie National Forest, Pine Valley Recreation Area, and Pine Valley Mountains Wilderness Area.
BLM, 225 West Bluff Street, St. George, UT 84770, 801/673-4654, or 801/628-4491.

St. George Municipal Airport is served by **Skywest/Delta Connection**, with service primarily to Salt Lake City, Las Vegas, Phoenix and Cedar City. For information phone 800/453-9417. Rental car agencies at the airport include **Avis**, 801/673-3686, or **National**, 801/673-5098. There are several other car rental agencies in town, including **Dollar**, 801/628-6549, and **Budget**, 801/673-6825.

Zion National Park

Zion National Park, Springdale, UT 84767, 801/772-3256, lies northeast of St. George and northwest of Lake Powell, in a stunning canyon filled with massive sandstone cliffs and oddly shaped rock formations ranging in elevation from 3,600 feet to 8,700 feet. Colorful mesas tower above convoluted canyons and lush valleys enlivened by waterfalls and rivers. Hiking trails are both plentiful and rewarding. Horseback trips are available.

Visiting the whole park takes a bit of trucking around. The main entrance to the park is north of Springdale, 60 miles due south of

Zion National Park

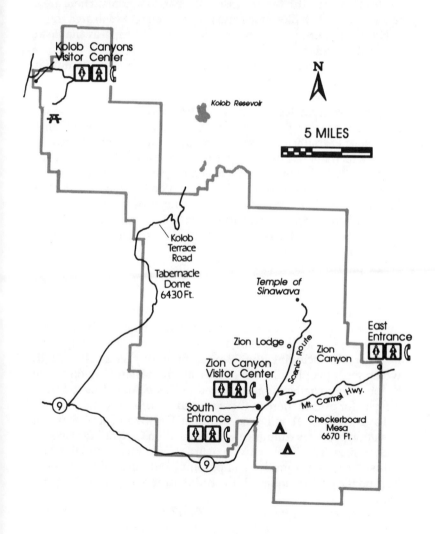

Cedar City. Alternatively it is 42 miles northwest of St. George, west of I-15, off UT 9.

There's also an east entrance to Zion from Mt. Carmel Highway (UT 9), west of the town of Mt. Carmel Junction. It goes through some of the most remote terrain in the park.

A third access road to Zion is 35 miles northwest of St. George, 16 miles south of Cedar City, off I-15, on the 5.5-mile-long Kolob Canyons Road. In this northwestern corner of the park a small Visitor Center is situated just inside the park boundary. There are a few small exhibits plus maps and information on Kolob area trails. Backcountry permits are required for overnight trips–available at the Visitor Center.

Beyond the Kolob Visitor Center, Kolob Canyons Road continues past numerous scenic stops characterized by colorful cliffs and mountainous terrain, through the **Finger Canyons of the Kolob**. The road ends at **Kolob Canyons Viewpoint** which overlooks many of the major geographic features of the park. Several hiking trails start at trailheads along the road, including a trail to **Kolob Arch**, which may be even longer than Landscape Arch in Arches National Park, depending on who's doing the measuring.

Yet another road passes through a portion of Zion Park–**Kolob Terrace Road**. To reach it from Kolob Canyons Road, return to I-15 and head south for 15 miles to UT 17. This meets UT 9 six miles west of the town of Virgin. Here the road starts to the north. It's paved only through the park.

The pavement ends after 20 miles, just before Lava Point, then turns to dirt and gravel the rest of the way to UT 14, five miles east of Cedar City.

The steep road, which is usually closed in winter, passes a number of scenic views of canyons and watercourses. It also provides access to some of the more remote backcountry hiking trails in the park, including the 13-mile, multi-day **West Rim Trail**, which most people hike the other way, from Zion Canyon to the Kolob. Other challenging trails lead to Kolob Arch. Contact park rangers for information on these rugged backcountry trails.

Lava Point is 21 miles northeast of Virgin, and its 7,890-foot elevation provides stunning views of the Zion Canyon Narrows, as well as sites much farther away, such as Cedar Breaks and the Pink Cliffs. There is a primitive campground and north of Lava Point, beyond the park boundary, is the **Kolob Reservoir**, for boating and fishing.

Springdale is a little town near Zion's south entrance. All visitors' services, including groceries, dining, accommodations, and RV parks are available. A side trip south from town leads to the ghost town of **Grafton**, where parts of *Butch Cassidy and the Sun-*

dance Kid were filmed and a cemetery marker memorializes a family killed by Indians in 1866.

Outskirts south of Springdale are good for hiking, biking and four-wheel driving far from the crowds of Zion Park. Contact the BLM office in St. George for information.

Zion Scenic Drive is a six-mile route that follows the North Fork of the Virgin River through 2,400-foot-deep **Zion Canyon**. It starts north of Springdale, a half-mile north of the year-round Visitor Center, which is filled with exhibits relating to park geology and geography, abundant park wildlife, Anasazi Indian artifacts and pioneer Mormon exploration. This is where you can pick up information on hiking trails and the permit you'll need for camping in the backcountry. In addition, many ranger-led interpretive programs and hikes are offered. A schedule is posted here.

At intervals along the scenic drive, parking areas are provided near spots with especially scenic views (**Court of the Patriarchs**, **Mountain of the Sun**, **Great White Throne**, and **Weeping Rock**). Hiking trails branch off from the scenic drive which ends at the **Temple of Sinawava**, a natural amphitheater of bright cliffs, distinguished by two tall spires in the middle.

Halfway up the scenic drive is the venerable **Zion Lodge**, originally built in 1925. It is set amidst a stunning setting, with the river running by and tall cliffs and rock outcrops soaring above. The lodge offers year-round accommodations, a dining room, snack bar, horseback rides, vehicle tours, and shuttles for hikers.

Kanab to Page, AZ/Glen Canyon/Lake Powell

Travelling east 24 miles from Zion National Park on the Zion-Mt. Carmel Highway leads through the southeastern portion of the park. This area is a maze of twisting canyons, hoodoos, slickrock and the aptly-named **Checkerboard Mesa**. The road eventually joins with US 89 at Mt. Carmel Junction.

Three and a half miles south of the junction is a turn-off on US 89 to **Coral Pink Sand Dunes State Park**, PO Box 95, Kanab, UT 84741, 801/874-2408. The paved road leads 11 miles southwest to the park, where half the desert terrain is sand dunes–some several hundred feet high, some tinted a definite pinkish color. Hiking trails criss-cross the park and there are special four-wheel-drive areas that are popular with dune buggy enthusiasts. There is also a campground.

Also on the way heading south on US 89, is **Moqui Cave**, a tantalizingly tacky gift shop in a cave, specializing in locally extracted rocks and minerals. There's also a museum displaying Indian arrowheads and pottery, as well as dinosaur tracks.

Kanab, 17 miles south of Mt. Carmel Junction on US 89, is filled with modest motels and restaurants, pioneer architecture and historic links with Hollywood movie and TV productions which were filmed here. One of the few vestiges of Hollywood's apparently played-out love affair with the area is **Lopeman's Frontier Movie Town**, 297 West Center Street, 801/644-5337, open April to November. It's a fake western town displaying western sets, false front shops, and fake shoot-outs. If you want to see the real Hollywood locations, ask here for directions to the sites of the opening scenes for the 50s TV series *The Lone Ranger* and *Rin Tin Tin*.

There are some possibilities for backcountry travel in the area—hiking trails and four-wheel-drive roads meander through the desert. For information contact **Kane County Information Center**, 41 South 100 East, Kanab, Utah 84741, 801/644-5033, or the local office of the **BLM**, 318 North 100 East, Kanab, Utah 84741, 801/644-2672.

You can drive straight south from Kanab to reach the North Rim of the Grand Canyon. To complete the tour of southern Utah, head to Page, Arizona. This is the main gateway to Lake Powell and is 75 miles east on US 89.

Travelling east from Kanab on US 89, the scenery becomes more desolate and desert-like. Nine miles east of town is the southern end of the **Skutumptah Canyon Road**, which is paved at this end and goes north through the Vermillion Cliffs, White Cliffs and Pink Cliffs. It leads to **Kodachrome Basin State Park** after 49 miles.

Forty-three miles east of Kanab is the BLM's Pariah Canyon Ranger Station, which administers the **Pariah Canyon Vermillion Cliffs Wilderness Area**, a remote area of little-visited canyons and watercourses spanning the Utah-Arizona border. There is a truly adventurous 40-mile hiking trip possible here, but only for the well-experienced, self-sufficient hiker. For information see below under Kanab to Page Hiking.

On US 89, 75 miles east of Kanab, is Page, Arizona, the largest town on the shore of **Lake Powell**. It was the construction base for the 710-foot-high **Glen Canyon Dam**, which created the 250-square-mile lake, most of which is in Utah. The dam was completed in 1964. Page has since developed as a major service town. There are motels, campgrounds, RV parks, restaurants, gas stations, and the all-important boat rentals are available at **Wahweap Marina**, a few miles north of town.

Most people don't spend a lot of time in Page–preferring the waters of Lake Powell–but coming and going through here, there are a few interesting attractions. These include the free tour of **Glen Canyon Dam**, 602/645-2511, and the **Carl Hayden Visitor Center**, which features a movie about Lake Powell, exhibits on the construction of the dam, and a Navajo rug display.

The **National Park Service**, PO Box 1507, Page, AZ 86040, operates an information booth in the Visitor Center adjacent to the dam. This is where you can get information on camping, hiking, and boating activities within Glen Canyon National Recreation Area.

John Wesley Powell Memorial Museum, at Lake Powell Boulevard and North Navajo Drive, 602/645-9496, displays an historical exhibit on the Colorado River and the people who have run it over the years. Other displays detail movie-making in the area, as well as more distant geological and social history.

Page/Lake Powell Chamber of Commerce, 716 Rim View Drive, PO Box 727, Page, AZ, 602/645-2741, offers information on town and lake activities, and also makes tour reservations.

Sky West/Delta Connection, 602/645-9200 or 800/453-9417, offers scheduled service connecting Page with Salt Lake City, Flagstaff, Phoenix and Las Vegas.

Avis, 602/645-2024, rents cars at the airport. **Budget**, 602/645-3977, has an office in town.

Lake Powell's 2,000 miles of shoreline extend throughout hundreds of branching fingers of sheer-walled canyons that range in color from pale tan to flaming orange. Networks of waterways intertwine through the canyons, offering ever-changing waters for a variety of watersports. Scuba diving to submerged Indian ruins in the lake is just one idea. Part of the adventure that lures three million travellers each year is the varying water level; you can never be sure to see the same coves, caves, or inlets again.

You can travel in your own boat or rent one at one of the many marinas. Stepping ashore you can find hiking trails into remote backcountry, including the Escalante River Canyon, Dark Canyon or the Grand Gulch Primitive Area.

Wahweap Lodge and Marina, Box 1597, Page, AZ 86040, 602/645-2433, is six miles north of Page and includes the **Rainbow Room** restaurant and an RV park.

Guided tours available include half-day or full-day boat tours to **Rainbow Bridge National Monument**. For information see below under Lake Powell Boating. Also offered are dinner and sunset tours on Wahweap Bay aboard *the Canyon King*–a stern-wheel paddleboat. All manner of boat and water accessory services can be found here; houseboats in various sizes, motor boats, jet skis, water skis, and fishing gear. You can stock up on provisions for your houseboat or picnic at the nearby campground operated by the Park Service.

Dangling Rope Marina, 602/645-2969, is situated 40 miles uplake from Wahweap and is accessible only by water. Facilities include a ranger station, grocery store, and marine gas station.

Adventures

Adventures in southern Utah's isolated backcountry can provide enlivening challenges, excitement, and fun. They can then swiftly turn into a disaster if you don't know what you're doing. For backcountry excursions a topographic map is a must. Always carry sufficient water for everyone, and it is highly recommended that you consult with Forest Service or BLM offices for updates on conditions and predicted weather changes. Roads and trails that are passable when dry may not be when wet. Canyon bottoms and washes may flood in sudden thunderstorms. River conditions change all the time. Extremely hot and dry weather can compromise your enjoyment in the shadeless backcountry. For state-wide weather reports call the **National Weather Service**, 801/524-5133.

A number of reputable outfitters are included below. For additional information contact **Utah Guides & Outfitters**, PO Box 111, Jensen, Utah 84035, 801/789-4952.

On Foot

There are thousands of miles of hiking and backpacking trails in Southern Utah. Many bike trails and jeep roads are also good for hiking.

Remember the following conditions:

- Always take the necessary precautions.
- Certain backcountry restrictions are enforced in National Parks.
- Fires are not usually allowed in the backcountry, so a backpacking cook stove is necessary.
- Where backcountry camping is permitted, campsites must be one half to one mile from roads, trails, or other improved facilities.
- Backcountry permits are required. These are available for free from the administering agency.

- All garbage must be carried out or deposited in provided receptacles.
- Pets must be on a leash at all times and are not allowed on hiking trails, river trips, or in the backcountry.
- All plants, animals and artifacts are protected. It is against the law to disturb them.
- Fishing is allowed with the proper license.

The Hiker's Guide to Utah, Dave Hall, Falcon Press, 1991, is a detailed and useful volume.

MOAB

There are enticing trails that start right in town, or close by. Look here for hikes with packstock or, for the skilled adventurer with adequate gear and a climbing partner, rock and ice climbing. Popular climbing areas are in the vicinity of Fisher Towers, Arches National Park, Potash Road, and Indian Creek.

Among the best hiking and backpacking areas are the following:

Mill Creek Canyon starts on Powerhouse Lane, at the end of Mill Creek Drive. It's a short hike skirting the edge of the creek to several shaded swimming holes, or you can keep going beyond a fork in the trail for a more challenging hike.

Hidden Valley Trail starts south of town, off US 191 to Angel Rock Road. Continue to a right turn onto Rimrock Lane. The trailhead is in a parking lot. It's a two-mile hike with a series of switchbacks to the Moab Rim. At the top is a satisfying view of Moab and Spanish Valley.

Corona Arch Trail starts 10 miles west of Moab, off UT 279 (Potash Road), near the railroad tracks in a parking lot. It's a mile and a half one-way to views of Corona and Bow Tie Arches.

Negro Bill Canyon starts off UT 128 (River Road), three miles past the junction with US 191. The parking lot is marked. Two miles up the trail is Morning Glory Arch; its 243-foot span makes it the sixth largest natural stone arch in the country. It is possible to continue hiking beyond the arch and all the way back to Moab (about 15 miles) but there is no maintained trail and a topographic map might come in handy.

The La Sal Mountains (Utah's second highest mountain range) cover an area 15 miles long and six miles wide. Ranging as high as 12,721 feet at Mount Peale, the La Sals are laced with nearly 100 miles of hiking trails.

The mountain terrain is extremely different from the sandy river country of giant rocks and canyons. The aspen- and spruce-forested La Sals are filled with streams, lakes, and wildlife–including black bears. For information on trails contact the U.S. Forest Service in Moab.

Moab Outabouts, PO Box 314, Moab, Utah 84532, 801/259-2209, runs guided hiking and backpacking trips in the Moab/La Sals/Canyonlands area.

ARCHES NATIONAL PARK

You can hike through the backcountry here or follow well-marked, established trails to Delicate Arch, and the Devils Garden Trail. The **Devils Garden Trail** leads to the greatest concentration of off-road arches in the park. A two-mile round-trip hike leads to **Landscape Arch**, 106 feet high and spanning 306 feet. Complete trail and backcountry information is available at the park's Visitor Center (PO Box 907, Moab, UT 84532, 801/259-8161).

ISLAND IN THE SKY DISTRICT

Neck Spring Trail starts on the other side of the road from the Shafer Canyon Overlook, a half-mile past the Visitor Center. It's a five-mile loop descending 300 feet to several springs, then returning to the canyon rim.

Lathrop Trail starts a mile past the Visitor Center and offers a challenging hike down to the Colorado River, descending 2,100 feet in nine miles. It is the only marked foot trail in this area that leads from the mesa top to the river. A primitive campground is on the edge of the river. Bring plenty of water. There's not much shade.

Mesa Arch Trail is much easier than Lathrop, covering only a half-mile for the entire round-trip to Mesa Arch. The trailhead is on the left, 5.5 miles from the Visitor Center.

Hands-on learning trips focusing on challenging real-life situations are offered by **Outward Bound**, 384 Field Point Road, Greenwich, CT 06830, 203/661-0797 or 800/243-8520, fax 203/661-0903. Wilderness trips run six to 29 days and are devised to build teamwork, trust, and concern for others. Itineraries include rock climbing, whitewater rafting, hiking, and kayaking.

NEEDLES DISTRICT

More than 50 miles of maintained trails wind through the Needles District. You can hike for an hour or many days in the backcountry. You can climb rocks, or you can find somewhere to be alone.

There may or may not be water available; any water you come upon would need to be treated. It's probably best to carry water, and don't forget insect repellent and sunscreen in the summertime.

A trail near the Squaw Flat Campground leads to **Peekaboo Trail**, a 10-mile round-trip past Indian ruins, including steep slickrock segments. The half-way point of this trail is Peekaboo Campground where petroglyphs can be seen on the surrounding rock walls. Other marked trails veer off through Squaw Canyon or Lost Canyon, and loop back to the Squaw Flats Campground. **Elephant Hill Trail**, at the picnic area, three miles past Squaw Flat Campground, leads to some of the park's most testing and beautiful terrain. **Chesler Park Trail** (off Elephant Hill Trail) is a six-mile round-trip through the slender, multi-colored rock spires that gave the Needles district its name. From **Chesler Park**, a meadow surrounded by towering sandstone needles, a five-mile trail loops around the entire park district.

The rather difficult **Lower Red Lake Canyon Trail** also begins from the Elephant Hill Trail and drops 1,000 feet in 10 miles to the Colorado River. Remember that it's another 10 miles back up. Don't consider this hike under the hot, mid-summer sun unless you're a reptile. Bring plenty of water.

The **Confluence Overlook Trail** starts at the end of the paved park road at Big Spring Canyon Overlook. It is an 11-mile round-trip leading to a 1,000-foot-high viewpoint of the Colorado River. There are excellent views of side canyons and the Needles along the way.

Wild Horizons Expeditions, West Fork Road, Darby, MT 59829, 406/821-3747, offers naturalist/conservationist-guided backpacking trips in Canyonlands National Park for a maximum of eight hikers. All must be willing to shoulder 30-40 pound backpacks for six to seven miles each day. Scheduled trips run from March to September and emphasize safe, low-impact hiking and camping. Also: Customized and family trips are available.

NATURAL BRIDGES NATIONAL MONUMENT

A nine-mile trail loops past the three natural bridges, the Horse Collar Ruins, and along the base of the White and Armstrong Canyons. It can be accessed from any of the bridge trailheads. Backcountry hiking is not permitted in the National Monument.

DARK CANYON/GRAND GULCH

Seeing Dark Canyon entails remote backcountry hiking far from any human intrusion or possible help. A number of shorter trails comprise a 40-mile-long trail that passes through Woodenshoe, Peavine, Hammond, and Upper Dark Canyons, among others, leading to Anasazi pictographs and refreshing desert water holes.

Although the actual hiking may not be difficult and no permit is required, it is recommended that you consult with BLM or National Forest information sources in Monticello for access road and trail conditions.

Hiking in Grand Gulch is similar to Dark Canyon; it's rugged going and you're on your own. You can camp anywhere; there are no developed sites and water sources may or may not be available. Trailheads on the east side of the Upper Grand Gulch area are at **Kane Gulch** and **Bullet Canyon**. A 25-mile trail connects the trailheads.

Collins Spring Trail is the western access to Collins Canyon and the Lower Grand Gulch area. It's a 40-mile hike from Kane Gulch to Collins Spring. No hiking permit is required, but again, check with the appropriate offices for current conditions. They can also provide hiking maps, and it's not a bad idea to let them know your travel plans.

Less visited, but no less absorbing, are hikes in the vicinity of **Fish Creek** and **Owl Creek** (east of Grand Gulch and UT 261, a mile south of Kane Gulch). There are Anasazi ruins throughout these canyons, plus arches and spring-fed rock pools. Twelve-mile-long **Slickhorn Canyon** contains numerous Anasazi ruins south of Grand Gulch to the San Juan River. Trail access is west of UT 261, 10 miles south of Kane Gulch. For current information and trail maps contact the BLM ranger station in Kane Gulch (see above, under Touring Natural Bridges National Monument) or the BLM office in Monticello (435 North Main, PO Box 7, Monticello, UT 84535, 801/587-2141).

A liberating alternative for backpackers is hiking with packstock. **Pack Creek Ranch**, PO Box 1270, Moab, UT, 84532, 801/259-5505, offers an opportunity to travel into some of Utah's most remote and intimidating terrain with a horse to carry your gear. Four-day trips are scheduled for a maximum of 12 hikers in April, May, September, and October. They include exploring, camping, and five to eight miles of hiking daily in one of the three following areas.

In **Lower Grand Gulch**, participants camp near Indian ruins and explore cliff dwellings, rock art, side canyons, and old trails before meeting a boat on the San Juan River for a final day of rafting.

On **Upper Grand Gulch** trips participants hike through deep, winding canyons, with an opportunity to explore ancient Indian ruins and Indian rock art panels.

Guided trips into **Dark Canyon** focus on Anasazi ruins and rock art, as well as splashing around in improbable, oasis-like, desert water holes.

Guided hiking trips of a half-day to six days in southeastern Utah are offered by **Tours of the Big Country**, PO Box 309, Bluff, UT 84512, 801/672-2281.

Hikers wishing to explore Dark Canyon can make arrangements for drop-off and pick-up services at Hite Marina.

HENRY MOUNTAINS

There are numerous old mining trails and jeep roads suitable for hiking in the Henrys, but most trails are unmarked and unmaintained. The BLM office in Hanksville (see above, under Touring Hanksville) can provide information. An excellent source for hikers in the Henrys and other remote parts of canyon country is *Canyon Hiking Guide to the Colorado Plateau*, by Michael R. Kelsey, Wasatch Book Distribution, PO Box 1108, 66 West 400 South, Salt Lake City, Utah 84110, 801/575-6735.

There is a partial trail from Lonesome Beaver Campground to Mount Ellen peak. It's an eight-mile round-trip with an elevation gain of 3,300 feet.

GLEN CANYON NATIONAL RECREATION AREA/THE MAZE DISTRICT/GOBLIN VALLEY STATE PARK

The many miles of trails and rugged jeep roads through the **Maze District** are largely unmarked and there are no services anywhere close by. Free backcountry permits are required for travel through here. These are available from the Hans Flat Ranger Station or from the National Park Service office in Moab (see above, under Touring).

Backcountry permits are not required for the **Glen Canyon National Recreation Area**, which adjoins the Maze. Any travel in this area is going to be challenging though, so check with the ranger station regarding area conditions before venturing out. Several hiking routes are accessed only after driving 35 miles from the ranger station, deep into the backcountry. For ideas, see below, under Maze District Jeeping.

Horseshoe Canyon, west of the Maze District and site of the Great Gallery, is a little easier to get around, though not by much. You can drive close to the trail leading to the Great Gallery, but you'll need a four-wheel-drive. To get there you bear left (north) at the Hans Flat Ranger Station and continue for seven miles. The trailhead is two miles south of the main road; there should be a sign to the trail on the west rim of the canyon. Follow the trail down 500 feet in one mile to the bottom of the canyon. The Great Gallery is to the right, about two miles away. There are a couple of primitive campsites in the canyon. Backcountry permits are required for camping, so when you're picking one up pick the ranger's brain about conditions in the area.

There are several hiking trails in **Goblin Valley State Park**, all accessed off gravel roads through the park. Most offer a two- to three-mile round trip, and there are several miles of slot canyons to explore on foot in **Little Wild Horse** and **Bell Canyons**, just outside the park boundaries to the west.

CAPITOL REEF NATIONAL PARK

The few roads through the park only take you to a small fraction of the most scenic areas. There are a number of short hiking trails suitable for daytrips within easy reach of the park's Visitor Center, or numerous longer backcountry trails are suitable for backpackers. Park rangers stationed at the Visitor Center can inform hikers of road and trail conditions and provide information for rock climbers about restrictions and areas where rock climbing is not allowed.

Most of the hiking in the park is fairly difficult. Some of the slickrock slopes and many of the trails are steep. Trail markings may be hard to follow. As for restrictions; no pets are allowed, backpackers may not camp within a half-mile of roads or trails, and no fires are permitted. You'll need a cook stove to prepare food, and your own water; water sources are unpredictable.

Summer is hot and buggy; preferred hiking seasons are spring and fall. Wisdom dictates avoiding low spots in washes which may flood rapidly in the event of a sudden downpour. Respect the weather; flash floods can carry away your tent or your car. Imagine what one could do to you.

A number of trails intersect throughout the park, so you can make long or short hikes. Good hiking trails include the following:

Grand Wash Trail (five miles east of the Visitor Center, on the south side of UT 24) is an easy, level route along a dry river bottom that slices completely through Capitol Reef. You can access Grand Wash from UT 24 or from the end of Grand Wash Road–a 4.5-mile drive from the Visitor Center–off the southwesterly scenic drive. From there it's a two-mile hike down the wash to the Fremont River.

Instead of hiking down, **Cassidy Arch Trail** climbs 1,000 feet in less than two miles. You can turn off this trail after a mile onto **Frying Pan Trail**, which reaches Cohab Canyon in three miles. Cohab was named for Mormon polygamists who once hid from the law there. **Cohab Canyon Trail** then drops a mile down to the Fruita Campground.

You can access Cohab Canyon and the above trails from the parking area for **Hickman Natural Bridge Trail**, two miles east of the Visitor Center. The trailhead is across the road, or follow a well-marked one-mile trail to the 133-foot-long, 75-foot-high natural bridge. On the way there's a classic view of Capitol Dome framed by the natural bridge.

The **Rim Overlook Trail** veers off the Hickman Natural Bridge Trail and covers two miles, one-way, to a 1,000-foot-high bird's eye perch over the Fremont Valley. Portions of the craggy park and mountains lie far beyond.

Three miles west of the Visitor Center is the trailhead for **Chimney Rock Trail**, a 3.5-mile loop leading to scenic views of the Reef. Access to Chimney Rock Canyon starts at the same place and follows the canyon for nine miles to the Fremont River at UT 24, four miles east of the Visitor Center. Avoid this route in wet weather. Flash flooding is a possibility and heavy rains will raise the water level in the river, which is normally low enough to cross on foot.

Capitol Gorge lies at the end of the Scenic Road, 11 miles from the Visitor Center. You can walk four miles through the slender gorge on the **Pioneer Trail**, which was the old state highway until 30 years ago, to Notom Road.

Another option is to climb two miles, more than 1,000 feet up the nearby **Golden Throne Trail**, for a fine view of the park from the bottom of the colorfully striated Golden Throne formation, one of the park's most prominent features, at an elevation of 6,500 feet atop the reef.

Many hikers follow the Pioneer Trail for only a mile, past some badly eroded petroglyphs and the Pioneer Register, where old-time travellers scratched their names and thoughts into the rock. Turnaround point for the short route is a level mile down the gorge, at the natural tanks, otherwise known as waterpockets.

Other hiking areas in the southern portion of the park may be accessed off Notom Road. These include the **Lower Muley Twist Canyon**, accessed off Burr Trail Road, two miles west of Notom Road. The canyon twists tortuously along the top of the Waterpocket Fold then down 900 feet to Halls Creek after 12 miles.

Several trails also veer off from **Upper Muley Twist Canyon**. The upper canyon starts west of Lower Muley Twist Canyon, a mile past the peak of the switchbacks over the fold on Burr Trail Road. If you have a jeep, you can drive a few miles up the canyon, then hike in six miles to the head of the canyon or climb a mile up the **Strike Valley Overlook Trail** at the end of the road for a scenic view.

Hiking in the northern section of the park can lead you to rarely visited canyons, the reverential monoliths of Cathedral Valley, and desert badlands. See below, under Capitol Reef National Park Mountain Biking for some ideas, or contact the ranger station for trail guides, reports on current conditions, the necessary backcountry permits, and topographic maps which are a must when travelling through this rugged backcountry.

ESCALANTE

There are numerous hiking possibilities in the canyon country around the Escalante River, from easy, short hikes to rivers for swimming, to overnight excursions past Indian ruins near incredible alcoves and amphitheaters. You can hike to caves and grottoes with hanging gardens, or all the way to Lake Powell, which is 85 miles from the town of Escalante. It's a remote area, though, and backcountry permits are required. Contact the BLM or National Park Service offices in Escalante (see above, under Touring Escalante), for permits and current information, including trailhead and hiking route maps.

Be prepared to get wet. Most routes include shallow river crossings, though sometimes the water is higher, and there is always a flash flood danger, particularly in summer. Spring and fall offer cooler weather and less chance of flooding. You can usually find water to drink, but you do need to purify it first. Bring insect repellent and sun screen. There are many spots where you can camp; just don't pick a low spot that might flood. Any hiking plans should include a copy of the book *Hiking the Escalante*, by Rudi Lambrechtse (Wasatch Publishers). It details numerous backcountry hiking routes and is as indispensable as the topographic maps you need to navigate this challenging wilderness of arches, buttes, and canyon networks.

Trails are accessed right in Escalante or from the UT 12 bridge, 15 miles east of town. A good hike that does not require extreme preparation connects those two spots. Head east down the river from town through the main canyon. In seven miles you reach **Death Hollow**, where you should find some swimming holes to the north where you can to cool off. You can take a side trip up Death Hollow, or continue east another five miles to **Sand Creek**,

with more swimming holes upstream. Or continue east past Escalante Natural Bridge, and in another two miles to the UT 12 bridge.

A longer hike starts at the UT 12 bridge and covers 25 miles to
Harris Wash. From there it's another 12 miles west through Harris
Wash to Hole-in-the-Rock Road. This hike takes you through numerous slot canyons and surprisingly fertile meadows, splashes
through quite a few streams and past arches, hanging gardens and
dry washes–in short, the full array of Escalante Canyon country
scenery. You need good maps for this trek.

A 65-mile, multi-day hike to Lake Powell starts at the **Harris
Wash Trail**, off Hole-in-the-Rock Road south of Escalante, and
requires a shuttle. You hike east through Harris Wash to the Escalante River, then down the river past Fence Canyon, Twenty-Five
Mile Wash, Moody Creek, the huge and impressive Stevens Arch
and into Coyote Gulch, a mile from Lake Powell. To get back to the
Hole-in-the-Rock Road, hike west up Coyote Gulch. In eight miles
you turn southwest on Hurricane Wash and it's seven miles from
there to the road, 45 miles south of Escalante.

Other canyon hiking possibilities are from numerous trailheads
off Hole-in-the Rock Road leading east to the Escalante River, or
from the Burr Trail Road east of Boulder, and south into the Escalante River canyons.

There are three canyons near the southern tip of Hole-in-the-
Rock Road that you can follow for relatively short hikes to Lake
Powell. Contact the BLM or National Park Service for details of
hiking **Fortymile Gulch**, a 12-mile round-trip, **Willow Gulch**, a
seven-mile round-trip, or **Fiftymile Creek**, a seven-mile round-
trip.

In addition, there are numerous mountain country hiking trails
north of Escalante off the 38-mile-long Hell's Backbone Road. Contact the BLM office in Escalante for details.

Wild Horizons Expeditions (West Fork Road, Darby, MT 59829,
406/821-3747) offers ecologically oriented, guided backpacking
trips of six to eight days through Escalante Canyon, March to
September.

Escalante Canyon Outfitters, PO Box 325, Boulder, UT 84716,
801/335-7311, offers guided hiking and backpacking trips.

Boulder Outdoor Survival School, PO Box 3226, Flagstaff, AZ
86003, 602/779-6000, runs educational programs in the pristine
outdoor setting of the Escalante River area, eschewing high tech
bells and whistles to focus on back to basics outdoor skills training,
primitive skills, survival training, and walkabouts.

BRYCE CANYON

Hiking trails here can be taken in large or small doses. Overnight trips are only allowed on **Under-the-Rim Trail** and **Riggs Spring Loop Trail**. Fires and wood gathering are not allowed in the park. Except for the Rim Trail, every trail goes down into the canyon, so the hiking is fairly strenuous coming back up.

Fairyland Loop Trail covers an eight-mile loop starting at either Fairyland Point or Sunrise Point. One of the hundreds of fantastical rock forms along the way is the monolithic Gulliver's Castle. An alternative to the entire loop is to hike down to the rock spires in the amphitheater and back up to where you started.

Queen's Garden Trail covers a two-mile round-trip from Sunrise Point, down into hoodoos deep in the amphitheater, including evocative forms such as Queen Victoria and Queen's Castle. Connecting trails from this route meet up with Navajo Trail, the Rim Trail and Peekaboo Loop Trail.

Navajo Trail descends a steep 500 feet in a half-mile from Sunrise Point into the midst of a battalion of hoodoos known as the Silent City, and also connects with several other park trails in the bottom of the amphitheater. Along the way, it passes forms known as the Turtle, Organ Grinder's Monkey, and Thor's Hammer.

Peekaboo Loop Trail is a four-mile loop that can be accessed from several different places, taking you through some of the park's best scenery. If you start at Bryce Point, or from Sunrise Point and the Queen's Garden Trail, you will have a seven-mile round-trip. From Sunset Point and the Navajo Trail it's a mile shorter.

Under-the-Rim Trail is the most ambitious hike in the park, covering a 23-mile, multi-day route. It passes below the Pink Cliffs and stretches from Bryce Point to Rainbow and Yovimpa points. You can tackle shorter segments of the trail from the scenic drive, such as the four-mile round-trip from Bryce Point to the mushroom-like Hat Shop formations.

Riggs Spring Loop Trail covers a nine-mile loop from Yovimpa Point or Rainbow Point and provides some of the best park views of the Pink Cliffs.

Just west of Bryce Canyon is the similar looking **Red Canyon** area of the Dixie National Forest. The main difference is that fewer people hike through Red Canyon.

Pink Ledges Trail offers a short, quarter-mile hike from the Visitor Center on UT 12, 10 miles west of UT 63, through startling pink and red rock formations.

Buckhorn Trail begins near Red Canyon Campground and leads you a mile up to the canyon rim.

For information, phone the **Red Canyon Visitor Center**, 801/676-8815, or contact the Forest Service office in Escalante (PO Box 246, Escalante, Utah 84726).

MountainFit, 663 Battery Street, Fifth Floor, San Francisco, CA 94111, 415/397-6216 or 800/926-5700, fax 415/397-6217, offers week-long, all-inclusive hiking tours in southwestern Utah. The tours stress pampered, healthy living for up to 14 adventurous participants who do not want to rough it too much. They include yoga each morning, jacuzzis, massages at night, spa cuisine, and accommodations in luxurious mountain lodges.

CEDAR BREAKS NATIONAL MONUMENT

There are several trailheads on the Cedar Breaks rim drive. **Wasatch Rampart Trail** covers a four-mile round-trip from the Visitor Center. It curves along the south rim of the amphitheater, through a sweet-smelling forest of ancient, thousand-year-old bristlecones at Spectra Point, followed by grassy meadows, then on to another rim overlook at trail's end.

Alpine Pond Loop covers a two-mile loop from Chessman Ridge Overlook, or from a trailhead a mile farther north. It dips below the rim and through a spruce and aspen forest to Alpine Pond, where you can fish if you have a Utah fishing license.

Bristlecone Pine Trail is a short trail from Chessman Point to a rim overlook.

Rattlesnake Creek Trail starts outside the park's north entrance and descends 3,500 feet in nine miles to Ashdown Creek, which you can hike upstream into the Cedar Breaks Amphitheater. You can also hike away from the park and head downstream through the Ashdown Gorge Wilderness Area.

CEDAR CITY/ST. GEORGE

There are miles of hiking trails in the Pine Valley Recreation Area, east of the town of Pine Valley. Contact the Pine Valley Ranger District (see above, under Touring Cedar City/St. George) for information and trail maps.

Brown's Point Trail (which starts at the Pines Campground), and **Whipple Trail** (which starts at North Juniper Campground), lead in four miles and six miles respectively to **Summit Trail**, a long trail, covering 35 miles one-way, in the adjacent 50,000-acre Pine Valley Mountain Wilderness Area. **Summit Trail** eventually climbs to the top of Signal Peak.

There are also many hiking trails in Snow Canyon State Park, 12 miles northwest of St. George. **Hidden Pinyon Trail** starts near the

Shivwits Campground and covers an easy 1.5-mile round trip to a canyon overlook.

West Canyon Trail is a seven-mile round trip starting close to the stables, a mile south of the campground. Several other trails branch off from the trail for backpacking excursions and overnight camping.

Lava Tubes Trail starts a mile north of the campground and covers a one-mile round trip to the park's lava caves.

ZION NATIONAL PARK

In general, spring and fall are the best times to hike through Zion. Summers are hot and also the most crowded time in the park, unless you travel the back road trails off Kolob Canyons Road or Kolob Terrace Road. Winters are pretty when it snows, but trails may be obscured and it gets mighty cool at night. A list of 165 miles of park trails is available from the Visitor Centers.

Maintained trails off Zion Scenic Drive lead to great spots you can't see from the road. In addition there are all sorts of backcountry trails suitable for rock climbers and mountaineers with the proper equipment and route-finding skills. Always check with park rangers first for current backcountry conditions and overnight camping permits.

There are several hiking trails that start from the Kolob Canyons Road in the northwest corner of the park. **Taylor Creek Trail** starts two miles from the Kolob Canyons Visitor Center and covers three miles one-way through the Middle Fork of Taylor Creek to Double Arch Alcove.

La Verkin Creek Trail starts four miles past the Kolob Canyons Visitor Center, at Lee Pass, and leads seven miles, one-way, to Kolob Arch. The trail initially drops 800 feet to Timber Creek, then crosses La Verkin Creek before reaching the 310-foot rock span, which is 330 feet tall. The arch really glows in the early morning light; for this reason, photographers prefer to make this an overnight trip.

Rugged and steep trails off the Kolob Terrace Road include the West Rim Trail and Hop Valley Trail, both of which start near Lava Point, 20 miles northeast of Virgin.

West Rim Trail covers 13 miles, all the way back to Zion Canyon.

Hop Valley Trail covers a 14-mile round trip to Kolob Arch.

Consult with a park ranger regarding trail conditions and backcountry permits before striking out on these challenging treks. Main Zion hiking trails take you away from the bustling crowds that overwhelm the park's scenic drive and overlooks in summertime, while leading to wonderful areas redolent in Indian history and eons of geological activity. Despite the presence of the National Park, the most frequent visitors here have always been wild creatures, not humans.

Travelling north on the 6-mile scenic drive, trails are as follows:

Watchman Trail is named for a 2,600-foot-tall sandstone rock that greets visitors near the park entrance. The trail starts in either Watchman or South campground and covers a 2.5-mile round trip, climbing 370 feet to views of Zion Canyon and Springdale.

Sand Bench Trail is often shared with horseback riders. It's an easy two-mile loop, gaining 500 feet in elevation from a trailhead near the stunning Court of the Patriarchs Viewpoint, providing excellent views of Lower Zion Canyon.

Emerald Pools Trails are three trails to waterfalls, rock pools, and views of the forested slopes of Zion Canyon. Two trails start near Zion Lodge on a paved trail leading a half-mile to Lower Pool. Middle Pool is a quarter-mile farther. A third trail starts at Grotto Picnic Area and also reaches the pools. Beyond the Middle Pool, a very steep, half-mile trail, with chain handholds embedded in the rock wall, leads to Upper Emerald Pool–the prettiest of all, with a sandy beach beneath stratospheric cliffs.

West Rim Trail is a fairly major undertaking, covering 13 miles round-trip and gaining 3,700 feet in elevation from Grotto Picnic Area to West Rim Lookout, or 13 miles one-way to Lava Point. The route does provide ethereal canyon views and it is conveniently paved to the end of Walter's Wiggles, a lengthy series of tight switchbacks that take you to the top of Scout Lookout (1,000 feet in elevation). At Scout Lookout you can hike a half-mile, gripping another chain hand-grip, to the top of Angels Landing–a stone tower 1,500 feet above the Virgin River. From Scout Lookout, it's 3.5 miles to West Rim Lookout, then another 6.5 miles to Lava Point.

Weeping Rock Trail starts at Weeping Rock parking area and is a short, easy, half-mile round-trip hike, gaining 100 feet in elevation, past drizzling, hanging gardens to a fine view of the Great White Throne, a multi-colored, 2,400-foot-tall stone outcrop. **East Rim Trail** covers a steep 7.5-mile round trip, gaining 2,150 feet in elevation to Observation Point. There are great views along the way, as well as access to the backcountry on the **Hidden Canyon Trail** and **Echo Canyon Trail**, which veer off the main route.

Gateway to the Narrows Trail starts at the end of the scenic drive, near the Temple of Sinawava–an immense rock amphitheater with two prominent stone towers in the middle–and covers a paved two-mile round trip into a slender canyon 2,000 feet high, yet only 20 feet wide at the Virgin River Narrows.

Orderville Canyon Trail goes a few miles farther into the Narrows, but hiking into this area leads to extremely rugged backcountry, without trails. Plan to get wet; you'll be hiking in the river and it could be above your waist, or higher. A backcountry permit is required for any travel in the Narrows, and although a "Narrow Canyon Danger Level" is posted daily at the Visitor Center, it is still a smart idea to talk to a ranger about current conditions.

Canyon Overlook Trail starts at the east side of the long tunnel on the Zion-Mt. Carmel Highway (UT 9). It's a one-mile round trip through desert-like terrain, offering views of prominent features on the east side of Zion Canyon.

KANAB TO PAGE, ARIZONA

For hikers seeking something more forgiving to sink their toes into than a rocky hiking trail, the sand dunes at **Coral Pink Sand Dunes** State Park, west of Kanab, could be the ticket. Just watch out for dune buggies; drivers of all-terrain vehicles also enjoy tracking through the dunes.

A possible week-long hiking trip is the **Pariah River Canyon**, a BLM wilderness area, starting 43 miles west of Kanab, south of US 89, and ending 40 miles later at Lee's Ferry, Arizona. The route starts in a 2,000-foot-deep gorge, winds through narrows, past arches and entails a fair bit of river wading before ending at the Colorado River. To negotiate this area you need to be able to read a map; the route is not well-marked. The trail is closed in threatening weather, particularly if there's a danger of thunderstorms, which can flood the narrows near the north end of the trail. Because of the flood danger, required permits are available no more than 24 hours in advance, and all hikers must start at the north end of the canyon, in Utah. The BLM ranger office on US 89, east of the Pariah River, provides permits, weather forecasts, and hiking maps. Information is also available from the BLM office in Kanab (318 North 100 East, Kanab, Utah 84741, 801/644-2672). Several other shorter and easier trails also lead to the Paria River.

LAKE POWELL/GLEN CANYON NATIONAL RECREATION AREA

Most of the hiking near Lake Powell is rugged and over difficult trails. Areas to consider are near Rainbow Bridge National Monument, which is equally far from any of the major marinas, or the Escalante River Canyons, Grand Gulch Primitive Area, and Dark Canyon Wilderness, which are most easily accessed through the northern marinas at Hite, Hall's Crossing, or Bullfrog. Contact park rangers at Lake Powell marinas for information.

A popular and relatively easy seven-mile hike is to **Rainbow Lodge Ruins**. The trail starts a mile past Rainbow Bridge National Monument, on the San Juan Arm of Lake Powell, and leads southeast through Horse Canyon to the site of a once fashionable lodge that counted John Wayne and Teddy Roosevelt among its guests. Several other trails veer off to nearby arches and rock formations. From the same spot, east of Rainbow Bridge, you can hike 13 miles northeast to Navajo Mountain.

These hikes are on Navajo land and hikers need permission from **Navajo Nation Recreational Resource Department**, Box 308, Window Rock, AZ 86515.

Llama Treks

Canyonlands Llamas, Box 1911, Moab, UT 84532, 801/259-5739, offers day trips and overnight pack trips with llamas.

Red Rock 'N Llamas, PO Box 1304, Boulder, UT 84716, 801/335-7325, offers guided, outfitted hiking trips with llamas packing all the gear and supplies through Capitol Reef National Park, along the Escalante River, or into the Glen Canyon National Recreation Area–in short, some of the most remote terrain anywhere. Scheduled trips of three to five days operate from March to October, with easy to moderately difficult day hikes from base camps into Hall's Creek Narrows, the Escalante River, Box Death Hollow, or Choprock Narrows. Day and customized trips are available.

By Horse

MOAB/CANYONLANDS/SAN JUAN COUNTY

Pack Creek Ranch (PO Box 1270, Moab, UT, 84532, 801/259-5505) offers the ultimate get away on overnight horseback trips to a base camp in the La Sal Mountains. Participants follow old cowboy trails, drink cold, clear, natural spring water, inhale the scent of pine forests, and take in stunning views of Utah's canyon country. Sleeping bag, tent, Dutch oven cooking, horses and tack are supplied. Bonuses are campfire stories, some of them true, about the Southwest. The family running this outfit has been in this area for a long time and knows it well.

Sunset Trail Rides, PO Box 302, Moab, UT 84532, 801/259-4362, offers trail rides by the hour in the La Sals and red rock country, or a two-hour evening ride, with a campfire dinner included. The rides leave from a ranch nine miles south of Moab on US 191.

Ed Black Horse Tours, Mexican Hat, Utah 84531, 801/739-4285, focuses mainly on the Monument Valley area, covered in the Navajo Nation & Hopiland chapter, but also offers customized canyon country horseback trips.

San Juan Horseback Tours, Mexican Hat, Utah 84531, 801/683-2283, offers horseback trips in San Juan County.

CAPITOL REEF NATIONAL PARK

Hondoo Rivers & Trails, PO Box 98, Torrey, UT 84775, 801/425-3519 or 800/332-2696, runs a number of pack trips into the deep backcountry of the Colorado Plateau. A five-day fall foliage ride is offered in late-September through Capitol Reef National Park, and the Escalante and Circle Cliffs Wilderness Areas. Other five-day trips into Capitol Reef are scheduled June through September.

Five- or eight-day rides in May explore the San Rafael Swell. A six-day trip in June coincides with the peak wildflower blooming season in the Wasatch Plateau, and another six-day trip through the Henry Mountains in July follows the trail of free-roaming herds of buffalo. Trips are for a maximum of 10 riders, and stick to good to rugged trails suitable for riders of all abilities, with options of challenging terrain for experienced riders. Trips begin and end in Torrey.

Outlaw Trails, Inc., Box 129, Hanksville, UT 84734, 801/542-3221 or 801/542-3421, offers multi-day horseback trips in Glen Canyon National Recreation Area, Canyonlands National Park Maze District, Capitol Reef National Park, and surrounding areas.

Rim Rock Ranch, Torrey, UT 84775, 801/425-3843, offers guided horseback trips in Capitol Reef National Park.

Color Country Outfitters, 2523 East Route 24, Torrey, UT 84775, 801/425-3598, offers guided horseback rides and overnight trips into the Capitol Reef area.

Horseback Outfitters

Escalante Canyon Outfitters (PO Box 325, Boulder, UT 84716, 801/335-7311) offers guided horseback trips in the Escalante River canyons.
Scenic Safaris, PO Box 278, Cannonville, UT 84718, 801/679-8536, runs guided trail rides and overnight pack trips in and around Kodachrome Basin State Park.

Canyon Trail Rides, PO Box 128, Tropic, UT 84776, 801/772-3967, offers half-day trail rides in Bryce Canyon and Zion National Parks.

Bryce-Zion Trail Rides, PO Box 128, Tropic, UT, 884736, 801/679-8665, has two locations: Bryce Lodge and Zion Lodge. They offer trail rides through Bryce Canyon and Zion National Parks. There are several trails at Bryce that are used for horseback trips. The Zion rides include a one-hour trip from the Zion Lodge to the Virgin River, a three-hour trip on Sand Bench Trail, or a day-long outing from the east entrance station on UT 9 (Zion-Mt. Carmel Highway) to Cable Mountain.

Ruby's Inn offers trail rides through Bryce Canyon National Park. For information, see below, under Torrey to Bryce Canyon Accommodations.

Eagle Basin Outfitters & Guide Service, PO Box 947, Parowan, UT 84761, 801/477-8837, runs guided horseback trips in the Markagunt Plateau area, in the vicinity of Brian Head.

Rick Marchal Pack Saddle Trips, Box 918, Hurricane, UT 84737, 801/635-4950, offers horseback trips in the Pine Valley Mountains Wilderness and surrounding areas.

Pine Valley Lodge operates guided horseback trips in the Pine Valley Mountains Wilderness Area. For information see below, under Cedar City/St. George Accommodations.

Snow Canyon Riding Stables, PO Box 140, Santa Clara, UT 84765, 801/628-2255, offers trail rides and overnight pack trips based out of the park, 12 miles northwest of St. George, off UT 18.

CATTLE DRIVES & ROUNDUPS

Dalton Gang Outfitters, PO Box 8, Monticello, UT 84535, 801/587-2416 operate a 200,000-acre ranch they consider a real cowboy outfit in the brushy, rocky deserts and canyons of the Blue Mountains, bordering Canyonlands National Park and the Colorado River.

A maximum of six guests can ride horses from dawn to dusk, eat Dutch oven meals, and camp out under the stars or in cabins without electricity, some with bathrooms, some without running water. Cattle work is done much the way it was 100 years ago and varies according to the time of year. It includes branding, round-ups, and trailing cattle and horses off the winter range in spring. In the fall you can haul hay, put out salt, round up yearlings for market, and drive cattle off the mountain. In winter you can cut ice and trail cattle to new ranges.

Pace Ranch, PO Box 98, Torrey, UT 84775, 801/425-3519 or 800/332-2696, is the headquarters for **Hondoo Rivers & Trails**. The ranch moves 700 head of cattle from winter to summer pasture and back again, in spring or fall. It's a six-day, 25-mile trip through

Capitol Reef National Park, passing through sculpted canyons featuring red rock spires and remote desert terrain.

On Wheels

A popular and relatively quick way to reach remote spots is by driving the many, many miles of four-wheel-drive roads that criss-cross Utah's public lands. Driving on some of these so-called roads can be hazardous. A certain level of off-road driving experience and skill is recommended.

A number of other scenic back roads are suitable for ordinary cars and, for those with the legs and lungs to make it, there are lesser tracks for bikes all over the area, ranging from short, easy loops, to multi-day, cross-country routes in extremely remote terrain. For bike riders who don't mind the companionship of gas combustion engines, jeep roads are generally pretty good bike routes, too, not to mention their appeal for cross-country skiers and snowmobilers in winter, when these roads are generally unplowed and inaccessible to automobiles.

Some of the more accessible driving, jeeping and biking routes in various areas are listed below. Route-finding can be a tricky affair; if you plan to travel in the backcountry you need to be prepared and self-sufficient. Accurate maps are a must and, since many of these excursions will take you far from the beaten path, it's wise to consider possibilities such as mechanical breakdowns in advance.

There are also restrictions to consider. On Forest Service and BLM land, off-highway vehicles are permitted only in designated areas. Consult with the administering agency for details, including brochures and maps for off-road vehicle use. There are also many four-wheel-drive areas within or near state parks. Off-highway vehicle use is not allowed in National Parks, wilderness areas or on lake shores. For information about highway road conditions in Utah phone 800/492-2400.

A brochure titled *Southern Utah's Byways and Backways* details a number of driving routes. It is available from Visitor Information Centers in Moab, Monticello or St. George.

Canyonlands Marketing Cooperative, PO Box 698, Moab, UT 84532, 801/259-8431, offers several useful books as part of a Canyon Country Off-Road Vehicles Trail Series. They include such titles as *Arches and the La Sals Areas*, *Canyon Rims and Needles Areas*, *Island Area*, and *The Maze Area*. In addition, they offer *Canyon Country Mountain Biking* and *Canyon Country Slickrock Hiking and*

Biking, as well as topographical maps of Arches and Canyonlands National Parks, Glen Canyon National Recreation Area and Grand Gulch Primitive Area.

Local bike shops can also provide information on bike trails. For additional information about the Moab/Canyonlands area, contact the **Grand County Tourism Council** (PO Box 550, 805 North Main Street, Moab, UT 84532, 801/259-8825 or 800/635-6622), US Forest Service, BLM, or National Park Service offices in Moab.

MOAB DRIVING TRIPS

You need not hug death-defying, cliff-side jeep roads to see the beautiful country around Moab. There are many short scenic drives that can be accomplished by careful drivers in ordinary vehicles.

Just north of Moab, **Scenic Byway 279 (Potash Road)** runs west off US 191. It follows the Colorado River for 12 paved miles, past Indian ruins and rock art sites.

The Potash Road Petroglyphs are a series of rock art panels lining sheer cliffs for two miles on the north side of the road, eight miles west of Moab. The panels contain human, animal, and geometric designs estimated to span periods from 7,000 B.C. to 1,300 A.D. There are several road turn-outs to the petroglyphs. The Potash Road turns to dirt at the Potash Plant (that gave the road its name) continuing on to the Shafer and White Rim Trails–this stretch is recommended for four-wheel-drives only.

Kane Creek Canyon follows the other side of the Colorado River, south of the Potash Road, and reveals a tremendous variety of canyon country scenery. The road passes numerous petroglyphs, then turns into gravel after four miles and winds its way for another six miles into remote, otherworldly sandstone cliffs. Four-wheel-drive vehicles can continue across Kane Springs Creek to Hurrah Pass.

La Sal Mountain Loop Road covers 60 miles starting and ending in Moab, varying in elevation from 4,000 feet to 8,000 feet. Open from May to October. You can drive the route starting at either end. Along the way, numerous jeep roads branch off from the main road.

If you drive north of Moab, the trip starts on US 191 north to UT 128 and passes Matrimony Springs on the way to the mouth of Negro Bill Canyon, a popular hiking and biking area, the Big Bend Recreation Area and White Ranch, where a number of movies have been filmed. The loop turns south on **Castle Valley Road** and climbs into the foothills of the La Sals. Five miles south is a good view of Castle Rock, and the Priest and Nuns formation. In another six miles you pass the remains of a mining town at Castleton.

A mile past Castleton, you can head off the main road to visit Pinhook Battlefield, where you can see the graves of eight settlers who were killed by Indians in 1881, or the area of Miner's Basin, where you can spot remains of an 1890s gold-mining camp at 10,000 feet elevation. Four-wheel-drive vehicles are recommended for these trips.

About 11 miles farther on the main road, another turn-off leads to Warner Lake, a five-mile trip on a good gravel road to a camp-ground, mountain lake, and hiking trails at 9,200 feet. A few miles farther is a turn-off at Mill Creek Bridge to Lake Oowah, site of another small lake and campground. Another mile or so farther is a fairly rugged dirt road leading to Gold Basin and Geyser Pass, at 10,600 feet.

The main loop road passes through prime habitat for deer and elk as it winds down the mountains. Farther on, it passes Ken's Lake, a reservoir supplying Moab's water and also a good spot for fishing, swimming, or windsurfing, before returning to US 191 south of Moab.

JEEPING/FOUR-WHEEL-DRIVE TRIPS

Moab

The **Moab Rim Trail** starts off Kane Creek Boulevard, 2.5 miles from the intersection with Main Street. The trail climbs for a mile and a half to the top of a plateau offering stunning views of Moab, Arches, and the La Sals. Hikers who follow this route can continue southeast to connect with the **Hidden Valley Trail** which leads five miles back to US 191. If driving, the jeep road continues to meander up steep slopes and down through several sandy washes, with separate short side roads leading to viewpoints, before ending near the top of the Hidden Valley Trail.

Pritchett Canyon Road is not for the faint-hearted, but it does provide good canyon views of several arches and the Behind The Rocks area–a maze of enormous rock fins without maintained trails. For directions see below, under Moab Mountain Biking.

Within Arches National Park, there is a dirt road turn-off from the main road, a mile before the Devil's Garden area. The road covers 8.5 scenic miles through Salt Valley, to Klondike Bluffs and Tower Arch.

Lockhart Basin Road is a 57-mile paved and gravel road that starts south of Moab, off US 191, and connects with UT 211, a few miles east of the Needles District Visitor Center.

Tag-A-long Expeditions, 425 North Main Street, Moab, UT, 84532, 801/259-8946 or 800/453-3292, fax 801/259-8990, is a major tour operator in canyon country, offering a variety of guided trips, including three-day overland jeep adventure in Canyonlands National Park. During the day, botanists and Canyonland specialists guide you through remote areas of the Needles District, with chances to hike to Indian ruins and rarely visited red rock grottoes.

Also scheduled are four-wheel-drive charters for three or more passengers, half-day and full-day Canyonlands trips to Island in the Sky or Angel Arch, and four-wheel-drive trips combined with jet-boat tours.

Lin Ottinger's Tours, 137 North Main, Moab, UT 84532, 801/259-7312, runs jeep trips to the most scenic view points and some of the best places for Indian petroglyphs, led by local rock specialists.

Great Jeep 'n Guide, 550 North Main, Moab, UT 84532, 801/259-4567, runs guided four-wheel-drive trips, as wel' as sunset safaris. On the safari, you follow one of their jeeps in your own four-wheel-drive vehicle. The route is a scenic tour around Moab and includes a trailside dinner of Navajo tacos on frybread.

Four-wheel-drive rentals (with or without bike racks) are available from **Certified Rentals**, 500 South Main Street, Moab, UT 84532, 801/259-6107.

North Main Service, 284 North Main, Moab, UT 84532, 801/259-5242, rents four-wheel-drives.

Farabee Rentals, 234, South Main, Moab, UT 84532, 801/259-7494, fax 801/259-2997, rents four-wheel-drive vehicles and offers trip planning assistance.

Island in the Sky District

Shafer Trail Road begins just past the Visitor Center in the Island in the Sky section of Canyonlands National Park. It was originally a cattle track, and was widened to accommodate vehicles used by uranium prospectors. It's not so bad going down the 1,200 feet in four miles, but it can be difficult coming back up. The road does connect with the White Rim Four-Wheel-Drive Road and the Potash Road (UT 279), so you don't need to drive up it if you prefer not to.

White Rim Four-Wheel-Drive Road gives the best variety of viewpoints of the awesome scenery found on various levels of Island in the Sky, including the high plateaus, the White Rim, and the Colorado River. Access is from the Shafer Trail Road or from the Potash Road.

This is a difficult 100-mile road for experienced drivers in four-wheel-drive vehicles only. Many travellers take a few days for this classic trip, with overnight camping at primitive campgrounds along the route. However, backcountry permits and reservations are required for the campgrounds; These may be obtained in person or by mail, for free, at the Visitor Center, or from the Moab office of the National Park Service. Remember: there are no services or water sources anywhere along this route so plan ahead.

North American River Expeditions & Canyonlands Tours, 543 North Main, Moab UT 84532, 801/259-5865 or 800/342-5938, fax 801/259-2296, offers jeep trips through the Island in the Sky and the Needles Districts of Canyonlands National Park.

Needles District/San Juan County

Interlaced canyon networks, arches, spires, pinnacles, Indian ruins and rock art petroglyphs are all found along four-wheel-drive trails in the Needles District backcountry.

Relatively easy four-wheel-drive roads go into **Lavender Canyon** and **Davis Canyon**, east of the park border, off UT 211. Round-trip distances on the roads are 26 miles and 20 miles, respectively.

Colorado Overlook Four-Wheel-Drive Road starts at the Needles ranger station and covers a 14-mile round trip, highlighted by slickrock terrain and a stunning river view.

Salt Creek Canyon Four-Wheel-Drive Road starts close to the Cave Springs Trail (see above, under Touring South of Moab/ Canyonlands (Needles District) and covers 30 miles round trip, including fascinating canyon territory and numerous arches. A side road goes from here to the often-photographed, 150-foot-tall Angel Arch.

Horse Canyon Four-Wheel-Drive Road veers to the left at the mouth of Salt Creek Canyon and covers a 13-mile round trip through similar scenery.

Elephant Hill Four-Wheel-Drive Loop Road starts at the Elephant Hill picnic area (see above, under Touring South of Moab/ Canyonlands (Needles District) and includes a challenging, steep climb up Elephant Hill over the 10-mile round trip. This is a demanding route, it has cramped slots barely wide enough for a car to squeeze through, rock stairs, and a spot where you must back up to the edge of a cliff to make a three-point turn. Several hiking trailheads can be reached from the road, plus other four-wheel-drive roads such as **Silver Stairs**, **Cyclone Canyon**, and **Devil's Chute**.

Elk Ridge Road is a dirt road that starts eight miles west of Newspaper Rock State Park on UT 211 and goes 48 miles south to Natural Bridges Road and UT 95. It passes overlooks of the Canyonlands National Park, Dark Canyon Wilderness Area, the Henry and La Sal mountains, and Monument Valley.

South of the Needles District, off US 191 in Monticello, the **Blue Mountain Loop** begins by heading west on 200 South and climbs to within a mile of Abajo Peak (elevation 11,362 feet) at its midpoint. The road covers 22 miles before ending three miles north of Blanding on US 191.

From the center of Blanding, a 38-mile jeep road heads west, traversing **Bears Ears Pass** in the Abajos (elevation 9,058 feet), on the way to Natural Bridges National Monument.

Farabee 4x4 Rentals, Highway 666, Monticello, UT 84535, 801/587-2597, or South US 191, Blanding, UT 84511, 801/678-2955, rents jeeps.

Henry Mountains

There are numerous rough dirt roads crossing the Henrys, but conditions vary from bad to worse. Check with the BLM office in Hanksville for current road conditions.

Bull Mountain Road starts on UT 95, three miles north of the north end of UT 276 (north of Lake Powell), and loops westward through the Henrys for 68 miles, ending on UT 276, five miles south of UT 95 (eight miles south of the starting point).

Glen Canyon National Recreation Area/The Maze District

Jeeps and four-wheel-drive vehicles are really the only motor vehicles that can negotiate the long, sandy, or hard-packed clay, washboard roads in the Maze and the surrounding Glen Canyon National Recreation Area.

Contact the Hans Flat Ranger Station or the National Park Service office in Moab (both listed under Touring) for road conditions. Always fill your tank with gas before entering these areas. If possible, carry extra gas, water, food, and emergency gear.

Horseshoe Canyon may be slightly more accessible than the Maze. To reach the very bad jeep road that leads to the oversize petroglyphs of the Great Gallery, you bear left (north) and drive 21 miles, past the Hans Flat Ranger Station, to the east rim of the canyon. It's a two-mile hike down the steep canyon to the Great Gallery.

The 35-mile road leading to the **Maze Overlook** starts at the ranger station. You can see or hike down to the melted-looking rocks called the Chocolate Drops from the overlook, and there are several other hiking trails that start here. One such trail descends into the canyon below, where you can see larger than life, ancient Indian rock paintings at Harvest Scene.

Capitol Reef National Park

A rough jeep road begins on the other side of Pleasant Creek, eight miles south of the Visitor Center on the scenic drive, then three miles south on **Pleasant Creek Road**.

The **Notom-Bullfrog Road** covers 60 miles along the eastern border of the Waterpocket Fold, between UT 24 and Bullfrog Marina, on Lake Powell. It's not strictly a four-wheel-drive road, but one is certainly recommended for any lengthy excursions.

Burr Trail Road bisects Notom Road 30 miles north of Bullfrog and 30 miles south of UT 24. It covers 40 miles, crossing the fold in a series of tight switchbacks between Notom Road and the town of Boulder, west of the Capitol Reef National Park, on UT Scenic Byway 12. The segment through the park is unpaved but normally accessible in a passenger car. It may be hazardous when wet. From the western park boundary to Boulder the road is paved.

Many other four-wheel-drive roads criss-cross the park, and the ones north of UT 24 lead to impressive sites such as Temple of the Sun and Temple of the Moon, in Cathedral Valley. These are pretty rotten roads; particularly so in wet weather. Get advice on conditions in these remote areas from the park rangers at the Visitor Center before heading north on **Hartnet Road**, near the eastern edge of the park off UT 24, or farther east off UT 24, on the **Caineville/Cathedral Valley Road**.

About 20 miles north on the Cathedral Valley Road, **Thousand Lake Mountain Road** starts to the west through Upper Cathedral Valley and loops back to the east, covering 35 miles and ending back on Cathedral Valley Road.

One road that may not be so bad covers 25 miles into Cathedral Valley from the west, through Loa and Fremont. It crosses Thousand Lake Mountain, then drops down into the valley.

Jeep rentals, guided day tours of Cathedral Valley and Hell's Backbone, and multi-day backcountry jeep trips and rock art seminars are offered by **Hondoo Rivers & Trails**, in Torrey (PO Box 98, Torrey, UT 84775, 801/425-3519 or 800/332-2696).

Escalante

There are numerous four-wheel-drive roads in this area. The BLM or National Park Service offices in Escalante can provide detailed information.

The **Burr Trail Road**, which is accessible to passenger cars in good weather, slices eastward across the Waterpocket Fold from Boulder, with a rough 30-mile jeep road leading south across Horse Canyon, Wolverine Canyon, Little Death Hollow, and Silver Falls Creek, where it loops back north to the Burr Trail Road.

Hell's Backbone Road follows the old pack train route between Escalante and Boulder for 38 miles through the mountainous terrain of the Aquarius Plateau. It is accessible to passenger cars in good weather, though not when the road is wet, and the area does get heavy snow which usually keeps the road closed until May. Many four-wheel-drive roads branch off from the main road to streams and fishing holes, including **Posey Lake Road**, which goes 40 miles north from Escalante, through Dixie National Forest. Access is through Escalante, or west of UT 12, three miles south of Boulder.

Hole-in-the-Rock Road follows a rugged 56-mile trail cut by Mormon settlers in 1878. It took them six weeks to build a road through Hole-in-the-Rock, overlooking what was then the Colorado River (today it's Lake Powell). They had to lower wagons and livestock through the hole and the historic journey, from Escalante to Bluff, took six months to complete. Today, you can drive from Escalante to near the edge of Lake Powell in a four-wheel-drive. In dry weather, passenger cars can make it most of the way. The road heads south, five miles east of Escalante, off UT 12, and crosses Harris Wash to Devil's Garden in 12 miles. The garden contains lots of improbable balanced rock forms. Farther on, after 36 miles, is Dance Hall Rock, a stone amphitheater near where the original Mormon settlers camped for several weeks while road construction continued farther up ahead. The last few miles of Hole-in-the-Rock Road are pretty rugged. At the road's end you can walk to the actual hole in the rock, through which you can see Lake Powell. You can't drive down the last half-mile to the lake, but you can hike it.

A shortcut to Lake Powell is the **Smoky Mountain Road**, a 78-mile dirt and gravel road, south from Escalante. On the way are great views of the lake, Navajo Mountain, Bryce Canyon, Table Cliffs, and Boulder Mountain. The southern end of the road is on US 89, at Big Water, 20 miles north of Page.

Bryce Canyon National Park/
Kodachrome Basin State Park

Tropic Reservoir, three miles west of the junction of UT 12 and UT 63, then south into Red Canyon, is the start of an extensive four-wheel-drive area known as the **East Fork Trail System**. For information contact the Powell Ranger District in Panguitch (see above, under Touring Torrey to Bryce Canyon National Park). The longest road in the trail system, **East Fork of the Sevier River Road**,goes south for 60 miles from the UT 12 intersection, three miles west of Bryce Canyon.

About 35 miles south of Escalante, a lengthy dirt road and a partially paved one (probably both best attempted in a four-wheel-drive vehicle), extend past Kodachrome Basin State Park to the south, emerging on US 89 between Kanab and Page, Arizona. The 49-mile-long, partly-paved, **Skutumptah Canyon Road** ends nine miles west of Kanab.

The 40-mile-long **Cottonwood Canyon Road** meets the highway 40 miles farther east, closer to Page.

Several multi-day hiking trails are accessed off these roads–in Hackberry or the Upper Paria River Canyons. Contact Kodachrome Basin park rangers for current conditions and information.

Ten miles south of the park, off the Cottonwood Canyon Road, is a one-mile turn-off to Grosvenor Arch, a giant-size double arch named for an official at the National Geographic Society.

Cedar City/St. George/Zion National Park

Five miles east of Cedar City is the north end of the **Kolob Terrace Road**, a partly-paved 50-mile stretch that passes through a little visited part of Zion National Park. The narrow, steep road passes the Lava Point Fire Lookout and Tabernacle Dome, on the Kolob Terrace Highlands, before terminating in Virgin, west of the main park entrance on UT 9, six miles east of I-15.

There are quite a few backcountry roads in the **Dixie National Forest** southwest of Cedar City and north of St. George. Contact the Pine Valley Ranger district office in St. George for information (see above, under Touring Cedar City/St. George). Other four-wheel-drive routes wind through areas south of Hurricane and Springdale to the Arizona border. Contact the BLM office in St. George (see above, under Touring Cedar City/St. Georg) for information on the **Sand Mountains** area.

Coral Pink Sand Dunes State Park, south of Mt. Carmel Junction, off US 89, is popular with dune-buggy fans. Guided tours in all-terrain vehicles are offered from April to November by the **United States Trail Riding Association**, PO Box 35, Mt. Carmel, UT 84755, 801/648-5358.

Page, Arizona/Lake Powell

Most people come to Lake Powell for the water, not the jeeping possibilities, which are limited by the fact that the area east of Page is largely Navajo land and is not generally open to unsupervised visitation. The safest bet is to take a guided jeep tour with **Lake Powell Jeep Tours**, 108 Lake Powell Boulevard, Page, AZ 86040, 602/645-5501.

MOUNTAIN BIKING

Fat tires and red rock terrain seem to have an affinity, or so it would appear from the profusion of mountain biking enthusiasts who are almost magnetically drawn to southern Utah. Although some of the popular trails may sometimes seem like a frat party, it's more than likely you can pedal your way into privacy if that is what you want to do.

Utah's slickrock desert and canyon country is legendary mountain biking terrain, with forested mountains and sagebrush range. Sometimes you can tour slickrock in the morning, before temperatures rise, then ride to a cool, alpine lake in the afternoon, when the desert heats up. In general, biking is restricted to designated trails or roads. Off-trail biking is the surest way to bring even tighter restrictions on mountain biking in the future.

Information on road and mountain biking is available from **Bicycle Utah**, PO Box 738, Park City, UT 84060, 801/649-5806, or for fat-tire aficionados, from **Utah Mountain Bike Association**, 801/476- East South Temple, Suite 246, Salt Lake City, UT 84111.

Moab

Moab has clearly become one of the prime mountain biking areas in the country, and for good reason. The canyonlands in the vicinity of the town provide absolutely incredible biking terrain, ranging from 13,000-foot peaks to high mountain meadows, and from high desert flats to harrowing canyon-side descents. In fact, you may feel out of place in Moab without a mountain bike strapped to your vehicle.

There are hundreds of backcountry trails within easy reach of town, as well as jeep trails and driving routes (see above) that are fine for mountain bike riders. Paved roads through such places as Arches and Canyonlands National Parks are certainly fair game for bike riders.

The Moab Slickrock Bike Trail is perhaps the best known Moab bike route, with a main loop covering 10.5 miles. It starts east of town, out past the town dump, 2.5 miles up Sand Flats Road. There is a 2.5-mile practice loop at the start of the trail, which is especially recommended for those not accustomed to biking on rock. The trail is painted with broken white lines, and yellow caution lines–it's a good idea to stick to these markings as diversions from the main route can get you lost or in serious trouble. There are numerous sheer drops near the trail. Even those following the main loop will probably spend part of the time walking their bike up steep slopes. The route is filled with tight switchbacks and has earned a reputation of being more than challenging. Don't be fooled by the distance, this is a tough ride, noted for technical difficulty as well as beauty. Allow four to six hours to complete the loop, more if you digress on side trails leading to scenic spots overlooking Moab, the La Sals, the Colorado River, and Negro Bill Canyon.

Hurrah Pass Trail covers 30 miles from the junction of 5th West Street and Kane Creek Road, at the south end of Moab. It's rated as easy to moderate, but it's no walk in the park. There are steep sections leading to the pass, but your sweat will be rewarded with a concentrated mini-version of the variety of scenery to be found throughout the region.

Scenic Byway 279 (see above, under Moab Driving Routes) is a scenic 28-mile round-trip road ride alongside the Colorado River, framed by colorful cliffs containing petroglyphs, and arches, including Jug Handle Arch, perched above the highway, two miles before the end of the pavement.

Monitor and Merrimac Trail starts 15 miles north of Moab's Visitor Center on US 191. Turn left past the railroad tracks and go a half-mile to the trailhead. This is rated a moderate trail and it covers a 13-mile round trip. Along the way you'll pass the Mill Canyon Dinosaur Site, Monitor and Merrimac Buttes, and Determination Tower.

Gemini Bridges Trail takes a full day to travel. A vehicle shuttle needs to be arranged for your return from the 14-mile one-way ride. Your efforts are rewarded by views of the Arches, the La Sals, and the Gemini Bridge formation–two massive rock spans hundreds of feet long that arch gracefully from a sheer cliff to the ground. The trail starts 12.5 miles north of Moab on UT 313, toward Deadhorse Point and is rated as moderate, with much of the trail heading downhill. A number of side trails off the main route lead to stunning view sites.

Pritchett Canyon Road starts on Kane Creek Boulevard, a little before the road goes up into Kane Springs Canyon and covers a nine-mile round-trip ride up the canyon to Pritchett Arch. This is also a tricky jeep road.

White Rim Trail in Island in the Sky, is another rugged jeep road that is good for a multi-day mountain biking trip. It covers 100 miles, 75 of which are in the National Park. The trail winds between the mesa top and the River District, descending 1,000 feet to the White Rim Sandstone Bench. On one side of the narrow trail, plunging sandstone cliffs drop 1,000 feet into maze-like canyons. On the other side, sheer rock walls, broken only by occasional hanging gardens watered by seeps, soar 1,500 feet above.

Kokopelli's Trail is probably the place to go for maximum mountain biking adventure. It is 128 miles long and connects Moab with Grand Junction, Colorado, encompassing dramatic canyon country and mountain scenery. It starts at the trailhead for the Slickrock Bike Trail and entails a 4,000-foot ascent.

The trip the other way, from Grand Junction, is suitable for active intermediate to advanced riders looking for rolling terrain, challenging climbs, and descents. It starts on a single-track trail hugging canyon walls along the Colorado River, and rises to expanses above the Colorado Plateau, with jagged snow peaks looming in the distance, in contrast to the horizontal red rock canyon terrain.

Climbing into the forested La Sals, the 12,000-foot snow caps are closer, while the canyons you've left behind drop abruptly below. The 4,000-foot descent into Moab begins amid high mountain pine and aspen, drops into sparser pinyon- and juniper-clad slopes, and ends on the sandstone domes of the Slickrock Trail.

Area bike shops can give you details about the Kokopelli Trail, which was named after the arched-back flute player whose image graced ancient Indian petroglyphs and pictographs. The Hopi Indians consider Kokopelli a magical creature. As with so many of these things, today you cannot avoid depictions of Kokopelli on souvenirs such as t-shirts and coffee cups. Despite commercialization of the image, the trail is indeed a magical journey. Vehicle support is recommended.

For further biking information or guided tours, as well as bike sales, service and rentals around Moab, contact the following sources:

Western Spirit Cycling, 38 South 100 West, Moab, UT 84532, 801/259-8732 or 800/845-BIKE, offers "civilized tours in uncivilized terrain," including guided and supported bike tours in Canyonlands Park, on the White Rim Trail, and in the Abajo Mountains. Bike rentals are available.

Poison Spider Bicycles/Nichols Expeditions, 479 North Main, Moab, UT 84532, 801/259-7882, offers rentals, sales, and service.

Kaibab Mountain/Desert Bike Tours, 391 South Main Street, Moab, UT 84532, 801/259-7423 or 800/451-1133, offers mountain bike sales and rentals, clothing, accessories, and camping equipment rentals. Also: Fully supported mountain bike tours, customized whitewater rafting/biking combination tours, and daily mountain biking descents are offered. Tours for between four and 12 riders follow hidden roads in deep, red-rock canyons and across towering mesas, including Canyonlands' White Rim Trail and routes in the rarely visited Maze District. Tours are planned to accommodate all levels of ability and include a fully-equipped support vehicle along with friendly, knowledgeable guides who attend to all details, including gourmet trail-side meals. Combination trips are also offered, mixing all outdoor activities in five- or seven-day trips. These include biking, rafting, and scenic flights.

Rim Cyclery, 94 West 1st North, Moab, UT 84532, 801/259-5333, offers bike rentals, sales and service, as well as camping and climbing equipment sales.

Descent River Expeditions & Mountain Bike Tours, 321 North Main, PO Box 1267, Moab, UT 84532, 801/259-7983 or 800/833-1278, fax 801/259-5823, offers guided, vehicle-supported bike trips on the White Rim, and in the Needles and Maze districts of Canyonlands National Park. Also: Mountain bike combination tours, meeting with watersport boats in Cataract Canyon, are available.

Slickrock Adventures, PO Box 1400, Moab, UT 84532, 801/259-6996, offers guided mountain biking excursions.

Scenic Byways Bicycle Touring, 942 East 7145 South, Suite 105, Midvale, UT 84047, 801/566-2662, offers guided, vehicle-supported mountain bike excursions of two to six days, with Dutch-oven meals included, for all levels of ability, in Utah's canyon country and mountains. Also: Custom trips, equipment rentals, and combination biking/river trips are available.

Backroads Bicycle Touring, 1516 5th Street, Berkeley, CA 94710, 510/527-1555 or 800/245-3874, fax 510/527-1444, offers six-day trips on off-road bike trails, jeep trails, and paved roads through Arches and Canyonlands National Parks.

Four Corners Center for Experiential Learning, 1760 Broadway, Grand Junction, CO 81503, 303/858-3607, fax 303/858-7861, offers customized bike trips of one to 12 days for two to eight riders in the Moab area. The excursions include descents to the Colorado River and all-day or overnight trips on the Kokopelli Trail between Moab and Grand Junction, CO.

Roads Less Traveled, PO Box 8187, Longmont, CO 80501, 303/678-8750 or 800/488-8483, offers guided, vehicle-supported bike trips for a maximum of 13 riders on quiet backroads and trails. Meals and accommodations are in century-old inns, secluded guest ranches, mountain huts, or tents. A five-day, five-night biking and camping tour, offered in late May or late September, covers the Kokopelli Trail between Grand Junction, CO and Moab. A five-day, four-night trip offered weekly in April, May, September, and October, along the White Rim in Canyonlands National Park, moves at a relaxed pace, with time for hikes to hidden canyons, Indian ruins, and afternoon swims. Special interest tours for singles, families with children over 12, or adults over 50 are available.

Holiday River & Bike Expeditions, 544 East 3900 South, Salt Lake City, UT 84107, 801/266-2087 or 800/624-6323, fax 801/266-1448, runs guided, vehicle-supported, four-day mountain bike trips on the White Rim Trail, or through the Maze District. Trips combining three days of biking on the White Rim or in the Maze, followed by four days of rafting in Cataract Canyon are available.

Needles District

The Colorado River Overlook mostly follows a jeep trail over 15 miles of moderate riding varying only 250 feet in elevation. The ride can usually be accomplished in three or four hours. Along the way there are magnificent views of deep river canyons, the Needles, Junction Butte, Island in the Sky, Deadhorse Point, the La Sals and the Abajos. The ride starts at the Needles District Visitor Center, 36 miles west of US 191 on UT 211, and essentially follows Salt Creek to its confluence with the Colorado River.

Beyond the Visitor Center, head north on the gravel road marked Colorado Overlook and follow it for 7.5 miles to a spectacular, multi-colored, layer-cake overlook of Salt Creek Canyon and the Colorado River extending for miles to the north and south.

There are many other good bike riding trails in the Needles District, including the challenging, steep **Elephant Hill Road**, beginning at the Elephant Hill picnic area. For information see above under Needles District Jeeping.

For additional information, including maps and other rides in this area, contact local bike shops or the BLM Grand Resource Area office in Moab.

Monticello

Hot desert biking gives way to cooler climes on the **Gold Queen Basin Trail**, a nine-mile route through the Abajo Mountains, west of town. The route starts on a paved road and leads to the inoperative Blue Mountain Ski Area. From there it winds through aspen and spruce forest along the way to views of 11,360-foot Abajo Peak, and finishes close to Loyd's Lake, near Monticello.

Bicycle rentals are available from **Monticello Cyclery**, 248 South Main, Monticello, UT 84535, 801/587-2138.

Mexican Hat

Valley of the Gods is a 27-mile loop rated as moderate. If you complete the whole loop without a vehicle shuttle, half of the ride is on paved highways, the other half on winding, dirt and gravel roads leading through remote territory sporting massive stone monoliths which rise from the valley floor. The ride can start at either end of the loop near small signs posted for the Valley of the Gods. One end of the loop is nine miles northeast of Mexican Hat on US 163. The other end is nine miles northwest of Mexican Hat on UT 261.

Muley Point Overlook is a short, easy, four-mile, one-way road that starts a mile north of the western terminus of Valley of the Gods on UT 261 and leads west. Muley Point Overlook offers outstanding views of Monument Valley, the Goosenecks of the San Juan River, Navajo Mountain, as well as the Abajos and Henrys.

Glen Canyon National Recreation Area/The Maze District/Goblin Valley

Panorama Point is a 17-mile ride that is considered moderate. No off-trail riding is permitted to Panorama Point, which affords staggering views of Utah's canyonlands and as far away as Colorado's San Juan Mountains. It's a long way to the start, though. Go 20 miles north of Hanksville on UT 24, then travel east for 25 miles at a sign for Hans Flat Ranger Station. At the ranger station you must pick up a free backcountry permit, then continue south for 2.5 miles to the sign for Panorama Point and the start of the bike trail. The road actually drops 500 feet in 8.5 miles on the way to the point. Several spots hug narrow cliff side rims and there are a few steep downhill sections. You can camp at the point or turn around and ride back.

For information about other bike trails within this area contact the Hans Flat Ranger Station (801/259-6513) or the Moab office of the National Park Service.

Goblin Valley State Park is named for the incredibly-shaped hoodoos that look like sculptured incarnations of a disturbing dream. Gravel park roads here are good for bike riding and several routes lead from the park into the San Rafael Reef area.

A few mountain biking possibilities follow, or contact the BLM's Hanksville office (Box 99, Hanksville, Utah 84734, 801/542-3461) for further information.

Little Wild Horse Trail covers around 22 miles from the campground at Goblin Valley, first heading north and out of the park, then west across Wild Horse Creek, passing close to the steep-walled narrows of Little Wild Horse Canyon and Bell Canyon, and through the bottom of Little Horse Creek. It's a moderate ride along the lower edge of the reef, with some sandy stretches, but only a 300-foot elevation change.

Temple Mountain Loop is a shorter but steeper ride, covering loops of eight or 19 miles, with a 1,500-foot change in elevation. Temple Mountain, which from certain angles resembles Mormon temple architecture, is the tallest point on the San Rafael Reef. The ride starts seven miles north of Goblin Valley State Park and turns west on a paved road past abandoned uranium mines and primitive Indian rock art sites. A half-mile after the pavement stops you can go straight for the longer loop, or turn right for the shorter one.

The short loop passes through a heavily-mined area, sticking close to the slopes of Temple Mountain. In another mile the long loop starts climbing and continues to do so for seven miles, passing through layers of rock and onto the top of a forested mesa. The route then turns back toward Temple Mountain, starting a rugged and rocky descent, followed by sandy downhill areas.

Capitol Reef National Park/ Scenic Byway 12/Escalante

Some people, including the author of the best reference book on mountain biking in Utah (see below), think the **Cathedral Valley Loop**, east of Capitol Reef National Park, is one of the premier multi-day mountain bike rides anywhere. It covers 65 miles, best accomplished in three days, with elevations varying by as much as 2,400 feet. Don't try this during rainy weather; you'll probably be slipping and sliding on foot, pushing your bike. Four-wheel-drive-vehicle support is a wise idea, as is alerting the Capitol Reef National Park Rangers about your plans in this remote and isolated area. The route starts 12 miles east of the Capitol Reef Visitor Center on UT 24, then north on **Cathedral Valley Road**, across the Fremont River. After going up and down short steep slopes, it climbs into scenic terrain overlooking the Waterpocket Fold, and briefly crosses the boundary of Capitol Reef National Park. You might want to camp in this area the first night. The route then climbs back through the National Park for another 12 miles, before swinging back on a park road 26 miles from UT 24, and over varied, difficult terrain in Upper Cathedral Valley. It then heads down into Lower Cathedral Valley, and up again over step-like stretches to a ridge-top approximately 55 miles from the start–a good place for another campsite. The third stretch covers more strenuous rugged terrain, along with more great views, that finally leads to UT 24, north of the starting point.

This is a serious outing, requiring a strategy and the logistical support to make your plan work. For more specific details contact park rangers at Capitol Reef National Park and consult the book *Mountain Biking in the Four Corners Region* by Michael McCoy (The Mountaineers 1990).

Notom-Bullfrog Road, a 60-mile-long dirt road along the east side of Waterpocket Fold, is good for biking. It starts nine miles east of the Capitol Reef Visitor Center on UT 24. About 30 miles south of UT 24 it intersects with the Burr Trail Road, which traverses the Waterpocket Fold across the southern portion of Capitol Reef National Park. In another 30 miles it reaches Bullfrog Marina.

Burr Trail Road is also good for biking, either west from the Notom-Bullfrog Road, or from Boulder in the east. From Boulder, the 40-mile-long, partly paved route starts in red hills, passes views of Lake Powell and the Circle Cliffs, and finishes at UT 276 north of Bullfrog Marina.

UT Scenic Byway 12, running south from UT 24 in Torrey, provides a good biking route and access through Boulder to the Burr Trail Road. Between Torrey and Boulder, it offers a sinuous ride over 45 miles of mountainous terrain, topping out at 9,200 feet on Summit Mountain Pass. From Boulder, the road drops down through canyon country for 30 miles into the town of Escalante.

Numerous bike routes branch off into the mountainous area north of Escalante, off **Hell's Backbone Road**, or south of Escalante, off **Hole-in-the-Rock Road**. For additional information contact BLM Teasdale or Escalante district offices.

Kodachrome Basin State Park/Bryce Canyon National Park/ Cedar Breaks National Monument/Zion National Park

Dirt and gravel roads suitable for mountain biking wind through **Kodachrome Basin State Park**–named by the National Geographic Society for its range of colorful sandstone formations–and farther south to connect with US 89 between Kanab and Page, Arizona. For details see above, under Kodachrome Basin State Park Jeeping.

The best riding in the vicinity of Bryce Canyon National Park is probably in Red Canyon, west of the park. Try jeep roads off the **East Fork of the Sevier River Road** (see above, under Bryce Canyon National Park Jeeping), or **Dave's Hollow Trail**, an easy eight-mile round trip. The trail starts a mile north of the National Park's Visitor Center and heads west into the forests of Red Canyon.

Bike rentals at Bryce are available from **Ruby's Inn**. For details see below under Accommodations.

You can ride a bike on **Bryce Park's Scenic Drive**, but it's a narrow road that does fill with traffic during the summer months. Try it in fall when the leaves are changing.

Once known to Indians as "The Circle of Painted Cliffs," Cedar Breaks National Monument contains a half-mile-deep amphitheater comprised of multi-colored rock carved into arches, columns, pinnacles, and terraces. A scenic, but difficult road ride into the area starts west of the park in Cedar City, climbing more than 4,000 feet on **UT 14** and **UT 148**. Although the route can be ridden in reverse, the views are less appealing and the tight switchbacks are actually harder to negotiate under speed, going downhill.

Cedar Breaks overlooks abound on trails crossing lava fields and bristlecone pine forests atop the 10,000-foot-high plateaus surrounding **Brian Head Ski Resort**. There are more than a dozen specified bike trails in the vicinity of Brian Head Peak, all maintained and well-marked by the Forest Service. You can ride one trail, or combine several for an in-depth tour of the mountainous terrain of the Markagunt Plateau.

One of the easier routes is the 10-mile **Scout Camp Loop Trail**. It starts south of the Brian Head Hotel on UT 143, which leads to Bear Flat Road, and from there you should follow the signs to Henderson Lake. Alternatively, try the six-mile **Pioneer Cabin Trail**, also well-signed from a turn-off on Bear Flat Road. A good road route comes down off the mountain from Brian Head onto the Cedar Breaks National Monument scenic drive. The round trip from the resort area on **UT 143** to the end of the scenic drive on **UT 148** covers 16 miles.

Brian Head Cross Country & Murphy's Bike Shop, 223 West Hunter Ridge Drive, PO Box 65, Brian Head, UT 84719, 801/677-2012 or 800/468-4898, is a bike sales, service, and rental operation in the lobby of the Brian Head Hotel. They can provide maps and information on local bike routes.

Another Brian Head area bike shop is **George's Ski Shop**, 612 South Brian Head Boulevard, Brian Head, UT 84719, 801/677-2013.

An advanced mountain biking trail, covering 39 miles one-way, starts 25 miles southeast of Cedar City on UT 14 at Navajo Lake. From the lake, ride south on **Forest Service Road 53** to the cliff tops overlooking the lake, then south on a mostly downhill route that crosses the Virgin River several times, connecting with UT 9 three miles west of the southeastern entrance to Zion National Park.

A similar 50-mile route, the **Kolob Terrace Road**, starts five miles east of Cedar City, but actually goes south through Zion National Park to the town of Virgin. For details, see above, under Cedar City/St. George/Zion National Park Jeeping.

Numerous bike routes are possible in the Dixie National Forest and Pine Valley area. Contact the Pine Valley Ranger District office in St. George (196 East Tabernacle, St. George, UT 84770, 801/673-3431) for information, or inquire at area bike shops (see below).

A popular bike trip is the 24-mile **Snow Canyon Loop**, which begins on pavement in St. George, at the northwest end of Bluff Street, follows UT 91 west through the village of Santa Clara, then heads north on UT 300 to Ivins. From there it becomes a dirt road eastbound to Snow Canyon State Park. The ride passes cacti-studded sand dunes, yucca and pinyon flats, red cliffs, and mesas that have served as backdrops for many movies.

The **New Harmony Trail** is a famed, four-mile single-track ride near the northwest corner of the Pine Valley Mountains Wilderness Area. It starts in the town of New Harmony, a mile north of Zion National Park's Kolob Canyons Road, and heads west.

The name of **Zion National Park's Scenic Drive** is an understatement. A seven-mile road starts at the park's south entrance, off UT 9, passes between purple cliffs and shining mesas, by Zion Lodge. It finishes at the Temple of Sinawava.

Zion-Mt.Carmel Highway cuts across the southeastern corner of the park to the south entrance and is considered an engineering marvel. The ride from Mt. Carmel to the south entrance covers 23 road miles. You first pass between Checkerboard Mesa and the White Cliffs, then the road drops sharply through two tunnels. Check first with the ranger station before riding through this area. Bike riders must be escorted or transported through the tunnels, one of which is a mile long, but with large windows cut in the stone for incredible scenic views of the canyon. Beyond the longer tunnel, a series of switchbacks aid another sharp descent, with views of the Great Arch, East Temple, and the Beehives. Upon reaching the Visitor Center, a number of other famous sights and rock formations can be seen.

Bike riders seeking to escape the congestion around Bryce might try heading south of Springdale into the area of the **Vermillion Cliffs**. The scenery's less spectacular than in the park, but you won't be muscling for road space with motor homes, and the 360 degree views of the park and environs are unforgettable. For information, contact the BLM office in St. George.

Area bike shops that can provide information, service, and bike rentals include the following:

Bike Route, 70 West Center, Cedar City, UT 84720, 801/586-4242, offers sales, service, trail maps, information, rentals, and free minor repairs.

Bicycles Unlimited, 90 South 100 East, St. George, UT 84770, 801/673-4492, offers sales, service, and maps.

Sports Cyclery, 175 West 900 South, St. George, UT 84770, 801/628-1119.

St. George Cyclery, 420 West 145 North, St. George, UT 84770, 801/673-8876.

Just outside of the south entrance to Zion National Park is **Zion Canyon Cycling Company**, 998 Zion Park Boulevard, Springdale, UT 84767, 801/772-3939.

The Road Less Traveled (PO Box 8187, Longmont, CO 80501, 303/678-8750 or 800/488-8483) offers combined biking and hiking trips in early June and early October around Bryce and Zion National Parks, with accommodations nightly at inns offering a pool or hot tub. Trips begin in St. George; some itineraries include walking through Mammoth Cave, visiting an ice cave, cycling the plateau rim above Sunset Cliffs, and riding a bike or a horse through Bryce's rock spires, canyon mazes, and hoodoos. All trips include an exhilarating 4,000-foot, switchback descent to Zion National Park and hiking in Zion.

Timberline Bicycle Tours, 7975 East Harvard, #J, Denver, CO 80231, 303/759-3804, runs five- to nine-day, guided, vehicle-supported bike tours, with overnight reservations at inns and mountain lodges. Itineraries include a road bike tour of Cedar Breaks, Bryce Canyon, Zion, and the North Rim of the Grand Canyon. Bike tours of the Grand Canyon, Sedona, and Colorado's San Juan Mountains are also available.

On Water

RIVER TRIPS

Moab/Canyonlands/Green, Colorado & San Juan Rivers

In Grand County (Moab) and San Juan County (Canyonlands National Park) the abundance of river recreation is staggering, ranging from the rugged wilderness areas of Cataract and Desolation-Gray Canyons, to many more easily accessible areas of the Colorado, Green and San Juan Rivers. There are whitewater rapids and flat water stretches well-suited to canoes, jet boats and small power boats.

For the most part, there are no facilities on the rivers (the San Juan does flow through the small town of Mexican Hat), so planning is critical. Regulations are available from the National Parks Service office in Moab, or the BLM office in Monticello. Among the most popular areas for river recreation are the following:

Westwater Canyon is northeast of Moab and the Fisher Towers. It is the first canyon on the Colorado River within Utah, just west of the Colorado state-line, and was the last stretch of the Colorado to be navigated. The brief, exciting run includes 11 rapids, passing through the oldest exposed rocks in Utah. These Precambrian black rock formations rise into 200-foot-tall, inner canyon walls, above which golden, rust-colored sandstone walls loom. Historic sites along the way include a miner's cabin and an outlaw cave.

The **Colorado River Daily** is located below Westwater, closer to Moab, along UT 128, between Hittle Bottom and Sandy Beach. On a day trip you can raft six rapids and take in red rock views of named formations such as Fisher Towers, Castle Rock, the Priest and Nuns. **Cataract Canyon**, one of the best-known whitewater sections, is within Canyonlands National Park, from the confluence of the Colorado and Green Rivers to Lake Powell, at Hite. The route includes 26 rapids below mammoth red rock walls and spires which tower over the river. Side trip hikes lead to Indian ruins and rock art.

Commercial outfitters take care of everything relating to river travel but independent travellers within National Park boundaries need to have a permit, life jackets, and fire pans for fires. Remember that all trash and solid human waste must be packed out. Contact the National Park Service office in Moab as far in advance as possible to insure you can meet all the permit requirements for independent travel.

Desolation/Gray Canyons are located north of the town of Green River on the river itself, in Utah's deepest canyon. Sixty-seven rapids await whitewater enthusiasts 5,000 feet below the canyon rim at Rock Creek. Along the way there are hundreds of shaded campsites in cottonwood groves, numerous examples of Indian rock art, stunning red-rock topography, and outlaw hideouts.

The San Juan River forms the boundary between the Navajo Nation and San Juan County and is one of the fastest flowing major rivers in the United States. It flows from Colorado's San Juan Mountains through New Mexico and into an uncrowded wilderness of broad sandy beaches and chiseled, striated canyons in Utah. With only moderate whitewater, it is popular for family rafting trips lasting three to five days. These typically run for 30 miles from Bluff to Mexican Hat. Despite the modest whitewater, the river currents can be tricky on the San Juan, which is noted for deceptive and wave. The river is not recommended for novice rafters, canoeists, or kayakers travelling without an experienced companion. Several outfitters offer guided trips. Otherwise, a permit is required. Contact the BLM office in Monticello (435 North Main, PO Box 7, Monticello, UT 84535, 801/587-2141) far in advance of any independent San Juan River trip.

Sand Island Campground, three miles southeast of Bluff, is a popular put-in site. You can walk from the campground to see more than a mile of petroglyphs on the north side of the river. A number of the carvings feature Kokopelli, while more modern designs include river runners' graffiti.

River House Ruin is west of Bluff on the San Juan and is six miles southwest of the Sand Island Bridge. It is a multi-room dwelling occupied by the Anasazi from 900 to 1300 A.D. It is constructed of sandstone and clay mortar and situated in a cave. River runners or those alighting here by land via US 163 can stop to walk freely through the walled ruins which are still littered with fragments of pottery and stone tools.

Moab is the epicenter of the river outfitting business for all these routes, with daily raft trip departures of half-day, one-day or overnight itineraries down Cataract, Westwater, and Desolation canyons. Also available are jet-boats, affording a quicker experience of the rivers and canyons, plus alternatives for rafters who do not want to paddle. And a number of operators based outside the Moab area also offer trips in the region.

Adrift Adventures, PO Box 577, Moab, UT 84532, 801/259-8594 or 800/874-4483, fax 801/259-7628, offers three- or four-day motorized trips, or a five-day oar-powered trip. The longer trip, through Cataract Canyon, is especially wild in May and June. A four-day trip through Desolation and Gray Canyons on the Green River is great fun for families. Three-day Labyrinth Canyon trips on the Green River provide 45 miles of rafting and canoeing in waters without rapids. There are half-day and full-day rafting trips on the Colorado River and combination adventures such as a morning of horseback riding in Arches National Park, followed by an afternoon of rafting the Colorado River. Two-day horseback trips in the La Sal Mountains can be combined with four days of rafting in Cataract Canyon. A three-day Cataract Canyon river trip can be combined with two days of jeeping through Canyonlands back to Moab. Any river trip can be combined with two days at Pack Creek Ranch.

Sheri Griffith Expeditions, PO Box 1324, Moab, UT 84532, 801/259-8229 or 800/332-2439, fax 801/259-2226, offers scheduled river trips on the Colorado and Green Rivers from May to August. They are soft on risk but high in adventure and pampering.

Trips from two to five days use paddle- and oar-powered boats in Cataract, Westwater or Desolation Canyons. For Colorado River trips minimum age is 10. On the Green River minimum age is 5 years old.

Also: A number of specialized trips are offered. These include trips for women only, personal and professional development seminars for adults, family trips, and Cataract Canyon luxury trips featuring Canyonlands sunsets while a waiter flambés your dessert.

Combination trips are also available. These can include three days of mountain biking combined with four days of river rafting (April through September) or two days of horseback riding in the La Sal Mountains (in summer) or Canyonlands (in spring and fall) combined with a raft trip in Cataract Canyon.

Tag-A-Long Expeditions (425 North Main Street, Moab, UT, 84532, 801/259-8946 or 800/453-3292, fax 801/259-8990) offers a variety of river trips in Cataract, Westwater, and Desolation Canyons. Major class whitewater trips of three or four days through Cataract Canyon are offered during high water season. A six-day trip combines Westwater and Cataract Canyons river trips with a half-day of land exploration of Arches National Park. An overnight stay at a Moab motel is included.

A Westwater Canyon "Rapid Escape" trip is a two-day whitewater trip. "Wilderness Accent Expeditions" are led by experts who focus on geology, natural history, desert ecology, and ancient and modern Indian cultures. Also: Half-day and full-day rafting trips, and winter backcountry ski tours are available.

North American River Expeditions & Canyonlands Tours (543 North Main, Moab UT 84532, 801/259-5865 or 800/342-5938), also offers river trips including full-day raft trips, half-day jet-boat trips, full-day tours combining jet boating and jeep touring, and two to four-day motorized raft trips through Cataract Canyon.

The San Juan Touring Company, PO Box 801, Moab, UT 84532, 801/259-RAFT, offers one- to five-day whitewater trips through the canyons of the San Juan River.

Downstream River Works, 401 North Main, Moab, UT 84532, 801/259-4121, fax 801/259-4122, offers half-day and full-day Colorado River rafting trips plus a sunset dinner float that includes a cook-out on a beach. Inflatable kayaks, rafts, and all necessary river equipment rentals are available. Custom trips can be arranged.

Tex's Riverways, Box 67, Moab, UT 84532, 801/259-5101, offers full-day and overnight raft trips, jet-boat trips into Canyonlands National Park, guided canoe trips, canoe rentals, and vehicle shuttles for Green River trips.

Canyon Voyages, 352 North Main, Moab, UT 84532, 801/259-6007, runs half-day or full-day trips plus overnight Colorado River rafting trips with inflatable kayaks. Free motel and campground pick-up is included.

World Wide River Expeditions, 625 North River Sands Road, Moab, UT 84532, 801/259-7515 or 800/231-2769, offers half-day or full-day Colorado River rafting trips and evening float trips.

Ross River Ed-Ventures, Monticello, UT 84535, 801/587-2859 or 800/525-4456, offers Colorado and San Juan River trips.

Wild River Expeditions, 101 Main Street, PO Box 118, Bluff, UT 84512, 801/672-2244 or 800/422-7654, runs one- to eight-day educational adventures guided by archaeologists and geologists on the Colorado and San Juan Rivers. Airport and river shuttle services plus river supplies are available.

Don and Meg Hatch River Expeditions, Box 1150, Vernal, UT 84078, 801/789-4316 or 800/342-8243, fax 801/789-4126, runs four- and five-day trips through Cataract Canyon employing oar- and paddle-powered rafts as well as inflatable kayaks.

Hondoo Rivers & Trails (PO Box 98, Torrey, UT 84775, 801/425-3519 or 800/332-2696) runs seven-day kayak trips and six-day oar-powered raft trips, with inflatable kayaks and paddle boats for those who want them, through Desolation Canyon. Kayak trips progress from gentle water through turbulent areas and include instruction for novice and intermediate kayakers. Oar-powered trips are well-suited to families.

Mind Body River Adventures, PO Box 863, Hotchkiss, CO 81419, 303/527-4466, runs four-day whitewater and flatwater trips on the Colorado and Green Rivers. These are actually retreats focusing on ecology, yoga, tai-chi, massage, or drawing and painting. They include vegetarian meals unless otherwise requested.

Also: Customized trips of one to six days through Westwater or Labyrinth Canyons on the San Juan River are run from April through October.

Adventure Bound River Expeditions, Inc., 2392 H Road, Grand Junction, CO 81505, 303/241-5633 or 800/423-4668, fax 303/241-5633, offers scheduled one- to five-day trips in oar, paddle, or pontoon boats, as well as inflatable kayaks, from May to September, through Westwater Canyon, Desolation and Gray Canyons, and Cataract Canyon. Custom charter trips are available in April, October, and November.

Holiday River Expeditions, 544 East 3900 South, Salt Lake City, UT 84107, 801/266-2087 or 800/624-6323, fax 801/266-1448, offers two- to five-day, oar-powered river trips on the Green, Colorado, and San Juan Rivers. Inflatable kayaks are available on request. Also: Special instructional trips focusing on kayaking or whitewater guiding. Canoe trips are available.

Western River Expeditions, 7258 Racquet Club Drive, Salt Lake City, UT 84121, 801/942-6669 or 800/453-7450, fax 801/942-8514, offers three- to six-day oar-powered trips scheduled from May to September through Westwater Canyon and motorized river trips through Cataract Canyon.

Colorado River and Trail Expeditions, PO Box 57575, Salt Lake City, UT 84157-0575, 801/261-1789 or 800/253-7328, fax 801/268-1193, offers river trips combined with off-river hiking in areas of the Colorado Plateau. These include a one-day rowing trip in the Fisher Towers area on the Colorado River, two- or three-day trips in Westwater Canyon, and five-day trips through Cataract Canyon. The longer trip through Cateract starts with a lazy float past slick-rock canyons and is followed by 15 miles of rapids. Also scheduled are spring hiking trips on the Green and Colorado Rivers, women's, youth, or senior camping trips on the Green River, and motorized raft trips in Cataract Canyon.

O.A.R.S., Inc., Box 67, Angels Camp, CA 95222, 209/736-4677, fax 209/736-2902, offers motorless Canyonlands river trips from one to 18 days, including options for oar-powered boats, paddle boats, inflatable kayaks, sea kayaks, and wooden dories.

Sunrise County Canoe Outfitters, Cathance Lake, Grove Post Office, ME 04638, 207/454-7708, offers nine-day springtime canoe trips on the Class I and II waters of the San Juan River.

Dvorak Expeditions, 17921 US Highway 285, Nathrop, CO 81236, 719/539-6851 or 800/824-3795, fax 719/539-3378, offers unusual whitewater canoeing skill seminars. They begin on flatwater and progress to mastering fast-moving water. Six-day trips are offered on Utah's Green River through Desolation and Gray Canyons. Also available are two- to five-day river rafting trips.

LAKE POWELL BOATING

You could spend a lifetime boating in the secluded coves and bays of Lake Powell and never see it all. Swimming is great at numerous Lake Powell beaches. Summer is by far the busiest season at Lake Powell but it gets hot, with daytime temperatures routinely topping 100 degrees. Make boat rental reservations far in advance. Fall is a much quieter time to visit. The water is still warm and great for swimming but the air temperatures are much lower.

Year-round marinas at **Hite Crossing, Bullfrog Basin, Halls Crossing,** and **Wahweap** are operated by **ARA Leisure Services,** PO Box 56909, Phoenix, AZ 85079, 800/528-6154, or fax 602/331-5258. All offer boat rentals for fishing, waterskiing, or houseboating on the enormous lake, as well as tours to Rainbow Bridge and other sites.

A floating marina at **Dangling Rope,** 602/645-2969, a quarter of the way up the 186-mile-long lake, can only be reached by boat. No boat rentals are available, but there is a ranger station, a store, and gas. Addresses and phone numbers for the ARA-operated marinas are listed above, under Touring. Additional information regarding marinas, boat tours and rentals, plus accommodations and restaurant, may be obtained from ARA Leisure Services. Below are a variety of "Explorer packages" available through ARA.

- The *Rainbow Explorer* trip combines a full- or half-day 100-mile guided tour from Wahweap or Bullfrog to Rainbow Bridge, side trips to several major canyons, lunch, and two nights lodging.
- *Colorado Combo Explorer* includes a half-day Colorado River float trip from Glen Canyon Dam to Lee's Ferry, a day-tour to Rainbow Bridge and three nights accommodations at Wahweap Lodge.
- A *Famous Monuments Explorer* offers three nights accommodations at Wahweap Lodge, a full-day guided cruise to Rainbow Bridge, a half-day tour of Monument Valley plus a scenic flight over both sites.
- *Houseboat/Lodging Explorer* packages combine a one-night houseboat rental with one night's lodging or two night's RV space at any of the ARA marinas.

ARA's houseboat rentals are particularly popular for navigating the scenic miles of Lake Powell. The lake offers astounding red-rock side canyons to fish from, featuring scenic buttes, spires and multi-colored striated cliffs that may be explored on foot. If you prefer, just kick back with a cocktail on the deck. Self-sufficient houseboats, which are similar to floating motor homes, range in size from 36 feet to 50 feet, and are available for rent year-round. The lowest rental prices are from November to March. Boating instructions are included with rentals. You can also rent an 18-foot powerboat to tow behind a slow-moving houseboat for daytime cruising and exploring, or other water equipment, such as water skis and jet boats.

There are National Park Service-operated boat ramps and campgrounds at all the marinas, except Dangling Rope, while each of the marinas has a ranger station.

Sailboating is popular around Wahweap Bay and Bullfrog Bay, where the most reliable winds are found, although storms and high winds can make any sort of boating treacherous.

Scuba diving allows you to explore Indian ruins that were covered by water when the lake was created by flooding Glen Canyon.

Blue Water Adventures, 697 North Navajo, Page, AZ 86040, 602/645-3087, is a full-service dive shop and offers guided trips for snorkelers and scuba divers, including overnight camping trips to Lake Powell.

Probably the most popular trip on Lake Powell is to **Rainbow Bridge National Monument,** 50 miles up the lake from Wahweap, and the same distance down the lake from Bullfrog or Hall's Crossing. The colorful, 290-foot-tall, 275-foot-wide natural bridge is the largest in the world and is instantly recognizable to anyone who has browsed through the local postcard displays. The actual site is accessible only by water, or by rugged foot or horseback trails through Navajo land. Details on land access, including required tribal hiking and camping permits, are included in the Navajo Nation & Hopiland chapter. No camping is permitted at Rainbow Bridge.

Other worthwhile sites on the lake include **Antelope Island,** south of Rainbow Bridge, which was a campsite for the first white explorers in the area, and **Cha Canyon,** 10 miles east of Rainbow Bridge on the San Juan River Arm, which is filled with ancient Indian rock art.

Wilderness River Adventures, 50 South Lake Powell Boulevard, Page, AZ 86040, 602/645-3279 or 800/528-6154, runs raft trips below Glen Canyon Dam and Lake Powell, on the Colorado River to Lee's Ferry. These excursions pass through the only land remnant of the original Glen Canyon.

The Jet Ski M.D., 136 Sixth Street, PO Box 3966, Page, AZ 86040, 602/645-3121, provides sales, service and repairs, along with a rental hotline for waverunners and jet skis.

High Image Marine Center, 920 Hemlock Avenue, PO Box 2004, Page, AZ 86040, 602/645-8845, provides sales and service for small and large boats plus all personal watercraft. They stock marine supplies and accessories as well as RV parts. A rental department offers boats, jet skis, water skis, skurfers, kneeboards, tubes, hydrosleds, water worms, windsurfers, beach canopies, diving equipment, wet suits, and camping equipment.

Outdoor Sports Lake Powell, 861 Vista Avenue, Page, AZ 86040, 602/645-8141, provides sales and service along with rentals of boats, waverunners, water toys, kneeboards, water skis, and rod and reel sets.

FISHING

Moab/Canyonlands/San Juan County

In the La Sal Mountains you can fish for native cutthroat trout in streams at higher elevations of for rainbow trout in **Mill Creek** and area reservoirs.

Ken's Lake, south of Moab on the La Sal Mountains Loop Road, is good for bass and rainbow trout. The laka is also excellent for swimming.

In the Monticello area fishing and non-motorized boating are available in **Loyd's**, **Monticello**, and **Foy lakes**.

Recapture Reservoir, four miles northeast of Blanding, is an excellent location for boating, water skiing and trout fishing. There are no visitor services here.

Escalante

With nearly 100 backcountry lakes and streams, the Aquarius Plateau country (west of Boulder and north of Escalante) offers good trout fishing. Best access is from the Hell's Backbone Road.

Posey Lake, 15 miles north of Escalante off the Hell's Backbone Road, contains rainbow and brook trout. A few miles farther north is **Blue Spruce Campground** and a stream nearby contains trout.

Wide Hollow Reservoir, in the Escalante Petrified Forest State Park, 1.5 miles northwest of Escalante, offers trout fishing and boating.

Tropic Reservoir, at the King's Creek Campground (three miles west of the UT 63-UT 12 junction, then seven miles south on East Fork River Road), contains rainbow and brook trout.

Fishing information, gear, tackles, and licenses are available from **The Outfitter**, 310 West Main, Escalante, Utah 84726, 801/826-4207.

Cedar Breaks

Duck Lake, 12 miles west of Long Valley Junction and north of UT 14, has trout fishing and a campground.

Duck Creek Village, two miles east of Duck Lake, is a year-round resort community. It comprises several resorts, restaurants, and equipment rental facilities for mountain biking, boating, cross-country skiing, and snowmobiling.

Navajo Lake, 16 miles west of Long Valley Junction, is a 3.5-mile lake offering trout fishing, a marina, boat ramps, boat rentals, several campgrounds, and a lodge. Ice fishing is popular in winter. Nearby is the Cascade Falls Recreation Trail, a one-mile round-trip hike to a waterfall that drains out of the Pink Cliffs from the lake.

Panguitch Lake is a 1,200-acre reservoir good for trout fishing. It is situated midway between Panguitch and Cedar Breaks National Monument on UT 143. There are three national forest campgrounds at the lake and another just a few miles north of the lake. There are also three fishing lodges featuring cabin accommodations, RV parks, restaurants, groceries, fishing supplies, and boat rentals. The campgrounds and most services are open mid-May to mid-September.

For information about Panguitch, Duck or Navajo Lakes contact the Forest Service office in Panguitch (Dixie National Forest, PO Box 99, Teasdale, Utah 84773, 801/425-3435) or the Garfield County Travel Council, also in Panguitch (PO Box 200, Panguitch, UT 84759, 801/676-2311).

Fishing is permitted in **Alpine Pond**, off Alpine Pond Trail in Cedar Breaks National Monument.

Eagle Basin Outfitters & Guide Service, PO Box 947, Parowan, UT 84761, 801/477-8837, runs guided fishing trips in the area north of Cedar Breaks National Monument.

Cedar City/St. George

Enterprise Reservoirs are two lakes for rainbow trout fishing. You can reach them by heading 30 miles west of Cedar City on UT 56, 12 miles south on UT 18 to the town of Enterprise, and 11 miles west to a signed turn-off. Facilities including boat ramps and a campground are a few miles farther south.

Pine Valley Reservoir, five miles southeast of Pine Valley, in the Pine Valley Recreation Area, offers trout fishing.

Baker Dam Recreation Site is two miles south of Central, off UT 18. It has rainbow and brown trout in a 50-acre lake administered by the BLM office in St. George. There is a campground and a boat ramp.

Gunlock Reservoir, four miles southwest of Veyo on UT 91, at Gunlock State Park, offers 266 acres of lake great for bass, catfish and bluegill fishing. It has boat ramps and docks, making it a great place for waterskiing.

Quail Creek State Park, PO Box 1943, St. George, UT 84770, 801/635-9412, contains a 600-acre lake stocked with trout, bass, catfish and bluegill. It has a boat ramp and campground. Waterskiing, jet-skiing and windsurfing are popular here. The park is three miles east of I-15 on UT 9, then two miles north.

There's fishing for trout and a boat ramp just north of Zion National Park at **Kolob Reservoir**, three miles north of Lava Point on the Kolob Terrace Road.

Sports shops that can provide area-wide fishing information, tackle, gear and fishing licenses include the following:

- **Ron's Sporting Goods**, 138 South Main, Cedar City, UT 84720, 801/586-9901.
- **McKnight's Sporting Goods**, 968 East St. George Street, St. George, UT 84770, 801/673-4919.
- **Allen's Outfitters & Guide Service**, 584 East 300 South, PO Box 77, Kanab, UT 84741, 801/644-8150.
- **Last Frontier Guide & Expedition**, 263 South 100 East, Kanab, UT 84741, 801/644-5914.

Lake Powell

Lake Powell is 186 miles long, with 1,960 miles of shoreline. The many species of fish found here include largemouth and striped bass, carp, catfish, walleye, northern pike, perch, bluegill, and sunfish.

Inquire at the marinas for the best places to fish. Experienced anglers head to the most remote waters up the various canyon arms, such as the extensive **Escalante River Arm** past Hole-in-the-Rock or the **West Canyon Arm**, 10 miles south of Dangling Rope. The ubiquitous houseboats seen on the lake are usually equipped with a fishing boat trailing behind on a tow line.

Since most of Lake Powell is in Utah, a Utah fishing license is required for those waters. To fish the Arizona portion of the lake, approximately the lower five miles, you need an Arizona fishing license. Appropriate licenses are available at the marinas.

Arizona Reel Time, PO Box 169, Marble Canyon, AZ 86036, 602/355-2222, runs guided fishing trips for largemouth, smallmouth or striped bass on the lake plus trophy trout fishing trips below the Glen Canyon Dam at Lees Ferry. For further details about fishing below the Glen Canyon Dam see the Northern Arizona chapter, under Fishing.

On Snow

Ruby's Inn, just north of Bryce Canyon National Park's Visitor Center on UT 63, offers ski rentals and cross-country ski tours on groomed trails in **Dixie National Forest** or into **Bryce Canyon**.

Bryce can feel remarkably close to magical during winter. Under a clear blue sky, clean white snow tops the radiant red and multi-colored rock scenery. The chances are that you can have the park pretty much to yourself. Skiers and snowshoers need to pick up a free permit from the Visitor Center; they also lend snowshoes at no cost.

You can ski from the motel complex along the rim of Bryce Amphitheatre on the **Paria Ski Trail**, a groomed five-mile loop or, the **Fairyland Ski Trail**, a 2.5-mile loop.

Panguitch Lake offers cross-country skiing and snowmobile trails plus ice fishing.

Brian Head Ski Resort, Box F, Cedar City, UT 84720, 801/677-2035 or 801/586-7101 (snow report 800/782-6752), offers seven chairlifts leading to 40 downhill skiing runs. This full-service ski area provides 20% beginner terrain, 40% intermediate terrain and 40% advanced terrain. Brian Head Peak tops out at 11,307 feet and the longest vertical run on the mountain is 1,150 feet. Contact the resort for details.

Brian Head Cross-Country Ski Center has 25 kilometers of groomed cross-country trails and provides back country maps to routes through Cedar Breaks National Monument and other local areas.

For information on resorts operating in **Duck Creek Village** see below, under Cedar City/St. George Accommodations. The village offers groomed trails for cross-country skiing and snowmobiling. Equipment rentals are available.

Also in the area is **Navajo Lake** with groomed cross-country ski and snowmobile trails plus ice fishing.

Pine Valley Recreation Area has an extensive network of trails for cross-country skiing and snowmobiling.

Cedar Mountain Complex, 30 miles east of Cedar City, is a large winter sports area with many trails. Note that the one into Cedar Breaks National Monument is not open to car traffic in winter.

MOAB/LA SAL MOUNTAINS

There are no developed ski areas in the La Sals, so you need to be careful. Good maps probably won't be much help in a sudden blizzard. A certain level of winter backcountry experience, including route finding, avalanche awareness skills and the appropriate equipment (avalanche beacons and shovel), may come in handy. This in mind, snow-packed mountain roads are open for cross-country skiing and snowmobiling. Cross-country skiing is good in **Beaver Basin, La Sal Pass,** and **Dark Canyon** among other sites.

Recent additions to cross-country skiing facilities in these parts are the backcountry huts in the **La Sal Mountain Hut System**. These provide accommodations with heating, lighting, cooking and sanitary facilities, plus kitchen supplies, mattresses and pillows. Large huts at Mount Tomasaki, Dark Canyon, or Beaver Lake sleep 10 to 12 skiers. Smaller cabins on the shore of Dark Canyon Lake sleep up to four skiers.

Huts may be reserved exclusively for your group. Information about backcountry skiing and the hut system is available from the following sources:

La Sal Mountain Adventures, 2200 Munsey Drive, Moab, UT 84532, 801/587-2859, runs guided backcountry ski tours.

Pack Creek Ranch (see below, under Moab Accommodations) offers guided cross-country tours in the La Sals and winter ski-accommodations packages.

Tag-A-Long Tours (425 North Main Street, Moab, UT, 84532, 801/259-8946 or 800/453-3292, fax 801/259-8990) runs customized backcountry ski tours in the La Sals and also offers car shuttles, trailhead transportation, overnight accommodations, and guide services.

SAN JUAN COUNTY

There are many trails for cross-country skiing and snowmobiling in the **Abajos**, west of Monticello and north of Blanding. Check with information sources listed under Touring for information and maps.

In Air

Redtail Aviation, Box 515, Moab, UT 84532, 801/259-7421, offers scenic flights year-round from Moab's airport, 18 miles north of town on US 191. Options include flights over Arches, Canyonlands, Capitol Reef National Parks or Dead Horse Point State Park.

Needles Outpost (see above, under Touring Canyonlands National Park/Island in the Sky) offers scenic flights.

Scenic Aviation, PO Box 67, Blanding, UT 84511, 801/678-3222 or 800/888-6166, offers a number of scenic tours including a one-hour flight over Canyonlands National Park or Monument Valley, the Goosenecks of the San Juan and Valley of the Gods. Charters and rentals are available.

Bryce Canyon Helicopters, Box 41, Ruby's Inn, Bryce Canyon, UT 84764, 801/834-5341, offers aerial tours.

Cedar City Air Service, PO Box 458, Cedar City, UT 84720, 801/586-3881, fax 801/586-8021, offers scenic flights and charters.

Kanab Air Service, 2378 South 175 East, #125, Kanab, UT 84741, 801/644-2904, offers scenic flights over the Kanab area and the Grand Canyon.

Lake Powell Air Service, 901 Sage, Page, AZ 86040, 602/645-2494 or 800/245-8668, fax 602/645-9318, offers numerous flightseeing itineraries from Page Municipal Airport. Options include half-hour trips over Lake Powell and Rainbow Bridge or longer flights to the Grand Canyon, Monument Valley, or Bryce Canyon. Customized charters are also available.

Eco-Travel & Cultural Excursions

Canyonlands By Night, 1861 North US 191, Moab, UT 84532, 801/259-5261, has been a popular tourist attraction for more than 25 years. The nightly trip combines a motorized sunset ride on a jet boat along the Colorado River with a slide and light show projected onto canyon walls. Accompanying narration describes local geology, Indian legends, pioneers and outlaws. The show is complete with synchronized music.

Canyonlands Field Institute, Box 68, Moab, UT 84532, 801/259-7750, is a non-profit organization promoting understanding and appreciation of the Colorado Plateau. They run a variety of educational tours year-round in settings throughout canyon country. Among the extensive offerings are: hiking with packstock and studying either Grand Gulch archaeology or Navajo culture; backpacking in Salt Creek Canyon; hiking across the Maze and Needles Districts of Canyonlands National Park; a nature trip, river rafting and canoeing on the Colorado River for women only; naturalist tours focusing on animal ecology, red rock geology, or ethnobotany; seminars on avalanche awareness and safety. A variety of specialized photo workshops add to your choices. Most trips are university accredited. Also offered are river safety and rescue seminars, half-day and full-day naturalist walks, private photography sessions, backpacking trips, summer morning outings for children aged between six and 10. Elderhostel trips are offerd for participants over 60 years old.

The Canyon's Edge is a 40-minute, multi-media, eight-projector slide production produced by CFI. It explores human relationships on the Colorado Plateau through Native American stories, photographs, and music. It is shown nightly at the Hollywood Stuntman's Hall of Fame in Moab (see above, under Touring Moab).

Cloud Ridge Naturalists, 8297 Overland Road, Ward, CO 80481, 303/459-3248, offers a range of field seminars for exploring Canyonlands National Park. Groups of 12 to 20 participants are led by knowledgeable instructors who have conducted first-hand research or have working experience in subjects such as dinosaur tracks, butterfly ecology, wildflowers, and desert rivers. Accommodations on these two- to 10-day trips vary from lodges to camping. They are scheduled May to October and you do not need a scientific background to enjoy them, only an interest in learning.

Four Corners School of Outdoor Education, East Route, Monticello, UT 84535, 801/587-2859 or 801/587-2156, a non-profit organization, runs a variety of outdoor and environmental education programs on archaeology, cultural studies, natural history, wilderness advocacy, geology, and wildlife. The school also teaches outdoor skills, natural sciences and land stewardship by creating a community of individuals who share interests through informal, relaxed, hands-on experiences.

Some of the programs include excavating archaeological sites, others offer hiking with pack stock to remote areas near Lake Powell, where you help record, map, photograph and analyze Anasazi sites. There are also trips rafting the San Juan combined with hiking in Grand Gulch. Itineraries run throughout the Four Corners and workshops for wilderness first-aid, photography and writing are offered.

White Mesa Institute, 639 West 100 South, Blanding, UT 84511, is associated with the College of Eastern Utah and offers educational programs focusing on archaeology, geology, pioneer life, wildlife, and modern Indians.

Hondoo Rivers & Trails (PO Box 98, Torrey, UT 84775, 801/425-3519 or 800/332-2696) offers naturalist-led trips in various areas of the Colorado Plateau from June to September. Participants are accommodated for five days in base-camps and have the option of riding a horse or travelling by jeep to prime habitats of elk, buffalo, bighorn sheep, antelope, and wild horses.

In addition, a five-day field seminar and canyon-country vehicle tour is scheduled in May, August, and September. A seven-day trip combines an Indian rock art seminar with rafting the Green River, camping and staying several nights at a Ute Indian-run lodge. Trips depart from Torrey, Utah.

Colorado River & Trail Expeditions (PO Box 57575, Salt Lake City, UT 84157-0575, 801/261-1789 or 800/253-7328, fax 801/268-1193) offers a series of "Earthway Education Expeditions" which explore Desolation and Gray Canyons from an ecological, historical, or recreational perspective. These guided tours for up to 15 participants expand the length, focus and participatory elements of river trips by teaching ecology through information collected in the field. They also focus on the specific interests and demographics of each group. Special itineraries include a seven-day ecology and conservation youth camp for high school students in June. This combines off-river hiking, paddling, field work, camp chores, fireside discussions, star-gazing, orienteering, knot-tying, and low impact camping. A senior citizens camp on outdoor skills and ethical views is run in August and a woman's camp called *The River as Metaphor* is offered in early June.

The Grand Circle, a multi-projector slide show with music, is presented nightly from late May to early September, at the O.C.Tanner Amphitheater, Springdale, UT 84767, 801/671-4811. It depicts highlights of Zion park and many other scenic areas of the southwest.

Audubon Ecology Camps and Workshops, 613 Riversville Road, Greenwich, CT 06831, 203/869-2017, are operated by the National Audubon Society and include a southwest Canyonlands itinerary offered in early October. The trip covers Bryce, Zion and the North Rim of the Grand Canyon National Parks. Participants travel with a naturalist-guide and explore the ecology of the area, learning how the landscape of pinnacles, spires, and shaded canyons was carved by rain, wind, ice, and snow. Also included are explorations of waterfalls, springs, unique plant life and weeping rocks. They also teach how to search for tracks left by ring-tailed cats and cougars. Listen for the calls of canyon wrens, golden eagles and pinyon jays.

Where to Stay & Eat

Moab/Canyonlands/San Juan County Accommodations

There are plenty of motels lining Main in Moab. Many of these have small pools. There are also other more interesting accommodations.

Castle Valley Inn, 424 Amber Lane, Moab, UT 84532, 801/259-6012, is 15 miles northeast of town on Utah 128, then south a couple of miles on La Sal Mountain Road.

The site provides views of red rocks and mountains and the 11-acre property has an orchard, five lodge rooms, three bungalows with kitchens, and an outdoor hot tub. Breakfast is included. Box lunches and a fixed-price dinner are available.

Pack Creek Ranch, PO Box 1270, Moab, UT 84532, 801/259-5505, fax 801/259-8879, is off the south end of La Sal Mountain Road, 16 miles southeast of Moab. The picturesque 300-acre ranch is set amid mountains and red rock scenery at 6,000 feet and offers one- to four-bedroom cabins with kitchens, a heated pool, and a hot tub. During high season all meals are included. The dining room is one of the area's best, serving a sort of gourmet-cowboy-style cuisine. It's open to the public by reservation only.

The ranch runs a variety of tours that are covered in the Adventures section. If you stay here, you can come back after your travels and have a massage, a dip in a jacuzzi, and a satisfying meal.

Cottonwood Condos, 338 East 1st South, Moab, UT 84532, 801/259-8897 or 800/447-4106, has full kitchens and cable.

Sunflower Hill Bed & Breakfast, 185 North 300 East, Moab, UT 84532, 801/259-2974, is a five-room B&B, with all private baths, in an old, remodeled adobe house. Situated close to downtown.

Cedar Breaks Condos, Center and 4th Street East, Moab, UT 84532, 801/259-7830, features two-bedroom condos with full kitchens. Breakfast foods are supplied. You prepare it yourself.

Kokopelli Lodge, 72 South 100 East, Moab, UT 84532, 801/259-7615, caters to bike riders with eight small rooms. Prices include a continental breakfast.

Slick Rock Inn, 286 South 400 East, Moab, UT 84532, 801/259-2266, is a cozy five-room B&B with shared baths.

Canyon Country Bed & Breakfast, 590 North Main, Moab, UT 84532, 801/259-5262 or 800/635-1792, offers five rooms, some of which share a bath. It also has bike rentals and runs guided tours.

Westwood Guest House, 81 East 100 South, Moab, UT 84532, 801/259-7283 or 800/526-5690, has seven one-bedroom apartments with full kitchens.

Moab/Canyonlands Central Reservations Service, PO Box 366, Moab, UT 84532, 801/259-5125 or 800/232-7247, is a complete reservation service for accommodations, tours, and transportation in the Moab area.

Home Ranch, PO Box 247, UT 46, La Sal, UT 84530, 801/686-2223 or 800/982-1540, is a working cattle ranch that accommodates guests in the mountains between Moab and Monticello.

The Grist Mill Inn Bed & Breakfast, 64 South 300 East, Monticello, UT 04535, 801/587 2597 or 800/645-3762, has six rooms with private baths in a remodeled flour mill. A full breakfast is included and there's a jacuzzi.

The Cottage, 649 Circle Drive, Monticello, UT 84511, 801/587-2597 or 800/645-3762, is a private cottage with a kitchen.

Day's Inn Monticello, 549 North Main, Monticello, UT 84511, 801/587-2458, is the largest motel in town with 43 rooms that are a cut above average for these parts. Continental breakfast is included and there's a pool and jacuzzi.

Cliff Palace Motel, 132 South Main, Blanding, UT 84511, 801/678-2264, is a comfortable, basic 16-room motel.

Best Western Gateway Motel, 88 East Center, Blanding, UT 84511, 801/678-2278, is a clean, standard motel with 56 rooms and a pool.

The Old Hotel Bed & Breakfast, 118 East 300 South Street, Blanding, UT 84511, 801/678-2388, has been in the same family for generations. It has seven rooms with private baths, or a private two-bedroom cottage. Open April to November.

Recapture Lodge and Pioneer House, PO Box 309, Bluff, UT 84512, 801/672-2281, is a basic motel with 32 rooms, some with kitchenettes. Also offered are geologist-guided tours, llama treks, slide shows, vehicle shuttles, bike rentals, and topo maps.

San Juan Inn & Trading Post, US 163 and the San Juan River, PO Box 535, Mexican Hat, UT 84531, 801/683-2220, is a river runners' favorite that offers 24 rooms, some with kitchenettes. They also sell camping supplies, Indian rugs, pottery, jewelry and baskets. There is a restaurant on the premises–**The Olde Bridge Bar & Grille**.

Moab/Canyonlands/San Juan County Restaurants

There are plenty of places to eat in booming Moab, some of them good. Farther south the pickings get slimmer.

Golden Stake Restaurant, 550 South Main, Moab, 801/259-7000, serves big and tender steaks.

Pack Creek Ranch (see above, under Accommodations) has an imaginative restaurant. Reservations are required for non-guests.

Mi Vida Restaurant, 900 North US 191, Moab, 801/259-7146, serves steaks and seafood north of town in a remodeled home. The house was once owned by a gentleman who went from being a down-on-his-luck prospector to a millionaire overnight, starting the uranium boom at the same time.

Grand Old Ranch House, North US 191, Moab, 801/259-5753, was built in 1896 and serves steaks and seafood. Open for lunch and dinner. Reservations suggested.

Westerner Grill, 331 North Main, Moab, 801/259-9918, serves breakfasts, burgers, and other diner fare 24 hours a day.

Center Cafe, 92 East Center, Moab, 801259-4295, is as close to chi-chi as you'll find around here. It serves grilled lamb sausage, spinach pesto and goat cheddar, espresso and much more.

Eddie McStiff's, 57 South Main, Moab, 801/259-2337, serves six types of home-brewed beer, home-made root beer, pizza, and burgers.

Sundowner Restaurant, North US 191, Moab, 801/259-5201, serves steaks, German and Southwestern dishes.

Elk Ridge Restaurant, North US 191, Blanding, 801/678-9982. As for eating out in Blanding, this is the best of a thin selection. Burgers, sandwiches, and other ordinary dishes are available and there is a modest salad bar.

Cow Canyon Trading Post & Restaurant, US 191 and 163, Bluff, 801/672-2208, serves much better than average Navajo dishes, plus Mexican and vegetarian fare. This place is a real find and is unquestionably the best restaurant in San Juan County. There's a real Indian trading post attached. It is set in an evocative log and adobe structure with a glassed-in patio where you can watch the San Juan River flow by. Open April to November.

The Olde Bridge Bar & Grille (see above, under San Juan Inn & Trading Post), serves breakfast, lunch, and dinner, featuring mainly Navajo-inspired dishes.

El Sombrero Restaurant, US 163, Mexican Hat, 801/683-2222. If you want Mexican food in Mexican Hat, here it is.

Northern Lake Powell Area Accommodations & Restaurants

The following offer modest individual trailer/housekeeping units with kitchens:
Hite Resort & Marina/ARA Leisure Services, Lake Powell, UT 84533, 801/684-2278 or 800/528-6154; **Halls Crossing Resort & Marina/ARA Leisure Services**, Lake Powell, UT 84533, 801/684-2261 or 800/528-6154, fax 801/684-2326; **Bullfrog Resort & Marina/ARA Leisure Services**, PO Box 4055, Bullfrog, Lake Powell, UT 84533, 801/684-2233 or 800/528-6154, fax 801/684-2312. Fully-equipped houseboat rentals are also available at the marinas.

Defiance House Lodge at Bullfrog Resort, offers 48 better-than-average rooms done in Southwestern decor overlooking Lake Powell or a garden area.

Anasazi Restaurant at Defiance House Lodge, the only restaurant for many miles, serves three meals a day. The steaks and Mexican dishes are average.

Hanksville/Torrey/Escalante Accommodations

Pickings are really slim in Hanksville; the best idea is to keep going or camp out. If you really need a place to stay there are two marginal B&Bs and the funky **Whispering Sands Motel**, UT 95, Hanksville, UT 84734, 801/542-3238.

Rim Rock Resort Ranch, 2523 East UT 24, Torrey, UT 84775, 801425-3843, is not very fancy but does provide good views of Capitol Reef National Park, to which it is the closest accommodations. There is a restaurant (see below) and the ranch also offers horseback trips.

Capitol Reef Inn & Cafe, 360 West Main Street, Torrey, UT 84775, 801/425-3271, is right in downtown Torrey. It has large, inexpensive rooms and the best restaurant in the area (see below).

Wonderland Inn, UT 12 & 24, PO Box 67, Torrey, UT 84775, 801/425-3775, fax 801/425-3212, has a pool and a restaurant.

Road Creek Inn, 90 Main Street, PO Box 310, Loa, UT 84747, 801/836-2485 or 800/38-TROUT, fax 801/836-2489, is a surprisingly nice 13-room hotel in a 1912 building, with a jacuzzi, exercise room, and restaurant.

There's no place to stay in Boulder, but there are 60 rooms in four extremely modest motels in Escalante.

Hanksville/Torrey/Escalante Restaurants

Tropical Jeem's, north of Hanksville on UT 24, looks frightening but actually serves good Mexican food and American standards.

Stage Coach Inn, the restaurant at Rim Rock Resort Ranch (see above), serves steaks, sandwiches, and typical western grub.

Capitol Reef Cafe, at Capitol Reef Inn (see above), actually serves vegetables, a rarity in these parts, also fresh trout, espresso and imported beers.

La Buena Vida Mexican Cafe, 599 West Main, Torrey, 801/425-3759, serves good Mexican food; open May to November.

Bicknell might be worth a side trip if you favor Western kitsch. It includes a dining room that looks like a garage sale of spurs, barbed wire, and animal skulls, among many other things, at the **Aquarius Cafe**, 240 West Main Street, Bicknell, 801/425-3835 or 800/833-5379. Try the pickle pie at the **Sunglow Cafe**, 63 East Main Street, Bicknell, 801/425-3821. Each of these establishments has a motel attached.

Road Creek Inn (see above) serves fresh trout many different ways.

Boulder and Escalante have a few western American eating establishments that don't seem to distinguish between food and feed. You might want to stuff yourself on pickle pie in Bicknell and bypass them. If you're really hungry try the **Circle 'D' Restaurant** in Escalante.

Bryce Canyon National Park Area Accommodations

Bryce Valley Inn, 200 North & Main Street, Tropic, UT 84776, 801/679-8811, fax 801/679-8846, is a standard motel.

Bryce Point Bed & Breakfast, 61 North 400 West, PO Box 96, Tropic, UT 84776, 801/679–8629, fax 801//679-8629, is a cozy five-room B&B with private baths.

Bryce Canyon Pines Motel & Restaurant, UT 12, PO Box 43, Bryce Canyon, UT 84764, 801/834-5330, has 50 rooms, a heated pool, and an above average coffee shop.

Best Western Ruby's Inn, PO Box 17, Bryce Canyon, UT 84764, 801/834-5341 or 800/528-1234, fax 801/834-5265, is the closest motel to Bryce Park. It has 216 rooms, an indoor pool, restaurant, bookstore, and gift shop. Vehicle tours, helicopter tours, car or bike rentals, horseback rides, cookouts, and winter ski rentals are available. Open year-round.

Bryce Canyon National Park Lodge, TW Recreation Services, 451 North Main Street, PO Box 400, Cedar City, UT 84720, 801/586-7686, fax 801/586-3157, is a classy, 1930s vintage, log and stone lodge offering accommodations in duplex cabins or motel rooms. The lodge is within walking distance of Bryce Canyon Amphitheater. The restaurant serves three meals a day but you need to make reservations for dinner. Also: General store, gift shop, laundromat, horseback rides and vehicle tours in a 1938 limousine. Make reservations far in advance. Open mid-April to November.

Meadeau View Lodge, PO Box 356, Duck Creek Village, UT 84762, 801/682-2495, is on UT 14, 10 miles west of US 89, 30 miles east of Cedar City. It offers nine rooms in a rustic lodge with breakfast included. Caters to bikers, hikers, fisher-folk and cross-country skiers in winter.

Pinewoods Resort, PO Box 1148, Duck Creek Village, UT 84762, 801/682-2512 or 800/848-2525, fax 801/682-2543, features two-bedroom suites with full kitchens, a restaurant, and numerous tours including mountain biking trips, boating on Navajo Lake, and excursions to Bryce Canyon, Cedar Breaks, and Zion.

Brian Head Hotel, PO Box 218, Brian Head, UT 84719, 801/677-3000 or 800/468-4898, fax 801/677-2211, has 180 rooms (some with kitchens), jacuzzis, a pool, sauna, and a good restaurant.

There are 3,000 rooms in Brian Head. For information contact **Brian Head Reservations Center**, PO Box 190055, Brian Head, UT 84719, 801/677-2042, or **Brian Head Condo Reservations**, PO Box 190217, Brian Head, UT 84719, 801/677-2045 or 800/722-4724.

Lake View Resort, PO Box 397, Panguitch Lake, UT 84759, 801/676-2650 (summer), 602/628-2719 (winter), is a rustic fishing lodge featuring 10 rooms with kitchens.

Panguitch has a number of small motels–nothing fancy. The same goes for Parowan, a little farther north of Brian Head and a possibility if everything else is full.

Bryce Canyon National Park Area Restaurants

Pizza Place, North Main Street, Tropic, 801/679-8888, serves a very edible pizza.

Bryce Canyon Pines (see above) serves soups and sandwiches.

Best Western Ruby's Inn (see above) has a large restaurant serving tolerable but unexceptional steaks and chicken.

Bryce Canyon Lodge (see above) serves above average fare in a nice log and stone restaurant.

Summit Dining Room, at the Brian Head Hotel (see above), serves seafood and pasta. Open for dinner only.

Cedar City/St. George Accommodations

Grand Circle Reservations, PO Box 1369, St. George, UT 84771, 801/673-7650 or 800/233-4383, fax 801/628-7359, is a booking reservation service for all areas of Southern Utah.

Cedar City has many chain motels run by Best Western, 800/528-1234, Holiday Inn/Quality Inn, 800/228-5151, and Rodeway Inn, 800/228-2000. One of the better ones is Holiday Inn Cedar City, 1575 West 200 North, Cedar City, UT 84720, 801/586-8888 or 800/432-8828. It has 100 rooms, a pool, jacuzzi, exercise room, and a restaurant.

Paxman Summer House Bed & Breakfast, 170 North 400 West, Cedar City, UT 84720, 801/586-3755, is a four-room B&B in a 100-year-old farmhouse. Rooms have private baths.

Pine Valley Lodge, 960 East Main, Pine Valley, UT 84722, 801/574-2544, is the only place to stay in the valley and features cabins. Horseback trips and backcountry guide services are available.

St. George has many of the same chain motels as Cedar City, except more of them, and some more unusual properties.

Greene Gate Village Bed & Breakfast, 76 West Tabernacle Street, St. George, UT 84740, 801/628-6999 or 800/350-6999, has 16 rooms in nine restored houses, a cozy garden setting, a pool, hot tub, and a restaurant.

Seven Wives Inn, 217 North 100 West, St. George, UT 84740, 801/628-3737, has 13 rooms with private baths. They are all done up in antiques and many have wood stoves or fireplaces. There's a pool.

Bluffs Motel, 1140 South Bluff, St. George, UT 84740, 801/628-6699, has 33 large rooms with microwaves and refrigerators, outdoor pool, and jacuzzi. A continental breakfast is included. Two king suites with private jacuzzis are available.

Holiday Inn Resort Hotel, 850 South Bluff, St. George, UT 84740, 801/628-4235, has decent rooms, indoor and outdoor pools, jacuzzi, tennis, an exercise room, and a restaurant.

Harvest House Bed & Breakfast, 29 Canyon View Drive, Springdale, UT 84767, 801/772-3880, has four rooms with private baths, great views, full breakfasts, and mountain bikes for guests.

Under the Eaves Guest House Bed & Breakfast Inn, 980 Zion Park Boulevard, PO Box 29, Springdale, UT 84767, has five rooms, some with shared baths, an outdoor jacuzzi and big breakfasts.

Cliffrose Lodge & Gardens, 281 Zion Park Boulevard, Springdale, UT 84767, 801/772-3234 or 800/243-UTAH, has 44 rooms with good views and a pool. It is set on five acres of lawns and gardens.

Flanigan's Inn, 428 Zion Park Boulevard, Springdale, UT 84767, 801/772-3244, has large or small rooms, a pool, and a restaurant.

Zion National Park Lodge, TW Recreational Services, 451 North Main Street, PO Box 400, Cedar City, UT 84720, 801/586-7686, fax 801/586-3157, was built in 1925, burned down in 1960 and then rebuilt. It's open year-round and offers rooms, suites, or cabins in a stunning setting surrounded by lush greenery and looming cliffs. A restaurant offers dinner by reservation only and there is a gift shop. Tram and bus tours in a 1936 bus with a convertible top are available.

Cedar City/St. George Restaurants

All the chains are represented along with a few stand-outs offering better than average selections.

Black Swan, 164 South 100 West, Cedar City, 801/586-7673, serves lunch and seven-course dinners (reservations only) featuring steaks, seafood, chicken, lamb, and pork dishes.

Market Grill, 2290 West 400 North, Cedar City, 801/586-9325, is a funky place serving solid western breakfast fare and steaks.

Yogurt Junction, 911 South Main, Cedar City, 801/586-2345, is one of the best spots in town for soups and sandwiches.

Milt's Stage Stop is five miles east of Cedar City on UT 14, 801/586-9344, but worth the drive for steaks and seafood. Dinner reservations are suggested.

Dis I'L Dew Steak House is 10 miles north of St. George, on UT 18, in Dammeron, 801/574-2757. You can cook your own steak for dinner. Closed Mondays and Tuesdays.

Libby Lorraine's, 2 West St. George Boulevard, St. George, 801/673-0750, serves imaginative breakfasts and lunches.

Andelin's Gable House, 290 East St. George Street, St. George, 801/801/673-6796, is the most upscale restaurant in St. George and offers five-course dinners of beef, seafood, chicken, and other lighter fare.

Flanigan's Inn Restaurant (see above) serves family fare.

Bit & Spur Saloon and Mexican Restaurant, 1212 Zion Park Boulevard, Springdale, 801/772-3498, looks funky but it's in the running for best Mexican restaurant in the state.

Driftwood Restaurant, 1515 Zion Park Boulevard, Springdale, 801/772-3224, serves family fare. Standard breakfasts and lunches, beef, chicken and seafood, including local trout, for dinner. It also has a motel, the Driftwood Lodge.

Zion Lodge Restaurant (see Zion Lodge above), 801/772-3213, serves three fairly ordinary meals a day, but the setting is terrific. Dinner by reservation only.

Kanab to Page, Arizona Accommodations & Restaurants

Thunderbird Best Western Motel, UT 9 & 89, PO Box 36, Mount Carmel Junction, UT 84755, 801/648-2203 or 800/528-1234, fax 801/648-2239, is a 66-room motel with a pool and restaurant. Consider this as an alternative to staying or dining in Kanab.

Shilo Inn, 296 West 100 North, Kanab, UT 884741, 801/644-2562, or 800/222-2244, fax 801/644-5333, is the best place to stay in Kanab. It offers 118 spacious rooms, continental breakfast, and a pool.

Inn at Lake Powell, 716 Rim View Drive, PO Box C, Page, AZ 86040, 602/645-2466 or 800/826-2718, is an above average motel.

Page Lake Powell Holiday Inn, 287 North Lake Powell Boulevard, PO Box 1867, Page, AZ 86040, 602/645-8851 or 800/232-0011, fax 602/645-5175, offers no surprises, but decent accommodations in 130 rooms. It has an outdoor pool and the **Family Tree Restaurant** that serves three meals daily and features Southwestern and American cuisine.

Lake Powell Suites, 602/645-3222 or 800/525-3189, six miles north of the Glen Canyon Dam, offers nightly or weekly rates for studio suites with full kitchens and laundry facilities in each.

Weston Inn, 207 North Lake Powell Boulevard, Page, AZ 86040, 602/645-2451 or 800/528-1234, is a standard 91-room motel. It has a pool and courtesy car service to the airport and Wahweap Marina.

Wahweap Lodge & Marina, PO Box 1597, Page, AZ 86040, 602/645-2433 or 800/528-6154, fax 602/645-5175, is similar to Defiance House Lodge and has a large pool. Wahweap's large **Rainbow Room** restaurant overlooks Lake Powell and serves a large amount of beef and poultry to a lot of people. It's not great, but then, neither are most of the other numerous family-style or chain restaurants in the Page area. Count on bacon and egg breakfasts, burgers, steaks, and other standard fare. You might do better whipping something up in the kitchen of your houseboat with provisions from the 24-hour **Safeway** at 650 Elm Street. Wahweap Marina also offers a dinner buffet nightly from 6 PM to 9 PM in the **Cathedral Room**, 602/645-2433, extension 6303.

The **Cookie Jar**, 602/645-1023, a cafe at the top of the ramp overlooking Wahweap Marina, provides three meals daily, from 6 AM to 8 PM.

Stromboli's Italian Restaurant and Pizzeria, 711 North Navajo, Page, AZ, 602/645-2605 serves lunch and dinner. The menu includes New York-style pizza, seafood, pasta, chicken, and salads. There's a children's menu, and they offer free delivery.

Camping

The extensive list of public camping areas that follows is offered because of Utah's splendor and the scarcity of decent accommodations in certain areas. Camping may be the preferred alternative in some cases or the only possibility for many miles in remote stretches. During the busy summer season, limited accommodations, even not very good ones, may be filled.

Camping in National Forests, National Parks, recreation areas, and on BLM land is generally first-come, first-served. For state parks, reservations can be made by calling 800/332-3770. For National Forest reservations call 800/284-2267.

Overnight camping or day-use fees are charged at most public campgrounds. Primitive sites are generally free but backcountry permits are usually required. These are available free from the administering agency. Backcountry restrictions regarding fires and off-road vehicles apply in certain areas. Check first with the administering agency.

There's usually room to pull in an RV at public campgrounds but hook-ups are not often available. Numerous private campgrounds on the outskirts of public lands can generally provide full service to RVs.

Moab/Canyonlands/San Juan County Camping

Arches National Park's Devil's Garden Campground is close to the end of the paved park road. It is open year-round but water is only available March to October.

Deadhorse Point State Park's Kayenta Campground offers year-round campsites with water and electrical hook-ups in summer, water only in winter. Reservations are recommended.

Among seasonal **La Sal National Forest** campgrounds are **Oowah Lake**, 22 miles east of Moab off US 191, and **Warner**, 26 miles east of Moab off US 191, both open June to October. **Dalton Springs**, five miles west of Monticello off US 191, and **Buck Board**, 6.5 miles west of Monticello of US 191, are open late May to late October.

Devil's Canyon, nine miles northeast of Blanding on US 191, is open mid-May though October.

All the National Forest campgrounds have drinking water in season and may be open in off-season without water.

Canyonlands National Park allows year-round camping in designated campgrounds located at **Willow Flat**, 23 miles southwest of US 191 on UT 313, north of Moab, in the Island in the Sky District, or at **Squaw Flat**, 35 miles west of US 191 on UT 211, in the Needles District. Backcountry camping is allowed, but a permit is required. **Newspaper Rock State Park**, 12 miles west of US 191 on Utah 211, has a year-round campground with 10 sites but no drinking water.

BLM's Canyon Rims Recreation Area offers year-round camping at **Wind Whistle** and **Hatch Point** campgrounds. Water is available only April to November.

BLM's Sand Island Recreation Area, three miles south of Bluff, offers primitive camping year-round, without water. It is set under cottonwood shade on the shore of the San Juan River.

Natural Bridges National Monument, 50 miles west of Blanding, has a 13-site campground open year-round. The only water available is from a tap at the Visitor Center, a quarter-mile away.

Northern Lake Powell Area Camping

There are public campgrounds at **Halls Crossing** (65 spaces, cold water showers), **Bullfrog Basin** (87 spaces), and **Hite Crossing** (12 spaces). There are also primitive campgrounds close to these areas. Contact local ranger stations for directions.

The BLM operates several campgrounds in the **Henry Mountains**. The sites may or may not have water and the rough dirt roads leading to them may not be in be very good shape; at the best of times they are probably only suited to four-wheel-drive vehicles. Contact the BLM office in Hanksville (see above, under Touring) for information about road conditions and the following sites:

Starr Springs Campground, 23 miles north of Bullfrog Basin and 43 miles south of Hanksville, off UT 276, is open year-round with water available May to October.

Lonesome Beaver Campground, 27 miles south of Hanksville on 100 East, is open May to October but there is no water available.

Hanksville/Torrey/Escalante Camping

Goblin Valley State Park has a year-round campground with water and showers, 21 miles north of Hanksville and 12 miles southwest of UT 24.

The 71-space, year-round **Fruita Campground** at **Capitol Reef National Park**, just south of the Visitor Center, is set amid fruit orchards watered by the nearby Fremont River.

The primitive, five-site, **Cedar Mesa Campground** is 25 miles south of the east entrance to Capitol Reef park, on the dirt Notom-Bullfrog Road. It's open year-round but has no water. Five other primitive campsites without water are 25 miles north on Hartnet Road, at **Cathedral Valley Campground**.

The **National Forest Service** operates several campgrounds between Torrey and Boulder, on UT 12. Three are open, with water available, only in the summer:

Singletree Campground is 15 miles south of Torrey. **Pleasant Creek** is 20 miles south of Torrey. **Oak Creek** is 21 miles south of Torrey.

Five miles east of Pleasant Creek, on a rough dirt road, is the primitive **Lower Brown's Reservoir Campground**. It is open year-round, has no water, but does offer trout fishing in the reservoir.

Calf Creek Recreation Area, 15 miles east of Escalante on UT 12, has a seasonal campground, open May to October, with 11 sites, restrooms, and drinking water.

Dixie National Forest seasonal campgrounds near Escalante include **Posey Lake** and **Blue Spruce**, 15 and 20 miles north of town respectively, on the Hell's Backbone Road. Both are open June to October with water available.

Escalante Petrified Forest State Park has a shaded 22-site year-round campground with restrooms and drinking water, around Wide Hollow Reservoir. The reservoir is used for trout fishing and boating. Short trails from the campground lead to areas filled with petrified wood. The park is a mile west of Escalante on UT 12, then a half-mile north.

Bryce Canyon National Park Area Camping

Kodachrome Basin State Park has a 26-site campground with restrooms, hot showers, and drinking water.

Bryce Canyon National Park is home to **North Campground** and **Sunset Campground**. North is next to the Visitor Center and open year-round, with restrooms and drinking water. Sunset is three miles farther south, across from Sunset Point, on the park's scenic drive. The campgrounds are quite popular in summer months so you may need to look outside the park for alternatives.

Three campgrounds are fairly close-by to Bryce Canyon. Ask Bryce park rangers for information on **Kings Creek Campground**, seven miles southwest of the Visitor Center at Tropic Reservoir; **Red Canyon Campground**, 14 miles west of the Visitor Center, off UT 12; **Pine Lake Campground**, eight miles northeast of the Visitor Center off UT 63. These Dixie National Forest campgrounds only supply drinking water from May to October but remain open year-round if weather permits. For additional information contact the Escalante Ranger District office in Escalante, or the Powell Ranger District Office in Panguitch (see both above, under Touring Torrey to Bryce Canyon).

Also administered by the Powell Ranger District: a campground at **Duck Lake**, eight miles west of Long Valley Junction; three campgrounds at **Navajo Lake**, 16 miles west of Long Valley Junction; a campground at **Cedar Canyon**, midway between Cedar Breaks National Monument and Cedar City on UT 14; and four campgrounds at **Panguitch Lake**, midway between Cedar Breaks National Monument and Panguitch on UT 143.

Cedar City/St. George Camping

Point Supreme Campground in Cedar Breaks National Monument is open mid-May to mid-October depending on snowfall, with flush toilets and drinking water. It has 30 spaces.

There are campgrounds all over the Dixie National Forest southwest of Cedar City and north of St. George. These include ones at **Pine Valley Recreation Area, Enterprise Reservoir,** and **Baker Dam Recreation Site**.

The campground at **Snow Canyon State Park** has restrooms with showers plus some trailer hook-ups.

Quail Creek State Park, 14 miles north of St. George, off I-15, has a campground on the shore of a 600-acre reservoir. For information see above, under Fishing.

Red Cliffs Recreation Site is three miles north of Quail Creek on I-15 to the Leeds exit, then three miles south on a frontage road and two miles west. For information about this small, scenically situated campground, contact the BLM office in St. George, phone 801/628-4491.

Zion National Park campgrounds include **Watchman** and **South**, with a combined total of 373 sites. Both campgrounds are near the south entrance to the park, off UT 9 to the north of Springdale. Both have drinking water, flush toilets and dump stations, and are situated near the Virgin River which provides excellent swimming.

Some sites are open in winter. **Lava Point Campground** is a primitive site on the Kolob Terrace Road with no drinking water.

Kanab to Page, Arizona Camping

Coral Pink Sand Dunes State Park, south of Mt. Carmel Junction, off US 89, has a year-round campground. Drinking water and showers may only be available from March to November. The BLM also maintains a primitive campground north of the park.

There's a 189-site, Park Service-operated campground at **Wahweap Campground**, north of Page, AZ, and several primitive campgrounds nearby on the shore of Lake Powell.

Camping is permitted almost anywhere on the 2,000-mile shoreline of Lake Powell, but not within one mile of developed areas.

For information contact the park ranger station west of Wahweap Lodge or the Carl Hayden Visitor Center at Glen Canyon Dam.

The Forest Service also operates a 54-space campground at Lees Ferry (below the Glen Canyon Dam).

Northern Arizona

The predominant feature in this area is, of course, the **Grand Canyon National Park**.

It is more than impressive; it is one of the seven wonders of the world and the term Grand scarcely does it justice. It is the largest hole in the earth, two billion years in the making, 277 miles long, and averaging a mile-deep and 10 miles wide. Hundreds of side canyons, creeks and trails lie within its boundaries.

There's no place else on earth where you can see so much of the earth's physical history on display. In the rock layers exposed over eons you can literally see to the beginning of time. The Grand Canyon's epochal depths and immense spaces contain extensive opportunities for adventures.

Ride the definitive North American river trip, floating the Grand Canyon's main architectural force, the **Colorado River**. Roll the wheels of your bike or jeep up to its edge. Hike down into its unimaginable depths or simply stand there on the lip of eternity, over a 5,000-foot-deep universe carved over eons.

The route through Northern Arizona starts near the **North Rim**, only 10 miles across from the far more popular and heavily used **South Rim**, but 214 circuitous miles away by road. Only one in 10 visitors to the Grand Canyon ever reaches the North Rim. This is not a small number, around 400,000 yearly, but with all visitor services clustered around the relatively compact North Rim facilities, there's a lot of space nearby for adventurous types.

The South Rim provides its own rationale, with a far larger commercial area, including the greatest concentration of visitor activities. Despite the relative congestion around the South Rim's **Grand Canyon Village**, particularly during the summer, you can still find plenty of space to get away from it all. You just have to venture a little farther off the best-known, well-worn paths of the South Rim.

From the South Rim, it's a short distance to explore around **Williams** and the **Flagstaff** area, a mountainous, cool region containing the biggest city covered in this book, plus the world's largest stand of ponderosa pines and Arizona's tallest mountains, the **San Francisco Peaks**.

From 7,000 feet in Flagstaff, the 30-mile descent through diverse forests and famed red rock scenery in **Oak Creek Canyon**, to nearby **Sedona** at 4,500 feet, is brief and captivating.

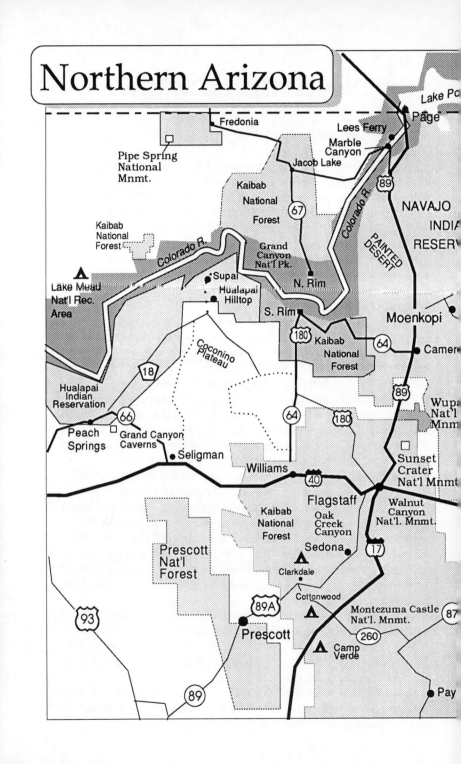

Northern Arizona

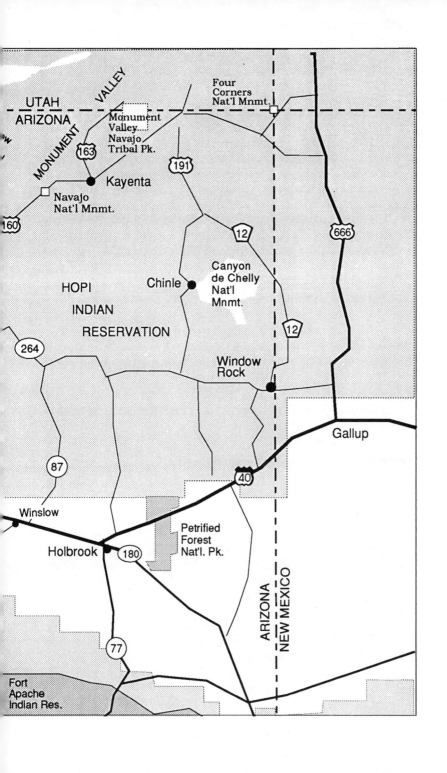

The area has lured artists and creative types for the last 100 years or so, including a relatively recent influx drawn to its supposedly commanding spiritual locale.

Is Sedona the locus of powerful forces of cosmic energy? No one has ever proven the presence of these so-called energy vortices, but that does not deter four million yearly visitors, including hikers, jeep riders, art buyers, crystal gazers, and vortex seekers. Perhaps Sedona's magical power resides in many finding what they seek in this accommodating area filled with colorful geology and characters.

The last stop in this chapter will be the area around the **Petrified Forest National Park** and the **Painted Desert**, a subtly colorful wilderness of little-used hiking and biking trails marked by jewel-like specimens of wood turned to stone. North across the Painted Desert lie the Navajo and Hopi Reservations.

Geography & History

A large part of Northern Arizona is made up of the Navajo Nation, the largest Indian reservation in the United States, containing 26,000 square miles and 250,000 residents, and Hopiland, far smaller and surrounded by Navajo land, but perhaps the most culturally intact Indian tribe in America.

These cultures have long exerted influence on the surrounding areas. You'll see Indian ruins, Indian goods for sale, exhibits pertaining to Indians in museums and Visitor Centers, and you'll even see Indians everywhere you go in Northern Arizona. But the reservation lands present unique perceptions of the world; some liken visiting there to a foreign country.

They miss the point. No place could be more American. The chapters of this book have circled these Indian lands, exploring the outside, saving the original heart of the High Southwest for last.

Although the Indians have been here the longest, today they're hemmed in by the route we're following through New Mexico, Colorado, Utah, and Arizona.

Yet how often do you find a stark and hauntingly scenic, largely undeveloped piece of US real estate the size of Vermont, New Hampshire and Massachusetts combined, with a culturally distinctive population and only 600 hotel rooms?

These Indian territories are covered in the next chapter.

The contrasts awaiting discovery in the areas of Northern Arizona range from the high, pine shaded, 9,000-foot plateaus of the Grand Canyon's North Rim, to the lingering pastel expanses of the

Painted Desert. Elevations range from 3,000 to more than 12,000 feet.

You can hike over red rocks and among cacti in the morning, then ski the San Francisco Peaks in the afternoon. Humphries Peak, northwest of Flagstaff, is Arizona's highest point, attaining a height of 12,633 feet at its summit.

The Grand Canyon has been likened to an upside down mountain, and any hike into it is considered strenuous. What goes down must come up in this case, and hiking out of the canyon takes at least twice as long as long as hiking in.

There are easier ways to go down there. A river raft is probably the least demanding approach. On the back of a mule is another option although many people prefer ministering to sore feet rather than a sore bottom. Others rave about the scenic swaying perch on the back of a large, well-trained and sure-footed animal on the narrow, precipitous trails.

As for the Colorado River, it flows in all its modern-day, dam-regulated glory through the Grand Canyon, still offering what many consider to be the premier rafting experience in the United States, if not the world. You can spend a day or as long as three weeks floating through here.

For those who prefer sinking a fishing line to boating through rapids, there's trophy fishing to the south of the Glen Canyon Dam, plus good fishing in numerous lakes through Arizona's high country.

The mountains and deserts surrounding Flagstaff make the area a year-round recreational wonderland. The terrain for hiking, biking, and jeeping is superb from spring to fall. Cool mountain summers and warm desert winters are fine for outdoor activities or, when the snow flies, the mountains become a winter sports mecca.

There are also upscale resorts and restaurants in this part of the High Southwest, mainly around Sedona, providing a stylistic counterpoint to accommodations and dining options found in certain other areas. There's even a steam train to the Grand Canyon from Williams. You can leave the driving to someone else and simply soak in the ambience of Northern Arizona.

Getting Around

The suggested route through this area of the High Southwest starts in Page, where the previous chapter finished, on the shores of Lake Powell. From there it's on to the Grand Canyon's North Rim and the **Arizona Strip**, the undeveloped northwestern corner of the state between the North Rim and the Utah border.

The North Rim's accommodations and services are only open from mid-May until the first snow, usually around mid-October. Accommodations are available outside the North Rim year-round and the area is accessible for winter sports, though without in-park services. For Arizona road and weather reports phone 602/638-7888.

From the North Rim it's necessary to backtrack to US 89 and head south along the western edge of the Navajo Nation to **Cameron**, where there is an evocative, old-time trading post not far from the eastern entrance to the Grand Canyon's South Rim.

The South Rim is open year-round and is the state's most visited attraction. There is snowfall on the South Rim too, but usually not enough to close trails into the canyon.

There are quite a few choices of South Rim accommodations and restaurants, though nowhere near enough to handle the flow of tourists in peak season. Make your plans as early as possible; reservations are accepted as far as 23 months in advance. The South Rim is also the center for all sorts of tours, including mule trips, scenic flights, and rafting excursions.

The Grand Canyon has already been forced into compromises in order to accommodate dramatic increases in visitors while protecting the scenery everyone is coming to see. Vehicle restrictions are enforced on parts of the South Rim in the summer. Even so, on a typical day, 6,000 cars still try to squeeze into 1,500 parking places. Further restrictions will surely be instituted for the South Rim and a permit system is being considered for the North Rim.

After touring the South Rim it's a short trip south to Williams, the terminal for the **Grand Canyon Railway**, a restored turn-of-the-century steam train. Then east to Flagstaff, a choice center for area-wide excursions. These include visits to three National Monuments: **Wupatki**, site of 800 Indian ruins dating to the 11th century; **Sunset Crater**, a 900-year old volcano; **Walnut Canyon**, containing 300 cliff dwellings built by Sinagua Indians a thousand years ago.

From Flagstaff the route heads south to Sedona and **Oak Creek Canyon**, a landscape of natural pools and rapids winding through 16 miles of sheer red rock cliffs. There's even a natural water slide at **Red Rock State Park**, between Flagstaff and Sedona.

After cooling off in the refreshing waters, the route turns eastward to the sandy deserts of Petrified Forest National Park, site of the largest concentration of mineralized wood in the world. The Painted Desert, north of the National Park, is the last stop before the Navajo and Hopi Reservations.

There are airports and rental cars in Flagstaff and at the Grand Canyon. Again, you really need to drive to make your way through the whole area covered in this chapter.

Time is of a special essence in Arizona which does not acknowledge daylight savings time. Mountain Standard Time is observed year-round. The exception is the Navajo Reservation which sets its clocks ahead one hour in May, then back one hour in October. To confuse this issue, the Hopi Reservation, which is completely surrounded by the Navajo Reservation, does not change its clocks for daylight savings time.

It may help to think of it this way: In summertime, most of Arizona is on the same time as California; in winter, it's on the same time as Colorado, New Mexico, and Utah; the Navajo Reservation is on the same time as Colorado, New Mexico, and Utah year-round.

Information Sources

Arizona Office of Tourism, 1100 West Washington, Phoenix, AZ 85007, 602/542-8687 or 800/842-8257.

Arizona Game and Fish Department, 2222 West Greenway Road, Phoenix, AZ 85023, 602/942-3000, fax 602/789-3924.

Arizona State Parks, 800 West Washington, Phoenix, AZ 85007, 602/542-4174, fax 602/542-4180.

Bureau of Land Management, 3707 North 7th Street, Phoenix, AZ 85011, 602/640-5501, fax 602/640-2398.

Touring

Marble Canyon/Lees Ferry/Arizona Strip

The **North Rim** offers what some consider to be the best views of the Grand Canyon. Don't get the wrong idea; the South Rim is mighty nice too, but it's a lot more crowded and sees 10 times the number of visitors as the North Rim. For some, this makes all the difference in the world.

To reach the North Rim from Page you drive southwest for 25 miles on US 89 to **Bitter Springs**, then north for 14 miles on US 89A to the **Navajo Bridge**, 616 feet long and 467 feet high. On the west side of the bridge is **Marble Canyon**, five miles south of **Lees Ferry**, the put-in point for many Grand Canyon river trips.

Marble Canyon doesn't have a lot of services to offer but the scenery is fine, with the river coursing through an 800-foot-deep gorge. Fishing is excellent in the trophy waters of the Colorado below the Glen Canyon Dam. There are places to stay in this vicinity: The **Cliff Dwellers Lodge & Trading Company**, eight miles west of Marble Canyon; **Lee's Ferry Lodge**, three miles west; **Marble Canyon Lodge**. You can also get gas and groceries, and there are camping areas here.

Lees Ferry was the original site of a ferry operated by a man named Lee, who was hiding out from the law because of his part in the 1857 Mountain Meadows Massacre in Utah. It took 20 years to catch him but he was eventually returned to the spot of the massacre north of Cedar City and executed by a firing squad.

For years, until the completion of the bridge in 1929, the ferry was the only way to get across the dangerous Colorado River. The bridge was, however, a little late for the last ferry passengers. Three people drowned on the final crossing of the ferry in 1928. The ferry sank in the turbulent, uncontrolled river. That was in the days before the dam, when the waters were less predictable.

There are old structures and equipment in the Lees Ferry area, including a log cabin, a ranch house and some orchards at **Lonely Dell Ranch Historic District**, a mile northwest of Lees Ferry, on the Paria River. Several old mine buildings, an old post office, a wrecked steamboat, and **Lees Ferry Fort**, close to the actual ferry crossing, are within the **Lees Ferry Historic District**.

There's a strenuous, steep, unmaintained hiking trail that starts near the remains of the steamboat and leads in a mile and a half to an overlook 1,500-feet above Marble Canyon.

The greatest usage of the Lees Ferry area is for launching river trips into the Grand Canyon. A boat ramp is also used for trips up-river to the Glen Canyon Dam. The 15 miles to the dam are popular for fishing.

For information, a ranger station is near the Lees Ferry Campground.

From Marble Canyon US 89A heads west across the **Vermillion Cliffs** for 40 miles to **Jacob Lake** and the junction with AZ 67, the only paved road leading to the North Rim of the Grand Canyon. US 89A continues northwest for 30 miles from this junction to **Fredonia**.

It meets US 89 seven miles north of Fredonia in Kanab, Utah. AZ 389 heads west from Fredonia to wilderness areas of the **Arizona Strip**, the remote area between the North Rim and Southern Utah, which is accessed off AZ 389 or UT 59. It's the same road, but the designation changes at the border between **Colorado City**, Arizona and **Hilldale**, Utah, two unusual small towns that have achieved

minor notoriety as the residences of modern-day Mormon polygamists. Colorado City, you may recall, was in the news in the early
1990s for expelling an elementary school student who had the
audacity to wear a *Batman* t-shirt to school.

UT 59 continues on to **Hurricane**, Utah in 23 miles from Hilldale,
or there is a dirt road turn-off seven miles northwest of Hilldale at
Big Plain Junction, Utah, offering a 10-mile back way to UT 9 and
Zion National Park.

If you can't wait to see the North Rim, or at least the part of lower
Marble Canyon that leads to it, the graded dirt **House Rock Buffalo Ranch Road** starts south 24 miles west of Marble Canyon, or
16 miles east of Jacob Lake, and leads 25 miles from US 89A to
several viewpoints in the vicinity of **House Rock Valley**, where a
rare herd of wild bison roams freely. The main road and spur roads
to overlooks should be passable in a passenger car if the weather is
dry.

At the end of House Rock Road you are only 15 miles east of AZ
67, near **Kaibab Lodge**. A rugged series of jeep trails connects these
areas but travellers in a passenger car will need to retrace the route
back to US 89A.

There's good hiking and backcountry camping near the end of
House Rock Road, in the vicinity of **Saddle Canyon** and nearby
Saddle Mountain.

Another dirt road, Forest Road 610 swings east from AZ 67,
south of Kaibab Lodge, 18 miles north of **Bright Angel Point**, to
these areas, linking up with rougher jeep trails that eventually lead
to House Rock Valley. See below for information on contacting the
Kaibab Forest office in Fredonia or the ranger station at Jacob Lake
for maps and detailed road information.

Although a certain amount of North Rim traffic comes from Page
and Lake Powell, the Arizona Strip and the North Rim are primarily and much more directly accessed through Southern Utah, on US
89 south from Kanab to Fredonia, or on various dirt roads branching off from AZ 389-UT 59. The main dirt roads that eventually lead
through the isolated backcountry of the Arizona Strip to the most
secluded parts of the North Rim are rugged and long. They should
not be taken lightly. These back roads are covered below, under
Arizona Strip/Grand Canyon National Park North Rim Jeeping.

Jacob Lake is primarily a service area for North Rim travellers
from May to October. Facilities include a motel, restaurant, grocery
store, and gas station. There are also seasonal campgrounds for
tents or RVs, open from May to October.

In the winter AZ 67, south of here to the Grand Canyon, is closed
by snow. Then Jacob Lake becomes a center for cross-country ski
trips. There are many gravel and dirt backroads, bicycle and hiking

trails, and primitive camping areas throughout the **Kaibab National Forest**, south of Jacob Lake.

A **Kaibab Forest Information Center**, 602/643-7295, is south of **Jacob Lake Lodge** and can provide information. If no one's around, the **North Kaibab Ranger District** office is located at 430 South Main Street, Box 248, Fredonia, AZ 86022, 602/643-7395.

Fredonia, 32 miles northeast of Jacob Lake on US 89A, boasts a population of around 1,400, which makes it the metropolis of the Arizona Strip. There are a few modest motels and restaurants, as well as the Kaibab Forest office.

About 15 miles west of Fredonia on AZ 389 is **Pipe Springs National Monument**, 602/643-7105. It was set aside by the federal government in 1923 to memorialize pioneer life at a one-time Mormon ranch. The original ranch buildings are collectively called **Winsor Castle** and, during the summer, costumed National Park Service interpreters offer recreations of frontier life, including blacksmithing, baking, and weaving demonstrations. There are also maintained orchards and gardens offering produce at harvest times, plus a Visitor Center and book shop. A snack bar is operated by the Paiute Tribe which also runs a campground just north of the Visitor Center.

If you do venture off the main paved roads of the Arizona Strip into the spacious backcountry, it is possible to visit no fewer than nine isolated wilderness areas.

Two areas are accessible off of I-15, 20 miles south of St. George, Utah. These are the 20,000-acre **Beaver Dams Wilderness**, north of the interstate and notable for the presence of rare Joshua trees, and the 85,000-acre **Paiute Wilderness**, south of the interstate.

There are no hiking trails in the Beaver Dams area but you can wander freely through the desert. Paiute Wilderness contains rugged hiking trails ranging from 2,000-foot-high desert terrain through 8,000-foot-high evergreen forests.

These areas are managed by the BLM out of their **Arizona Strip District Office**, 390 North 3050 East, St. George, UT 84770, 801/673-2545. The office can provide maps and other information about the areas.

The same Arizona Strip BLM office administers **Cottonwood Point Wilderness**, a 6,000-acre tract containing tall cliffs and plunging canyons, plus the anomalous fertility of **Cottonwood Point**, where unexpectedly verdant flora is surrounded by desert. The area lies east of Colorado City off AZ 389 and south of Hilldale, Utah on dirt roads.

Several other wilderness areas administered by this office are accessed off the dirt roads south from St. George, Colorado City and Pipe Springs Monument which lead to the North Rim. These include the virtually inaccessible **Grand Wash Cliff Wilderness Area**, due south of the Paiute Wilderness and 30 miles south of I-15. It contains 36,000 acres of isolated canyons along the western border of the Colorado Plateau. The only road access is by very rough, unmaintained dirt roads. **Mount Logan Wilderness** and **Mount Trumbull Wilderness** may be reached by any of the main dirt roads from the north. The areas lie just north of the National Park boundary, close to the North Rim's **Toroweap Point**. Together the two areas encompass 22,000 forested acres laced with rugged hiking trails, including ones to the top of 7,866-foot **Mount Logan**, and 8,028-foot **Mount Trumbull**.

Along with miles of remote backcountry there are several little-visited Anasazi sites in the Arizona Strip, including **Little Black Mountain Petroglyph Interpretive Site**. It is eight miles southeast of St. George at the base of a 500-foot sandstone mesa covered by a lava flow. It contains a wide variety of designs in 500 individual petroglyphs or elements carved into boulders and cliffs stretching for 800 yards. Although it's not far from St. George, gravel and dirt back roads to the site are rough. Four-wheel-drive is recommended.

Information is available from the **Shivwits Resource Area**, 225 North Bluff, St. George, Utah 84770, 801/628-4491.

Farther south, in the vicinity of Mount Trumbull, a site called **Nampaweap**, meaning "Foot Canyon" in Paiute, also contains hundreds of petroglyphs on boulders beneath a lava wall. The site is also known as **Billy Goat Canyon**. It is administered by the BLM's Vermillion Resource Area, at the same address and phone as the Shivwits office, above.

The southwestern portion of the 77,000-acre **Kanab Creek Wilderness**, which contains the largest canyon network near the North Rim, is also administered by the BLM offices in St. George. The rest of the area is administered by the North Kaibab Ranger District office in Fredonia.

Within the Kanab Creek Wilderness are numerous backcountry trails, including a multi-day hike along **Kanab Creek** to **Kanab Point** overlooking the Colorado River. The area is accessed west of AZ 67 by a network of back roads through the **Kaibab National Forest**.

Also administered by the North Kaibab office is the 40,000-acre **Saddle Mountain Wilderness**, east of AZ 67 and just north of the Grand Canyon on the **Kaibab Plateau**. There's good fishing and plenty of trails for hiking and horseback riding here.

The **Paria Canyon-Vermillion Cliffs Wilderness** encompasses 110,000 acres north of US 89A between Jacob Lake and Lees Ferry, and extending into Southern Utah. For information on this area, see the Southern Utah chapter, under Kanab to Page Hiking.

Grand Canyon National Park

NORTH RIM

Travelling south on AZ 67, from Jacob Lake toward the North Rim, you gain elevation through the northern portion of the Kaibab National Forest.

The road is also known as the **Kaibab Plateau-North Rim Parkway**. The pine and spruce forests surrounding mountain wildflower meadows are full of wildlife such as mule deer and elk. This road is usually closed in winter which means, most years, driving access is limited to a May to October season.

It's 45 miles south from Jacob Lake to the end of the paved road at the North Rim's **Bright Angel Point**, which is adjacent to the classic, cut-stone **Grand Canyon Lodge**. There are, however, unpaved backroads along the way leading to even more isolated North Rim viewpoints.

Twelve miles south of Jacob Lake you can turn west and follow signs through the Kaibab Forest for 26 miles to **Crazy Jug Vista**. To return to AZ 67 and the main North Rim service area, you can backtrack for 16 miles. Instead of continuing east and following the road you came in on, turn south along **Lookout Canyon**, at the first dirt road junction, and follow the road for 17 miles back to the pavement, just south of **Kaibab Lodge**.

The lodge offers the closest accommodations and dining outside the North Rim and offers mountain bike and cross-country ski rental. The full list of services are detailed under North Rim Accommodations & Restaurants and various Adventures categories below.

Another viewpoint is reached by a turn-off to the east onto Forest Road 611, a mile south of Kaibab Lodge, off AZ 67. The gravel road is usually accessible to passenger cars and there are signs showing the way in only five miles to the **East Rim Vista**.

Since the area is outside the park boundaries, you can camp in the expansive Kaibab Forest backcountry without a permit. It might be handy to remember this if you don't have reservations for camping space on the North Rim in high season.

From Kaibab Lodge it's 18 miles on AZ 67 to the end of the road at the North Rim which, on average, is 1,200 feet higher than the

South Rim. It's a quarter-mile walk on a paved trail from the parking lot at the end of the road to Bright Angel Point.

Because of the colder, wetter weather at the higher elevation, there are many more trees, and larger ones, than at the South Rim, adding a touch of liveliness to the scenery that the rocky faces of the South Rim lack.

The big difference is really the shortage of crowds at the North Rim, allowing for a more intimate experience of the Grand Canyon, which looks absolutely incredible and humbling wherever you stand. You'd have to be numb or dead not to sense the power of the place.

The **Grand Canyon Lodge** is an imposing stone and log structure where all visitor services are located, including information on hiking trails and tours, mule trips into the depths, and rafting excursions. Camping supplies and gas are also available here. And there is a restaurant as well as various accommodations in lodge rooms, cabins, or a campground. The 1.5-mile **Transept Trail** heads along the North Rim from the lodge to the campground.

A ranger station, where backcountry information is available, is located a quarter-mile north of the campground. It is generally open from mid-May through October.

A list of scheduled ranger-led activities is posted at the Grand Canyon Lodge. During the summer season these include campfire talks on geology, nature and history, ranger-guided hikes, and special children's programs.

Although the Grand Canyon Lodge, ranger station, and roads are closed in winter, visitors are still permitted to hike (best accomplished with snowshoes) or ski in the area of the North Rim.

There is only one paved road leading to canyon overlooks on the North Rim. It starts three miles north of the Grand Canyon Lodge and heads northeast for eight miles to **Point Imperial**, elevation 8,800 feet, affording the highest rim views of the park. Alternatively, you can turn south at the Point Imperial turn-off and drive 15 miles to **Cape Royal**. You reach Cape Royal by walking a half-mile from the parking lot at the end of the road. There are several other viewpoints on the way to Cape Royal, including **Vista Encantadora** and **Walhalla Overlook**.

The only other road in this area of the North Rim is a 17-mile four-wheel-drive road west of Grand Canyon Lodge to **Point Sublime**. It starts 2.5 miles north of the lodge.

There are a number of trails from the North Rim leading down into the Grand Canyon. These are detailed below under North Rim Hiking.

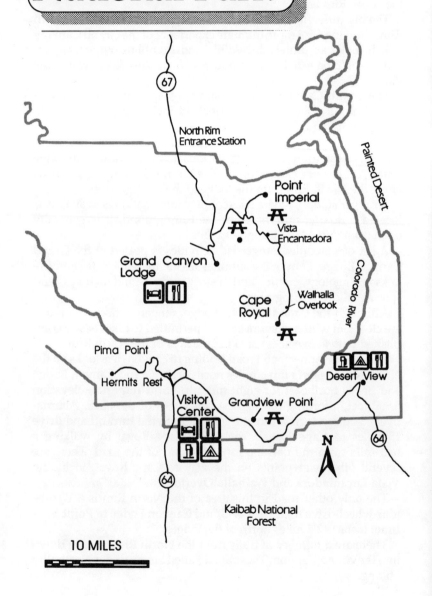

SOUTH RIM

To reach the South Rim by car from the North Rim you have to backtrack all the way to Marble Canyon and south to Bitter Springs on US 89A, a distance of 95 miles. Continue south on US 89 through the western edge of the Navajo Nation for 59 miles to **Cameron Trading Post**, Box 339, Cameron, AZ 86020, 602/679-2231 or 800/338-7385, where accommodations, a restaurant, a campground which accommodates RVs, a grocery store, and a gas station are located. Cameron has been an operating trading post since 1916 and offers a large range of goods. **Cameron Collector's Gallery**, next door to the main trading post, is where they keep the good stuff.

The quickest way to the South Rim is to turn west, a mile south of the Cameron Trading Post, onto AZ 64, which leads in 32 miles to the **East Entrance Station** of the National Park. There's an overlook of the **Little Colorado River** 15 miles west of Cameron.

The first stop past the entrance station on the East Rim Drive is **Desert View**, the highest point on the South Rim, elevation 7,500 feet. You can see the bend in the Colorado River as it flows out of Marble Canyon into the Grand Canyon and there is a structure here, the **Desert View Watchtower**, which was built in 1932. It's 70 feet tall and you can climb to the top for a better view of the river and the Painted Desert. There is also a ranger station, a gas station, a snack bar, a grocery store, and a campground.

Lipan Point, two miles west of Desert View, offers one of the better viewpoints for assessing the incredible scope of the geological history contained in the park.

Tusayan Ruin is a mile west of Lipan Point and contains a small Anasazi ruin. There is also a small museum focusing on the Anasazi and more modern Indian tribes.

Other viewpoints and several picnic areas are along the 26 miles between Desert View and **Grand Canyon Village**. These include **Moran Point, Grandview Point**, and **Yaki Point**, the closest to the South Rim Visitor Center.

Grandview Point is close to the mid-point of the East Rim Drive, 14 miles west of Desert View, and offers one of the best rim overlook views of any site you can drive to in the park.

A number of trails start at the various East Rim overlooks.

Most visitor facilities are in the vicinity of Grand Canyon Village, 26 miles west of Desert View, at the western end of the East Rim Drive.

Coming from the East Rim Drive you first pass **Mather Point**, a popular view site, then the **Yavapai Museum**. There are big windows in the museum overlooking the canyon and visible sites are named, so you know what you're looking at. Displays include rocks from the various geologic layers, billion-year-old fossils, and a geologic clock that clicks off 11-million-year segments of geological activity. There are also scientific exhibits and displays revealing Indian legends about how the Grand Canyon was formed.

A mile west of the museum is the **South Rim Visitor Center**, featuring an outdoor display of various water craft that have been used to ply the waters of the Colorado River and indoor displays relating to natural and human history of the Grand Canyon. Exhibits recount the lives of ancient Indians, early explorers, miners, and the annals of tourism in the area. Other displays recommend ways to explore the park. A listing of ranger-led activities is posted. Books, maps, and information are available here and a ranger is on duty.

Clustered around the Visitor Center are a number of services including the **Backcountry Reservation Office**, **Mather Center**, a grocery store, bank and post office, an RV dump station, a gas station, **Yavapai Lodge**, and **Mather Campground and Trailer Village**, with hook-ups for RVs, shower and laundry facilities.

A mile west of the Visitor Center are additional visitor services at Grand Canyon Village, including **El Tovar Hotel**, **Maswik Lodge**, **Kachina Lodge**, **Thunderbird Lodge**, a ranger station, movie theaters, several souvenir shops, and the railway station where the steam train from Williams arrives and departs.

Over the Edge! Theater, PO Box 600, Grand Canyon, 602/538-2229, a block east of Maswik Lodge in Grand Canyon Village, shows a 30-minute multi-media slide presentation on the history and geology of the Grand Canyon.

A free shuttle loops through Grand Canyon Village during the busy summer season.

West Rim Drive starts just west of the **Bright Angel Lodge** and is closed to automobile traffic in the summer. You can, however, ride a bike or a free shuttle bus along the drive. The West Rim shuttle starts at Bright Angel Lodge and stops at all the West Rim viewpoints, including **Powell Memorial**, **Hopi Point**, **Mohave Point**, and **Pima Point**. You can get on and off as often as you like. The drive covers eight miles to **Hermit's Rest** where there are bathrooms and a snack shop.

Sightseeing bus tours that are not free depart from El Tovar, Maswik Lodge, Yavapai Lodge and Bright Angel Lodge. Options include tours to Hermit's Rest and Desert View (or both). A short sunset tour is also offered. For information contact **Bright Angel Lodge Transportation Desk**, Grand Canyon National Park Lodges, PO Box 699, Grand Canyon, AZ 86023, 602/638-2631, extension 6577.

The more challenging hiking trails from the South Rim are detailed below, under South Rim Hiking.

Among the easier rim-top trails is the popular **South Rim Nature Trail** is an option for those who want to stay atop the South Rim. A short, half-mile unpaved section leads east from Yavapai Museum to Mather Point. It's paved for 3.5 miles from Yavapai Museum to **Maricopa Point**, on the West Rim Drive, then continues for five unpaved miles to Hermit's Rest. You can get off the trail and onto the free shuttle bus every half-mile or so along the West Rim Drive.

Many additional services and facilities are a few miles south of the park entrance on AZ 64 in **Tusayan**. These include motels and restaurants, which are listed below, RV parks, **Grand Canyon Airport**, gas stations, stores and shops, miniature golf and bowling. There's a McDonald's and a movie theater showing popular Grand Canyon-related fare.

Tusayan-Grand Canyon Shuttle, 602/638-2475, operates bus service between Grand Canyon Village and Tusayan and includes stops at the airport.

Grand Canyon IMAX Theater, AZ 64/US 180, PO Box 1397, Grand Canyon, AZ 86023, 602/638-2203, fax 602/638-2807, shows a feature called *Grand Canyon: The Hidden Secrets* on a seven-story-high screen with six-track Dolby sound.

There's a Taco Bell at the theater complex and an **Arizona Tourist Information & Visitor Center**, where you can book scenic flights and other tours.

Getting There

Scheduled Grand Canyon air service operates out of **Grand Canyon Airport** in Tusayan, six miles south of the park on AZ 64/US 180.

Air Nevada Airlines, 5700 South Haven, Las Vegas, NV 89119, 702/736-8900 or 800/634-6377, runs daily flights between the Grand Canyon and Las Vegas.

Grand Canyon Airlines, 6005 Las Vegas Boulevard South, Las Vegas, NV 89119, 702/798-6666 or 800/634-6616, runs flights between the Grand Canyon and Las Vegas or Los Angeles.

Scenic Airlines, 241 Reno Avenue, Las Vegas, NV 89119, 702/739-1900 or 800/634-6801, runs scheduled service between the Grand Canyon and Las Vegas.

Arizona Air, 602/991-8252 or 800/445-8738, and **Arizona Pacific Airlines**, 602/242-3629 or 800/221-7904 in Arizona and

800/974-4280 out of Arizona, also offer daily service to and from the Grand Canyon.

Rental cars at the Airport are available from **Budget**, PO Box 758, 100 North Humphreys Street, Flagstaff, AZ 86002, 602/638-9360.

Fred Harvey Transportation Company, 602/638-2822, offers taxi service and airport transfers, plus narrated sightseeing tours based at the South Rim. Half-day Grand Canyon tours to the West or East Rim or a Yaki Point sunset tour are available. Tours leave from El Tovar, Maswik, Yavapai, and Bright Angel lodges. Also: Full-day tours are offered outside the park. These include itineraries covering the East Rim Drive, Wupatki, Sunset Crater and Walnut Canyon National Monuments, Flagstaff's Museum of Northern Arizona, Monument Valley, or a rafting tour to Marble Canyon. Reservations can be made through the transportation desks at Bright Angel, Maswik or Yavapai Lodges.

Nava-Hopi Tours, PO Box 339 Flagstaff, AZ 86002, 602/774-8687 or 800/892-8687, fax 602/774-7715, runs daily buses to the Grand Canyon from Phoenix, Flagstaff, and Williams and offers guided sightseeing bus tours.

Transportation between the rims of the Grand Canyon is offered by **Trans Canyon Van Service**, Box 348, Grand Canyon, AZ 86023, 602/638-2820.

Additional Information Sources

Grand Canyon National Park, PO Box 129, Grand Canyon, AZ 86023, 602/638-7888. The phone number will give you a recorded message on how to reach appropriate park divisions or receive an informative Trip Planner.

Grand Canyon Chamber of Commerce, PO Box 3007, Grand Canyon, AZ 86023.

South Rim Travel, PO Box 3651, Grand Canyon, AZ 86023, 602/638-2748 or 800/682-4393, provides central hotel reservations, air and ground tours, plus air and car rental reservations.

Grand Canyon Natural History Association, 602/638-2481, provides a substantial number of books, videos, and maps focusing on the Grand Canyon.

For those who overdo it on the back of a mule or hiking around, **Grand Canyon Massage Therapy**, 385 Park Circle, 602/638-9468, is inside the park and offers half- and 1-hour massages, sport massage, and acupressure.

If massage doesn't work, **Grand Canyon Health Center**, 602/638-2551 (after hours 602/638-2477), offers 24-hour emergency service and a pharmacy (602/638-2460).

Tusayan Ranger Station, PO Box 3088, Grand Canyon, AZ 86023, 602/638-2443, administers the area of the Kaibab National Forest just south of the South Rim. The office is south of the park, near Moqui Lodge, and can provide information on camping, hiking, and other recreational activities.

Havasupai and Hualapai Indian Reservations

It's 35 air miles from Grand Canyon Village to **Havasu Canyon** but a lot longer ride by car. The most common route from the South Rim is to drive 56 miles south on AZ 64/US 180 to Williams. Then drive 43 miles west on I-40 to **Seligman**. Here you can cruise a short motel strip, perhaps eat a meal, and definitely fill the tank with gas; it's likely to be the last chance for fuel on the 180-mile-trip to Havasu Canyon and back.

For information contact **Seligman Chamber of Commerce**, East Chino Avenue, PO Box 65, Seligman, AZ 86337, 602/422-3352.

From Seligman it's 30 miles northwest on AZ 66, and 61 miles northeast on Indian Route 18 to **Hualapai Hilltop**. You'll pass **Grand Canyon Caverns**, 602/422-3223, on AZ 66, 25 miles northwest of Seligman, 13 miles east of Peach Springs, or seven miles east of Tribal Road 18 to Hualapai Hilltop. The vaulted limestone caverns lie 21 stories underground. You can take an elevator down to the cave for a 45-minute tour. There's a year-round motel and campground, plus a restaurant.

There are dirt road short cuts west from Tusayan and points farther south off AZ 64 that shave the distance to Tribal Route 18 and Hualapai Hilltop by two-thirds. You'll save miles, but the trip will probably take just as long on these bad roads with poor or non-existent signs. These back routes are recommended for map-reading four-wheel-drivers only.

The Havasupai Tribe, who have lived in this area for a long time before there ever was a National Park, don't want an easier or shorter road from Grand Canyon Village. The tribe's 200,000-acre reservation includes the area around Hualapai Hilltop. This is where most visitors park and prepare to hike or ride a horse or mule down 2,000 feet in eight miles to the main village of **Supai**, on the bank of **Havasu Creek**.

To get into the village you must pay a fee. There is a small grocery store in Supai and a cafe. If you want to stay in Supai at the **Havasupai Lodge** or campground, which are the only places you can stay, you need a reservation. The only way you really have time to see the waterfalls and canyon scenery the tribe has protected for hundreds of years is to stay overnight.

For campground information contact **Havasupai Tourist Enterprises**, Supai, AZ 86435, 602/448-2121. This is the same office that handles the necessary reservations needed to secure transportation from Hualapai Hilltop to Supai by horse or mule, or a seat on a mule or horse's back for a scenic tour from Supai to the waterfalls. You may bring your own horse if you prefer.

For Supai Lodge information contact **Havasupai Lodges**, Supai, AZ 86435, 602/448-2111.

The great scenery starts a mile down the rushing waters of Havasu Creek from Supai. Three impressive waterfalls are clustered in a space of only two miles. **Navajo Falls** is 75 feet high. Nearby, **Havasu Falls** plunges 100 feet into a rock-rimmed pool of turquoise water that has graced many postcard views of the Grand Canyon. You can swim in the pool. **Mooney Falls** is the farthest of these three waterfalls from Supai. It's also the tallest, dropping 196 feet into another pretty blue pool. It's harder to get to this pool, though. You have to hike a narrow trail through two tunnels, then grab onto chain handholds and metal stakes to lower yourself to the swimming hole.

Two miles farther down Havasu Creek is **Beaver Falls**. It's four miles from there to the Colorado River. Remember that the only permissible camping is at the campground near Mooney Falls. If you decide to go to the river this way, make sure you are fully prepared to make it back the same day.

The **Hualapai Indian Reservation** covers almost a million acres, including areas of the South Rim. Any travelling on reservation land requires a permit which may be obtained in **Peach Springs**, on AZ 66, 55 miles north of Kingman, or seven miles west of Tribal Route 18 on AZ 66.

The are two things that most people want to do here. One is to drive the **Diamond Creek Road**, the only road to the Colorado River within the Grand Canyon. The second is to ride the tribal-run motorized rafts through the Lower Grand Canyon into Lake Mead. For information about the raft trips see below, under Grand Canyon River Trips.

Diamond Creek Road covers 21 gravel miles from Peach Springs to **Diamond Creek** on the Colorado River. Four-wheel-drive is only necessary in wet weather. There are picnic tables and outhouses at the end of the road. To drive it you must first obtain a backcountry permit from the Hualapai River Runners office (see below, under Grand Canyon River Trips).

Williams/Flagstaff

There are three highway routes to Flagstaff from the South Rim:

- You can drive 51 miles out the East Rim Drive to Cameron, then south on US 89 for 45 miles into town.
- Drive south for 56 miles from Grand Canyon Village on AZ 64/US 180 to Williams, then east on I-40 for 32 miles to Flagstaff.
- Twenty-eight miles south of the South Rim on AZ 64/US 180, the third route to Flagstaff splits off in a southeasterly direction at **Valle**, home of **Bedrock City**, 602/635-2600. Bedrock City features camping areas for tents or RVs and has the added allure of models of *Flintstones'* characters wired for sound in a little cement theme park. AZ 64 continues south to Williams at I-40 while US 180 cuts southeast through the **San Francisco Peaks** for 52 miles from Valle to Flagstaff. Many mountain activities based in this area are covered below under Adventures.

Williams is the closest town to the Grand Canyon on the interstate, so plenty of traffic passes through here on the way to somewhere else. The town is unimpressive but it's geared for tourism and there are many gas stations and restaurants. It's also easier to reserve a room in one of Williams' 30 or so motels than at the Grand Canyon and rates are lower than the South Rim.

The National Park is only 2.5 hours north on the **Grand Canyon Railway**. The train offers a practical, stress-reducing alternative to automobile and bus traffic at the South Rim. For information see below, under Rail Trips.

The forested areas around Williams, elevation 6,780 feet, offer opportunities for hiking, camping, fishing. and other activities, including winter sports.

The **Sycamore Canyon Wilderness Area**, southeast of Williams, might be thought of as the back side of Sedona's Oak Creek Canyon, a scant 15 miles east as the crow flies, though many more miles by road. The forested red rock terrain is essentially the same, the main difference being that Sedona attracts millions of visitors yearly and undeveloped Sycamore Canyon sees a lot more wildlife and only a small fraction of those people.

The only nearby access road to the wilderness area, which is otherwise accessible only to hikers or horseback riders, is 23 miles southeast of Williams at **Sycamore Canyon Point**, where a panoramic view site overlooks the west rim of the 21-mile-long, five- to seven-mile-wide canyon. To reach the overlook drive eight miles south of Williams on Fourth Street, then 15 miles east on Forest Road 110.

Sycamore Canyon can also be approached from the south, on a dirt road north from **Tuzigoot National Monument**, 15 miles southwest of Sedona off US 89A, or from Forest Road 525C, northwest from US 89A on the edge of West Sedona.

Another scenic drive near Williams is the road to the top of **Bill Williams Mountain**, which is probably best enjoyed in a four-wheel-drive. It starts five miles south of Williams on Fourth Street. From there it's seven miles west to the 9,255-foot peak.

For Kaibab National Forest information regarding the areas south of Williams, contact **Williams Ranger District**, Route 1, PO Box 142, Williams, AZ 86046, 602/635-2633. For areas east of Williams contact **Chalender Ranger District**, 501 West Bill Williams Avenue, Williams, AZ 86046, 602/635-2676.

For general information about Williams and the Grand Canyon contact **Williams-Grand Canyon Chamber of Commerce**, 820 West Bill Williams Avenue, PO Box 235, Williams, AZ 86046, 602/635-4061.

Flagstaff is 32 miles east of Williams on I-40 or 45 miles south of Cameron on US 89. There's a worthwhile detour 20 miles south of Cameron at **Wupatki National Monument**. It adds only 20 miles to your trip if you follow a scenic 35-mile road loop east through Indian ruins at Wupatki, then turning south. After 15 miles it leads to a volcanic cinder cone at **Sunset Crater National Monument**. The loop returns to US 89 three miles west of Sunset Crater and 15 miles north of Flagstaff.

Wupatki National Monument, Box 444A, Flagstaff, AZ 86001, 602/527-7040, contains primitive masonry ruins built by Indians who lived and farmed here from 1100-1300 AD. Only a few sites, out of an estimated 2,000 here, have been excavated and much of the reserve is protected by restricted access. Overnight hiking is prohibited, except for special ranger-led hikes offered in April and October.

Entering Wupatki from the north means the Visitor Center, 14 miles east of US 89, is one of the last places you'll reach on a drive through here. There are small exhibits of ancient Indian artifacts and other historical displays, as well as information pamphlets, maps, and activity schedules. You don't really need the Visitor Center brochures to find the several ruins sites that can be driven to on the well-signed park road. From the north these are **Lomaki Ruin**, **Citadel Ruin**, **Wukoki Ruin** and, the largest site, **Wupatki Ruin**, near the Visitor Center, containing 100 rooms. Short trails to each site provide views of other scattered ruins.

Directly south of Wupatki is the **Strawberry Crater Wilderness Area**, containing 10,000 acres of sparsely vegetated volcanic lava fields, and **Sunset Crater National Monument**, Route 3, Box 49, Flagstaff, AZ 86004, 602/527-7042, 11 miles south of the Wupatki Visitor Center.

Sunset Crater is a black, volcanic cinder cone 1000 feet high. Not much has grown near the crater in the 700 years since the last eruption, so the area is good one to observe the effects of a volcano.

You can hike the short **Lava Flow Trail**, around the base of the crater, but hiking up the crater is prohibited.

Nearby, **Lenox Crater** is open to hikers, or a quarter-mile west of the Sunset Crater Visitor Center is a turn-off for Forest Road 545A which goes north for five steep miles to the 8,965-foot summit of **O'Leary Peak**. From the peak you can look down into Sunset Crater.

Sunset Crater Visitor Center is near the southwestern entrance to the park, 3.5 miles east of US 89. Displays deal mainly with the forces of volcanism. Ranger-led activities schedules are posted. A campground is situated nearby and is open May through October.

Flagstaff is 12 miles south of Sunset Crater on US 89. Its population of 46,000 more than doubles any other city in this book and, if you're just passing through on the main roads, you will see undeniable evidence that Flagstaff does have more gas stations, motels, and restaurants than any other place this book covers. It's the biggest city between Albuquerque and Los Angeles on I-40, which runs coast-to-coast, so it's definitely a major stop on the interstate.

Flagstaff is well situated amid cooling pine forests at 7,000 feet to provide central access to the many adventurous things to do in the area on a year-round basis, including hiking or biking in Arizona's highest mountains, the **San Francisco Peaks**, just northwest of the city, skiing there in winter, or fishing on numerous lakes. There are Indian ruins, volcanoes, and wilderness areas nearby, as well as an historic downtown district, museums, an observatory where astronomers first spotted Pluto, a university community that contributes nearly 20% of the city's population, and numerous galleries.

Northern Arizona University is situated on 700 acres, just seven blocks south of downtown. Free shuttle buses travel across the large campus.

A lot of things are generally going on here, including changing shows at **NAU Art Gallery**, 602/523-3471, sporting events, plus theatrical and musical performances. For the school's information desk, phone 602/523-2391.

A few blocks south of the University, **Riordan State Historic Park**, 1300 Riordan Ranch Road, Flagstaff, 602/779-4395, offers guided tours of Flagstaff's largest home, circa 1904. The log and volcanic rock structure contains original interior furnishings.

Lowell Observatory, 1400 West Mars Hill, Flagstaff, 602/774-3358, is where the planet Pluto was discovered in 1930. It's still a functioning space research facility and is just a mile west of downtown Flagstaff. A Visitor Center offers exhibits and a slide show about the observatory. You can also see the observatory's original 1896 telescope.

You can see stars for yourself through a modern telescope, not the 24 inch antique, several nights a week during the summer, once monthly the rest of the year. Call for schedules. You can also look through a telescope one night a week at **NAU Campus Observatory**, 602/523-7170.

You may see stars of a different nature at the **Museum Club**, 3404 East Santa Fe Avenue, Flagstaff, 602/526 9434, a genuine Western night club, complete with mounted trophy animals on display in a cavernous log cabin structure. The dance floor straddles five tree trunks. Check the schedule; big names have appeared.

Pioneer Historical Museum, 2340 North Fort Valley Road, Flagstaff, 602/774-6272, is two miles northwest of downtown on US 180. Displays focus on Flagstaff's pioneer history and include an 1880s pioneer cabin. An exhibit on Lowell Observatory's founder Percival Lowell includes a mechanical computer he built in the early 1900s. Other exhibits display the work of early local photographers, farm equipment and machinery, ranching and logging paraphernalia, old wagons, cars, and a stuffed bear.

Coconino Center for the Arts, 2300 North Fort Valley Road, Flagstaff, 602/779-6921, is a block north of the Pioneer Museum. It offers regional folk art exhibits, musical, dance and theatrical performances, and workshops. The primary focus of the museum is on western and Indian arts and each year the center hosts a summer-long **Festival of Native American Arts**. From late June through early August, Indians from the Four Corners lead craft workshops and demonstrations as part of a special series of displays, dances, lectures, concerts, and theatrical performances related to the Indian cultures of the Southwest. For information contact **Festival of Native American Arts**, PO Box 296, Flagstaff, AZ 86002, 602/779-6921.

Art Barn, 2320 North Fort Valley Road, Flagstaff, 602/774-0822, is next door to the Coconino Center and offers gallery sales of paintings, photographs, pottery, rugs, jewelry, and other regional creations.

Museum of Northern Arizona, 301 North Fort Valley Road, Flagstaff, 602/774-5211, is a mile farther northwest of the Coconino Center on US 180 and features a highly-regarded collection. Exhibits on archaeology, ethnology, biology, geology, Indian and Western fine arts, and modern Indian folk arts are displayed. One exhibit includes a replica kiva. There's also a well-stocked Southwestern bookstore and a large Southwestern research library.

An annual, ten-day **Hopi Artists Exhibition** has been a tradition for the last 60 years over the fourth of July weekend. Three weeks later a **Navajo Artists Exhibition** has been a successful annual event for the last 40 years.

A half-mile northwest of the Museum of Northern Arizona, **Shultz Pass Road** turns to the northeast for 12 scenic, unpaved miles, skirting the southeastern border of the San Francisco Peaks and the **Kachina Peaks Wilderness Area**, and passing to the west of **Mount Elden**. All are popular areas for outdoor recreation. It's a scenic, short drive that can usually be achieved in fair weather by passenger cars. It returns to the paved US 89 near Sunset Crater National Monument. From the end of the dirt road it's 11 miles south on US 89 to Flagstaff.

Getting There

Several bus lines, as well as **Amtrak**, 800/872-7245, offer service through Flagstaff. Amtrak's service connects Chicago, Albuquerque, Flagstaff, and Los Angeles.

Limited air service is offered from Flagstaff Municipal Airport, five miles south of town. **America West**, 602/525-1346 or 800/247-5692, provides daily service to the Grand Canyon, Phoenix, and Las Vegas. **Skywest/Delta Connection**, 602/774-4830 or 800/453-9417, offers daily service to Phoenix or Page.

Rental cars are available at the airport from **Avis**, 602/774-8421, **Budget**, 602/779-0306, or **Hertz**, 602/774-4452. Several in-town car rental services are also available. Motorhome rentals are available from **Cruise America**, 824 West Route 66, Flagstaff, AZ 86001, 602/774-4797.

Additional Information

Flagstaff Chamber of Commerce Visitor Center, 101 West Santa Fe Avenue, Flagstaff, AZ 86001, 602/774-9451 or 800/842-7293, provides free information on area attractions and services, including a self-guided historic downtown walking tour.

Flagstaff Current Events Hotline, 602/779-3733.

Coconino National Forest Supervisor, 2323 East Greenlaw Lane, Flagstaff, AZ 86004, 602/556-7400, administers areas north and south of Flagstaff.

Peaks Ranger Station, 5075 North US 89, Flagstaff, AZ 86004, 602/526-0866, deals specifically with areas north of Flagstaff.

Mormon Lake Ranger District, 4825 Lake Mary Road, Flagstaff, AZ 86001, 602/556-7474, operates the southern district.

Road conditions: 602/779-2711.

Weather conditions: 602/774-3301.

Oak Creek Canyon/Sedona

Sedona is 28 miles south of Flagstaff on US 89A. The two towns are separated by another remarkable piece of scenic geography called **Oak Creek Canyon**. The road descends 2,600 feet on the trip. Coming down off the forested rim into Oak Creek Canyon, you pass through eight major plant communities, surrounded by vertical, monolithic red rocks and mazes of leafy subordinate canyons at 4,400 feet elevation in Sedona. It's less than 30 miles south but the elevation change means Sedona is usually 15 to 20 degrees warmer than Flagstaff, though still considerably milder than the scorching deserts and cities to the south.

The terrain includes the extremely popular Oak Creek area, **Slide Rock State Park**, eight miles north of Sedona on US 89A, and many other camping, fishing, horseback riding, biking and hiking spots. Four-wheel-drive tours are a booming industry here. It's all set amid dramatic canyons and rocks, borderland forests, stark mesas and buttes giving way from the cool alpine and evergreen slopes near Flagstaff, to the hot, lowering deserts of southern Arizona.

Wildlife is apparently attracted to these climes; the area contains more than 50 species of mammals, approximately 175 species of birds, several dozen species of reptiles, and 20 species of fish living along Oak Creek amid more than 500 varieties of flowering plants.

For a small town of around 12,000 residents, Sedona's cachet as a world-class resort owes its foundations to the incredible scenery. Mountain-sized, smooth-faced, bare red rocks sprout through wreaths of low-lying broad-leaf foliage, a fringe of greenery tracing the flow of Oak Creek. Sedona lies in a basin at the lower end of Oak Creek Canyon. The picturesque locale has attracted visitors, artists, and film makers to the area since the 1920s.

Sedona has had a long time to become a sophisticated tourist town, so inevitably commercial and public interests have made certain inroads on the natural environment. There are a lot of places to stay, including deluxe golf resorts and B&Bs, and there are excellent restaurants. There are around 40 art galleries and many,

many shops, from unusual ones offering one-of-a-kind items, to factory outlets in the **Village of Oak Creek**, south of Sedona on AZ 179.

An entire sub-culture of New Age believers in crystals, vortices, power centers, UFOs, and para-normal phenomenon has also made a visible impact on Sedona. Several bookstores specialize in New Age materials. Racks throughout town offer brochures touting jeep tours, balloon flights, motels, restaurants, tarot-card readers, crystal and cosmic energy experts, fortune tellers, and spiritual healers.

Many claim, from one perspective or another, that the distinctive red rocks glowing through a palette of crimson shades according to the angle of the sun, the interplay of clouds and shadow, emanate extraordinary cosmic power. Enthusiasts postulate that, among other things, the vigorous energy emitted by **Bell Rock** stimulates activity while, in contrast, the soothing strength of **Cathedral Rock** reduces stress. It all has to do with so-called vortices, the places where powerful lines of energy that criss-cross the earth intersect. Some people think that Sedona's supposed to be a magical place because it has as many as a dozen of these uncommon junctions nearby. To others, the vortex conception remains theoretical.

It is well-known that the iron-tinged red sandstone terrain provides a colorful landscape for extraordinary adventures, ranging from numerous guided tour options, including some to otherwise inaccessible areas, to roughing it on your own in the backcountry, to channeling the vibes–if that's the wavelength on which you're broadcasting.

Travelling south from Flagstaff on US 89A, you enter narrow **Oak Creek Canyon** nine miles south of Flagstaff. This is the preferred direction to travel for maximum scenic impact. You can get pretty good views of the canyon from a car but, if you want to look more closely, there are many turn-offs and parking areas with short walks to scenic view sites.

At the head of the canyon the rim drops away at **Oak Creek Overlook**, providing a view of 1,200-foot canyon walls and the road dropping down through 15 twisting miles to Sedona, where the canyon walls are twice this size. Driving down the steep, narrow road, vegetation changes around each lowering switchback. At differing elevations each turn reveals a new perspective of the red, yellow, and white cliffs and rock forms that rise out of the mile-wide canyon. It's stunning anytime but be prepared for especially slow-going due to heavy traffic on a summer weekend, or in September and October, during Arizona's most colorful autumn display, as aspens, oaks, and maples shed their leaves. A good thing about fall travel is that although the main roads are crowded, the backcountry is not.

Sterling Springs Fish Hatchery sits near the bottom of the switchbacks, at the head of Oak Creek. The rainbow and brown trout found in Oak Creek come from here.

About a mile farther south, adjacent to **Pine Flat Campground**, is a short but steep half-mile hike on **Cookstove Trail** to the east rim.

Several miles farther south is **Slide Rock State Park**, PO Box 10358, Sedona, AZ 86336, 602/282-3034, which was created to further environmental education. Its 286 acres include stunning red rocks, short and long hiking trails, orchards and a primal water theme park along Oak Creek, terraced rock pools and natural water slides created amiably over thousands of years by nature.

There is, of course, the famous **Slide Rock**, a slippery but not-so-smooth chute (wear long pants and shoes) plunging into Oak Creek. Other wading or swimming areas in smaller pools stretch along the creek and broad tiers of horizontal red rocks beckon swimmers to dry out beneath the Arizona sun or just work on a tan. Many people do exactly these things. Too many people for some tastes on a summer weekend. Picnic sites, a nature trail, a snack bar and restrooms are available. There is no camping permitted although the park is open for day-use year-round.

Sedona has its surrounding scenery and well-honed tourism infrastructure offering abundant services to recommend it. Remarkable sites in town are mostly unique stores, resorts, or good restaurants. If you enjoy shopping or just browsing, and perhaps a round of tennis or golf followed by an excellent meal, you can find these things here.

Sedona Arts Center, at the north end of town on US 89A at Art Barn Road, 602/282-3809, is a good place to get a handle on the Southwestern sensibilities favored by local artists. Local talent is featured in art exhibitions. Also: Concert, dance, and theater performances are regularly scheduled here.

A popular site is **Tlaquepaque Arts & Crafts Village**, a recreated Mexican village and market featuring restaurants, gift shops, and art galleries in a vine-draped, adobe-walled, tree-shaded courtyard complex. It's a quarter-mile south of US 89A, off AZ 179.

Three miles south of town on AZ 179, then a mile east on Chapel Road is the **Chapel of the Holy Cross**, set dramatically on a hill-top, nestled among looming red rocks.

Shrine of the Red Rocks, two miles west of Sedona on US 89A, on **Table Top Mountain**, offers a very large wooden cross and views looking down at the red rocks.

As for the most popular vortex sites, common interpretations credit Sedona's enchanted appeal to the sites' invisible powers of magnetism or electricity, their perfect Oriental balance of grace and harmony, or ancient mysteries contained here in hidden well springs of Indian shamanic wisdom, sometimes all of the above at once.

Regardless of the explanation, believers ascribe enhanced creativity, psychic talents, and sensations of passion to particular rocks.

Bell Rock Vortex, five miles south of US 89A, on the east side of AZ 179, between Sedona and the village of Oak Creek, is sometimes called the **Electric Vortex**. It is thought by many to be a preferred landing zone for extraterrestrial space travellers. **Cathedral Rock Vortex** is in West Sedona, situated 4.5 miles west of AZ 179 on US 89A to Red Rock Loop Road. Turn south two miles to a "Slow" sign and follow signs for another mile and a half on dirt roads to a parking area. Although quite solid in stature, this large rock is felt by some to radiate a tender tranquility. Its magnetic effects are said to project 500 yards from the rock, which is plenty of room for an idyllic picnic in its shadow.

Another vortex site is **Boynton Canyon Vortex**, the largest of the vortices and considered to radiate electromagnetism. Its effects are supposed to radiate several miles, but if you want to visit the actual spot northwest of Sedona go three miles west of AZ 179 on US 89A to Dry Creek Road, then north five miles on a well-signed route to a parking area and several hiking trailheads. It's a mile hike to reach the rock.

Other hiking trails wind among red hills, cliffs, and dry washes dropping from narrow canyons topped in pinyon and juniper.

Airport Mesa Vortex, another electric vortex, is a mile west of AZ 179 on US 89A, to Airport Road, then south a few blocks to a parking area beside the road. The vortex is on the east side of the road and several short trails lead up a hill to a cliff overlooking the valley. The electrical energy can supposedly be felt over a field of 100 yards from the hilltop.

Capital Butte, Chimney Rock, and **Lizard Head,** are other famous rock formations around town.

A site that has appeared in thousands of photographs illustrating Sedona is called **Red Rock Crossing**. It's four miles west of AZ 179 on US 89A, then south on paved Red Rock Upper Loop Road/Forest Road 216. Bear left after two miles onto Forest Road 216A for a half-mile to Red Rock Crossing. It's designated a day-use area by the Forest Service. There are picnic sites and areas where you can wade in Lower Oak Creek.

Schnebly Hill Scenic Drive starts east off AZ 179, a half-mile south of US 89A, and covers 12 partly-paved miles, through red rocks and possibly the best scenic views of the area, to I-17, 20 miles south of Flagstaff. The road should be accessible to passenger cars.

There is a small airport a few miles southwest of Sedona on Airport Road off US 89A. Daily service to Phoenix is provided by **Air Sedona**, 602/282-7935 or 800/228-7654.

Car rentals are available at the airport from **Budget**, 602/282-5602. There are several taxi services in town and there is bus service to Phoenix, Flagstaff, and other Arizona locations several times each day.

Additional Information

Sedona-Oak Creek Chamber of Commerce, Forest Road and North US 89A, PO Box 478, Sedona, AZ 86336, 602/282-7722 or 800/288-7336.

Sedona Ranger District, 250 Brewer Road, PO Box 300, Sedona, AZ 86336, 602/282-4119, provides maps, hiking trail guides, plus camping and road information.

South of Sedona

Cottonwood is 19 miles southwest of Sedona on US 89A. The town has motels and restaurants, plus old western false Front Street in **Historic Old Town Cottonwood**.

Just north of town is **Tuzigoot National Monument**, PO Box 219, Cottonwood, AZ 86326, 602/634-5564, site of excavated Sinagua Indian ruins 600 to 900 years old. A Visitor Center contains displays of artifacts retrieved from the ruins and exhibits pertaining to the Sinagua culture. A short trail leads from the Visitor Center to the ruins.

Dead Horse Ranch State Park, 602/634-5283, is located on the north end of Cottonwood, east of Tuzigoot, and offers fishing for bass, catfish and trout, hiking along the Verde River, and a campground.

Little **Clarkdale** has some old buildings and it is the terminal for the **Verde River Canyon Rail Trip**, which is detailed below, under Rail Trips. Clarkdale is situated two miles northwest of Cottonwood. For additional information contact **Verde Valley Chamber of Commerce**, 1010 South Main Street, Cottonwood, AZ 86326, 602/634-7593.

Jerome, situated atop a hill overlooking the Verde Valley, six miles west of Cottonwood on US 89A, is an old, partly-restored copper mining boom town, now taken over by galleries, shops and cafes. Among sites of interest are the following:

- **Jerome State Historic Park**, 602/634-5381, is a museum of mining and local history situated in a 1917 mansion at the lower end of town.
- **Jerome Historical Society Mine Museum**, 602/634-5477, contains more mining era memorabilia on the corner of US 89A and Jerome Avenue.
- **Gold King Mine Museum**, 602/634-0053, has lots of big, old pieces of mining equipment and a petting zoo, a mile northwest of Jerome on Perkinsville Road.

For information contact **Jerome Chamber of Commerce**, 317 Main Street, Jerome, AZ 86331, 602/634-5716.

To cover another interesting nearby area you could drive east on AZ 260 from Cottonwood, or 15 miles south from Sedona on AZ 179 to I-17 at **Camp Verde**. AZ 260 continues east to **Clints Well** and ultimately northeast to **Winslow**, on I-40, midway between Flagstaff and the Petrified Forest. There's good hiking, biking, fishing, and camping terrain through these areas, plus several interesting historic sites.

Three miles north of AZ 260 on I-17 is **Montezuma Castle National Monument**, PO Box 219, Camp Verde, AZ 86332, 602/567-3322. It contains a five-story structure that you can see but not enter, built under a protective cliff by Sinagua Indians in the 1300s. It also has a campground and a Visitor Center featuring exhibits describing primitive but effective irrigation and farming techniques and clearly durable building techniques employed by Sinagua and earlier Hohokam Indians.

Ten miles northeast of the castle is **Montezuma's Well**, a water-filled sinkhole nearly 500 feet across and site of other Indian ruins.

Two miles east of I-17 on AZ 260 is **Fort Verde State Historic Park**, Lane Street, Camp Verde, AZ 86332, 602/567-3275. In the 1870s the US Army cavalry headquarters located here all but terminated local Indian disturbances. Exhibits in four restored adobe structures, an administration building, commanding officer's quarters, doctor's office and bachelor's quarters, include displays on frontier life, with illustrations pertaining to Indians, soldier's and their families, Indian scouts employed by the Army to root-out other Indians, and settlers.

For area information contact **Camp Verde Chamber of Commerce**, PO Box 1665, Camp Verde, AZ 86332, 602/567-9294.

The **Yavapai-Apache Visitor Center**, 602/567-5276, sits beside I-17 at the Montezuma Castle/Camp Verde exit. Displays describe area attractions and travel information is available.

For details about public lands west and south of Camp Verde contact **Verde Ranger District**, Main Street, PO Box 670, Camp Verde, AZ 86322, 602/4567-4121.

These include the 20,000-acre **Pine Mountain Wilderness**, 15 miles south of Camp Verde on I-17, then 20 miles east on a Forest Service Road. In addition, river rafters and kayakers can receive information from this office on running the Verde River south from Camp Verde for as far as 60 miles to **Horseshoe Lake**. The best time of year for this trip is the desert spring, February and March. There are commercial river trips offered on the Verde River in late spring. See below, under River Trips, or contact the chamber of commerce for information.

For information about areas east and north of Camp Verde contact **Beaver Creek Ranger District**, Box 240, Rimrock, AZ 86335, 602/567-4501.

These regions include two exceptionally rugged wilderness areas where you are likely to discover solitude, wildlife, and swimming holes.

West Clear Creek Wilderness can be driven to 12 miles east of Camp Verde. It contains 13,000 acres of virtually pristine canyon country.

Wet Beaver Creek Wilderness is accessed 12 miles north of Camp Verde and east of I-17, adjacent to the Beaver Creek Ranger office.

In addition, the Beaver Creek office can supply information on the **General Crook National Recreation Trail**, a restored 135-mile section of a 200-mile-long military supply route initiated in the 1870s. It runs right through Camp Verde and starts 115 miles east, near **Show Low**. The western end of the trail is 20 miles west of Camp Verde.

For information about forests in the vicinity of Clints Well contact the **Blue Ridge Ranger Station**, Box 300, Happy Jack, AZ 86024, 602/477-2255.

Sedona to Petrified Forest/Painted Desert

From Sedona the quickest way to reach **Petrified Forest National Park** is to return to I-17 North and take I-40 East for 120 miles.

The shortest and most scenic route to the interstate is travelling east out of Sedona on **Schnebly Hill Scenic Drive** to I-17, 20 miles south of Flagstaff. Otherwise, you can drive north on US 89A, back through Oak Creek Canyon, or south on AZ 179 for 15 miles to I-17, 40 miles south of Flagstaff.

Seven miles east of Flagstaff on I-40 and three miles south on a well-signed paved road, is **Walnut Canyon National Monument**, Walnut Canyon Road, Flagstaff, AZ 86004, 602/526-3367. The site was occupied by Sinagua Indians for 100 years in the 1100s. A Visitor Center displays ancient Indian tools and household items, along with descriptions of Sinagua life. Two short trails start near the Visitor Center.

Island Trail covers a paved mile and a descent from the Visitor Center of 185 feet. It leads to more than 20 ruins built into cliff walls. The half-mile long **Rim Trail** is not as steep. It leads to several view sites and stabilized ruins.

Forty miles east of Flagstaff, 20 miles west of Winslow and south five miles on I-40, is **Meteor Crater**, a privately-owned, enormous cavity created 50,000 years ago when a meteor hurtling through space crashed on this spot. Although the space rock was only 100 feet in diameter, it made a hole nearly 600 feet deep and more than 4,000 feet wide.

A Visitor Center contains exhibits relating to meteorites and US lunar astronauts who trained here during the Apollo program. Unlike the astronauts you cannot go down into the crater but you may walk a 3.5-mile rim trail encircling the world's first proven and best preserved meteorite impact crater.

Winslow is a convenient but unexciting city on I-40, 50 miles west of the Petrified Forest. Noted mainly for the profusion of motels and restaurants that decorate the interstate passing through this community of 9,000, Winslow also has interesting natural areas nearby.

McHood Park, 602/289-3082, five miles southeast of town, is operated by the city and offers fishing for catfish, trout and bass, boating, and a campground.

Two miles northwest of Winslow is **Homolovi Ruins State Park**, 523 West Second Street, Winslow AZ 86947, 602/289-4106, possibly one of the last areas occupied by Anasazi Indians. The park includes a half-dozen large and small pueblos among 300 archaeological sites. Nine miles of paved roads lead to various sites that include ancient Indian rock art panels and a cluster of 1,400-year-old pit houses. There is a Visitor Center with a small museum. A mile-long hiking trail leads to two main ruins sites.

Little Painted Desert County Park, 602/524-6161, 15 miles north of Winslow off AZ 87, contains 900 acres of Painted Desert

Petrified Forest National Park

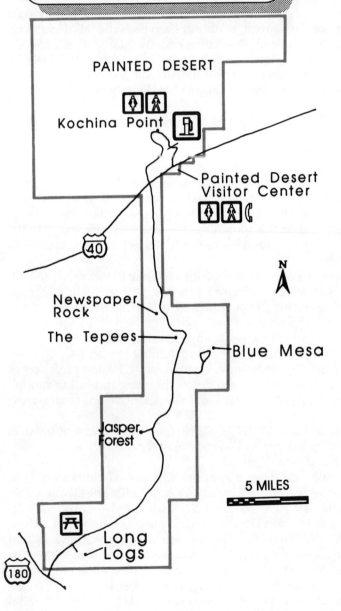

PAINTED DESERT

Kochina Point

Painted Desert
Visitor Center

40

N

Newspaper
Rock

The Tepees

Blue Mesa

Jasper
Forest

5 MILES

Long
Logs

180

scenery at 5,500 feet. There's a two-mile scenic drive and a mile-long hiking trail down into the eroded gullies at the bottom of 300-foot hills, all shaded in differing muted, earthy colors that take on a spectral glow early or late in the day.

For area-wide information contact **Winslow Chamber of Commerce**, 300 West North Road, Box 600, Winslow, AZ 86047, 602/289-2434. Winslow is served by major bus lines and **Amtrak**, 800/872-7245.

Holbrook, population 6,000, is 32 miles east of Winslow and 18 miles west of Petrified Forest National Park, on US 180. It provides the nearest accommodations, dining and picnic supplies to the National Park but mainly it's just another interstate pit-stop, replete with modest motels and restaurants and a not surprising number of shops offering petrified wood specimens for sale. Stock up here. You're not allowed to pocket samples from the National Park. The oldest shops in town are **Sun West Trading Co.**, 905 West Hopi Drive, and **J&J Trading Post**, 104 Navajo Boulevard.

Navajo County Museum, 100 East Navajo Street, Holbrook, AZ 86025, 602/524-6558, contains historic exhibits in a restored 1898 court house ranging from the prehistoric Indian era, through wild west shoot-em-up days, and contemporary affairs.

For area information, the **Holbrook Chamber of Commerce**, 602/524-6558, is in the same building and shares the same address with the museum.

The 93,533-acre **Petrified Forest National Park** can be reached either from the north by travelling 26 miles east on I-40 from Holbrook or, from the south, by travelling 18 miles east US 180, which you pick up a mile south of Holbrook off AZ 77. The two routes lead you to opposite ends of a 28-mile scenic drive through the park.

This is the final stop before heading north to the Navajo Reservation and Hopiland. The suggested route through the park starts at the southern end of the drive and ends at I-40. You can make the drive from either direction.

The attractions of the Petrified Forest are more subtle than many of the other overwhelming beauty sites in the Southwest but the austere, pastel-shaded hills contain more than 200 million years of fossils, including the world's largest concentration of petrified wood. These are ancient trees felled by primeval rivers then turned to stone by the interaction of minerals present in the water. The multi-colored, crystalline wood turned to stone looks like stained glass. When specimens catch the light they glimmer through a range of jeweled hues amid cacti and desert wildflowers.

Outside the park, just north of US 180, the **Petrified Forest Museum and Trading Post**, offering the last gas station and campground before entering the park, is across the road from **Crystal Forest Museum and Gift Shop**. These privately-owned shops sell rocks and exhibit some impressive specimens of petrified wood. Since the penalty for pocketing petrified wood from the park is jail time and a fine, these places offer a preferable alternative.

At Petrified Forest Trading Post you can actually pay a fee to gather samples from the 6,000-acre grounds. Rock hounds are given a map to the best sites. Hammer and chisel rentals are available.

Petrified Forest National Park, PO Box 2217, Petrified Forest National Park, AZ 86028, 602/524-6228, has a year-round Visitor Center, food services, and ranger facilities at both ends of the scenic drive. There are no services in between for 25 miles. There are no camping facilities or other accommodations inside the park.

Backcountry permits are required for overnight camping in designated wilderness areas. These are available from the ranger stations along with backcountry maps and other information.

Rainbow Forest Museum and Visitor Center is two miles north of the south park entrance on the scenic drive. Exhibits portray ancient reptiles, sea creatures who lived here millions of years ago, plus other ancestral area residents, including much more recent Anasazi Indians, who may have lived in the vicinity for nearly 1,000 years. There's a snack bar and a souvenir shop across the road and a picnic area nearby.

Behind the Visitor Center is a half-mile walking loop, **Giant Logs Trail**, lined with glittering, fallen, petrified logs, some five to six feet in diameter.

Every few miles along the scenic drive are turn-offs for parking areas and short trails displaying more petrified wood. Among the more interesting stops are the following:

- A quarter-mile past the Visitor Center is a turn-off to **Agate House**, an unusual reconstructed Indian ruin. Seven hundred years ago it contained seven rooms made of bejeweled blocks of petrified wood. Park rangers rebuilt two rooms in the 1930s.
- Agate House is just off the main **Long Logs Trail** which covers a half-mile through the greatest convergence of petrified wood in the park, including numerous petrified trees specimens more than 100 feet in length.
- Seven and a half miles north of the Visitor Center is **Agate Bridge**, a large petrified tree. It's 111 feet long, with its ends encased in sandstone, and stretches horizontally across an eroded ravine 40 feet wide.

- Three miles north of Agate Bridge and three miles east on a side road, midway through the park, is **Blue Mesa**. A mile-long trail provides good, close-up views of badlands. It descends into the low, red, orange, white, and blue striped hills, sloping steeply above scattered samples of petrified logs.

- Three-and-a half miles north of Blue Mesa, at **Newspaper Rock**, you can look through a telescope to see Indian petroglyphs carved into a big rock down below. A number of petroglyph sites in the park appear to be connected with solar cycles and primitive astronomy.

- A mile farther north is **Puerco Ruins**. It contains petroglyphs, a kiva and foundations of a 76-room pueblo that was abandoned 600 years ago.

- Six miles north of Puerco Ruins, a mile after you cross over I-40 into the northern section of the park, is the first of five **Painted Desert overlooks** of the epic expanses to the north and west.

- A sixth overlook, **Kachina Point**, nine miles north of Puerco Ruins, is also the trailhead for the backcountry at the north end of the park. It's adjacent to the **Painted Desert Inn Museum**, originally a Route 66 roadside inn in the 1920s, now an historic adobe structure with displays relating to the natural and human history of the area. Two rooms contain murals by a famous Hopi artist and there is a good Southwestern bookstore in the basement.

- As you loop south toward I-40 from the northernmost point on the scenic drive there are two more overlooks of the Painted Desert. They show the most expansive and colorful part of the park, best appreciated in early morning or late evening when the low angle of the sun casts long shadows. From the overlooks you can see the undulating layers of mineralized desert mauves, purples, reds, pinks, and oranges to the best advantage.

- A half-mile before returning to I-40 is the **Painted Desert Visitor Center**, featuring a film about the park, fossil displays, a ranger station for permits or information, a cafeteria dining room, a gift shop, and gas station.

Adventures

On Foot

There are a number of specific hiking guides published on trails in Northern Arizona and the Grand Canyon. Usually a selection of these are available at gift shops or bookstores in the area. Among the better ones are: *The Hiker's Guide to Arizona*, by Stewart Aitchison and Bruce Grubbs (Falcon Press, 1987); *Hiking the Southwest*, by Dave Ganci (Sierra Club Totebook, 1983); *A Naturalist's Guide to Hiking the Grand Canyon*, by Stewart Aitchison (Prentice Hall, 1985) which includes route maps for 30 Grand Canyon trails.

ARIZONA STRIP

There are nine wilderness area in the Arizona Strip plus portions of the Kaibab National Forest (see above, under Touring), all offering hiking possibilities for a few hours or days on end. Among these are the following:

Beaver Dam Wilderness, 20 miles south of St. George, Utah, accessed from an I-15 rest area, offers no trails but easy terrain leading through a Joshua tree forest.

In the **Mount Trumbull Wilderness Area**, 55 miles south of Fredonia, on the way to Toroweap Point, you can hike to the top of Mount Trumbull and back in a few hours. It's only a three-mile round-trip with an elevation change of 1,500 feet.

GRAND CANYON NATIONAL PARK

Any hiking into the Grand Canyon is arduous. It's frequently over 100 degrees in the summer. At night, even in the summer, you will require some warm clothes. It's always cooler at the North Rim than the South Rim.

There are a few places on certain trails to stop for water but, for the most part, independent hikers need to plan on being self-sufficient and prepared for extreme conditions.

You don't need a permit for day-hiking or if you have reservations for accommodations at **Phantom Ranch**, in the canyon bottom. Otherwise, a backcountry permit is required for overnight travel in the Grand Canyon. These permits are available by mail or in person from the from the **Backcountry Reservations Office**, Box 129, Grand Canyon, AZ 86023, 602/638-2474. The office is located on the South Rim, just south of the Visitor Center. Permits are also available from the **North Rim Ranger Station**, a quarter-mile north of the campground, and from the **Tuweep Ranger Station**, near Toroweap Point, west of Bright Angel Point. These sources are also good ones for backcountry hiking information.

The number of permits available in a given area at a given time is limited by park rangers. It's a good idea to plan as far ahead as possible. Reservations are accepted at any time for the rest of the year, and after October 1 for the following year.

There are a lot of interconnecting trails that can be hiked though some are unmaintained. Experienced hikers with proper equipment, including ropes, can find many completely remote, off-trail areas to spend time. Depending on the time of year and conditions, it's a good idea to consult with park rangers for possible routes. Pick up a Grand Canyon hiking guide from the Visitor Center on the South Rim or at the Grand Canyon Lodge on the North Rim.

Unless you are in exceedingly good shape and ready for a major challenge, it's probably not wise to try to hike down to the Colorado River and back up in a single day. Even a very strong hiker would probably need at least 12 hours for the most direct round-trip. Most people plan on taking at least two days for the round-trip hike.

You need to carry water and food and generally be well-prepared for hot weather and no shade in summer. You need to have reservations for Phantom Ranch or established camping areas at **Indian Gardens**, **Bright Angel** or **Cottonwood**; no other camping is permitted on maintained park trails. Unmaintained trails are a different story; you still need a permit and route-finding and map-reading skills are essential to reach remote areas in the park where primitive backcountry camping is allowed.

It is possible to hire a mule to carry your gear to or from Phantom Ranch. For information see below, under Grand Canyon Horseback & Mule Trips. If you decide to hike from one rim to the other and need a ride back contact **Trans Canyon Van Service**, 602/638-2820.

If the logistics of self-sufficiency seem overwhelming, you don't have to go it alone into the Grand Canyon. A number of outfitters offer guided hiking trips, among them the following:

The busiest hiking concessionaire is probably **Grand Canyon Trail Guides**, Box 735, Grand Canyon, AZ 86023, 602/638-2391, or c/o **Canyoneers/North Rim Hikes & Tours**, Box 2997, Flagstaff, AZ 86003, 602/526-0924 or 800/525-0924. Their Grand Canyon office is adjacent to the Backcountry Reservation Office on the South Rim and is open April to October. They offer a number of standard guided hiking trips or customized trips year-round, plus equipment rental and repair service. Among North Rim options are half-day to two-day guided hikes in the Kaibab National Forest from May to October.

Museum of Northern Arizona Ventures, Route 4, Box 720, Flagstaff, AZ 86001, 602/774-5211, runs a variety of guided hiking trips. Some involve extended hiking while others call only for short excursions from a car or motel. Trips are led by naturalists, biologists, geologists, and historians.

Expeditions, Inc., RR 4, Box 755, Flagstaff, AZ 86001, 602/774-8176 or 602/779-3769, operates guided backpacking trips in the Grand Canyon. They also run a complete backpacking and river running store at 625 North Beaver Street, Flagstaff, 602/779-3769.

The Open Road, 1622 East Gardenia, Phoenix, AZ 85020, 602/997-6474 or 800/766-7117, operates a variety of wilderness hiking and backpacking trips, with departures from Phoenix. These focus primarily on the Grand Canyon area but include a range of locales throughout the High Southwest. Grand Canyon trips are scheduled from January through November and include the following: A five-day backpacking trip in January, March or November, from the South Rim to the Havasupai Reservation; a four-day January backpacking trip from Grand Canyon Village to Bright Angel Campground with day hikes to Angel Falls and Phantom Canyon; a five-day backpacking trip offered in March, April, and October from the South Rim, on the Hermit Trail, across the Tonto Trail to Indian Gardens and out on the Bright Angel Trail, including camping at Hermits Camp, Monument Creek, and Horn Creek or Indian Gardens; five days hiking and camping in June on the North Rim of the Grand Canyon and Zion National Park; nine days hiking and mountain biking in August, on the North Rim of the Grand Canyon, Bryce and Zion National Parks. Other trips are also available.

Willard's Adventure Club, Box 10, Barrie Ontario, L4M 4S9 Canada, 705/737-1881 or 705/728-4787, offers guided eight- to 10-day expeditions into the Grand Canyon in April and May.

On an eight-day, late-April Arizona Grand Canyon Base Camp Trip, the tour meets in Las Vegas and travels to the South Rim. Five days of hiking are based out of dormitory accommodations at Phantom Ranch. The hikes vary from strenuous to easy and include hiking the Inner Canyon trails to Ribbon Falls, Clear Creek, and Indian Gardens.

A nine-day Arizona Grand Canyon Expedition in early May includes seven nights camping and six days hiking on a full backpacking expedition exploring the North and South rims. It starts in Las Vegas and includes five nights at wilderness campsites within the Grand Canyon, with two nights of camping on the South Rim.

All Adventure Travel, 5589 Arapahoe Road, Suite 208, Boulder, CO 80303, 800/537-4025, fax 303/440-4160, offers a Grand Canyon Hiker tour in May and October. It lasts six days and heads to the South Rim, including hiking Bright Angel Trail and to the Havasupai Reservation. An Indians of the Grand Canyon itinerary, offered the same months, is a six-day tour focusing on Indian culture and includes a scenic flight to the Havasupai Reservation and day hikes.

North Rim

There are some easy trails on the North Rim. The following trails stay on the rim and lead to canyon overlooks.

Widforss Trail starts a quarter-mile south of the turn-off for Cape Royal, heading west off the North Rim road. It doesn't go down into the canyon but winds over milder terrain along the forested rim for five miles to Widforss Point, which affords views of Haunted Canyon and the South Rim. The 10-mile round-trip can usually be accomplished in six hours.

Ken Patrick Trail is another 10-mile rim trail that starts at Point Imperial and descends only 560 feet to the North Kaibab Trailhead, which is two miles north of the Grand Canyon Lodge. You can hike three- or seven-mile portions of the trail. The entire hike should take six hours.

Another rim trail is the **Uncle Jim Trail**, which starts on the Ken Patrick Trail at the North Kaibab Trailhead, then veers southeast to Uncle Jim Point for stunning rim views. The round-trip hike is five miles. This trail is also used for mule rides.

Then there are harder North Rim trails that descend into the Grand Canyon:

The most popular North Rim trail is probably the **North Kaibab Trail**. It starts just north of the ranger station, at the head of Roaring Springs Canyon, and covers 14 miles one-way, with a descent of 5,840 feet, to Phantom Ranch. In five miles, after a 3,100-foot descent past vertical rock faces that shed water in rivulets after a storm, there is a picnic area with water available at Roaring Springs (at the head of Bright Angel Creek). There are also some swimming holes nearby and this is as far as most day-trippers go. It's another two miles along the creek to Cottonwood Campground where there is water in summer and a ranger station. You need reservations for the campground. In another mile and a half you can take a side-trip to verdant Ribbon Falls, before the trail bottoms out at Phantom Ranch and Bright Angel Campground.

From there you can hike back to the North Rim or cross a suspension bridge to continue up to the South Rim by the Bright

Angel Trail or South Kaibab Trail. This is the only North Rim trail into the canyon with drinking water available along the way.

Clear Creek Trail starts off the North Kaibab Trail, a quarter-mile north of Phantom Ranch, and covers nine miles along the bottom of the Grand Canyon to Clear Creek. There's additional rugged hiking in side canyons feathering off Clear Creek or you can hike up the creek to Chevaya Falls.

The only other North Rim trail in the vicinity of Bright Angel Point is **Nankoweap Trail** and it is definitely not for those who are afraid of heights, nor for those who don't know how to read a topographic map. Don't even think about this trail if you don't know what you're doing. It's a narrow and steep unmaintained trail that starts 2.5 miles northeast of Point Imperial. The closest driving access to the trailhead is by Forest Road 610 or House Rock Buffalo Ranch Road, which are detailed above under Touring Arizona Strip. From the end of either road it's a three-mile hike to the trailhead, then 14 miles to the river.

Several other difficult trails descend below the North Rim from points farther west that are accessible by back roads through the Kaibab Forest. They incude the short but treacherous trail from the Toroweap area to Lava Falls.

To reach the trailhead you drive west on a jeep road midway between the ranger station and the campground. The trail starts where the road ends and descends a vertiginous 2,500 feet in only two miles. Despite its brevity, the strenuous round-trip hike takes the better part of a day. As always, before tackling extreme backcountry, consult with park rangers for helpful hints and details on conditions.

South Rim

There are maintained and unmaintained trails all along the South Rim leading into the Grand Canyon.

One unmaintained trail, the 92-mile **Tonto Trail**, threads through the inner canyon, staying 1,200 feet above the river, from mid-way on the East Rim Drive to far west of Hermit's Rest. It also links with many other rim trails. There are specified backcountry campsites along part of the Tonto Trail.

There are enough linked trails from the South Rim so that you can hike down one trail and back up a different one. The most popular South Rim trails are Bright Angel Trail and South Kaibab Trail, which are also used for mule-back trips.

Bright Angel Trail starts on the west side of Bright Angel Lodge and descends in the most easily managed steps to the Colorado River in eight miles. The steps include rest stops equipped with emergency phones and drinking water at 1.5 miles and 3 miles from the rim.

It's 4.5 miles from the rim to Indian Gardens Campground, and a bit over three miles from there to the river. Day hikers usually go as far as Indian Gardens. The more ambitious push on another mile and a half past the campground to Plateau Point, a wedge of land protruding 1,300 feet straight above the Colorado River and offering unobstructed views of the inner canyon in all directions.

River Trail connects a distance of a mile and a half from the bottom of the Bright Angel Trail to the bottom of South Kaibab Trail. It is bisected by two suspension bridges across the river to Bright Angel Creek and the North Kaibab Trail.

South Kaibab Trail starts from a trailhead 4.5 miles east of Grand Canyon Village, near Yaki Point, and descends 4,800 feet in the 6.5 miles leading to the river. It's shorter and steeper than the Bright Angel Trail. The only emergency phone is 4.5 miles below the rim at the Tonto Trail, which connects in four miles with Indian Gardens on the Bright Angel Trail.

Hermit Trail starts near Hermit's Rest at the end of the West Rim Drive and descends 4,300 feet in 8.5 miles to the river. A mile and a half from the rim it connects with a 1.5-mile section of **Dripping Springs Trail**, for a good day-hike.

You can also connect with **Boucher Trail** from the Dripping Springs Trail and descend 3,500 feet to the Tonto Trail, where there are signs to Boucher Creek, which leads 1.5 miles to the river. Many hikers on multi-day trips then hike east on the Tonto Trail, back to Hermit Trail. Others make a multi-day loop by hiking the Hermit Trail to the Tonto Trail, then heading east along the Tonto Plateau to Bright Angel Trail.

There are hiking trails into the western end of the Grand Canyon's South Rim through the Havasupai Reservation. These require special permits from the tribe (see above, under Touring).

Other trails are found along the South Rim's East Rim Drive.

Grandview Trail, from Grandview Point on the East Rim Drive, descends 2,600 feet in three miles to Horseshoe Mesa, making an attainable round-trip day hike. If you want to continue, there are several trails that lead from the mesa to the Tonto Trail.

Farther east, along the East Rim Drive, **New Hance Trail** starts from a trailhead between Grandview Point and Moran Point. It descends 4,400 feet in eight miles to the river at Hance Rapids, which is also the eastern end of the Tonto Trail. Rock cairns mark the faint **Escalante Trail** that extends for 15 miles up river from Hance Rapids to Tanner Canyon Rapids.

Tanner Trail starts farther east, near Lipan Point on the East Rim Drive, and covers a 4,700-foot descent in 10 miles to the river at Tanner Canyon Rapids.

Beamer Trail starts at Tanner Canyon Rapids and runs alongside the river for four miles to Palisades Creek. Another five miles takes you to the confluence of the Little Colorado River.

WILLIAMS/FLAGSTAFF

West of Flagstaff, near Williams, are a number of hiking areas that haven't yet seen the overcrowding that sometimes plagues areas such as Sedona's Oak Creek Canyon.

There are several easy trails at **Dogtown Lake**, seven miles southeast of Williams, including a two-mile loop around the lake and a short nature trail.

White Horse Lake, 19 miles southeast of Williams, is a year-round recreation area, providing nearby access to **Sycamore Falls Trail**, which is two miles north of White Horse Lake Resort on Forest Road 109. Two waterfalls are a short distance on the trail but they run only in rainy weather or during spring run-off.

Sycamore Trail covers 11 miles in Upper Sycamore Canyon and can be hiked for short or longer stretches with access through Sycamore Falls and several other trailheads.

Two trails to the top of Bill Williams Mountain are open June through September. **Bill Williams Trail** covers a seven-mile round-trip up the north side of the 9,255-foot mountain. It starts from the Williams Ranger Station, 1.5 miles west of Williams on the I-40 frontage road. **Benham Trail** covers a six-mile round-trip up the south side of the mountain. To reach the trailhead go three miles south of Williams on Fourth Street, then a half-mile west on Benham Ranch Road.

Information on Williams area trails is available from the Williams or Chalender Forest Service offices listed above, under Touring Williams/Flagstaff.The same offices can provide information on the two following hiking areas:

An unusual trail is 33 miles northeast of Flagstaff, off US 180, 18 miles southeast of Valle. **Red Mountain Trail** is a short, easy hike through a cleft in the side of a volcanic cone leading directly into the crater. You don't have to climb up the 1000-foot-high volcano to get inside it, although you can reach the top by hiking or driving a rough dirt road. This is probably the most easily accessed volcanic crater in the Southwest.

Access to the small **Kendrick Peak Wilderness Area** is west of US 180, 15 miles south of the Red Mountain turn-off, 18 miles northwest of Flagstaff. Kendrick Peak, elevation 10,418 feet, is lower than the famous San Francisco Peaks to the east. A gravel forest road crosses the southern border of the wilderness area and several signed hiking trails lead north in six- to 12-mile round-trips to the peak. Trails are generally open June through September.

Flagstaff's great variety of trails, many within a short distance of the city, climb to the highest peaks in the state, wind through wilderness areas restricted to hiking or horseback access, and pass by Indian ruins and volcanic fields.

Many trails start right in Flagstaff from the Peaks Ranger Station on Santa Fe Avenue/US 89. The office is the main information source for trail guides and conditions.

Mount Elden Lookout Trail ascends steeply from the ranger station, climbing 2,400 feet up the east slope in just three miles, for a 9,299-foot view of Flagstaff, the area around Sunset Crater, and vistas far beyond in all directions.

Several other trails lead to the top of Mount Elden, including the five-mile-long **Oldham Trail** which is not as steep as the Lookout Trail. It starts at the north end of town, off Cedar Avenue at Buffalo Park Trail, and ascends around 2,300 feet.

An easy day-hike to sample the scenery might cover a mile up the Oldham Trail from the **Buffalo Park Trail**, or a half-mile up the Elden Lookout Trail, then follow the level three-mile **Pipeline Trail** that connects the two trails around the base of Mount Elden.

Other popular hiking areas close to Flagstaff start from many trailheads along Shultz Pass Road or Mount Elden Road, both accessed three miles northwest of town, off US 180. Shultz Pass Road links US 180 with US 89 near Sunset Crater. Mount Elden Road climbs to the top of Mount Elden.

Rocky Ridge Trail starts at Schultz Creek Trail, a mile and a half north of US 180 off Shultz Pass Road, and connects with the Oldham Trail in two fairly level miles.

Sunset Trail starts four miles north of US 180 on Shultz Pass Road, at **Shultz Pass Trail**, and climbs 1,300 feet in four miles to the top of Mount Elden.

Schultz Creek Trail covers three easy miles, linking the trailheads for the Rocky Ridge and Sunset Trails.

The Peaks Ranger Station also administers the Kachina Peaks Wilderness Area, encompassing 18,200 acres of the San Francisco Peaks, including Humphrey's Peak, Arizona's highest mountain at 12,633 feet, plus other impressive but slightly smaller mountains that are accessible only to hikers or horseback riders.

Two main trails into the Kachina Peaks area are accessible on the north side of Shultz Pass Road, across from the parking area at Schultz Pass Trail. These are as follows:

Weatherford Trail was once an automobile road into the Kachina Peaks. Today, only hikers or horseback riders can use it to reach Humphrey's Peak in 10 miles.

Kachina Trail covers six miles, linking the main road and trails through the Mount Elden area with the main road and other trails through the Kachina Peaks Wilderness. It starts at either of two places, off Schultz Pass Road at 8,000 feet or at the 9,300-foot Snowbowl Ski Area. You could conceivably hike Kachina Trail to Sunset Trail and on to the top of Mount Elden.

The most direct access to Humphrey's Peak is from the ski area, seven miles northwest on US 180 to the Snowbowl Road, then north. On the way there's a short, easy trail five miles up the road from US 180. It starts beside a small parking area for the **Lamar Haines Memorial Wildlife Area**. The trail's a mile long and leads to a peaceful spring-fed pond.

At the end of the Snowbowl Road, seven miles north of US 180 at the ski area, **Humphrey's Peak Trail** covers a nine-mile round-trip to the 12,633-foot summit of Arizona's tallest mountain. The trail starts in evergreen and aspen forests and emerges around 12,000 feet into Alpine tundra. It's usually free of snow June through September but the weather can change dramatically year-round so it's a good idea to pack foul-weather gear. There's no camping or fires allowed above 11,400 feet so most hikers make this a day-trip.

Humphrey's Peak Trail joins the Weatherford Trail a mile and a half from Humphrey's Peak, at around 11,800 feet. It's eight miles on the Weatherford Trail from there to Schultz Pass Road, or around three miles to the ski area on Humphrey's Peak Trail.

The **Inner Basin** day-use area on the north side of the San Francisco Peaks offers additional hiking trails ranging from 8,500 feet to more than 11,000 feet. No overnight camping is permitted here. The turn-off to Forest Road 552 is a mile north of Sunset Crater off US 89. It reaches Lockett Meadow, site of several trailheads, in five miles. Parking and camping are permitted in the vicinity of Lockett Meadow.

Southeast of Flagstaff the terrain becomes less vertical, leveling into high, forested plateaus marked by lakes for fishing, boating, and camping.

There are some short hiking trails around Mormon Lake, and more extensive and challenging trails in the **West Clear Creek Wilderness Area**, between Happy Jack and Clints Well. Sometimes the only trail through the West Clear Creek Wilderness Area is the creek itself and hikers need to be prepared to get wet. Floating gear on a small inflatable raft usually prevents it from getting wet.

For trail information and conditions contact the following offices:

Mormon Lake Ranger District Office (4825 Lake Mary Road, Flagstaff, AZ 86001, 602/556-7474).
Happy Jack Ranger Station, PO Box 68, Happy Jack, AZ 86024, 602/527-7371. The office is on Lake Mary Road, 12 miles south of Mormon Lake.
Blue Ridge Ranger Station, Box 300, Happy Jack, AZ 86024, 602/477-2255. The office is eight miles northeast of Clints Well, on AZ 87.

SEDONA

Despite the overcrowded conditions that sometimes compromise the allure of Sedona, hiking trails around Sedona and Oak Creek Canyon do eventually lead to out-of-the-way places, including narrow canyons stretching vertically hundreds of feet and wilderness areas where the four-wheel-drive vehicles cannot travel.

You can hike for an hour or week and the season runs year-round. It's hot in mid-summer and some areas get a fair bit of snow in winter. The following are a sampling of interesting, readily accessible trails out of the many the region offers.

Pumphouse Wash is not really a trail but you can trek over rocks and through the stream flowing in this side canyon for 3.5 miles one way. The lower trailhead is at the bottom of the switchbacks, next to the Pumphouse Wash Bridge, 13.5 miles north of Sedona on the east side of US 89A. It's 800 feet lower than the upper trailhead which is 16.5 miles north of Sedona on the east side of US 89A. There are good swimming spots along this route.

The popular **West Fork Trail** begins 10 miles north of Sedona, on the west side of US 89A in Oak Creek Canyon, a mile and a quarter south of Cave Springs Campground. It covers 14 mostly level miles but you'll be getting your feet wet crossing the tributary of Oak Creek repeatedly. The first six miles of the trail contain dramatic vertical canyon faces and the flowing waters feed brimming foliage. Unique vegetation found here prompted designation of this portion of the trail as part of the Oak Creek Research Natural Area in the 1930s, long before it was incorporated into the Red Rock-Secret Mountain Wilderness Area. No camping or fires are allowed in this portion of the canyon.

Part of the reason day-hikes are popular along segments of this route is because the middle miles of the trail entail rock scrambling and possibly swimming, which tends to discourage all but the most intent backpackers. Towards the end of the trail at Woody

Mountain Road/Forest Road 231, where you may want to have a car shuttle waiting, the trail gets faint.

A mile and a half south of West Fork Trail, on the west side of US 89A across from Bootlegger Campground, is the start of the **East Pocket Trail**. It covers a strenuous two miles one way, up more than 30 switchbacks and gaining 2,000 feet in elevation to reach the East Pocket Fire Lookout which provides 360 degree views of the canyon and surrounding landscape.

Red rock buttes and spires begin to appear prominently as you pass Slide Rock State Park. Five and a half miles north of Sedona, a mile north of the Encinoso Picnic Area, is **North Wilson Mountain Trail**. It covers 2.5 miles one way, gaining 1,700 feet in elevation, to the top of Wilson Mountain. Another way to reach the same place is to drive south to Midgely Bridge, spanning Wilson Canyon, two miles north of Sedona. Wilson Mountain lies to the north and **South Wilson Mountain Trail** offers a more gradual, but longer ascent of 2,300 feet to the summit. It meets and merges with North Wilson Trail a little past half-way on the 5.5-mile one-way hike.

Four miles west of AZ 179 on US 89A, in West Sedona, Dry Creek Road goes north for two miles to Sterling Canyon Road and Forest Service-maintained trailheads for Devil's Bridge Trail, Brins Mesa Trail, Secret Canyon, and Vultee Arch Trail.

Devil's Bridge Trail is a mile northeast of Dry Creek Road off Sterling Canyon Road. The short trail gains 400 feet in elevation in just under a mile, ending at the base of Devil's Bridge, a graceful natural arch. A side trail leads to the crown of the arch.

The trailhead for **Vultee Arch** is three miles farther on Sterling Canyon Road from the Devil's Bridge Trailhead. It gains 400 feet in elevation covering a mile and a half one-way to a small natural bridge named after a pilot who crashed nearby in the 1930s.

Boynton Canyon, of vortex fame, is considered by many to be the strongest local power spot of all. It's also the site of the 2.5-mile one way **Boynton Canyon Trail** that gains 440 feet in elevation, through the wooded red rock canyon filled with Indian ruins.

To reach the trailhead, follow directions to the north off US 89A in West Sedona onto Dry Creek Road. Beyond the turn-off for Sterling Canyon Road, Dry Creek becomes Boynton Pass Road. Watch for trailhead signs.

At the south end of the village of Oak Creek, south of Sedona on AZ 179, Jack's Canyon Road/Forest Road 793, goes east three miles to **Jack's Canyon Trail**. The 6.5-mile trail climbs 2,000 feet, providing the main route into the 18,000-acre Munds Mountain Wilderness Area.

Jack's Canyon Trail ends in a saddle between Munds Mountain and Schnebly Hill. **Munds Mountain Trail** leads 2.5 miles from the saddle, and another 450 feet higher to the mountain top, which offers excellent views of the red rock scenery.

Complete trail and back road information is available from the Forest Service office in Sedona.

PETRIFIED FOREST NATIONAL PARK

Park rangers estimate that only one in a thousand visitors to the Petrified Forest ever hikes through the backcountry. There aren't even really trails out there; it's pretty much open desert terrain that you can wander through at will.

There are two designated wilderness areas in the park, Rainbow Forest Wilderness, filled with petrified wood, in the south, and Painted Desert Wilderness, a pastel-shaded wilderness of bare hills and badlands, in the north. Overnight camping is permitted in these areas; a backcountry permit is required and these are available at no charge from the Visitor Centers at the north or south park entrance.

The 7,400-acre Rainbow Forest Wilderness is accessed from the **Flattops Trail**, five miles north of US 180 off the scenic drive. The area contains a lot of petrified wood among eroded badlands and desert spiked by scrub grass. The trailhead, though, is only that; there are no proper trails in the wilderness area.

The 43,000-acre Painted Desert area is accessed a mile north of I-40, off the scenic drive, at **Kachina Point**. It contains the majority of ancient Indian sites found in the park, hidden ruins, and rock art amid gnomish badlands, with horizontally-striated mesas and buttes extending to a distant horizon. The highest point in the park, 6,235-foot high Pilot Rock, is six miles from the trailhead. The trail, such as it is, descends only a short distance from Kachina Point. Then you're on your own to pick out your own overland route.

Horseback/Mule Trips

GRAND CANYON NATIONAL PARK

The famous mule-back trips into the Grand Canyon generally require reservations far in advance, although occasional cancellations do occur.

A variety of trips are offered year-round from the South Rim, but only in summer from the North Rim. These range from an hour to overnight. Even though you will be sitting, the trips are formidable and it does take some energy to hang on. If heights are bothersome to you, be aware that the mules step very close to the edge of the narrow trail and it's a long way down. In addition, there are restrictions applied to the mule trips: Riders must speak English, stand over four feet seven inches tall and weigh less than 200 pounds fully clothed. If you don't qualify or decide you'd prefer to hike, a mule can be hired to carry your gear.

North Rim mule trips are offered when the Grand Canyon Lodge is open, usually mid-May to late-October. For information contact the lodge or **Canyon Trail Rides, Inc.**, Box 128, Tropic, Utah 84776, 602/638-2292 or 801/679-8665 (off-season), which runs one-hour to full-day trail rides at the North Rim.

South Rim mule trips are run under the auspices of **Grand Canyon National Park Lodges**, PO Box 699, Grand Canyon, AZ 86023, 602/638-2401. They offer popular one- or two-day mule rides into the canyon on the Bright Angel Trail. Day-trips go as far as Plateau Point. Overnight trips cross the river and include accommodations at Phantom Ranch. The return to the South Rim the following day is accomplished on the South Kaibab Trail.

Make reservations as far in advance as possible. Booking space a year ahead of time is common. Information and reservations are also available from the **Bright Angel Transportation Desk**, 602/638-2631.

Apache Stables, PO Box 158, Grand Canyon, AZ 86023, 602/638-2891 or 602/638-2424, is at Moqui Lodge, a quarter-mile south of the park's south entrance. The stables offer one- or two-hour trail rides, a half-day East Rim ride, and a campfire wagon and trail ride.

Wild & Scenic, Inc., Box 460, Flagstaff, AZ 86002, 602/774-7343 or 800/231-1963, runs five-day horseback trips to the Grand Canyon, Zion, and Bryce National Parks.

Havasupai Tourist Enterprises, Supai, AZ 86435, 602/448-2121, operates overnight mule trips to Havasupai Canyon.

FLAGSTAFF

Hartman Outfitters, 448 Lake Mary Road, Flagstaff, AZ 86001, 602/774-7131, runs horseback rides daily (May to September) from the Hitchin' Post Stables into Walnut Canyon, the ancient home of cliff-dwelling Sinagua Indians. The canyon is said to be five miles and 100 years from town. The choice of trips include breakfast rides, steak rides, one- or two-hour rides, half-day, full-day or multi-day rides, all offering opportunities to see pictographs, explore caves or hiking trails from the ranch campsite where meals are provided and overnight camps are made. Also: Horse-drawn wagon rides are available.

Ski Lift Lodge Stables, US 180 and Snowbowl Road, Flagstaff, 602/774-0729, runs trail rides in the San Francisco Peaks.

SEDONA

Kachina Stables, Lower Red Rock Loop Road, PO Box 3616, West Sedona, AZ 86340, 602/282-7252, offers year-round trail rides among the red rocks to supposedly sacred Indian ceremonial sites. Scheduled rides are offered for one or two hours, or a full day. Customized overnight pack trips are also available.

On Wheels

RAIL TRIPS

Grand Canyon Railway, 800/843-8724, runs a train powered by a turn-of-the-century steam locomotive. Trips run to the South Rim of the Grand Canyon from I-40 in Williams. Passengers ride in authentically restored 1920s Harriman Coach cars and there is on-board entertainment that includes a fake train robbery, as well as complimentary refreshments.

Since there are free shuttles available at the South Rim and traffic is a problem, this is certainly a legitimate alternative mode of transportation that helps ease overcrowding and allows you to sit back and enjoy the scenery. Round-trip service is available daily and if you're planning to stay at the Grand Canyon you can arrange to take the train back when you need to.

Verde River Canyon Excursion Train, PO Box 103, Clarkdale, AZ 86324, 602/639-1630, fax 602/639-1653, is based out of Clarkdale, 30 minutes southwest of Sedona by car. The two-hour train ride winds through Coconino and Prescott National Forests and has been compared to the Durango-Silverton train for scenic splendor with a Southwestern flair. It follows the Verde River through red rock scenery to Perkinsville, a small ranch site, and is the only way, aside from travel on foot, to view the riparian habitat of numerous bird and wildlife species, as well as Indian ruins, in this federal wilderness area that has no roads.

Passengers travel in pullman-style coach seats or first class cars that are more like living rooms, with access to open-air gondola cars for sightseeing and photography. The train operates year-round, Wednesday through Sunday, with extra Monday departures and two departures daily in April, May, October, and

November. There is a food and beverage service on board. Also: Moonlight rides are offered in June, July, and August. Room, Ride and Meal packages are available. They include overnight accommodations at the Railroad Inn in Sedona.

JEEPING/FOUR-WHEEL-DRIVE TRIPS

Arizona Strip/
Grand Canyon National Park (North Rim)

There's a network of backroads through the Arizona Strip leading to the North Rim of the Grand Canyon. These are not the best roads although the Forest Service does consider them passable in ordinary cars in good weather. Four-wheel-drive is a much better idea and make sure you start with a full tank of gas plus extra water and food. Tools and spare parts are not a bad idea. There should be signs along the way but these could be missing at certain points, so be sure to have a good map along.

The roads from **St. George** and **Pipe Springs** are maintained to some extent, but it's a long drive to the North Rim on any of these roads and you're unlikely to find help in an emergency. The road to the North Rim from **Colorado City** is the shortest but also in the worst condition. The last few miles to Toroweap Point are very poor. Remember: no water, gas, food, or any other supplies are available anywhere along these routes, and no services are available once you reach these remote areas of the North Rim.

The best road of the lot heads south off AZ 389, six miles east of Pipe Springs National Monument, and runs through deserted backcountry for 40 miles until it joins another dirt road, heading south from AZ 389, near Colorado City. This second dirt road covers 45 miles from AZ 389 to the wilderness junction. From there, it is another 20 miles south to **Toroweap Point** (sometimes called Tuweep) on the North Rim.

There is a year-round Tuweep Ranger Station a few miles north of a primitive campground at Toroweap. From the point you have the opportunity to experience the Grand Canyon at its narrowest point, barely a mile across. The Colorado River flows through 3,000 feet below and the voices of river rafters float up the tight canyon walls.

If you plan to camp here you will need a backcountry reservation, available at the ranger station. For other ways to obtain the permit see below, under Camping.

Other dirt roads eventually leading to Toroweap Point start south from **Hurricane** and **St. George,** in Utah. Of these, the one from St. George is probably the better.

Also in this area are several fascinating BLM-maintained petroglyph sites. Little Black Mountain Petroglyph Site, and Nampaweap/Billy Goat Canyon are detailed above, under Touring Arizona Strip.

Museum of Northern Arizona Ventures (Route 4, Box 720, Flagstaff, AZ 86001, 602/774-5211) runs four-wheel-drive tours on the Colorado Plateau, offering an alternative to ranging through this area on your own.

Grand Canyon National Park (South Rim)

A rough dirt road starts north from **Desert View** on the East Rim Drive and covers 15 miles to Cape Solitude, overlooking the confluence of the Colorado and Little Colorado rivers. Other rugged and remote roads branch off to more backcountry. Consult with park rangers for reports on road and weather conditions.

Several gravel and dirt roads head west from AZ 64/US 180 in the vicinity of **Tusayan,** more or less paralleling the South Rim all the way to Tribal Route 18, south of Hualapai Hilltop on the Havasupai Reservation. Take good maps.

Williams/Flagstaff

The only road access to the **Sycamore Canyon Wilderness Area** is 23 miles southeast of Williams at **Sycamore Canyon Point.** A panoramic view site overlooks the west rim of the 21-mile-long, six-mile-wide canyon. To reach the overlook, drive eight miles south of Williams on Fourth Street, then 15 miles east on Forest Road 110.

The seasonal road to the top of **Bill Williams Mountain** is probably more enjoyable in a four-wheel drive. It starts five miles south of Williams on Fourth Street, then heads west for seven miles to reach the 9,255-foot-peak. The road is open May to October.

Flagstaff's back roads are plentiful. A popular jeep route is **Mount Elden Road** to the top of 9,299-foot Mount Elden, just north of town. The road starts three miles north of downtown, a little north of the Museum of Northern Arizona. Continue driving straight (east) when Shultz Pass turns left to the north. Numerous hiking and biking trails cross the road before it reaches the mountain top. The view encompasses Flagstaff, Oak Creek Canyon, the

Painted Desert, volcano fields, including Sunset Crater, and mountains.

North of Sunset Crater and west of US 89, a network of jeep roads leads to remote hiking trails of the Inner Basin of the San Francisco Peaks. These north slope trails are open only to hikers and horseback riders. You can drive by the lower trailheads, west to US 180, in 14 miles. From there it's 20 miles southeast on US 180 to Flagstaff.

The area southeast of Flagstaff is laced with four-wheel-drive roads, many leading to good fishing lakes. For details see below, under Fishing.

Sedona

Some of Sedona's back roads are challenging while others are threatening. It's helpful to know the difference. A large numbers of visitors opt for guided jeep tours rather than independent journeys.

Guided jeep tours to vortex and ceremonial sites, isolated backcountry, overnight camping trips, or jeeping and hiking combination tours are offered by several companies. Friendly competition runs high among the most popular guides, who are known for their humorous routines. Most jeep tours operate year-round.

Pink Jeep Tours, Box 1447, Sedona, AZ 86336, 602/282-5000 or 800/283-3328, runs some of the most popular one- to three-hour, scenic, vortex and historic jeep tours in the backcountry around Sedona, including some over rugged terrain.

Sedona Red Rock Jeep Tours, 260 North US 89A, PO Box 10305, Sedona, AZ 86336, 602/282-2026, competes with Pink Tours for exciting trips and the funniest guides. Their Cowboy West Tour explores Sedona's western history on Soldiers Pass Trail, an old cavalry route from the 1870s, and Sedona's Indian history, including how Indians lived off the land and why the red rocks were sacred to them.

Another tour follows the Old Bear Wallow Stage Route and emphasizes opportunities to photograph wildlife such as elk, deer, great blue herons, wild turkeys, and red foxes. Also: Customized Photography Tours can be arranged to suit a photographer's specifications.

The same company operates **Sacred Earth Tours**, 260 North US 89A, Sedona, AZ 86336, 602/282-6826 or 800/848-7728, offering what they claim to be Sedona's original authentic Vortex tour, visiting the sacred spots of concentrated energy.

In addition, full-day Ancestral Hopi Mesa Tours are offered, including stops at three Hopi villages on First Mesa and craft demonstrations.

Time Expeditions, 276 North US 89A, Sedona, AZ 86336, 800/999-2137 or 602/282-2137, offers a variety of scheduled trips that consider the vortices scientifically. The specialty of the company is its historic Indian ruins tours. Also: Customized tours are available.

Sedona Adventures, Uptown Mall, Sedona, AZ 86336, 602/282-4114, offers two-hour jeeping and hiking tours, vortex tours, and overnight tours.

Sue Winters, 602/282-4320, specializes in photography tours.

Earth Wisdom Tours, 293 North US 89A, Sedona, AZ 86336, 602/282-4717, specializs in vortex trips with an unabashed New Age-slant; driver-guides are versed in the domain of crystals, auras, healing plants, and Indian symbolism.

For back roads information and maps contact Sedona's Chamber of Commerce or the local Forest Service office.

MOUNTAIN BIKING

Arizona Strip/Grand Canyon

You can't ride a bike on park trails, but you can ride one on specified park roads on the North and South Rims. Better biking may be found outside the park in areas of the Arizona Strip, such as **Antelope Valley**, **Mount Trumbull** and **Mount Logan**, and **Kaibab National Forest**. The dirt roads through the Arizona Strip to Toroweap Point or other remote viewpoints make challenging bike trips. For details see above, under Touring and Jeeping, or contact the ranger station south of Jacob Lake for maps and information.

The rough jeep road to **Cape Solitude** from the East Rim Drive is a difficult, 30-mile, multi-day bike trip. You need a backcountry permit to camp.

AZ 67, from Jacob Lake to the North Rim, has been called one of the prettiest roads in America. There's not as much traffic as along roads leading to the South Rim, but there is traffic, so bikers beware of large travel trailers and the like.

On the South Rim heavy vehicle traffic takes some of the fun out of biking, but the **West Rim Drive**, though closed to cars in summer, is open to bicyclists. The **East Rim Drive** can make for good biking, though probably in low season, not when contending with summertime traffic.

There are extensive backroads between **Grand Canyon Village** and the **Havasupai Reservation**, west of AZ 64/US 180, as well as east of the highway in the Kaibab National Forest, south of the East Rim Drive.

Williams/Flagstaff

There's good biking in the forests around Williams. The curlicue road to the top of **Bill Williams Mountain**, 4.5 miles south of town, is a challenging seven-mile ride to the 9,255-foot summit. Three miles south of that turn are several gravel roads leading to White Horse Lake and Sycamore Canyon Point.

There are hundreds of miles of bike routes surrounding Flagstaff on all sides. Right in town is the **Urban Trails System and Bikeways System**. It connects the university area with downtown. Contact the Visitor Center or university for information.

A major network of bike trails traverses the Mount Elden area on the north end of Flagstaff.

The longest trail to the top of Mount Elden starts in North Flagstaff, at the Buffalo Park Trailhead, off Cedar Avenue. **Oldham Trail** climbs 2,300 feet of the west side of Mount Elden in five miles.

Other major trail access is off Schultz Pass Road or Mount Elden Road, three miles northwest of downtown Flagstaff, and north off US 180.

Shultz Pass Road edges the San Francisco Peaks and the Kachina Peaks Wilderness northwest of Flagstaff for 12 miles to US 89. You can bike back to Flagstaff in 10 miles along US 89.

Sunset Trail starts four miles north of US 180 on Shultz Pass Road, at Shultz Pass Trail, and climbs 1,300 feet in four miles to the top of Mount Elden.

Mount Elden Road is a longer but more gradual ascent of six miles on a rugged jeep road that starts where the Shultz Pass Road turns north, a mile north of US 180.

An easy 4.5-mile ride, on mostly level ground, starts on the Oldham Trail but turns east after one mile onto the **Pipeline Trail**. The trail follows the base of Mount Elden to the Elden Lookout Trail, a half-mile from the Peaks Ranger Station. **Elden Lookout Trail** goes to the top of Mount Elden from there in 2.5 miles. It's a steep climb of 2,400 feet and suitable only for strong and fearless bike riders.

The forest office, on North Santa Fe Avenue/US 89 at the Elden Trail, can provide current information on the entire Mount Elden trail network.

Four miles northwest of Shultz Pass Road on US 180, the seven-mile **Snowbowl Road** offers a steep, 2,000-foot ascent to the ski area. The fun part of this is the descent.

Flagstaff Nordic Center, 602/774-6216, 15 miles northwest of Flagstaff on US 180, offers bike and equipment rentals. It opens up its cross-country ski trail network to bike riders from May through September.

A moderate road bike ride is the route through **Wupatki** and **Sunset Crater National Monuments** off US 89, north of Flagstaff. It covers 35 miles one-way so you might consider a vehicle shuttle.

There's a network of jeep roads good for biking four miles north of Sunset Crater on US 89, then west across the northern boundary of the Kachina Peaks Wilderness and the San Francisco Peaks. You can't ride a bike in the wilderness area, but you might ride on rough forest roads from US 89 to US 180 in 14 miles. From there it would be 20 road miles on US 180 southeast to Flagstaff.

Information on area biking routes is also available from the following area bike shops. They provide sales, service, and rentals.

Absolute Bikes, 18 North San Francisco Street, Flagstaff, 602/779-5969.

Cosmic Cycles, 113 South San Francisco Street, Flagstaff, 602/779-1092.

Mountain Sports, 1800 South Milton Road, Flagstaff, 602/779-5156.

Southwest Cycle Expeditions, PO Box 30731, Flagstaff, AZ 86003, 602/526-4882, rents bikes and related equipment, and offers guided bike tours throughout the Four Corners, including Verde Valley, Oak Creek-Sedona, and the Grand Canyon.

Sedona

Just about anywhere you bike around Sedona is going to be scenic. Roads in the immediate vicinity of Oak Creek Canyon and Sedona are bound to be heavily trafficked, but back roads and trails are still a good bet for getting away from it all.

The 2eight-mile ride down **Oak Creek Canyon** from Flagstaff on US **89A** to Sedona is a nice downhill road trip if there's not too much traffic. Try starting early in the morning and avoid weekends.

Red Rock Loop Road, south of US 89A in West Sedona, to Red Rock Crossing is a short, easy ride to a beautiful spot.

Schnebly Hill Scenic Drive, from Sedona to I-17, includes a steep ascent of Schnebly Hill on the 11-mile ride. A lot of bike riders turn around midway and enjoy the easy coast back into town.

Several rugged jeep roads start from Schnebly Hill and offer good bikeways. For details see above, under Touring Sedona.

Backroads Bicycle Touring, 1516 5th Street, Berkeley, CA 94710-1740, 510/527-1555 or 800/245-3874, fax 510/527-1444, runs six-day bicycle tours along the southern edge of the Colorado Plateau's mesas, buttes, and towering cliffs, with nights in lodges and inns.

Timberline Bicycle Tours, 7975 East Harvard, Denver, CO 80231, 303/759-3804, runs a Grand Canyon Biker/Hiker tour from Flagstaff that includes five-days of biking through Oak Creek Canyon and Sedona, followed by a van shuttle to the Grand Canyon's South Rim for two days of hiking into the canyon. Five-day Bike trips focusing exclusively on the Sedona area are also available. They also customize tours to suit you.

All Adventure Travel (5589 Arapahoe Road, Suite 208, Boulder, CO 80303, 800/537-4025, fax 303/440-4160) offers a six-day mountain bike tour of Sedona's red rock country in May, June, September, and October. Accommodations in country inns and hotels are included while touring through Flagstaff, the Verde Valley, Mormon Lake, Red Rock Secret Wilderness, and the Prescott National Forest. Also available during these months is a seven-day Grand Canyon Hike/Biker Tour, including accommodations in lodges or hotels, while travelling by bike or on foot through the Prescott National Forest, Tuzigoot National Monument, Montezuma's Castle, and the South Rim of the Grand Canyon.

Sedona area bike shops offering sales, service, rentals and biking information include **Canyon Country Mountain Bikes**, 245 North US 89A, Sedona, 602/282-6985, and **Mountain Bike Heaven**, 1449 West US 89A, Sedona, 602/282-1312. For additional biking information contact the Forest Service's Sedona office (see above, under Touring).

Painted Desert/Petrified Forest National Park

The nine-mile road through **Homolovi State Park**, north of Winslow, is a possible bike route.

The 28-mile scenic drive through **Petrified Forest National Park** is a fairly easy bike ride with some long, low hills. Start early from Holbrook and make a day-trip out of the 64-mile loop comprised of 18 miles east on US 180 from Holbrook to the park, then 28 miles north on the scenic drive, and 18 miles west to Holbrook along I-40. There's not much shade along this route so the trip is probably best suited to a time other than mid-summer. Carry plenty of water.

On Water

GRAND CANYON RIVER TRIPS

This is the cat's meow as far as Southwestern river trips are concerned, offering adventure, exploration, and discovery. You travel though time on this stretch of the Colorado River, back a billion or so years into prehistory. You can touch and climb rocks millions of years old and visit prehistoric Indian sites. Watch for the wildlife such as bighorn sheep, deer, birds, and reptiles, along with contrasts in vegetation, from desert cacti on precipitous canyon slopes to cottonwoods and thirsty ferns near waterfalls. Retrace the steps of explorers and challenge the rapids.

Just about all the experts agree that the best times of year for the Grand Canyon are April to May and September to October. Be aware that on partial canyon trips, put-in or take-out will require hiking a 5,000-feet-deep trail. Sometimes arrangements can be made for mule-back transportation and there are several guided trips offering helicopter transportation. To facilitate cooperative scheduling, arrangements should be made through your outfitter.

Only concessionaires licensed by the National Park Service are allowed to run trips through the canyon. A number of tour operators offer Grand Canyon trips but these are operated through licensed concessionaires.

It probably pays to shop around for the trip that best suits your interests. Outfitted trips are run in paddle- or oar-powered rafts, motorized rafts, and wooden dories. Their duration ranges from day-trips to three-week expeditions.

The main boat launching area for Grand Canyon river trips is at Lees Ferry, northeast of the National Park. The boat ramp there also provides access to the trophy rainbow trout fishing waters between Lees Ferry and the Glen Canyon Dam.

For additional information or reservations for any Grand Canyon river trips, contact the **River Subdistrict Office**, Grand Canyon National Park, PO Box 129, Grand Canyon, AZ 86023.

Rivers & Oceans, PO Box 40321, Flagstaff, AZ 86004, 602/525-4575, 800/473-4576, is also a central reservation office for Grand Canyon river trips.

For experienced river runners it is possible to create your own private river trip through the canyon, but start planning early. There is quite a bit of Park Service bureaucracy to wade through for the appropriate permit. Allow extra time for this process. For information phone the **River Permits office**, 602/638-7843.

The following outfitters offer a variety of river running options through the Grand Canyon:

O.A.R.S. Inc., Box 67, Angel's Camp, CA 95222, 209/736-4677, fax 209/736-2902, runs five- to 15-day river trips from April to October in wooden dories, oar-powered rafts, paddle boats, or inflatable kayaks.

Colorado River & Trail Expeditions, PO Box 57575, Salt Lake City, Utah 84157-0575, 801/261-1789 or 800/253-7328, fax 801/268-1193, offers rowing through the canyon in April or August and motorized trips of four, six, or nine days from May to September. All trips include opportunities for off-river hiking explorations.

ARA's Wilderness River Adventures, PO Box 717, Page, AZ, 602/645-3296, or 800/992-8022, offers motorized and oar-powered trips through the canyon. Itineraries include four- or six-day trips from Lees Ferry to Phantom Ranch, five or seven days from Phantom Ranch to Bar 10 Ranch, or seven or 14 days from Lees Ferry to Bar 10 Ranch. Also available are one-day float trips from Glen Canyon Dam to Lees Ferry. Customized trips and charters are also offered.

Arizona Raft Adventures, 4050 East Huntington Drive, Flagstaff, AZ 86004, 602/526-8200 or 800/786-7238, fax 602/526-8246, runs river trips with participant involvement in rowing and paddling. The trips include hiking, swimming the small rapids, helping in the kitchen, learning the natural history, or flat-out relaxing; you can do as much or as little as you want. Trips scheduled from April to October begin and end in Flagstaff and include eight-day itineraries in motorized rafts, or six- to 14-day trips with a choice of vessels.

Special interest trips include a Natural History Lab trip, emphasizing geology, origins, botany, climate, and environmental impacts of the Glen Canyon Dam. Also offered are professional seminars and psychologist-led outdoor retreats. Two- to six-day trips are offered from April to September on the San Juan River in Utah. Customized special interest trips may be arranged for groups of 16 or more.

Grand Canyon Dories, PO Box 216, Altaville, CA 95221, 209/736-0805, runs river trips in dories, a compartmentalized, rough-water, motorless boat made of aluminum, fiberglass, or marine plywood. These vessels ride higher and drier than rafts, don't bend or buckle in the waves, and don't get soft when it's cold. A guide travels in each boat but you can take the oars and learn to run the rapids. Another option is to test your skill in a two-person inflatable kayak.

Groups are limited to a maximum of 20 people per trip. If you're seeking a longer, slower, quieter voyage, as compared with other

Grand Canyon river trips, with time to observe, understand and savor the canyon from the water and the land, this is for you. A 277-mile trip takes 16 days.

Five- to 11-day trips are also offered from Lees Ferry or Phantom Ranch. You do need to hike in or out of the canyon or arrange for mule-back transportation to participate on a shorter trip. Full-length trips start and end in Flagstaff. Also available: Grand Canyon rafting trips of six, eight or 13 days; six-day trips in June through Desolation and Gray Canyons on the Green River; nine-day trips in June on the Colorado River through Canyonlands National Park; eight-day trips on the San Juan River in May or June.

A 47-day trip retracing the complete voyage of John Wesley Powell is offered from Green River, Wyoming to the Virgin River arm of Lake Mead, in Nevada. The Powell trip is divided into four portions of eight, 10, 12 and 17 days that may be taken separately.

Grand Canyon Expeditions, PO Box O, Kanab, Utah 87471, 801/644-2691 or 800/544-2691, fax 801/644-2699, runs the entire 277-mile length of the Grand Canyon from April to September on eight-day motorized or 14-day oar-powered dory and raft trips. Trips emphasize comfort and safety in negotiating nearly 200 rapids while passing through one of the earth's most spectacular geological exhibits. They've had 25 years to perfect their skills while running specialized trips for the National Geographic Society, Smithsonian Institution, and Cinemax, among others. Scheduled special interest trips highlight canyon history, geology, photography, ecology, archaeology, and astronomy. Trips include round-trip transportation from Las Vegas, sleeping bags and pads, ground cloth and rain shelter, waterproof river bags for sleeping gear, cameras and personal items, all meals on the river, cold beer, soft drinks, wine or champagne with evening meals, and ice is available throughout the trip. Also: Customized charters are available.

Outdoors Unlimited, 6900 Townsend-Winona Road, Flagstaff, AZ 86004, 602/525-9834 or 800/637-7238, runs trips from May to October in oar- or paddle-powered boats that hold five to six passengers and a guide. Itineraries include 12-day trips from Lees Ferry to Lake Mead, five-day trips from Lees Ferry to Phantom Ranch, and eight-day trips from Phantom Ranch to Lake Mead. Trips starting at Lees Ferry include overnight accommodations at Marble Canyon. Trips ending at Lake Mead include shuttle service to Las Vegas.

Western River Expeditions, 7258 Racquet Club Drive, Salt Lake City, UT 84121, 801/942-6669 or 800/453-7450, fax 801/942-8514, offers six-day motorized trips through the Upper Grand Canyon, or three- and four-day trips in the Lower Grand Canyon, including helicopter transfers to or from the Colorado River below Lava Falls. Once a year they run a 12-day rowing trip. Trips are scheduled May to September.

Museum of Northern Arizona Ventures (Route 4, Box 720, Flagstaff, AZ 86001, 602/774-5211) runs Grand Canyon rafting trips.

American River Touring Association, 24000 Casa Loma Road, Groveland, CA 95321, 209/962-7873 or 800/323-2782, runs six- to 13-day Grand Canyon raft trips.

Arizona River Runners, Box 47788, Phoenix, AZ 85068-7788, 602/867-4866 or 800/477-7238, runs three- to eight-day Grand Canyon rafting trips.

Canyoneers, Inc., Box 2997, Flagstaff, AZ 86003, 602/526-0924 or 800/525-0924, runs two- to 14-day Grand Canyon trips in motorized rafts or paddle powered rowboats. Seven-day, six-night trips in powered pontoon boats cover the whole 277 miles from Lees Ferry to Pierce Ferry. Two-day, two-night trips in the same motorized vessels cover 89 miles from Lees Ferry to Bright Angel Beach, near Phantom Ranch. A 14-day, 13-night paddle-powered rowboat trip covers 225 miles from Lees Ferry to Pierce Ferry and includes round-trip transportation from Flagstaff.

Canyoneers also operates the Kaibab Lodge on AZ 67 north of the North Rim. Among a variety of tours they offer are winter cross-country ski trips.

Canyon Explorations, Box 310, Flagstaff, AZ 86002, 800/654-0723, runs six- to 15-day Grand Canyon raft trips.

Diamond River Adventures, Box 1316, Page, AZ 86040, 602/645-8866 or 800/343-3121, runs four- to 12-day motorized and oar-powered river trips through the Grand Canyon.

Expeditions, Inc. (RR 4, Box 755, Flagstaff, AZ 86001, 602/774-8176 or 602/779-3769) runs five- to 18-day Grand Canyon river trips. Five- to six-day trips cover 87 miles and entail a nine-mile hike out of the canyon at the end. Eight- to nine-day trips cover the second portion of the Grand Canyon for 139 miles and require a seven-mile hike to the put-in spot. Twelve- to 18-day trips cover 226 miles on the river.

Trips are in oar-powered rafts with options available for those who prefer paddle boats or kayaks. All trips include leisure time and hiking time for exploring side canyons. Also included is transportation from Flagstaff to Lees Ferry or the Grand Canyon, depending on the put-in point. Return transportation from Diamond Creek is provided at the end of the full Grand Canyon trip to Flagstaff. All trips include a sleeping bag and foam pad, vehicle and valuables storage at a Flagstaff warehouse, all meals, plus hotel and motel pick-up in Flagstaff.

Complete outfitting services, tent and pack rentals, and shuttle services for vehicles to the South Rim or Diamond Creek are available. Customized trips for special interests, such as kayaking clinics, management training seminars, art and photography workshops, and experiential education programs are also offered.

Georgie's Royal River Rats, Box 12057, Las Vegas, NV 89112, 702/798-0602, runs three- to eight-day Grand Canyon river trips.

Moki Mac River Expeditions, Box 21242, Salt Lake City, Utah 84121, 801/268-6667 or 800/268-6667, runs six- to 14-day Grand Canyon oar-powered raft trips, or eight-day motorized raft trips.

Sleight Expeditions, Box 40, St. George, UT 84770, 801/673-1200, offers five- to 12-day Grand Canyon raft trips.

Ted Hatch River Expeditions, Box 1200, Vernal, Utah 84078, 801/789-3813, or 800/433-8966, offers seven-day Grand Canyon rafting trips.

Tours West, Inc., Box 333, Orem, Utah 84059, 801/225-0755 or 800/453-9107, offers three- to 12-day Grand Canyon rafting trips.

Wild & Scenic, Inc. (Box 460, Flagstaff, AZ 86002, 602/774-7343, or 800/231-1963) runs trips of a half-day to 13 days in rafts or sportyaks on the Colorado River through the Grand Canyon.

Hualapai Tribal River Trips & Tours, PO Box 246, Peach Springs, AZ 84634, 602/769-2219 or 602/769-2210, runs one- or two-day raft trips from Diamond Creek on the Colorado to Pearce Ferry on Lake Mead. Two-day trips include one day of rapids.

VERDE RIVER TRIPS

Canyon River Equipment Outfitters, PO Box 3493 Flagstaff, AZ 86003-3493, 602/526-4663 or 800/637-4604, fax 602/526-4535, runs guided whitewater raft, cataract, canoe, inflatables, and kayak trips on the Verde River, as well as the Lower Colorado River through the southern part of the Grand Canyon and the San Juan River in Utah. They can also provide complete outfitting for private river runners, including food, equipment rental (rafts, canoes, kayaks or inflatables), and shuttle packages.

ARIZONA STRIP FISHING

Some of the prime waters for rainbow trout fishing are along the 15-mile stretch of the Colorado River between the **Glen Canyon Dam** and **Lees Ferry**. There is a boat ramp at Lees Ferry and a Park Service-maintained fish cleaning station.

You need a permit from the Park Service to head downriver into the Grand Canyon but only an Arizona fishing license to try your luck in the trophy waters north of Lees Ferry. There are several endangered species of fish in these waters and these must be thrown back in. For details contact the ranger station next to the Lees Ferry Campground (see below, under Camping).

GRAND CANYON FISHING

Rainbow trout can sometimes be found in **Bright Angel Creek**, accessible from the North Kaibab Trail off the North Rim. Other creeks below the North and South Rims may have decent fishing at times. Consult with park personnel regarding conditions.

WILLIAMS/FLAGSTAFF FISHING & BOATING

There is fishing and boating available at four Forest Service campgrounds in the vicinity of Williams. For details see below, under Camping.

Information on fishing and boating site regulations in the area is available from a local office of **Arizona Game & Fish Department**, 310 Lake Mary Road, Flagstaff, AZ 86001, 602/774-5045.

For information about the following areas contact the Mormon Lakes Ranger District (4825 Lake Mary Road, Flagstaff, AZ 86001, 602/556-7474).

Close to Flagstaff, **Upper** and **Lower Lake Mary**, eight miles southeast on Lake Mary Road, are stocked with catfish, walleye, and northern pike. There are boat ramps on both lakes. You can water ski on the upper lake. There is a Forest Service campground.

Ashurst Lake, 18 miles southeast of Flagstaff on Lake Mary Road, and four miles east on Forest Road 82E, offers fishing for rainbow trout, a boat ramp, and two campgrounds.

You can also fish for rainbows in **Coconino Reservoir**, a mile south of Ashurst Lake.

Under the same jurisdiction is **Mormon Lake**, 20 miles southeast of Flagstaff on Lake Mary Road, containing 2,000 acres stocked with northern pike and catfish. The average water level is only 10 feet (sometimes lower), so there's no waterskiing or boat ramp. You carry your boat into the water and, if that's not enough exercise, there are short, easy hiking trails in the area. Two campgrounds, two lodges offering room or cabin accommodations, a cafe, and store are situated by the lake. The area is also popular for winter sports.

Kinnikinick Lake lies 25 miles southeast of Flagstaff on Lake Mary Road, near the south end of Mormon Lake, then 11 miles east on Forest Roads 125 and 82. There are trout in the lake. There is also a boat ramp and a free campground.

Stoneman Lake, 8.5 miles farther south from the turn-off for Kinnikinick Lake on Lake Mary Road, then six miles east on Forest Road 213, has been the location for state record-setting catches of yellow perch. There is a boat ramp but no campground.

SEDONA FISHING

Rainbow and brown trout are stocked in **Oak Creek.** Other cold water fish found mainly in Upper Oak Creek include cutthroat trout, grayling, sunfish, smallmouth bass, and bluegill.

The water is warmer farther south and four species of warm water catfish–yellow, channel, black, and flathead–are found in Lower Oak Creek, along with largemouth bass and carp.

There is fishing for a fee at **Rainbow Trout Farm,** 602/282-5799, three miles north of Sedona off US 89A in Oak Creek Canyon. You don't need a license and they supply the gear.

Dead Horse Ranch State Park, on the north end of Cottonwood, east of Tuzigoot National Monument, offers fishing for bass, catfish, and trout. There is also a campground here.

WINSLOW/HOLBROOK FISHING

McHood Park, 602/289-3082, located five miles southeast of Winslow, offers swimming, boating, camping facilities and fishing for catfish, trout, and bass.

Twenty-four miles east of Winslow, off I-40 at Joseph City, is **Cholla Lake Park.** It offers boating and fishing in the shadow of a power plant.

On Snow

ARIZONA STRIP/GRAND CANYON NATIONAL PARK

There's an active winter sports area from Jacob Lake south on AZ 67 to the North Rim.

Canyoneers, Inc. operates the winter sports facilities in the Kaibab National Forest between Jacob Lake and the North Rim. From December to March there are various tour packages available that include accommodations, meals, and equipment rentals. Guided tours and a helicopter service from the South Rim to Kaibab Lodge are also offered. Canyoneers-operated facilities include the following:

- The **North Rim Nordic Center** is a half-mile south of Jacob Lake on Forest Road 579 and offers 30 kilometers of groomed cross-country ski trails, guided backcountry tours, equipment rentals, and instruction. This is the only Kaibab Forest facility that you can reach by car. You can park here and ski to the following areas or Canyoneers can provide transportation.
- **Kaibab Lodge**, 26 miles south of Jacob Lake, is usually snowed-in during the winter but you can ski in or take a shuttle.
- Accommodations are available at the lodge or across the road at the **North Rim Winter Camp**, 602/638-2383, next to the North Rim Country Store. The winter camp provides mostly backcountry skiing access and accommodations in heated Mongolian yurts.

Most tours leave from the lodge, some from the winter camp. **Papillon-Grand Canyon Helicopters** (see below, under In Air) operates helicopter service to the Kaibab Lodge in winter from the South Rim.

All North Rim services within the park are closed in winter but you can ski in. Camping is permitted with a backcountry permit.

WILLIAMS/FLAGSTAFF

The mountains near Williams offer cross-country skiing, snowmobiling, plus ice fishing for trout or catfish at **White Horse Lake**, 19 miles southeast of town.

The small **Williams Ski Area**, 602/635-9330, is on the 9,255-foot **Bill Williams Mountain**, five miles south of town. Vertical drop is only around 700 feet. Downhill and cross-country ski rentals are available.

Cross-country skiing is popular on Forest Service land 20 miles northeast of Williams. For information and maps contact the Chalender Ranger District office (see above, under Touring Flagstaff).

Arizona Snowbowl, 602/772-1951, is 14 miles northwest of town and offers four chairlifts, more than 30 downhill trails, and a vertical drop of 2,300 feet. Conditions are highly variable throughout the December through March ski season, so it's a good idea to call 602/779-4577 for current reports. Equipment rentals are available and there is a ski school.

Cross-country skiing is offered at **Flagstaff Nordic Center**, 602/774-6216, providing 26 miles of groomed trails for all levels of skiers, telemark skiing areas, ski rentals, and instruction. The area is 15 miles northwest of Flagstaff on US 180.

Backcountry skiing is popular in the San Francisco Peaks. Several forest roads located 10 miles northwest of Flagstaff, and north of US 180, lead to such areas as **Wing Mountain** and **Hart Prairie**. For information contact the Peaks Ranger District Office (see above, under Touring Flagstaff).

Mormon Lake Ski Center, 602/354-2240, is 20 miles southeast of Flagstaff, then eight miles south on Mormon Lake Road, across from the Mormon Lake Lodge. The center offers 26 miles of groomed trails, equipment rentals, and instruction.

Montezuma Nordic Ski Center, 602/354-2221, four miles north of Mormon Lake at Montezuma Lodge, near Dairy Springs Campground, opens 13 miles of groomed trails and offers equipment rentals and instruction.

In Air

GRAND CANYON NATIONAL PARK

Grand Canyon scenic flights are not allowed to go below the rim but they're still pretty spectacular.

Grand Canyon Airlines, Box 3038, Grand Canyon, AZ 86023, 602/638-2407 or 800/528-2413, offers scenic flights over the canyon from the Grand Canyon Airline Terminal, Grand Canyon Airport, near Tusayan, six miles south of the South Rim Visitor Center. Hourly flights are operated by two pilots in a 19-seat, twin-engine Vistaliner. The wings are over the top of the plane so they don't obstruct the view.

Air Grand Canyon, Main Terminal Building, Grand Canyon Airport, PO Box 3339, Grand Canyon, AZ 86023, 800/247-4726, guarantees window seats and provides video camera hook-ups. Also: Customized flight itineraries are available.

Air Star Helicopters-Airlines, Main Terminal Grand Canyon Airport, PO 3379, Grand Canyon, AZ 86023, 602/638-2622 or 800/962-3869, runs scenic flights in fixed-wing aircraft or helicopter tours.

Windrock Aviation, Main Terminal Grand Canyon Airport, PO Box 3125, Grand Canyon, AZ 86023, 602/638-9591 or 800/247-6259, offers scenic flights over the Grand Canyon, Monument Valley, and Lake Powell, plus customized tours. Narrated flights are in high wing aircraft and every seat is by a window.

The following operators offer scenic helicopter flights departing from Grand Canyon Heliport, on AZ 64, a mile and a half south of the lower entrance to the National Park.

Papillon Grand Canyon Helicopters, Box 455, Grand Canyon, AZ 86023, 602/638-2419 or 800/528-2418, offers 30- or 50-minute scenic flights over the Grand Canyon. Also available are six-hour air and ground trips to Havasu Falls by helicopter and horseback, or overnight trips including accommodations at Havasupai Indian Village. Also offered are helicopter flights to Kaibab Lodge in winter for flight/ski packages.

Kenai Helicopters, Box 1429, Grand Canyon, AZ 86023, 602/638-2412 or 800/541-4537, offers scenic flights over both rims of the Grand Canyon.

FLAGSTAFF

Alpine Air Service, 602/779-5178, offers scenic flights to Meteor and Sunset craters, Sedona and Oak Creek Canyon from Flagstaff's Pulliam Field, five miles south of town off I-17.

SEDONA

Air Sedona, 602/282-7935, at the airport south of town off US 89A, offers local tours, longer scenic flights adding the Grand Canyon and the Havasupai Reservation, or deluxe tours to Meteor Crater, Lake Powell, Canyon de Chelly, and Monument Valley. Also: Charter flights and customized tours are available.

A variety of helicopter tours based at Sedona Airport are offered by **Arizona Helicopter Adventures,** 602/282-0904.

You can float over the red rocks at dawn in your choice of guided hot air balloon flights. Contact **Northern Light Balloon Adventures,** PO Box 1695, Sedona, AZ 86336, 602/282-2274, or **Red Rock Balloon Adventure,** 3230 Valley Vista Drive, Sedona, AZ 86336, 602/284-0040 or 800/258-3754.

Eco-Travel & Cultural Excursions

A number of ecologically-oriented tours and cultural explorations are offered by various outfitters listed throughout individual adventure categories above.

Specialized tours are offered by the **Four Corners School of Outdoor Education,** PO Box 78, East Route, Monticello, Utah, 801/587-2156. These include a nine-day, eight-night, **Grand Canyon Winter Traverse–North Rim to South Rim.** The trip, offered only in mid-March, involves skiing 43 miles over a five-day period to reach the North Rim, carrying a backpack, camping, and eating meals prepared by the staff. At the rim you tie your skis to your pack and descend 14 miles to Phantom Ranch, while a geologist-guide explains the surrounding scenery. After a layover day on the canyon floor, you hike up 12 miles to the South Rim for the last night in a motel. Recommended only for people who can ski seven to nine miles per day with a 50 pound pack.

Another trip is called **High Desert Dynamics–North Rim Grand Canyon**, and it is also offered only once a year in early October. It includes six days and six nights accommodations at the North Rim's Grand Canyon Lodge, with five- to eight-mile daily hikes led by a three-person team consisting of a biologist/river guide, an anthropologist/archaeologist, and a geologist. Evening seminars and slide shows are shown in the lodge.

Williams hosts a **Bill Williams Rendezvous** on a weekend in late-May, featuring authentically-clothed and outfitted mountain men competing in cow-chip throwing contests, black powder shooting, and other events. The town's **Arizona Cowpuncher's Reunion and Old-Timer's Rodeo**, held the first week in August, includes a rodeo, cowboy parade, and barn dance.

Coconino Center For the Arts, in Flagstaff, presents numerous exhibits and performances of cultural interest. These include the following yearly art exhibits: **Youth Arts Month**, in spring; **Trappings of the American West**, in June, focusing on the American cowboy; **Festival of Native American Arts**, from June to August, featuring fine arts and crafts created by Indians of the Four Corners, as well as contemporary and traditional Indian music; **Wood, Fiber, and Clay**, in fall, featuring works of Northern Arizona artists.

Northern Arizona University, in Flagstaff, offers frequent concerts, art shows, theatrical performances, and sporting events. Flagstaff's **Museum Club** puts on local culture shows nightly. See above, under Touring Flagstaff for information.

Many consider Sedona something of a cultural phenomenon under normal circumstances. The town also offers a variety of yearly special events, including **Hopi Days**, **Fiesta del Tlaquepaque**, and concert festivals featuring jazz, pop, or chamber music. For information contact Sedona Chamber of Commerce.

Jerome's **Spirit Room**, a bar in the Conner Hotel on Main Street, provides live music on weekends and genuine western culture all the time.

Where to Stay & Eat

Arizona Strip Accommodations & Restaurants

Cliff Dwellers Lodge and Trading Co., Inc., US 89A, Marble Canyon, AZ 86036, 602/335-2228 or 800/433-2543, is nine miles west of Navajo Bridge. It has 20 air-conditioned rooms, a restaurant, store, and gas station. Also: Guided fishing trips, river rafting, scenic flights, and hikers shuttle service.

Lee's Ferry Lodge, 541 1/2 US 89A, Box 1, Vermillion Cliffs, AZ 86036, 602/355-2231, offers nine modest rooms, a restaurant, gift shop, and fishing store.

Marble Canyon Lodge, PO Box 1, US 89A, Marble Canyon, AZ 86036, 602/355-2225 or 800/726-1789, fax 602/355-2227, has air-conditioning, 51 rooms, 10 suites, a coffee shop, and a dining room. Also: Guided fishing trips are available.

Jacob Lake Lodge, Jacob Lake, AZ 86022, 602/643-7232, is 44 miles north of the North Rim, offering motel rooms, cabins, dining room, gas station, and post office.

Kaibab Lodge, North Rim Grand Canyon, Jacob Lake, AZ 86022, has the closest accommodations to the North Rim and is 26 miles south of Jacob Lake, 18 miles from the National Park. Mailing address is c/o Canyoneers, Inc., PO Box 2997, Flagstaff, AZ 86003. To reach the lodge phone 602/638-2389; for information phone 602/526-0924 or 800/525-0924. The lodge has 26 units, jacuzzi, restaurant, gift shop, store and gas station. Also: Horseback riding, mountain bike rentals and guided tours, guided hikes and vehicle tours are available May through October.

The lodge becomes a cross-country ski center from December to mid-April. It has ski equipment rentals, lessons, tours, groomed trials, and set-track including skating lanes. Early reservations are suggested.

Grand Canyon Accommodations & Restaurants

Last-minute cancellations do occasionally crop up but reservations are usually needed at least six months to a year in advance to secure a room in the Grand Canyon National Park area. The operator of the lodges and dining rooms in Grand Canyon Village, on the South Rim, accepts reservations up to 23 months in advance. Outlying areas, even as close as Tusayan, just a few miles from the South Rim, may be able to accommodate you on short notice. The farther away you go, the easier it is to get a room or campsite. Plan especially far in advance for the summer season, May through October, which attracts the largest crowds.

Grand Canyon Lodge, North Rim Grand Canyon, AZ 86023, 602/638-2611, provides the North Rim's only accommodations. It includes an appropriately grand 1930s stone and timber main lodge, with huge windows overlooking the North Rim. Standard motel rooms and three choices of cabins are available. Pioneer Cabins are close to the lodge and sleep five people. Frontier Cabins are closer to the rim and come with a double plus a single bed. Western Cabins are the fanciest with two double beds and a porch with a choice canyon view. The lodge is open May to October. Reservations are accepted up to 23 months in advance. For information contact the same company that manages the lodges inside Bryce Canyon and Zion National Parks, **TW Recreational Services**, PO Box 400, Cedar City, UT 84720, 801/586-7686, fax 801/834-3157.

The **Grand Canyon Lodge Dining Room**, 602/638-0611, serves three ordinary meals a day in a stunning, spacious, log-beamed dining room with stone walls and enormous windows overlooking the canyon. Reservations are necessary for lunch and dinner. A cafeteria in the lodge serves three meals daily.

Grand Canyon Lodge is an information center for all park activities.

Cameron Trading Post, PO Box 339, Cameron, AZ 86020, 602/674-5875, is an active trading post year-round, including a post office, store, gift shop, restaurant, a small museum, and a modest motel on a bank of the Little Colorado River.

Eight and a half miles south of Cameron, the **Anasazi Inn-Gray Mountain**, PO Box 29100, Gray Mountain, AZ 86016, 602/679-2214, fax 602/679-2334, is a spartan 100-unit motel, with coffee shop, gift shop, and pool.

Grand Canyon National Park Lodges, PO Box 699, Grand Canyon, AZ 86023, 602/638-2401, fax 602/638-9247, operates the following South Rim properties:

Desert View Trading Post Cafeteria features a self-service cafeteria 23 miles east of Grand Canyon Village on the East Rim Drive.

El Tovar Hotel is a dramatic structure, four stories high, built from limestone and logs in 1905. It's the most elegant and expensive South Rim property, looking like a sporting lodge favored by

Napoleonic-era European royalty, offering rooms and suites, some with staggering views, a gift shop, dining room, and concierge service.

El Tovar Dining Room, 602/638-6292, serves steaks, seafood and Continental fare in a formal environment, although casual clothing is permissible. El Tovar's guests may make reservations, but others must wait for a table.

Bright Angel Lodge is a less expensive alternative to El Tovar, yet retaining distinction in its 1930s-era stone and log construction. The property includes a steak house, coffee shop, gift shop, and beauty salon. Several rustic rim cabins are also available.

Bright Angel Restaurant, 602/638-2631, serves three standard American meals daily, while the **Arizona Steakhouse** serves dinners only, including steaks, seafood and a salad bar. Open March through December.

Thunderbird Lodge and **Kachina Lodge** are modern motels which do not have their own dining rooms, but you can walk to those at Bright Angel Lodge or El Tovar.

Maswik Lodge has modern motel rooms and some cabins for the lowest available South Rim rates. On the premises, at the southeast corner of Grand Canyon Village, is the **Maswik Cafeteria** and a gift shop.

Yavapai Lodge is the largest South Rim lodge, situated across from the Visitor Center and a mile from the rim, offering standard motel rooms, the **Yavapai Cafeteria** and, serving faster food, the **Yavapai Grill**. It also has a gift shop.

Babbitt's Delicatessen, in the general store near Yavapai Lodge, serves sandwiches and salads to eat-in or take-out.

Hermit's Rest Snack Bar is at the end of the West Rim Drive, serving cold drinks, ice cream, candy, and hot dogs.

Phantom Ranch provides the only accommodations in the bottom of the Grand Canyon, at the end of the North Kaibab Trail and across the river from the bottom of Bright Angel and South Kaibab trails. Guests stay in stone cabins beneath shading trees or in four, 10-person hiker dormitories with bunk beds. The cabins are usually reserved for overnight mule-back travellers; the only other ways to get here are on foot or by river raft. Meals are available. Reservations are taken as much as a year in advance.

Moqui Lodge is managed by the Grand Canyon Lodges, but actually situated outside the park. It's a modern, airy structure, with motel rooms, a dining room, gift shop, horseback riding and tennis.

Moqui Lodge Dining Room, 602/638-2424, serves Mexican and American food. Summer chuckwagon cook-outs, with live western music are offered.

There are a number of motels and family-style restaurants, including a McDonald's, a few miles outside the park's South Rim in Tusayan.

Grand Canyon Squire Inn, PO Box 130, Grand Canyon, AZ 86023, 602/638-2681, fax 602/638-2782, is a Best Western with 150 motel rooms, dining room, coffee shop, gift shop, pool, tennis, bowling, sauna, jacuzzi, and billiards.

Quality Inn Grand Canyon, PO Box 520, Grand Canyon, AZ 86023, 602/638-2673 or 800/221-2222, fax 602/638-9537, contains 185 rooms, a restaurant, coffee shop, and a pool open only in summer.

Havasupai Lodge (Supai, AZ 86435, 602/448-2111) is the only motel in the village of Supai. It has 24 rooms and reservations are necessary. A restaurant, creek swimming, hiking and horseback riding are available here.

Relatively near Supai, at least within 80 miles of the Indian village, **Grand Canyon Caverns**, PO Box 180, Peach Springs, AZ 86434, 602/422-3223, offers 48 motel rooms, a restaurant, and a gift shop. Western cook-outs and guided cave tours are available.

Williams Accommodations & Restaurants

Grand Canyon Inn, PO Box 702, Williams, AZ 86946, 602/635-2345 or 602/635-2809, is 28 miles north of Williams at the junction of US 180 and AZ 64 near Valle. The 61-room motel has a restaurant, gift shop, and gas station. Helicopter and fixed-wing scenic flight reservations can be made here.

Comfort Inn, 911 West Bill Williams Avenue, Williams, AZ 86046, 800/228-5150, has 54 rooms, a pool, and a restaurant.

El Rancho Motel, 617 East Bill Williams Avenue, Williams, AZ 86046, 602/625-2552 or 800/228-2370, offers 25 rooms and a pool.

The Mountain Side Inn, 642 East Bill Williams Avenue, 602/635-4431 or 800/462-9381, fax 602/635-2292, is situated within walking distance of the Grand Canyon Railway, offering 95 rooms, a pool, jacuzzi, restaurant, and room service.

Quality Inn Ranch Resort, Route 1, PO Box 35, Williams, AZ 86046, 602/635-2693 or 800/221-2222, is six miles east of Williams, off I-40. The motel offers 69 rooms, a restaurant, coffee shop, pool, tennis, jacuzzi, and horseback riding. Locations for skiing and fishing are nearby.

Flagstaff Accommodations

Flagstaff is glutted with chain motels and fast foods, as well as other standard accommodations and restaurants. There are three **Best Westerns** (800/528-1234), two **Travelodges** (800/255-3050), a **Howard Johnson's** (800/654-2000), a **Quality Inn** (800/228-5151), a **Ramada Inn** (800/325-2525), two **Rodeway Inns** (800/228-2000) and an above-average **Residence Inn by Marriott** (800/331-3131) on the east side of town. Most have pools, many have restaurants, and some offer courtesy car service.

You can usually find a place with a vacancy unless some major event is in town. If you plan ahead, there are several unusual places to stay and dine.

Best Western Woodlands Plaza Hotel, 1175 West US 66, Flagstaff, AZ 86003, 602/773-8888, fax 602-773-0597, is a cut above the average Best Western, offering 125 large rooms, several restaurants (see below), pool, indoor and outdoor jacuzzis, sauna, and an exercise room. Room service and complimentary limousine service are offered.

Monte Vista Hotel, 100 North San Francisco Street, Flagstaff, AZ 86001, 602/779-6971, fax 602/779-2904, used to be frequented by western movie stars. Today it's a partly-restored historic hotel, with 64 rooms, in a 1920s structure. You can actually stay in a room that was once occupied by Walter Brennan. Some rooms share a bath.

Little America Hotel, 2515 East Butler, PO Box 3900, Flagstaff, AZ 866003, 602/779-2741 or 800/FLAG-FUN, fax 602/779-7983, offers 244 large rooms set on 400 acres of treed grounds, including a two-mile jogging trail and pool. A restaurant and gift shop are open 24 hours a day.

The Inn at Four Ten, 410 North Leroux Street, Flagstaff, AZ 86001, 602/774-0088, is an antique-filled B&B with three suites, including kitchen areas and private baths, or two rooms that share a bath. It is close to the downtown area and occupies a 1907 structure.

There are several character-laden youth hostels downtown. Contact the Chamber of Commerce for information.

Ski Lift Lodge, US 180 North & Snowbowl Road, Flagstaff, AZ 86001, has 28 rooms and cabins plus a restaurant. Situated six miles from the Arizona Snowbowl Ski Area.

Arizona Mountain Inn, 685 Lake Mary Road, Flagstaff, AZ 86001, 602/774-8959, has standard B&B rooms in a main house, and cabins with one- to five-bedrooms, fireplaces, and kitchens.

The inn's location southeast of town provides good access to hiking and cross-country skiing.

Mormon Lake Lodge, PO Box 12, Mormon Lake, AZ 86038, 602/774-0462, fax 602/354-2356, offers lodge rooms and cabins, a popular western-style restaurant featuring western music (see below), and a full slate of year-round activities, including hiking in summer, along with ice fishing, snowmobiling, and cross-country skiing in winter. The property includes a grocery store, fishing supplies, and gas station.

Flagstaff Restaurants

There are a lot of ordinary places to eat in Flagstaff and some more unusual ones. Chain restaurants are well-represented. Because of the college crowd there are plenty of spots for cheap eats. More upscale establishments are beginning to appear, including some imaginative choices.

Horseman Lodge Restaurant, 8500 US 89 North, Flagstaff, 602/526-2655, serves good steaks in a large western log structure.

Cottage Place Restaurant, 126 West Cottage Avenue, Flagstaff, 602/774-8431, serves Continental-inspired beef, poultry, and vegetarian dishes in a cozy, little, early-1900s cottage.

Sakura, in the Woodlands Plaza Hotel (see above), serves sushi, tempura, and beef, chicken or seafood teriyaki. **Woodlands Cafe**, also in the hotel, serves poultry, seafood, and beef dishes with a Continental flare in a Southwestern-style dining room.

Chez Marc Bistro, 503 North Humphreys Street, Flagstaff, 602/774-1343, is in an old, historic house, decorated in French country antiques, serving nouvelle cuisine, soups, salads, and sandwiches for lunch and dinner.

Main Street Bar & Grill, 4 South San Francisco Street, Flagstaff, 602/774-1519, is a college hang-out, serving barbecued ribs, sandwiches, and Mexican food.

Little America Hotel (see above) serves a popular Sunday brunch.

Macy's European Coffee House and Bakery, 14 South Beaver, Flagstaff, serves good coffees, teas, and baked goods.

Cafe Express, 16 North San Francisco Street, Flagstaff, 602/774-0541, serves good breakfasts, sandwiches, salads, and fresh baked goods.

Mormon Lake Lodge Steak House & Saloon, at Mormon Lake Lodge (see above), has been an old west steak house since the

1920s, servings beef, ribs, chicken, and fresh trout, all cooked over an open fire.

Sedona Accommodations

High season here is April to November and you need reservations during those months. Prices drop a little the rest of the year but there are not many bargains. The well-situated or deluxe resorts are very expensive and the more modest properties charge top dollar for what they offer. There are a lot of places to stay in Sedona, but you have to look outside of town for less expensive lodgings, in the Cottonwood-Jerome area or around Camp Verde or Flagstaff, which is less than 30 miles north. Upscale resort properties include the following:

Enchantment Resort, 525 Boynton Canyon Road, Sedona, AZ 86336, 602/282-2900 or 800/826-4180, contains 168 units, including private, two-bedroom, adobe cottages called "casitas," and One-bedroom suites with kitchenettes. The resort also offers six pools, a fine restaurant (see below), 12 tennis courts, croquet, and a six-hole pitch & putt golf course, all situated beside the trailhead to the Boynton Canyon Vortex in a red rock canyon.

L'Auberge de Sedona Resort, 301 L'Auberge Lane, Sedona, AZ 86336, 602/282-1661 or 800/272-6777, fax 602/282-2885, has 96 lodge rooms and luxurious cabins decorated in elegant French country style, with fireplaces and porches, on Oak Creek. The property includes a pool, a coffee shop, and a very good dining room (see below), all situated on 10 acres uptown. A different section of the resort, **The Orchards at Auberge**, offers modern Southwestern-style rooms.

Junipine Condo Resort, 8351 North US 89A, Sedona, AZ 86336, 602/282-3375 or 800/742-PINE, fax 602/282-7402, is in Oak Creek Canyon, a mile north of Slide Rock State Park. It contains 38 modern wood and stone units, either One-bedroom, One-bath, or two-bedrooms, two-baths, each with a fireplace, kitchen, and deck. Facilities include a restaurant, jacuzzi, volleyball, basketball, and horseshoes. There's no pool but you can swim or fish in Oak Creek, and explore hiking trails adjacent to the property.

Los Abrigados, 160 Portal Lane, Sedona, AZ 86336, 602/282-1777 or 800/521-3131, fax 602/282-2614, has 175 deluxe, modern Mexican-style suites with kitchens, fireplaces and patios. There is also a pool, restaurant, tennis, and health spa. Located next to the Tlaquepaque shops, the resort shares the same architectural inspiration. Its courtyards and walkways connect with the shopping area. Accommodations are available in a 1930s stone structure on the property which has been converted to a two-bedroom, $1,000 per night, ultra-deluxe retreat.

Poco Diablo Resort, 1752 South AZ 179, PO Box 1709, Sedona, AZ 86336, 602/282-7333 or 800/352-5710, fax 602/282-2090, is two miles south of US 89A and AZ 179. It contains 124 rooms, some with fireplaces and indoor jacuzzis, a good Southwestern restaurant, two pools, three jacuzzis, four tennis courts, nine-hole golf course, and racquetball.

Bell Rock Inn, 6246 Highway 179, Sedona, AZ 86336, 602/282-4161, is seven miles south of US 89A and AZ 179. The adobe-style resort contains 47 units decorated in a Southwestern desert style, a pool, jacuzzi, tennis, and dining room. Guests receive nearby golf privileges.

Garland's Oak Creek Lodge, Oak Creek Route/PO Box 152, Sedona, AZ 86336, 602/282-3343, offers creek-side accommodations, with breakfast and dinner included in daily rates, eight miles north of town, in Oak Creek Canyon. Open April though October. The dining room is open to non-guests by reservation only. The lodge and the restaurant are often booked solid far in advance.

Chains and standard motels are best represented by the following properties:

Best Western Arroyo Roble Hotel, 400 North US 89A, Sedona, AZ 86336, 602/282-4001, offers 53 rooms and six luxury villas, in-room coffee, tennis, racquetball, billiards, indoor/outdoor pool, exercise room, and jacuzzi. Villas contain two bedrooms, 2.5 baths, two fireplaces, and private balcony overlooking Oak Creek.

Quality Inn King's Ransom, PO Box 180, Sedona, AZ 86336, 602/ 282-7151 or 800/221-2222, has 65 units, heated pool (March 15 to November 30), jacuzzi, dining room, and coffee shop.

Railroad Inn at Sedona, 2545 West US 89A, Sedona, AZ 86336, 800/858-RAIL, fax 602/282-2033, is a standard motel, with a pool and restaurant. Special Room, Ride & Meal Deal packages are offered in conjunction with the Verde River Canyon Excursion Train.

Individualistic, moderately-priced properties include the following:

Graham's Bed & Breakfast Inn, 150 Canyon Circle Drive, Village of Oak Creek, AZ 86336, 602/284-1425, six miles south of Sedona, has five rooms, a jacuzzi, and provides a complimentary hot breakfast.

Greyfire Farm, 1240 Jack's Canyon Road, Sedona, AZ 86336, 602/284-2340, accommodates guests and their horses. There are many horseback riding, hiking and biking trails in the vicinity of this B&B south of town.

Red Rock Lodge, PO Box 537, Sedona, AZ 86336, 602/282-3591, offers 14 rooms and 0ne cottage, with in-room jacuzzis, fireplaces, and kitchens, near the north end of Sedona.

Cedar's Resort, PO Box 292, Sedona, AZ 86336, 602/282-7010, has 38 units on Oak Creek, a pool, jacuzzi, and fishing.

Oak Creek Terrace Resort, 4548 North US 89A, Sedona, AZ 86336, 602/282-3562 or 800/658-5866, beside Oak Creek, five miles north of town, offers 16 units with fireplaces, kitchenettes with refrigerators, and private patios with barbecues. Two-bedroom suites come with an in-room double jacuzzi. A Honeymoon Suite is in an A-frame house on Oak Creek.

Slide Rock Cabins, Oak Creek Canyon, Sedona, AZ 86336, 602/282-6900, has four small cabins in Oak Creek Canyon, six miles north of Sedona, offering access to hiking, fishing, and creek swimming.

Don Hoel's Cabins, Oak Creek Canyon, Sedona AZ 86336, 602/282-3560, are simple cabins in Oak Creek Canyon, nine miles north of Sedona.

Healing Center of Sedona, 25 Wilson Canyon Road, Sedona, AZ 86336, 602/282-7710, offers accommodations in geodesic domes and a vegetarian dining room. It also offers a sauna, jacuzzi, flotation tank, acupressure massage, herbal or crystal treatments. Channeling and rebirthing assistance are available at the center.

Recommended properties outside Sedona include the following:

Best Western Cottonwood Inn, 993 Main Street, Cottonwood, AZ 86326, 602/634-5575 or 800/528-1234, fax 602/255-0259, has 64 rooms, a restaurant, pool, and jacuzzi.

The Jerome Inn, 311 Main Street, Jerome, AZ 86331, 602/634-5094, offers utilitarian accommodations amid Victorian decor in Jerome's oldest hotel. Some rooms share a bath.

Nancy Russel's Bed & Breakfast, 3 Juarez Street, PO Box 791, Jerome, AZ 86331, 602/634-3270, overlooks the Verde Valley, with two antique-filled guest rooms in an old, restored miner's house. Breakfasts include fruit from Ms. Russel's garden.

Best Western Cliff Castle Lodge, PO Box 3430, Camp Verde, AZ 86322, 602/567-6611 or 800/622-7835, fax 602/567-9455, is at I-17 and Middle Verde Road, with 82 rooms, a pool and a restaurant.

Sedona Area Restaurants

The **Yavapai Room** at Enchantment Resort (see above), overlooks Boynton Canyon and serves a Southwestern menu, including selections of wild game. A champagne brunch, accompanied by live jazz, is offered on Sundays. Reservations are required.

L'Auberge Restaurant, 602/282-1667, in L'Auberge de Sedona Resort (see above), serves an elegant, expensive, French prix fixe, six-course dinner overlooking Oak Creek. The menu changes daily. Reservations are required. The resort also has more casual choice, **Orchards Restaurant**, 602/282-7200.

The Willows at Poco Diablo, 602/282-7333, at Poco Diablo Resort (see above), serves Southwestern dishes in a dining room overlooking a small golf course and a red rock canyon. Reservations suggested.

Canyon Rose at Los Abrigados, 602/282-ROSE, serves Southwestern dishes indoors or outdoors. Reservations suggested. Also: Sunday brunch.

Rene at Tlaquepaque, 602/282-9225, is located in the ersatz Mexican village shopping area, serving French food in a Spanish colonial setting. Be prepared to pay dearly for a great meal. Reservations required. **El Rincon**, 602/282-4648, serves Mexican food in the same upscale shopping complex.

Irene's Restaurant, Castle Rock Plaza, Oak Creek Village, 602/284-2240, serves American home-style cooking, including baked goods. Also in Castle Rock Plaza, the **Mandarin House**, 602/284-2525, serves Chinese food.

Heartline Cafe, 1610 West US 89A, Sedona, 602/282-0785, serves unusual salads and dishes made with fresh herbs, fruits, and vegetables.

Phil & Eddie's Diner, 1655 West US 89A, Sedona, 602/282-6070, is a throwback to the heyday of Route 66, serving classic diner fare, burgers, ice cream sodas, and breakfast anytime.

Thai Spices Natural, 2986 West US 89A, Sedona, 602/282-0590, in the White House Motel, serves Thai food prepared with organic ingredients.

Rainbow's End Steak House & Saloon, 3235 West US 89A, Sedona, 602/282-1593, serves up flame-grilled steaks and has country-western music.

In Jerome, **House of Joy**, on Hull Street, 602/634-5339, still looks like the brothel it was at one time, but now serves popular Continental cuisine. Open only on Saturdays and Sundays for dinner. Reservations are suggested far in advance.

Jerome Palace, Clark Street, Jerome, 602/634-5262, serves up barbecue with a view. The Verde Valley unfolds beneath the second-story dining room windows.

Macy's European Coffee House & Bakery, Main Street, Jerome, 602/634-2733, offers a similar menu, featuring coffees, teas, sandwiches and pastries, as their shop in Flagstaff. Open for breakfast and lunch.

Winslow/Holbrook
Accommodations & Restaurants

Chain motels are often, though not always, the best bet in this area. Food will be modest, especially if you're coming from Sedona, and it's going to be mostly standard American fare, meat and potatoes, scarce vegetables, that sort of thing.

Best Western Adobe Inn, 1701 North Park Drive, Winslow, AZ 86047, 602/289-4638, fax 602/289-5514, has 72 rooms, a restaurant, and an indoor pool.

Casa Blanca Cafe, 1201 East 2nd Street, Winslow, 602/289-4191, serves Mexican and American food.

Wigwam Motel, 811 West Hopi Drive, Holbrook, AZ 86025, is reason enough to stay overnight in Holbrook; accommodations are in 15 stucco tipis. How often do you see one of those, let alone sleep in it? Rooms contain handmade wooden furniture.

Best Western Arizonian Inn, 2508 East Navajo Boulevard, Holbrook, AZ 86025, 602/524-2611 or 800/528-1234, has 70 rooms and mini-suites, free HBO movies, a pool, restaurant and coffee shop. Also: This is one of the few properties in Holbrook that specifies no pets.

Comfort Inn, 2602 Navajo Boulevard, Holbrook, AZ 86025, 602/524-6131 or 800/228-5150 offers 61 rooms, a heated pool and a complimentary continental breakfast.

Budget Inn Motel, 602 Navajo Boulevard, Holbrook, AZ, 80625, 602/524-6263, has 38 rooms and a pool.

Aquilera's Cafe, 200 Navajo Boulevard, Holbrook, AZ 602/524-3806, serves big plates of Mexican and American food.

Camping

Arizona Strip Camping

Lees Ferry has four campgrounds situated in Marble Canyon, just south of the Lees Ferry Historic District. Boat camping is permitted at a site north of Lees Ferry, below the Glen Canyon

Dam. For information contact the **Lees Ferry Ranger Station**, 602/355-2234.

Heart Campground, operated by the Paiute Tribe, offers campsites and RV spaces a quarter-mile north of Pipe Springs National Monument, off AZ 389.

Jacob Lake Forest Camp, 44 miles north of the North Rim on AZ 67, is open May through October.

De Motte Forest Camp, just south of Kaibab Lodge off AZ 67, 18 miles north of the North Rim, is open June through September.

Grand Canyon National Park Area Camping

The following phone numbers provide information about **Grand Canyon National Park**, Box 129, Grand Canyon, Arizona 86023: Visitor activities & programs, 602/638-9304; Park information, 602/638-2245; Park headquarters, 602/638-7888.

Backcountry camping requires a free permit available from the **Backcountry Reservations Office**, Box 12, Grand Canyon, AZ 86023, 602/638-7875. Permits are limited and reservations are necessary. For a Backcountry Information line phone 602/638-7888.

During high season it may be easier to find camping sites outside the park. Reservations for Grand Canyon campgrounds may be made by writing to **MISTIX**, PO Box 85705, San Diego, CA 92138-5705, or by phoning 800/365-2267, with a credit card.

There is a primitive campground at **Toroweap Point** on the North Rim of the Grand Canyon. A permit is required and is available at the North Rim Ranger Station, located a few miles north of the campground or, by mail, from the Backcountry Reservations Office.

On the North Rim, **North Rim Campground**, is a mile and a half north of the Grand Canyon Lodge and is usually open only from May to October.

Below the South Rim two campgrounds, **Bright Angel** and **Cottonwood**, are for backpackers only, who may stay only two days. Reservations are often required months in advance.

Desert View Campground, on the East Rim Drive, 25 miles east of Grand Canyon Village, does not accept reservations. Camping limit is seven days. Open May through September.

Mather Campground, south of the Visitor Center on the South Rim, has tent sites and trailer sites with year-round hook-ups in the adjacent **Trailer Village**. Flush toilets and showers are available.

There is a seven-day limit. You can make reservations up to eight weeks in advance for the busy March 1 to December 1 season. The rest of the year the campground functions on a first-come, first-served basis. For reservations see the above contacts, or Grand Canyon Lodges, listed above under Accommodations.

Ten-X Campground is three miles south of Tusayan, near the South Rim. It's open from May through October.

Havasu Campground is the only place you can camp in Havasu Canyon. The camping area starts below Havasu Falls and stretches for nearly a mile along Havasu Creek to Mooney Falls. There are no fires permitted. Campers need a cook stove. There is as small grocery store in the village of Supai, 2.5 miles away.

Williams/Flagstaff Camping

There are four campgrounds near Williams, all on fishing and boating lakes.

Cataract Campground, two miles northeast of Williams, is only open May through October. The others are open year-round but may have water only in the summer. These include, **Kaibab Campground**, four miles northeast of Williams, **Dogtown Campground**, seven miles southeast of Williams, and **White Horse Lake Campground**, 19 miles southeast of Williams.

Bonito Campground, at Sunset Crater National Monument, is open May through October, with 44 sites for tents and RVs.

Fort Tuthill County Park, 602/774-3464, three miles south of Flagstaff off US 89A, has a 103-site campground amid 355 acres of wooded nature trails.

Lakeview Campground, across from Upper Lake Mary, 15 miles south of Flagstaff on Lake Mary Road, is the closest campground to Upper and Lower Lake Mary. Drinking water is available.

Ashurst and **Forked Pine campgrounds** are situated on opposite shores of Ashurst Lake, 18 miles southeast of Flagstaff on Lake Mary Road, and four miles east on Forest Road 82E.

Pinegrove Campground is 18 miles southeast of Flagstaff on Lake Mary Road and a mile east on Forest Road 651

There are two Forest Service campgrounds at Mormon Lake, **Dairy Springs** and **Double Springs**, with a combined total of 45 sites. To reach the campgrounds drive 20 miles southeast of Flagstaff, on Lake Mary Road, then turn east and south on Mormon Lake Loop Road, which follows the west shore of the lake. You'll come to Dairy Springs in four miles. Double Springs is two miles farther south.

Sedona Area Camping

There are five Forest Service campgrounds in Oak Creek Canyon, all situated along US 89A within a 12-mile stretch starting six miles north of town. The campgrounds are usually open March through September and they are the only spots where camping is permitted in Oak Creek Canyon. Several of the Forest Service campgrounds can accommodate trailers but no hook-ups are available. Private campgrounds nearby provide hook-ups.

Dead Horse Ranch State Park, north of Cottonwood, has a year-round campground with hookups for RVs and showers.

Two campgrounds are located near Camp Verde. **Beaver Creek** is 12 miles north of town and east off I-17. **Clear Creek** is five miles south on Main Street.

A small campground is at **Clints Well**, near the junction of Lake Mary Road and AZ 87.

Winslow/Holbrook Camping

There's a campground at **McHood Park**, six miles southeast of Winslow.

The Navajo Reservation and Hopiland

The route through the previous chapters of this book has circled these Indian tribal lands, now reaching, in a round-about way, the area some consider to be the heart of the High Southwest. This arid, high desert plateau country, ranging from 4,000 to more than 7,000 feet in elevation, is the central spot where many believe human occupation of the Colorado Plateau started. At the least, this is where travellers experience the most direct links with the prehistoric past.

Geography & History

The Navajo religion teaches that there are two classes of beings: Earth People and Holy People, with Holy People possessing the power to help or hurt Earth People. Centuries ago the Holy People taught the "Dineh," the Navajo people, how to live correctly and conduct the acts of everyday life, including how to live in harmony with Mother Earth, Father Sky, and all the other elements, such as man, animals, plants, and insects.

The Holy People defined Navajoland by specifying its limits within an area enclosed by four sacred mountains. Thus, in Navajo lore, the eastern border of their lands is Mount Blanca, east of Alamosa, Colorado. The southern border is Mount Taylor, near Grants, New Mexico. The western edge of Navajoland is in the San Francisco Peaks, close to Flagstaff, Arizona, and the northern limit is Mount Hesperus west of Durango, Colorado.

These cardinal points help define the boundaries of this book, an area where the past is never far away. It is perhaps closer than elsewhere in Navajoland, and even closer in neighboring Hopiland.

The **Navajo Nation** covers 26,000 square miles. This includes practically all of northeastern Arizona lying east of the Grand Canyon and north of I-40. It also includes a slice of northwest New Mexico, roughly from the Arizona border to Farmington and south to I-40, plus the area of southeastern Utah from Page, Arizona to the Colorado border, south of the San Juan River.

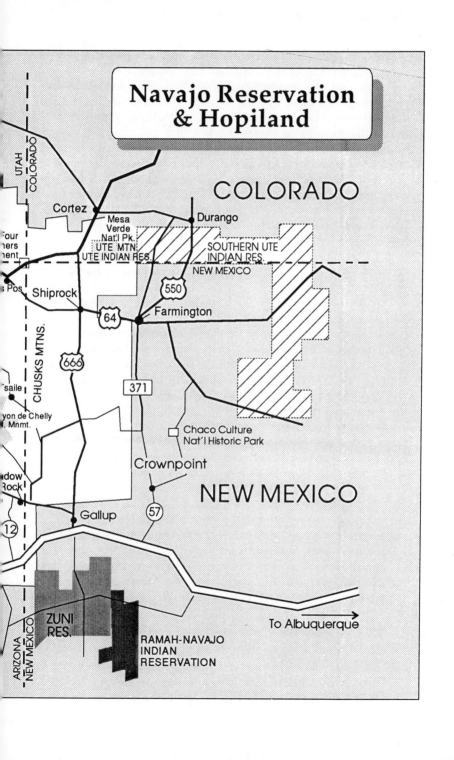

Sweeping panoramas of epic space unfold across the Navajo Reservation, perched atop the Colorado Plateau.

Navajoland contains two National Monuments located in canyons occupied long ago by the Anasazi, a tribal park consisting of desert flats and sand dunes sprouting protrusions of random rock monoliths, buttes and mesas the size of a skyscraper, or larger, numerous historic sites, and even popular fishing lakes situated among forested mountains along the New Mexico border.

You can visit ancient Anasazi Indian sites at **Navajo** or **Canyon de Chelly National Monuments**. Then you can see how the ancient ways link with the present beneath the 500-foot-tall cliffs of **Monument Valley Navajo Tribal Park**, where Navajo ranchers herd sheep as they have done for centuries. Or sink a line into the cold, clear waters of **Wheatfields Lake** in the **Lukuchukai Mountains**, one of a dozen major fishing lakes operated by the Navajo people.

The Dineh consider the land to be their mother and themselves an integral part of a universe in which they must do everything possible to maintain balance and harmony on Mother Earth.

Of course, in 1864 the United States Army took historical exception to some of the Navajo's efforts. The tribe had a well-known antisocial habit which entailed maintaining an even distribution of wealth by helping themselves to newcomers' possessions, including those of white settlers'.

US troops forced the Long Walk, which was the involuntary relocation of the Navajo People from these lands their ancestors had farmed and lived on for hundreds of years, to even bleaker surroundings in eastern New Mexico. The experimental effort at acculturation predictably failed, but not before many Navajos died and many spirits among the Dineh were broken. In 1868, the Navajo people were permitted to return to this area. They had to start from scratch as their homes and farms were destroyed from neglect and their minds subtly infiltrated by the white man's ways.

Among various modern proscriptions enforced to protect and control the reservation lands granted the Dineh by the federal government are certain restrictions to backcountry travel:

• You can't go biking or jeeping on back roads.
• Hikers need to pay a fee for a permit.
• You're not allowed to wander around very far on your own in Canyon de Chelly, Monument Valley, or Navajo National Monument, where guided tours are the only option for backcountry travel.

The nature of adventure takes an introspective turn in these parts. You may still ride a horse, a bike, or a jeep, but you do so as a guest in a different cultural milieu.

Among the contrasts you may see in Navajoland are some you might notice in any dramatically poor, chronically unemployed, Third World country trying to balance inherent contradictions.

On the one hand the Navajos like cashing in on their scenery, history, and traditions. They'd like to maintain the dignity of their traditions, which is where many challenges lie. Conflicts are inevitable while balancing economic growth and historic reserve while incorporating the unavoidable, good and bad changes wrought by an increasingly modern way of life.

Everything is symbolic in Navajo tradition. A basket, for example, represents the well-being of an individual, based on the creation by the Holy People of the First Man and First Woman, who made baskets for ceremonial uses. Each part of a basket has significance. Navajo people still use baskets ceremonially but workshops churn out hundreds a day for sale and today Navajos also use them for decorative touches at home.

Sand paintings are another symbolic art that originated with the Holy People, for ceremonial usage. The paintings represent numerous rituals and sacred songs. Today, many Navajo artisans mass-produce these ceremonially significant objects for commercial sales throughout Navajoland. Every gallery, gift shop, and gas station is equipped with a display rack for sand-painted refrigerator magnets.

And then there is the Navajo love-affair with the media. Film makers, television producers, and advertising art directors have long treasured the burnished, dramatic vistas stretching across the mother of the Dineh.

No problem, no conflict here. The Navajo impose fees for commercial photography. Individuals vehemently decline to participate in your snapshot, or you can snap away all you like for a dollar.

What seems perfectly rational to you may not seem so to a Navajo and vice versa, so don't expect a perfectly-oiled tourism machine in these parts. Some of the kinks are still being worked out. Time, for example, tends to have a different, non-specific meaning on the reservation. Slow down; a stranger putting on airs is not taken seriously anyway.

The Navajo people consider adapting to the demands of nature, as defined by themselves, a higher calling than conforming to the dominion of man, at least, generally speaking, non-Navajo man.

It should be understood that accepting a guest's formal responsibility to treat those concerns with respect is the only way to gain more than a superficial understanding of this place, and even that might not be enough to open the doors.

According to the Navajo Tourism Department, rules and regulations regarding visits to the Navajo Reservation are as follows:

- Respect the privacy and customs of the Navajo people. Enter home areas only upon invitation. Do not wander across residential areas or disturb property. Obtain permission before taking pictures. A gratuity may be expected.
- Please keep Navajoland clean. Do not litter! Do not burn or bury it. Please place all refuse in trash containers.
- Do not disturb or remove animals, plants, rocks, or artifacts as these are protected by Tribal Antiquity and Federal laws enforced on the Navajo Reservation. Rock hunting is prohibited.
- Possession and consumption of alcoholic beverages is prohibited.
- The use of firearms is not allowed on the reservation.
- The Navajo Nation is not responsible for any injuries, accidents, or thefts of personal property while travelling through the reservation.
- Appropriate dress is required. Please, no swim wear or bikinis.
- Please maintain pets on a leash or in a confined area. All actions of pets are the responsibility of the owner.

Hopiland is even harder to crack. It is bisected by AZ 264, running between US 160 in the west and US 191 in the east, and is surrounded by the southwestern corner of the vastly larger Navajo Reservation.

The Hopi Reservation was established in 1882, four years after the creation of the Navajo Reservation, granting the Hopi lands along the southern end of Black Mesa, where their families had lived for at least 650 years.

Hopiland includes three angular, flat-topped mesas jutting over the rock-strewn, scrub and cacti desert. Hopi villages include one called **Oraibi** which was settled in 1050, making it the oldest consistently occupied community in North America. Other villages, comprised of small clusters of homes, are located on **First Mesa**, **Second Mesa** or **Third Mesa**.

Despite the long-time proximity of their reservations, Hopis and Navajos come from different roots and differ in cultural beliefs.

Navajo people are descended from nomadic Athabascan tribes that filtered into this area from Canada, and Asia before that, around 600 years ago.

The Hopi are considered to be linked with the vanished Anasazi and have resided on the craggy, remote mesas for the past 1,000 years.

Protracted and embittered boundary feuds concerning the low-lying, arid gullies, lonely pastel buttes, and radiant, phantasmagoric mesas twinkling in the torrid desert like distant ships at sea, are still a problem with no readily apparent solution.

Ranging as high as 7,200 feet, Hopiland is a very different place than the Navajo Reservation. For one thing, the Hopi people are more clearly protective of their privacy. They tend to live close together in small villages while the Navajo tend to like more space between themselves and their neighbors.

In addition, no photographs, recordings, or drawings are permitted in the Hopi villages and backcountry travel is prohibited.

Particular ceremonies or dances are open only to tribal members. Other less significant ceremonies, often held on summer weekends, including distinctive dances, are considered public events, although would-be photographers are liable to have camera equipment confiscated by tribal police.

Officials will not hesitate in asking you to leave if they catch you screwing around. Leave your ego and vanity at the gate; the Hopi people are the real thing, baby. Therein lies adventure.

Complete guidelines for visitors to Hopiland are as follows:

- The Hopi asks you to be mindful while attending ceremonies; they call for the same respect due any sacred event, neat attire and a respectful disposition.
- Disruption of shrines or removal of articles/artifacts are strictly prohibited and possession of such items may subject the possessor to federal prosecution. All archaeological sites on the reservation are protected by federal laws and Hopi tribal ordinances.
- Photography, recording, and sketching villages and ceremonies are strictly prohibited.
- Overnight camping is allowed, but there are no facilities available.
- Alcoholic beverages and drugs are strictly prohibited by law on the Hopi Reservation.
- Before spending any length of time in the villages, permission should be obtained from the village leader. Non-Indians may not reside on the reservation without consent of the respective chief or official.
- Please observe all rules and regulations established by the villages. The villages are autonomous and have the authority to

establish their own governing policies supported by the Hopi Tribal Council. It is advisable to check with village Community Development offices before going into the village to visit or witness a ceremony.

- Policy signs are posted outside each village. For additional information about specific Hopi Villages contact the following village offices:

Bacavi, 602/734-2404.
First Mesa, 602/734-2670.
Hotevilla, 602/734-2420.
Kykotsmovi, 602/734-2474.
Mishongnovi, 602/737-2520.
Moenkopi, 602/283-6684.
Shungopavi, 602/734-2262.
Sipaulovi, 602/734-2570.

Getting Around

Private vehicles or organized tours are just about the only way to travel in this area of Indian country. There are a few private landing strips, but no commercial airports.

There are only 600 hotel rooms in all of the Navajo Nation and Hopiland. Reservations are highly recommended, particularly in summertime when hotels near popular Monument Valley and Canyon de Chelly are likely to be fully booked.

Coming from the Petrified Forest National Park area on I-40, it's 43 miles east on the interstate to a junction with Tribal Route 12 north, just a few miles west of the New Mexico border.

Window Rock, the Navajo capital and a good place to start, is 26 miles north on Tribal Route 12. There are several interesting shops and attractions in Window Rock and several possibilities for overnight accommodations.

Twenty-nine miles west of Window Rock on AZ 264 is **Hubbell Trading Post National Historic Site,** an original and still-operating trading post, where you can buy corn flakes, barbed wire, or Indian rugs. It is managed by the National Park Service. From Hubbell, it's 35 miles north on US 191 to Chinle, AZ.

Three miles east of Chinle on Tribal Route 7 is Canyon de Chelly National Monument. A paved South Rim Drive ends at a rugged dirt road better suited to intrepid mountain bikers than cars. A North Rim Drive leading to overlooks along the rim of the upper **Canyon del Muerto** also leads east 25 miles to Tsaile, AZ, location of **Navajo Community College**, the **Ned Hatathlie Cultural Center** and the main access to adventurous possibilities in the **Chuska** and **Lukachukai Mountains**, straddling the Arizona-New Mexico border.

From this area it is possible to travel south to the volcanic **Black Pinnacle** or **Wheatfields Lake**, east to **Shiprock**, NM and the **Four Corners National Monument**, and ultimately west to **Kayenta**, AZ, gateway to Monument Valley.

Monument Valley lies 24 miles north of Kayenta off US 163 or 25 miles south of Mexican Hat, Utah. From there, continuing to explore the Navajo Nation, you have to backtrack to Kayenta and travel 19 miles west on US 160 and nine miles north on AZ 564 to Navajo National Monument. **Tuba City** is 40 miles west on US 160 and is on the way to the **Navajo Mountain-Rainbow Bridge** area near Lake Powell.

Hopiland is accessed from the west by AZ 264 which meets US 160 in Tuba City. The two-lane state highway crosses to the eastern border of the small reservation 60 miles west of Window Rock.

About time: The Navajo Reservation keeps the same time as Colorado, New Mexico and Utah. The Hopi Reservation keeps the same time as the rest of Arizona.

Information Sources

Navajo Times, PO Box 310, Window Rock, AZ 86515, 602/871-6641 or 871-7357, fax 602/871-6177, is the tribal newspaper which contains, among reservation and other news, information about special events.

Commercial photographers in Navajoland need a permit from **Office of Broadcast Services**, PO Box 2310, Window Rock, AZ 86515, 602/871-6655 or 602/871-6656.

Permits are required for visits by non-Navajos to archaeologically, historically and culturally significant Navajo reservation sites, as well as for any archaeological or anthropological research. If you question whether or not a place you want to visit fits into one of these categories, it's probably better to ask first.

For information or required permits contact **Navajo Natural Historic Preservation Department**, PO Box 2898, Window Rock, AZ 86515, 602/871-6437.

In addition, **Navajo Tribal Rangers**, responsible, like their counterpart US Park Rangers, for certain lands, may be reached at the following numbers: **Window Rock**, AZ, 602/871-6701. **Chinle**, AZ, 602/674-5250. **Crownpoint**, NM, 505/786-5532. **Shiprock**, NM, 505/368-4522. **Tuba City**, AZ, 602/283-4644. **Montezuma Creek**, UT, 801/651-3673.

Touring the Navajo Nation

Window Rock

Window Rock, the capital of the Navajo Nation with a population of more than 3,000, is situated at 6,750 feet, 17 miles west of Gallup, New Mexico. The town boasts a modern motel, a relative rarity in Navajoland. You can also find several fast food options, including a Dunkin' Donuts, food markets, and gas stations, making Window Rock a functional base for day trips to Hubbell Trading Post and the Chuska Mountains.

In Window Rock you can see the octagon-shaped Navajo Nation Council Chambers, built to resemble a traditional, ceremonial hogan or Navajo home, on the short drive from downtown to **Window Rock Navajo Tribal Park**. The park and the Council Chambers are a half-mile north of AZ 264 on Tribal Route 12, and a half-mile east. This is the site of a large, red, sandstone outcrop containing a hole 47 feet in diameter. This is the window after which the town was named. The park has a picnic area and a hiking trail.

Tours of the **Council Chambers**, which are decorated with murals illustrating Navajo history, may be arranged by phoning 602/871-7171 or 602/871-6417. If the 88-member council, representing 100 chapters and communities, is in session, you may be able to listen to debates spoken in Navajo, the baffling language used to successfully transmit military codes during World War II.

Navajo Tribal Museum, PO Box 308, Window Rock, AZ 86515, 602/871-6673, has a collection of arts and artifacts, plus exhibits describing the reservation lands, its ancient and current residents, with craft displays of various styles in silver jewelry and weaving. It is next to the Navajo Nation Inn, north of the junction of AZ 264 and Tribal Route 12 North.

Navajo Arts & Crafts Enterprises, 602/871-4090, shares the same building as the tribal museum and offers one of the more comprehensive collections in the Four Corners of high caliber natural turquoise, coral, onyx, lapis, and sterling silver jewelry, along with baskets, handwoven rugs, Navajo pottery, t-shirts, and postcards. NACE, a non-profit organization, was founded in 1941 by the Navajo Nation to promote traditional Navajo crafts. Today the operation has grown to offer works by other Southwestern Indians and craft supplies, such as beads, silver, and woolen yarns.

The same company operates a **Navajo Arts & Crafts Enterprise** store in Chinle, 602/674-5338, and the shop at Cameron Trading Post, 602/679-2244, in the western Navajo Nation near the Grand Canyon.

Tse Bonito Navajo Tribal Park is a half-mile east of Tribal Route 12 on AZ 264 in Window Rock. It marks the site where the Navajo people camped before starting the Long Walk to Fort Sumner, New Mexico, in 1864. There is a small campground, but no facilities.

Behind Tse Bonito park, **Navajo Nation Zoo & Botanical Park**, PO Box 308, Window Rock, AZ 86515, 602/871-6573, near the Arizona-New Mexico state-line on AZ 264 in Window Rock, features animals native to the Navajo Reservation and domestic animals that are culturally important to the Navajo people. You can see rattlesnakes, eagles, wolves, mountain lions, black bears, elk, coyotes, and Navajo sheep.

St. Michael's Historical Museum, three miles west of Window Rock on AZ 264, is a 1937 stone church containing exhibits relating to the history of the Catholic Church and the Navajo people.

Window Rock Enterprises, PO Box 1389, Window Rock, AZ 86515, 602/871-4294 or 602/871-4562, provides tours, transportation, and information about the Window Rock area.

Navajo Transit System, 602/729-5449, operates a bus service connecting Window Rock with communities throughout the Navajo and Hopi Reservations.

For further information contact the **Navajoland Tourism Department**, PO Box 663, Window Rock, AZ 86515, 602/871-7371, fax 602/871-7381. The tourism office has been working out of a trailer two miles west of Tribal Route 12 on AZ 264 for years, but ground was broken in August 1993 to build a new Visitor Center, museum, and library in Window Rock, scheduled to be open in the summer of 1994.

Hubbell Trading Post National Historic Site

Situated 29 miles west of Window Rock on AZ 264 and a mile west of Ganado, **Hubbell Trading Post National Historic Site** is operated by the U.S. National Park Service, but in much the same way as the property has been run for more than 100 years, as a functioning trading post. In these parts that means you can find crafts and fine arts that have been traded here for corn, beans, flour, hardware, and tools. You can also buy or presumably trade for these things yourself.

Many things changed for the Navajo people after the Long Walk in 1864, followed by the Navajo's return in 1868 to these ancestral lands. For one, the Navajo people had to start from scratch, eking out subsistence livings from the land that had been left unattended. For another, where they had once been able to live modestly and self-sufficiently, they had now been introduced to the ways of the white man. They were becoming reliant on sweets, coffee, canned foods, tools, needles, thread, cloth, and other items. But having never been part of the cash culture, Indians could only trade the common items of their lives such as blankets, rugs, pottery, baskets, and jewelry. Cash was never exchanged at trading posts run by entrepreneurial whites.

Long into the 1900s Hubbell Trading Post and other scattered outposts across the reservation provided the sole connection between rural Indians and the encroaching society that had altered for all time their ancient ways of life.

John Lorenzo Hubbell opened the doors to his trading post here in 1878 and the property remained in continuous operation by the same family until 1965, when it was sold to the Park Service.

J. L. Hubbell died in 1930. His grave is on the side of a hillock surveying the trading post and his original homestead. A free tour is offered several times daily of his antique-decorated home, kept up in the historically accurate-style of the 1880s frontier. After the short tour you can step into the trading post to buy a cold drink, a candy bar, a quart of milk, motor oil, a hammer, canned green beans, a silver bracelet, a kachina doll, or perhaps one of high quality, hand-spun and dyed, Navajo rugs.

The really fine work is stored in a big, old vault. Beware the hefty price tags. Asking prices are intentionally high here to leave room for negotiations. Selling prices may be considerably lower depending on the negotiating skill of the buyer.

In addition, during the summer months, Navajo weavers and silversmiths display their skills at demonstrations in a small museum and gift shop adjacent to the trading post.

Canyon De Chelly National Monument

Five miles northwest of Hubbell Trading Post on AZ 264 then 35 miles north on US 191, is **Chinle**, a fairly large community that has developed alongside **Canyon de Chelly National Monument**, PO

Box 588, Chinle, AZ 86503, 602/674-5436. There are several motels, restaurants, a Burger King, gas stations, and markets.

Canyon de Chelly National Monument is actually two main canyons, the 35-mile-long **Canyon del Muerto** to the north and the 26-mile-long **Canyon de Chelly** to the south, which converge at their lowest depths in Chinle.

The canyon walls are only 34 feet high near Chinle, but they reach a height of 1,000 feet at the western end of the National Monument. Enclosed within those vertical sandstone walls are 83,800 acres containing numerous primitive Indian sites. Yet modern Navajo farmers still tend flocks of sheep and cultivate bean fields on the fertile canyon bottom. There may be nowhere else in Indian country where the natural continuum between ancient and modern Indian life is so clearly visible in such an unaffected way.

A Visitor Center is located three miles east of Chinle on Tribal Route 7. There is a small museum with a full-size round log hogan outside. Information is available about the rim drives to overlooks into the canyons and Navajo-guided tours are offered. Museum exhibits in the Visitor Center describe elements of the span of Indian occupation of the canyons.

The earliest occupants were nomads who discovered the area more than 2,000 years ago. Anasazi periodically used the canyons before eventually settling to live in hole-in-the-ground pit houses and farm the canyon bottom around 500 A.D. Successive generations evolved primitive masonry skills, eventually constructing kivas and above-ground pueblos. By the 12th-14th centuries, when they attained their cultural peak, a population of 1,000 was scattered in numerous small villages. Then, like the rest of their mysterious Anasazi brethren, they disappeared into the sands of time.

Some may have gone to nearby Hopiland. For the next 300 years only Hopis farmed the canyon bottom. The Navajos arrived in the 1700s and appreciated the many places they could hide in the canyons after looting forays against other local residents, including Spanish settlers and other Indians. In retaliation for these lootings, counter-attacks were launched that killed many Navajo braves and captured women and children for slaves.

Kit Carson, leading US Army troops, cleared out the last contentious canyon dwellers in 1864 by burning fields and killing livestock to starve the Navajo into submission. The Canyon de Chelly Navajos joined many others in the walk to New Mexico.

Survivors began filtering back in 1868. Today, their descendants still live in summer hogans to farm or raise livestock in the bountiful, moist canyon bottom, right beside incredible Anasazi pueblo ruins. The main difference is that the farmers now retreat during the cold and sometimes snowy winters to live in homes with satellite dishes on the canyon rim or in Chinle.

Another difference is the tours that pass through the canyon. In general, visitors are not allowed to enter Canyon de Chelly without a park ranger or a Navajo guide.

There is one trail, to **White House Ruin**, that can be hiked unescorted, but that's it as far as exploring the inner canyon on your own is concerned. You can drive the rim drives and stop at scenic overlooks. If you want to get inside you can hire a private guide or take one of the many tours that are offered.

The pair of 21-mile, one-way drives along the stark sandstone rims of this Navajo spiritual center begin at the Visitor Center. Well-marked parking areas provide access to scenic overlooks revealing 11 million years of geological history and 20 centuries of Indian habitation, distinguished by approximately 100 primitive ruins, many of which you can see far below the rim drive turn-offs.

On the South Rim, sites include **Tunnel Canyon Overlook**, **Tsegi Overlook**, and **Junction Overlook**, where Canyon del Muerto veers north. Six miles from the Visitor Center is **White House Overlook**.

In the deep canyon the vertical walls that appear to have been sliced neatly, as if with a chisel, blend somehow gracefully into eccentric, bulging rock forms, some forming arched rock overhangs that once offered protection against the elements to the Anasazi.

Intriguingly, amid all this rock, prosperous cultivation occurs on the canyon bottom, but even on the near-sheer walls, where trees and shrubs seem to sprout from boulders, natural cycles continue. Canyon de Chelly is a special place for observing that sort of thing.

Other stops on the South Rim Drive include **Sliding House Overlook**, **Wild Cherry Overlook**, and **Face Rock Overlook**.

The last stop before the paved rim drive turns into a rugged, impassable-when-wet, dirt road beyond the Park Service boundaries is the famous **Spider Rock Overlook**, a spot that figures prominently in Navajo religious tradition. Spider Rock is an 800-foot-tall spire rising from the canyon floor. From the 1,000-foot-high overlook you can see this Navajo deity and a slightly smaller spire next to it, **Speaking Rock**.

The North Rim Drive follows Tribal Route 64 northeast from the Visitor Center along the rim of Canyon del Muerto. Stops include **Ledge Ruin Overlook**, **Antelope House Overlook**, sites revealing easily-visible but tiny-looking ruins in the canyon far below. **Mummy Cave Overlook**, 18.5 miles northeast of the Visitor Center, is a ruins site where two mummified corpses were discovered by 19th century canyon explorers. The name Canyon del Muerto, which means Canyon of the Dead, also came from this early archaeological find.

Massacre Cave Overlook, the last stop on the North Rim Drive, is where more than a hundred Navajo were killed by Spanish soldiers in 1805.

You can return to Chinle on the North Rim Drive or continue on paved Tribal Route 64 for 13 miles to the small town of **Tsaile**, at the junction with Tribal Route 12. Tsaile is the modest, northerly jumping-off point for access to Tsaile Lake and Wheatfields Lake, and it is the location of Navajo Community College, home to the **Ted Hatathlie Museum & Gallery**, 602/724-3311.

The entrance to the college is a mile west of Tribal Route 12 off Tribal Route 64 and the Hatathlie Museum is on the east side of the small campus in a six-story cultural center shaped like a hogan. Exhibits explain primitive and modern Indian cultures. There is a gift shop and bookstore.

Wheatfields Lake is 10 miles south of Tsaile off Tribal Route 12. It's a popular fishing lake in a mountainous location. There is a campground and the Lakeside Store.

Tsaile Lake, Assayi Lake, Bowl Canyon Recreation Area and several other lakes are in the mountains south of Wheatfields Lake and north of Window Rock. These areas are detailed below, under Fishing and Camping.

Fifteen miles south of Wheatfields Lake on Tribal Route 12 is a junction with NM 134, which can be followed for 20 miles northeast across the scenic **Chuska Mountains** to US 666. From there it's 43 miles north on US 666 to **Shiprock**, New Mexico, a large Navajo community named after **Shiprock Peak**.

The 1,500-foot volcanic rock is visible 10 miles southwest of town, looming high over the desert. There are no services near the landmark; the Navajo spiritual site is off limits to hikers and climbers and can only be viewed from a distance.

Shiprock is not a particularly interesting town. One good thing in town is a supermarket. It is not a gas station/convenience store, but a real market. There are also several trading posts in the vicinity offering a range of Indian goods, including **Foutz Trading Company**, Shiprock, NM 87420, 505/368-5790, three miles west of town on US 64. Two other trading posts are 15 miles east of town on US 64 in Waterflow, New Mexico.

From Shiprock following US 64 west for 26 miles leads to **Teec Nos Pos**, a tiny, practically invisible community with a small motel and the **Teec Nos Pos Trading Post**, noted for sales of distinctive, locally-made rugs.

Six miles northeast of Teec Nos Pos on US 160 is **Four Corners Monument Navajo Tribal Park**, a small park marking the only site in the United States where the borders of four states–Arizona, New Mexico, Colorado, and Utah–meet. Strangely, there's little to see here in the actual center of this amazing territory of mountains, canyons, rivers, and deserts that form the Four Corners region. The exact spot is marked by a stone slab in the ground which you may stand on, officially being in four places at one time. A typically disconsolate assortment of Indian vendors offers t-shirts and mass-produced souvenirs from rickety wooden stalls.

From the Four Corners Monument it's 40 miles north on US 160 to Cortez, Colorado, and 28 miles north to the Ute Mountain Casino, providing insight into another aspect of modern Indian culture and perhaps even insight into the drab Four Corners monument.

Continuing west in Navajoland on US 160 it's 70 miles to **Kayenta**, the next reservation town of any magnitude and the gateway to **Monument Valley**.

Monument Valley

Kayenta is at the junction of US 160 and US 163, 23 miles south of Monument Valley Navajo Tribal Park.

The town provides basic services, several motels, restaurants, a market, and gas stations. It may not seem like much to offer, but there is only one motel and a campground in the extremely popular Monument Valley. Many travellers secure accommodations in Kayenta as a base for excursions north and, 28 miles west of town, to **Navajo National Monument**.

One of the more interesting sites in Kayenta is located in the Burger King. It is an exhibit of memorabilia relating to the Navajo code-talkers of World War II. Navajo servicemen relayed vital information in their native language, which baffled enemy cryptographers.

Eight miles north of Kayenta, on the way to **Monument Valley Navajo Tribal Park**, PO Box 93, Monument Valley, UT 84536, 801/727-3287, lunar-looking **Agthala Peak**, a 1,500-foot volcanic outcrop, looms to the east over desert flats, hinting at the magnitude of the geological wonders to come.

The 30,000-acre Navajo tribal park straddles the Arizona-Utah border east of US 163, 23 miles north of Kayenta and 25 miles south of Mexican Hat, Utah. You have to enter the park through Utah, on a three-mile entry road east of US 163, but the main scenic attractions are back across the border in Arizona. Near the highway the side of the entry road supports a row of stands offering frybread, Navajo tacos, mutton sandwiches, silver jewelry, and rugs.

At the end of the road there is a Visitor Center with bathrooms, gift and book store, campground, tour guides and traditionally-dressed models who will pose for photographers at a small cost. Otherwise, the closest services are at **Goulding's Lodge**. The lodge, a mile west of US 163 across the highway from the park entrance, includes a motel, restaurant, gift shop, museum, tour services, landing strip, grocery store, and gas station.

The next closest services are in Kayenta or Mexican Hat. If you're shopping for antique Indian arts and crafts try the **Oljeto Trading Post**, nine miles northwest of Goulding's. Follow the paved road running past the Goulding's complex for some unusual finds.

Monument Valley's year-round Visitor Center is adjacent to a campground, open in summer only. From this area you can look out over red buttes, mesas, and pinnacles rising off the valley floor in distinctive individual majesty, like a proud tribe turned to stone. If it all seems somehow familiar, it's probably because the vistas, back roads, washes, gullies, and canyons have appeared as settings in dozens of western movies, television shows, commercials, and print ads. Monument Valley is particularly known as one of the favorite locations of Hollywood director John Ford, who filmed several John Wayne movies here. Other stars such as Henry Fonda appeared in Ford's classics *Fort Apache* and *My Darling Clementine*, made here. *The Searchers*, *The Trial of Billy Jack*, and *The Legend of the Lone Ranger* are among other features filmed in Monument Valley.

There is a 17-mile loop road through the valley that is open to private vehicles, but no backcountry exploration is permitted without a Navajo guide. That deserted-looking back road that beckons is probably a Navajo family's driveway.

There are numerous view site turn-offs within the park and ample opportunity to stop and admire craft items offered at strategic locations in open-sided, thatch roof sheds or simply displayed on a blanket.

The scenic drive, a rather confusing and virtually un-marked sandy track filled with numerous opportunities for wrong turns, passes named sites, some with special spiritual significance to the Navajo people, as well as **John Ford Point**, honoring the movie-maker who masterfully employed the valley's mystique to immortalize his film legacy and the epic scenery at the same time. Other activity on the valley floor, aside from car, bus, and jeep tour traffic, includes Navajo herdsmen trailing sheep through gullies and canyons studded with juniper, pinyon, and wind-blown, dusty sage, overshadowed by the mammoth, vertical rocks.

Even without being allowed to wander very far on your own, the views from the valley bottom drive are impressive, but a lot of people want to see more, hence the booming local industry in guided tours. An encampment of operators outside the Visitor Center offer a variety of scheduled or customized tour services throughout the day and night. Special photography tours depart before dawn or in the late afternoon to capture long valley shadows. Full moon evening tours are scheduled and wildlife tours depart at certain hours depending on the animals being sought. You can generally book a scheduled tour on the spot for the same day, although the valley does get crowded in the summer and tours are in great demand.

The elegantly expansive valley seems to stretch forever into time, the eons marked by the dominating monoliths, volcanic steeples, isolated buttes, and mesas. **The Mittens, Merrick Butte, Elephant Butte, Three Sisters, Camel Butte, Sentinel Mesa, Totem Pole,** and **Yei Bei Chei,** are just some of the massive, human-humbling, independent-standing, angular stone sentinels that form the archetypal landscape instantly recognizable as the Southwest.

The fascinating details incorporated in that image, found in the nooks and crannies of Monument Valley, encourage the allotment of a day or more for surveying prehistoric Indian ruins, pictographs, hidden arches, and sandstone pinnacles standing atop the desert landscape. If you only see one Southwestern sunset, this is the place to plant yourself on a rock escarpment and watch the shadows lengthen across the desert flats, the slanting rays of late-day sun coloring the rocky sandstone, enlightening a subtle range of pinkish hues, darkening into shades of red. A feverish glow radiates under a dimming blue sky, finally giving up the last daylight in bright bands of mauve, pink, purple, and red near the horizon, colors transposed from the rocks, now in silhouette.

Monument Valley is popular in summertime and there may be crowds around the Visitor Center, campground, and Goulding's Lodge. The busiest part of the scenic drive is the first mile or so, near the Visitor Center. After the sharp descent into the valley bottom there are different ways to go, so the traffic disperses. Still, you are not likely to have a transcendent private experience in here unless you arrange for some sort of guided tour into the hinterlands of the tribal park. The park's popularity and the lack of extensive accommodations in the area means you should not count on a last minute reservation at Goulding's between May 15 and September 15. During this period it also gets extremely hot here (in the 100 degree range). Even if you're just going out for an hour or two on the scenic drive, carry water and food.

Springtime is beautiful in the desert, with wildflowers; fall is usually comfortably warm.

Navajo National Monument/Navajo Mountain

Twenty miles west of Kayenta on US 160, then nine miles north on AZ 564, is the largest of the prehistoric Indian pueblo-type ruins in Arizona, at **Navajo National Monument**, PO Box 3, Tonalea, AZ 86044, 602/672-2366 or 602/672-2367.

There is a Visitor Center with a small museum, a small but tasteful gift shop, and information on guided tours, which are the only way you can get close to the ruins in this park. The museum offers a free film on the Anasazi and artifacts, such as pottery, are on display.

A paved, half-mile trail from the Visitor Center leads to an overlook from which you can see the **Betatakin Ruins,** carved into a mammoth 450-foot-tall, 370-feet-wide, and 135-foot-deep alcove, set in a slender, steep-walled canyon. The only way you can visit the 135-room ruins is on a daily, ranger-guided, five-mile round-trip hike offered May through August, and limited to 20 people. The round-trip hike is scheduled to take five hours and entails a 700-foot descent from the 7,300-foot canyon rim. Bear in mind that what goes down must come up and you will have to hike that same distance back to the rim.

Keet Seel Ruins are open from late May to early September and can only be reached by a strenuous eight-mile trail from the monument's Visitor Center. Because of the fragile condition and remote location of the ruins only 20 hikers a day are allowed to visit them. A round-trip in a day is possible for strong hikers. You can also choose to camp near the isolated ruins and return the following day. Backcountry permits are required and are available at the Visitor Center. Arrangements can also be made there for a horseback trip with a Navajo guide. The horseback trips reach the ruins and return the same day.

Bring water and food along on any hikes in this area. Be sure to plan sufficiently ahead and make reservations. Although cancellations do occasionally occur on the day of each scheduled hike, the limited numbers of people allowed to view these ruins makes planning ahead a virtual necessity. Horseback trips are a little easier to secure on short notice, but numbers on these are also restricted.

Navajo Mountain, northwest of Navajo National Monument, is the tallest peak on the reservation at 10,388 feet, rising east of **Rainbow Bridge National Monument,** near the shore of the San Juan Arm of Lake Powell. The only road access is 13 miles west of AZ 564 on US 160, then northwest 12.5 miles on AZ 98 to a turn-off north on Tribal Route 16. Route 16 is paved for 13 miles, then turns to dirt for the balance of the 24-mile distance to the west side of the mountain or the 29 miles to the east side of it. You can hike to Rainbow Bridge National Monument from trailheads on either side of Navajo Mountain.

On the east side of Navajo Mountain, **Navajo Mountain Trading Post,** Tonalea, AZ 86044, offers guided horseback and hiking tours of Navajo Mountain and Rainbow Bridge National Monument. Backcountry permits issued by the Navajo Tribe are required for any off-road travel in this area and these are available by mail or in person from the **Navajo Parks & Recreation Department** (PO Box 663, Window Rock, AZ 86515, 602/871-7371, fax 602/871-7381) or in person from the Cameron Visitor Center, at the junction of US 89 and AZ 64, on the western edge of the Navajo Nation.

If you were to continue northwest on AZ 98 past the turn-off for Navajo Mountain, in 60 miles you would reach Page, Arizona.

Continuing west on US 160 leads instead to **Tuba City,** hardly a metropolis, though it does boast a population of more than 5,000 on the western edge of Navajoland. Situated 70 miles west of Kayenta on US 160, it's mainly a good place to get gas or groceries, have a meal, or spend a night, but there's really little to see and do in town.

Five miles west of town, on the north side of US 160, are some purported dinosaur tracks. Five miles beyond the dinosaur tracks is US 89. Fifteen miles south on US 89 is Cameron. From here, you can access the Grand Canyon to the west or Wupatki and Sunset Crater National Monuments and Flagstaff to the south.

Touring Hopiland

Tuba City does provide access to the western edge of **Hopiland.** In Tuba City turn south from US 160 on to AZ 264 which leads south and west for 40 miles across bare desert to Third Mesa. This is the start of the main Hopi settlements stretched along the two-lane highway for the next 40 miles or so to **Keams Canyon.**

Old Oraibi, thought to be the oldest continually occupied village in the United States, dating to 1100, is on **Third Mesa,** a short distance south of AZ 264. A lot of people think the Hopi people are descendants of the Anasazis and the stone houses clustered on the rim of the mesa here resemble nothing so much as the ancient ruins scattered all over the Southwest, except with 20th century people living in them. Several craft shops are found in dilapidated-looking structures in this tiny village.

Kykotsmovi is two miles east of the Old Oraibi turn-off on AZ 264. This is the site of the Tribal Government offices, which are a mile south of the highway. Several shops and a small grocery store are located in town and the **Hopi Civic Center** is just east of town on the highway. It's a community center, gymnasium, and the site for special events such as the **Reggae Inna Hopiland** shows, detailed below under Eco-Tours and Cultural Excursions.

Six miles east of Kykotsmovi on **Second Mesa** is the **Hopi Cultural Center**, a modern complex with a motel, restaurant, campground, and a museum featuring exhibits that explain aspects of the Hopi culture and way of life. The displays are circumspect. The Hopi continue to be publicly reticent to divulge certain features of their customs or beliefs. There are several craft shops in the Cultural Center complex and still more on the adjacent highway. Other shops are farther east on Second Mesa, in the villages of **Secakuku** or **Shungopavi**. Throughout all the Hopi villages private artisans often sell wares directly out of their homes. Look for a small sign in the front window.

Hopis are particularly recognized for silver overlay jewelry, enclosing polished stones behind intricately hand-cut silver silhouettes. You can also find rugs or cottonwood-carved kachina dolls representing Hopi spiritual beings, colorful woven sashes, hand-coiled pottery, and coiled baskets. Serious shoppers probably need to spend a few days here. Inquire locally about the finest crafts people and arrange personal visits for the best selections or custom-ordered work.

A good place to start is the **Hopi Arts and Crafts Silvercraft Cooperative Guild**, PO Box 37, Second Mesa, AZ 86043, 602/734-2463. This shop, next to the Hopi Cultural Center, represents the work of hundreds of Hopi artists, offering silver jewelry, weavings, baskets, pottery, and kachina dolls. You can usually see artisans at work here and make arrangements to meet them privately.

First Mesa is the location of **Walpi**, another very old Hopi village that appears to have developed organically out of the mesa rim and one that visitors are not permitted to enter without a guide. Half-hour tours leave from a Visitor Center outside this village that has never been hooked up to running water or electricity. Craft work is often offered for sale by villagers. For information about tours or this tiny, 30-person village, phone 602/737-226 or 602/737-2670.

Keams Canyon anchors the eastern edge of Hopiland. It has a motel, restaurant, trading post and federal government offices. The modern town is seemingly made of trailers and is lacking any charm whatsoever.

Keams Canyon Arts & Crafts, PO Box 607, Keams Canyon, AZ 86024, 602/738-2295, offers a wide variety of souvenirs and also has a back room with extremely high quality Indian goods.

For information on Hopi ceremonies phone the **Hopi Indian Agency** in Keams Canyon, 602/738-2228. For information about the Hopi Villages contact the tribal headquarters, **Hopi Tribe**, PO Box 123, Kykotsmovi, AZ 86039, 602/734-2441.

Villages tend to have their own sets of rules in addition to the tribal rules and these are generally posted just outside each village. In some cases, such as when visiting Walpi, this means you cannot enter the village without a local guide. For specific information the phone numbers for each village are given above, under the introduction to The Navajo Nation & Hopiland.

Adventures

Where backcountry activities on Navajo land are allowed, permits and fees are required. Information is available from **Navajo Parks & Recreation Department**, PO Box 308, Window Rock, AZ 86515, 602/871-6645 or 602/871-6646. The office is next to the zoo. Permits are available by mail or in person and there is a walk-in permit station at the **Cameron Visitor Center**, south of Cameron Trading Post on US 89 at the junction with AZ 64.

On Foot

Rock climbing and off-trail hiking are prohibited on the Navajo Reservation. In many places, loose, fragile rock and unfamiliar terrain may make climbing and hiking hazardous.

If you get a permit at the Visitor Center and hire a Navajo guide, you can hike through Canyon de Chelly National Monument and even camp overnight within the canyon. Ranger-led hikes are also offered by the center in the summer. Reservations are accepted.

In Canyon de Chelly summer weather is quite hot. Bring water, insect repellent and wear a hat. Winters can be snowy and cold. Early spring is usually wet. May-June and September-October are the best months for hikers.

The only hiking you can do on your own in Canyon de Chelly is the **White House Ruin Trail**. The trailhead is at the White House Overlook, six miles east of the Visitor Center on the South Rim Drive. The trail descends 500 feet in a mile and a half to White House Ruin, an Anasazi site containing remnants of more than 50 rooms and several kivas.

Hiking without a licensed guide is not permitted in Monument Valley. Guided hiking tours in Monument Valley, Mystery Valley and Hunts Mesa are offered by **Fred's Adventure Tours**, PO Box 310308, Mexican Hat, UT 94531, 801/739-4294. Otherwise, inquire of the local tour operators around the Visitor Center for hiking guide services by the hour or extended overnight backpack trips. A number of these operators are listed below, under Jeeping.

At Navajo National Monument the eight-mile hike to **Keet Seel Ruins** offers an overnight backpack trip through Keet Seel Canyon to Arizona's largest Anasazi ruin. Elevation change is 700 feet from the 7,000-foot canyon rim to the ruins below and most of this change occurs in the first mile from the Visitor Center. The majority of the trail follows the canyon bottom and is considered easy. It is open from late May to early September and access is limited to 20 people per day. Reservations may be made as far as two months in advance through the Visitor Center. There is a primitive campground near the 160-room ruins, but you should bring your own water. Any water found in this area would need to be treated before consumption.

Ranger-guided hikes to Navajo National Monument's **Betatakin Ruins** are detailed above, under Touring.

Provided you have the appropriate permits, hiking and backpacking are permitted around **Navajo Mountain** or to **Rainbow Bridge National Monument**. To reach the trailheads follow the directions from AZ 98 (see above). The east fork of the road leads to the Navajo Trading Post and the trail from there to Rainbow Bridge is 14 miles one-way. If you start on the west side of Navajo Mountain you can drive as far as the **Rainbow Lodge Ruins**. The trail from there is 12 miles one-way to the National Monument. You can't camp at Rainbow Bridge, but you can camp out along the trails, which are poorly marked and unmaintained. A topographical map is recommended if you do not have a Navajo guide. No services are available anywhere along either trail.

The trail from Rainbow Lodge is considered the classic hike to Rainbow Bridge and is the route used by most guided trips. Allow at least two days for the round-trip hike which starts at an elevation of 6,300 feet, in the shadow of Navajo Mountain, and descends to 3,300 feet at Rainbow Bridge. The canyon country is rugged and the trail is not well-marked. Many hikers take three days to complete this trip.

The trail from the east side of Navajo Mountain is longer, less-used and even rougher, skirting the northern edges of Navajo Mountain and the red rock canyons between the mountain and Lake Powell.

Four Corners School of Outdoor Education, PO Box 78, East Route, Monticello, UT 84535, 801/587-2156, offers a six-night hiking tour with llamas in mid-September, called "Stories From Navajo Bridge & Rainbow Mountain." The trip covers a 30-mile hike around and through side canyons on rough trails with significant changes in elevation. Llamas carry the gear. As you circle the base of Navajo Mountain and explore side canyons stretching to Rainbow Bridge, an archaeologist-naturalist guide team directs discussions emphasizing the natural and cultural history of Navajo Mountain, an area that has figured into Navajo mythology and legend for thousands of years.

The **Antelope Creek Canyon** area south of Page off AZ 98, also known as **Corkscrew Canyon**, offers rugged unmaintained trails through marble-walled canyon country for experienced hikers. Hiking permits are available at the **Lee Chee Chapter House**, three miles southwest of Antelope Creek Canyon on Tribal Route 20.

By Horse

Two Navajo-run stables offer horseback trips in Canyon de Chelly. You can also ride your own horse if you hire a Navajo guide to travel with you. Information is available from the Visitor Center or the following outfitters:

> **Justin's Horse Rentals**, PO Box 881, Chinle, AZ 86503, 602/674-5678, is located near the start of the South Rim Drive and offers guided horseback trips by the hour or multi-day, overnight pack trips.
>
> **Twin Trail Tours**, PO Box 1716, Window Rock, AZ 86515, 602/674-5985, offers trips into Canyon del Muerto, including full-day trips featuring a 700-foot descent into the canyon and visits to such sites as Mummy Cave, Standing Cow Ruin, and Antelope House Ruin. Overnight pack trips are available.

Horseback trips into other parts of Navajoland are offered by the following outfitters:

Bigman's Horseback Tours, Kayenta, AZ 86033, 602/677-3219, offers a variety of trips in the areas around Mitchell Butte, Mystery Valley, Rain God Mesa, and Big Chief, all south of Monument Valley.

Ed Black's Horseback/Monument Valley Trailrides, PO Box 155, Mexican Hat, UT, 84531-0155, 801/739-4285 or 800/551-4039, offers customized horseback trips for four to 25 riders in Monument Valley, Mystery Valley, Hunts Mesa, and Horse Canyon.

With Navajo guides you explore these areas for an hour, a day or on camping trips lasting up to five days, riding through ancient Anasazi and Navajo lands.

On longer trips the guides lead you to remote places visited by few non-Indians where broken pottery shards litter the ground beneath boulders packed with petroglyphs, while coyotes howl at night in the moon shadows of the monoliths.

This is a Navajo-run company. Two or more guides accompany each trip. Overnight packages include food, sleeping bags, and tents (if you bring your own gear there is a dramatic difference in price). A truck meets the group nightly with supplies and food. Trips are offered year-round.

Triple Heart Ranch Tours, Mexican Springs Trading Post, Mexican Springs, NM 87320, 505/733-2377, offers horseback trips in the vicinity of Mexican Springs, the Chuska Mountains, Chinle, Rough Rock, Kayenta, and Monument Valley.

Don Donnelly Stables, 6100 Kings Ranch Road, Gold Canyon, AZ 85219, 602/982-7822 or 800/346-4403, runs trips exploring the beauty of Arizona and Utah from the comfort of a well-made western saddle, including a Monument Valley ride offered in spring and fall. The trip starts with airport pick-up in Gallup and features comfortable camps set up with spacious tents, cots, toilets, hot showers, a dinner tent, gourmet chef, and evening entertainment. Indians and ranchers sometimes drop by to share stories around the campfire. Gear and equipment are transported by four-wheel-drive truck.

Rainbow Trails & Tours, PO Box 7218, Shonto, AZ 86045, 602/672-2397, offers horseback trips to Rainbow Bridge National Monument.

On Wheels

The Navajo Tribe asks that visitors please restrict travel to designated trails and established routes. Travel by four-wheel-drive vehicles, dune buggies, jeeps, and motorcycles is prohibited on backcountry roads.

JEEPING & FOUR-WHEEL-DRIVE TRIPS

Other than hiking or horseback riding with an Indian guide, a four-wheel-drive tour is the only way to see the bottom of Canyon de Chelly. Most people take the organized, guided tours in large, open-sided, almost amphibious, jeep/trucks. These are able to easily negotiate the boggy low spots and deceptive sandy washes containing quicksand and other obstacles that typically challenge travellers on the canyon bottom.

You can drive your own four-wheel-drive vehicle if you procure a permit from the Visitor Center and hire a Navajo guide to ride along with you. Contact the Canyon de Chelly Visitor Center for information.

Thunderbird Tours, at Thunderbird Lodge, offers year-round, half-day or full-day tours of Canyon de Chelly and Canyon del Muerto in heavy-duty, six-wheel, four-wheel-drive touring vehicles. These are commanded by knowledgeable Navajo guides who know their way around the canyons' quicksand and muck. The guides point out deep red walls, natural monuments of sculpted sandstone, steep cliffs, ancient dwellings built in seemingly inaccessible caves, and the hand and toe holds by which these sites were reached. The tour takes you close to such sites as Mummy Cave and Antelope House Ruin.

Four-wheel-drive vehicle tours in Monument Valley and other areas generally inaccessible otherwise are offered by the following tour companies:

Goulding's Tours, PO Box 1, Monument Valley, UT 84536, 801/727-3231, fax 801/727-3344, offers half-day or full-day tours with Navajo drivers well-versed in cultural, geological, and historical information. Tours are scheduled March 15 through October and are available on request during winter months.

Golden Sands Tours, PO Box 458 Kayenta, AZ 86033, 602/697-3684, operates jeep tours of Hunts Mesa, Hoskinnii Mesa, and Monument Valley.

Tours of the Big Country, PO Box 309, Bluff, UT 84512, 801/672-2281, offers vehicle tours of Monument Valley.

Crawley's Monument Valley Tours, PO Box 187, Kayenta, AZ 86033, 602/697-3463, offers vehicle tours of Monument Valley, Mystery Valley and Hunts Mesa.

Totem Pole Guided Tours, PO Box 360306, Monument Valley, UT 84536, 801/727-3230, offers vehicle tours of Monument Valley, Mystery Valley, Hunts Mesa, Poncho House, Paiute Farms, and Hoskinnii Mesa.

Navajo Guided Tours, PO Box 36056, Monument Valley, UT 84536-0375, offers vehicle tours of Monument Valley and Mystery Valley.

Jackson's Guided Tours, PO Box 360375, Monument Valley, UT 84536-0375, offers vehicle tours of Monument Valley, Mystery Valley and Poncho House.

Bennett Guided Tours, PO Box 360285, Monument Valley, UT 84536, 801/727-3283, offers vehicle tours of Monument Valley and Mystery Valley.

Jeep Tours/Roland C. Dixon, PO Box 131, Kayenta, AZ 86033, 800/377-9370, offers jeep tours of Monument Valley.

MOUNTAIN BIKING

Backcountry mountain biking is prohibited on both reservations, but there are still some pretty good bike routes.

The rim drives at **Canyon de Chelly** are well-suited to biking. A round-trip on either drive from the Visitor Center runs about 40 miles. On the South Rim Drive, at the end of the paved road near the Spider Rock Overlook, the dirt **Tribal Route 7** continues for 35 miles to Tribal Route 12, six miles north of Window Rock.

In the Chuska Mountains, **Tribal Route 12** from Tsaile to Window Rock is a 52-mile stretch of paved road through mountainous terrain, fishing lakes, and pine-studded high country.

The **Monument Valley Loop Road** covers 17 miles one way over sandy, dusty terrain mostly in the valley bottom, but with some short, steep climbs.

The nine-miles of **AZ 564** between US 160 and Navajo National Monument are all uphill to the Visitor Center, but there are lots of trees and shady spots for cool rest stops overlooking scenic Tsegi Canyon.

Tribal Route 16 north from AZ 98 in western Navajoland to Rainbow Lodge, covers 40 miles to Navajo Mountain and Lake Powell. A camping permit would be needed from Navajo Parks & Recreation Department (PO Box 663, Window Rock, AZ 86515, 602/871-7371, fax 602/871-7381) for overnight travel in this area.

You might not be able to gain access to certain villages with a bicycle, but the route from Tuba City through Hopiland on **AZ 264** to US 191 is a good moderate one for a bike rider. There's not much shade and two-wheelers will have to share the narrow road with motorized traffic, but there are several motels and free campgrounds in Hopiland so it's possible to make a multi-day road ride out of the 120-mile stretch.

On Water

The Navajo tribe operates 12 major fishing lakes. All are open to fishing year-round unless otherwise noted. Among the ones reported to be the best are the following:

- **Ganado Lake** is two miles east of Ganado on AZ 264 then a mile north on Indian Route 27. Camping is permitted but there are no facilities.
- **Tsaile Lake**, just south of Navajo Community College in Tsaile, offers fishing for bass, catfish, and trout.
- **Wheatfields Lake**, 10 mile south of Tsaile on Tribal Route 12 is a popular lake for rainbow and cutthroat trout fishing.
- **Whiskey Lake**, five miles south of Wheatfields Lake, is stocked with rainbow and cutthroat trout, open May 1 to November 30.
- **Asaayi and Berland Lakes**, off Tribal Route 12 between Wheatfields Lake and Window Rock, and **Chuska Red Lake**, north of Gallup off US 666 in New Mexico, are stocked with channel and warm water catfish.
- Try **Morgan Lake**, east of Shiprock off US 64, which is near the mammoth Four Corners Power Plant, a coal-burning, smoke-belching behemoth. The plant tends to detract from the wilderness experience, but not from the trophy-size largemouth bass.
- **Many Farms Lake**, 14 miles north of Chinle, off US 191, might be a better bet for peace and quiet. You can fish for channel catfish and largemouth bass.
- **The Navajo Adventurers**, c/o Anthony Lee, PO Box 124, Bloomfield, NM 87413, 505/632-3893, specializes in personalized, step-on fishing guide services in the Carrizo, Chuska, Lukachukai, and Beautiful Mountains east of Canyon de Chelly. This means you provide the vehicle and Mr. Lee rides along, imparting his local wisdom, directing you toward views spreading as far away as Navajo Mountain or the San Francisco Peaks, pointing out scenery that might otherwise go unnoticed, and leading you straight to where the fish are biting. All trips are customized to the client's specifications.

A permit is required for fishing any lakes or streams under jurisdiction of the Navajo Nation. These and information on fees and dates, as well as boating regulations, are available from **Navajo Fish & Wildlife Office**, PO Box 1480, Window Rock, AZ 86515, 602/871-6451 or 602/871-6452. You don't need a state license to fish on the Navajo Reservation, only the Navajo-issued one.

Considering the size of the Navajo reservation there are relatively few places offering information on fishing, boating or permits. Use the following sources:

Lakeside Store Wheatfields, PO Box 2309, Window Rock, AZ 86515, 602/724-3262.

Fed Mart Store, PO Box 269, Window Rock, AZ 86515, 602/871-4724.

K-Mart Store #7361, 1312 West I-40 Frontage Road, Gallup, NM 87301, 505/722-7261.

Swift's Sporting Goods, 1725 South 2nd Street, Gallup, NM 87301, 505/863-9331.

Wal-Mart, 1308 West Metro, Gallup, NM 87301, 505/722-2296.

Wal-Mart, 700 Mike's Pike Boulevard, Winslow, AZ 86047, 602/289-4641.

Ross Sporting Goods, 204 West Main, Farmington, NM 87401, 505/325-1062.

Zia Sporting Goods, 500 East Main, Farmington, NM 87401, 505/327-6004.

Four Corners Windsurfing, PO Box 751, Fruitland, NM 87406, 505/598-6688.

Kirtland Pawn Shop, PO Box 166, Kirtland, NM 87417, 505/598-6969.

Handy's Bait & Tackle, 504 Aztec Boulevard, Aztec, NM 87410, 505/ 334-9114.

Bonds & Bonds, PO Box 640, Shiprock, NM, 87420, 505/368-4448.

City Market, PO Box FF, Shiprock, NM 87420, 505/368-4248.

Copper Village Development Corp., Sheep Springs Trading Post, **Sheep Springs,** NM 87364, 505/732-4211.

Tsaile Trading Post, PO Box 66, Tsaile, AZ 86556, 602/724-3397.

Kayenta Trading Post, PO Box 175, Kayenta, AZ 86003, 602/697-3541.

CSWTA Inc., Environmental Consultants, PO Box 790, Tuba City, AZ 602/283-4323.

Cow Springs Trading Post, Tonalea, AZ 86004, 602/283-5377.

Red Barn Trading Post, PO Box 245, Sanders, AZ 86512-0245, 602/688-2762.

Four Corners School of Outdoor Education (East Route, Monticello, UT 84535, 801/587-2859 or 801/587-2156) offers a week-long river trip in mid-May on the San Juan River, led by a Navajo biologist who interprets the meaning of the natural communities along the river to the Navajo people. Part of this trip is devoted to assisting the Navajo people in the ongoing study to identify and record non-native plants and animals that live in the riparian zone along the river.

The Navajo Natural Heritage Program, associated with The Nature Conservancy, is studying the ribbons of precious riparian habitat found along the river and its tributary creeks as part of an effort to protect native species and habitats found in otherwise austere country. While drifting the San Juan River in mid-May, participants help assess the changing ecological relationships caused by invasion of non-native flora and fauna.

Eco-Travel & Cultural Excursions

Dances, festivals, rodeos, and tribal fairs are among the seasonal cultural events to be found in those areas.

Navajo Nation Fair, 602/871-6478, held in Window Rock in early September, is billed as the World's Largest American Indian Fair. Although the people who run the Gallup Inter-Tribal Ceremonial might dispute that claim, this is undeniably a big event, attracting 200,000 participants and visitors during its five-day run, including Navajo people from 110 far-flung, big and mostly little communities spread across the 26,000-square-mile reservation.

Activities at this over-sized county fair include a free beef brisket barbecue dinner for 8,000 guests, a Saturday morning parade, animal exhibits, carnival rides, rodeos, nightly country-western concerts featuring nationally-known acts, traditional Indian song and dance contests, and Pow Wow dances performed by traditionally-outfitted Indians from all over North America, including members of the Navajo, Apache, Sioux, Taos, Tewa, Ute, and Zuni tribes.

A beauty pageant to crown Miss Navajo Nation is held and crowns are presented to Navajo beauty pageant royalty in the persons of Miss Teen Navajo and Miss Northern Navajo. Indian foods, such as mutton and frybread are available from vendors, mainly women wearing traditional clothing and jewelry. There's a contest for the best frybread. In addition, prize-winning pottery, jewelry, rugs, baskets, and paintings are displayed and offered for sale.

Also in Window Rock each October is a popular **Coyote Calling Contest**. For information contact Navajo Fish & Wildlife Department.

Shiprock Navajo Nation Fair, PO Box 1893, Shiprock, NM 87420, 505/368-5108, 505/368-4679 or 505/368-4892, also known as the **Northern Navajo Fair**, is the oldest Navajo tribal fair. It is held in the reservation's largest city during the first week in October to celebrate the harvest. The fair coincides with the an ancient Navajo healing ceremony: *The Night Way* or *Yei Bei Chei*, a nine-day chant. This complex, detailed ritual is usually held after the first frost and the public is permitted to view parts of the ceremony during the fair. Among the colorful rituals are *Two Yei's Come*, a Saturday afternoon dance, and masked *Yei Bei Chei Dancing*, starting on Saturday night and continuing until dawn on Sunday morning.

You can watch, but don't even think about taking photographs. "There is Absolutely No Pictures to be taken in the YEI BEI CHEI," according to tribal literature.

There's a free barbecue to open the fair on Thursday, a rodeo, an ongoing midway and carnival, 10K run, and a western dance. Other activities include social, as opposed to ceremonial, dancing and singing groups. You will also see Pow Wow contestants from all over the Navajo Nation and North America, outfitted in their best traditional attire. There are exhibits of livestock, arts and crafts, and there is an Indian Market where arts and crafts, as well as farm produce, are offered for sale. A big parade is held on Saturday morning, featuring local, regional, off-reservation, and national entries.

Other regional Navajo fairs, similar in style, though a bit smaller in size than the two above, include the following:

- **Western Navajo Fair**, 602/283-5452, held in Tuba City, AZ, in late October.
- **Southwestern Navajo Nation Fair**, held in Dilcon, AZ, 602/657-9244 or 602/657-3376.
- **Central Navajo Fair**, 602/647-5877, held in Chinle, AZ, near Canyon de Chelly, in August.
- In addition, there is a **Chinle Agency Navajo Song and Dance Pow Wow Festival**, 602/674-5201, extension 201, held each March.
- **Eastern Navajo Fair**, held in Crownpoint, NM, in July, 505/786-5841 or 505/786-5244.

Fairs and rodeos aside, there are aspects of Navajo and Hopi culture that are virtually impossible for an outsider to penetrate. It may be nearly impossible for an outsider to gather significant insights into Hopi culture, but Navajo religion and philosophy lecturers who may be able to help answer questions about Navajo society and its manners include the following:

Benny Silversmith, St. Michael's, AZ 86511, 602/871-7229.
Eddie Tso, PO Box 442, St. Michael's, AZ 86511, 602/871-6378 or 602/871-4531.

Herbert Bennally, Navajo Community College, Shiprock, NM 87420, 505/368-5291.

Carl N. Gorman, PO Box 431, Window Rock, AZ 86515, 602/729-2218.

Andrew Becenti, Navajo Academy, 1200 West Apache, Farmington, NM 87401, 505/366-6571.

Wilson Arnold, Navajo Community College, Tsaile, AZ, 602/724-3311.

Alfred Yazzie, Rough Rock Demonstration School, PO Box 217, Chinle, AZ 86503, 602/728-3311.

Steve Darden, 2160 North 4th Street, Flagstaff, AZ 86004, 602/536-2911.

Ed McCombs, Navajo Community College, Tsaile, 602/724-3311, organizes personalized Navajo culture tours. For example, a trip combining three days hiking and two nights camping in the Chuska Mountains, focusing on native healing plants and Navajo lore, might be arranged.

Special interest tour guides and other useful institutions are listed below.

Four Corners School of Outdoor Education (PO Box 78, East Route, Monticello, UT 84535, 801/587-2156) offers a 10-day study-tour in April, July and August called "Native Cultures of the Southwest." The tour focuses on Hopi, Ute, and Navajo cultures, explores mythology and native arts and includes visits with educators and tribal elders. The group attends dances and visits with moccasin makers, basket weavers, potters, kachina makers, weavers, buckskin makers and others. This trip provides an unusual opportunity to learn legends and gain understanding of aspects of Indian culture that would be impossible without meeting these people in their homes, among their families, perhaps while munching on piki bread prepared with bare hands and cooked on a 400 degree sandstone slab.

Canyonlands Field Institute, PO Box 68, Moab, UT 84532, 801/259-7750, offers two van tours with motel accommodations, that include the Navajo and Hopi Reservations. Tours begin and end in Bluff, Utah.

An "Ancient Skywatchers: Archaeo-Astronomy" tour runs for five days in late September, around the time of the Autumnal Equinox, and studies how astronomy can teach about ancient people. The trip includes a pre-dawn visit to Hovenweep National Monument to observe sunrise alignments at the site. A full day at Chaco Canyon includes stops at a famous pictograph of a thousand-year-old supernova that was also recorded in China. There's a stop at Aztec Ruins National Monument to consider the Great Kiva. Driving across the Chuska Mountains to the Navajo Museum at Tsaile allows time for a discussion of astronomical features of hogans, distinctive landforms, and sand paintings, followed by a day exploring Canyon de Chelly's prehistoric and modern Indian sites.

The Hopi tour, offered in May, runs for three-days and two-nights and explores Hopi culture, history, and religion, along with Anglo influences and other contemporary issues. Tribal members explain Hopi history and life ways, as well as the techniques and symbolism incorporated into renowned Hopi silver, pottery, and kachina carving.

CFI also offers a four-day, three-night "Monument Valley Photography" tour twice a year in March and October. The tour is recommended for intermediate photographers and includes intense field sessions at Hovenweep National Monument, the Goosenecks of the San Juan, and Monument Valley. Tours are run with a Navajo guide from a base at Recapture Lodge in Bluff, UT. Overnight film processing is available. You should be prepared to hike 0ne to five miles with camera gear.

Special Expeditions, 720 Fifth Avenue, New York, NY 10019, 212/765-7740 or 800/762-0003, fax 212/265-3770, offers a 13-day tour of the Grand Canyon, focusing on Anasazi, Navajo and Hopi cultures, and ending in Monument Valley. Groups are limited to a maximum of 10, who explore the mystique of the Southwest through prehistoric ruins, geologic wonderlands, arts and crafts, and traditions of contemporary Pueblo and Navajo people. Trips are scheduled in May, September, and October, and include transportation and accommodations in lodges or inns.

Western Indian Tours, 11431 North 23rd Street, Phoenix, AZ 85028, 602/992-4845, fax 602/482-2256, operates cultural and scenic tours of Navajoland, including Monument Valley and Canyon de Chelly. Tours begin in Phoenix, Albuquerque or Las Vegas.

As for the far more secretive Hopis, people find unusual things on their desert mesas. Some find inspiration or spirituality in the remote open spaces and ancient villages. Others lay claim to renowned Hopi arts or observe traditional ceremonies, but it may be safe to say that no one ever expected to find dreadlocks in Hopiland; these appear in leonine profusion during irregularly scheduled **Reggae Inna Hopiland** shows.

Jamaican reggae is urban-bred, street-wise island music. The Hopi are private and traditional-minded, nothing if not laid-back, land-locked dirt farmers in far-off northeastern Arizona. Yet the world's top reggae bands have been quietly slipping into Hopiland to play since 1984. As many as 10 shows are scheduled yearly, featuring groups such as Third World, or the late Bob Marley's band, The Wailers. Freddie McGregor, a Jamaican mega-star, traveled more than a thousand miles out of his way by bus and accepted a reduced fee to play Hopiland in between shows in Los Angeles and New Orleans.

Hopis greet the Jamaicans with tribal drummers chanting in ancient rhythms. Traditionally-clothed Hopi dancers move on to the floor, stepping to the beat of this prehistoric Indian reggae as it fills the Hopi Community Center, actually a gymnasium.

Visiting musicians, many sporting the long, dark tangles of hair known as dreadlocks, peer over stacked equipment from the small stage, entranced. Hypnotic chants and steady drumming energize the dancers, their colorful feather and bone garments trailing in sweeping arcs.

Black Jamaicans, weather-worn Hopis, and a few lucky pale faces coalesce: racial and cultural differences vanish in the moment.

"One love," as the Jamaicans might say, "one destination."

A typical inter-cultural reggae show, such as one that featured Sugar Minott of Kingston, Dread Flimstone of Los Angeles, and the Wailing Coyotes, a local group comprised of Hopi and Navajo musicians, will draw 1,000 or more on a weekend. More than 500 people materialized out of the desert to see McGregor on a week-night. Even the biggest international reggae bands play Hopiland for fees far lower than they could command in a big city. Why?

Outside the community center before a show, horses grazed in the parking lot. The moon rose over the nearest mesa where lights twinkled amid sandstone outcrops on the hillside. It was warm, quiet, a conversation could be carried by whispers.

"We love the music," said a tribal member, "and the musicians appreciate an opportunity to be in this special place."

During a first set by Maxi Priest, Freddie McGregor sat smiling on a folding chair in the middle of the gym. While the audience swayed and danced, children flowed around and over him, scaling his knees and fingering his tight dreadlocks. Many of the young-sters wore long hair, too.

"We play for the love of the people," McGregor said later, "not for the money. These people, they don't have a lot and we used to be there. This is sort of a gift. And we are appreciated here."

"These Hopis were moved here, forced here, and we Jamaicans were all slaves. We come to Hopiland because of the spirit of the people. The Hopi people and our people share the struggle. How would you like it if someone came into your home and tell you to move, if you were pushed out here to this dirt? We see everything on tour, the good, the bad and the evil, and I tell you something, I'd like to come out here for a week, it's so quiet and peaceful. Hopiland is the best stop on the tour, one of the best places to play.

"We know the money isn't here, but the love of the music is. It's an experience, for the love and the culture."

For Reggae Inna Hopiland information contact the Tribal Office (PO Box 123, Kykotsmovi, AZ 86039, 602/734-2441).

For more traditional dancing in Hopiland, the Hopi practice their beliefs through the year with different ceremonies for various phases of the annual cycle. Visitors are welcome. The Hopi believe the ceremonies are intended for the benefit of all people although, while on the reservation, remember that you are guests of the Hopi and act accordingly.

Some of the more popular ceremonies or dances, are the **Social Dances** held in January and February, the **Bean Dance** held in February, and the **Kachina Dances**, held throughout the summer, ending with the **Home Dance** in August. The **Snake Dance** and **Flute Dance** are held in August in alternating years in Shungopavi and Mishongovi only. The **Flute Dance** is also held in Walpi every two years. Typically rhythmic drumming and chanting set the pace for the elaborate steps performed by dancers wearing intricately feathered and beaded costumes, often with masks or painted headgear.

Where to Stay & Eat

Window Rock Accommodations & Restaurants

Navajo Nation Inn, US 264, PO Box 1687, Window Rock, AZ 86515, 602/871-4108, fax 602/871-5466, offers modern rooms and suites decorated in a utilitarian Southwestern/Navajo-style and there's a heated pool. A restaurant and coffee shop serve traditional Navajo dishes, including Navajo tacos, blue corn pancakes, and frybread, plus American food.

Step-on tour guides are also available here. You provide and operate your own vehicle. A guide comes along to narrate a tour of the Window Rock area, Hubbell Trading Post or Canyon de Chelly. **Paulina Watchman**, PO Box 278, Navajo, NM, 505/777-2703, offers B&B accommodations or straight room rentals.

Los Verdes, 602/871-5105, in St. Michael's three miles west of Window Rock, serves Mexican combination plates stuffed sopapillas, chimichangas, menudo, chile rellenos, and taco salads. It also has American, Mexican, and Navajo sandwiches.

Chinle Accommodations & Restaurants

Canyon de Chelly Motel, PO Box 295, Chinle, AZ 86503, 602/674-5875, is a comfortable, modern motel with 68 rooms, a heated indoor pool, and a clean coffee shop, the **Junction Restaurant**, 602/674-8443. The restaurant offers three meals a day, including Mexican food, Navajo tacos, sandwiches, burgers, and steaks.

Thunderbird Lodge, PO Box 548, Chinle, AZ 86503, 602/674-5841 or 602/674-5842, is the classic place to stay at Canyon de Chelly, offering 71 modern motel rooms in standard and deluxe categories, as well as 0ne- to four-person suites.

The lodge's restaurant, **Thunderbird Lodge Cafeteria**, offers daily lunch and dinner specials or a choice of five lunch entrees served cafeteria-style. It's located in the original trading post built here in 1896 and features an all-Navajo staff. The lodge also has a gift shop and a rug room with a complete line of Indian jewelry, crafts, and Navajo rugs.

Thunderbird Tours, based at the lodge, offers year-round tours of Canyon de Chelly and Canyon del Muerto.

Holiday Inn Canyon de Chelly, PO Box 1879, Chinle, AZ 8653, 602/674-5000 or 800/465-4329, features 120 air-conditioned rooms, a heated pool, and a gift shop.

Garcia's, in the Holiday Inn, serves three meals a day from a menu that includes a blue cornmeal breaded rainbow trout with pinyon nut butter, lamb stew, vegetable lasagna, Mexican food, steaks, burgers, and sandwiches.

Coyote Pass Hospitality, PO Box 91, Tsaile, AZ 86556, 602/724-3383 or 602/674-9655, offers B&B accommodations near Navajo Community College, the Chuska Mountains, and Canyon de Chelly. It's not your typical B&B. Guests are accommodated in a dirt-floor hogan and the restrooms are situated in an outhouse.

This may be the closest experience you can find on the reservation of what typical living conditions are like for many of the Navajo people. Tours of the Navajo Nation and cultural consulting are available.

Kayenta/Monument Valley Accommodations & Restaurants

Navajo Trails Motel, Teec Nos Pas, AZ, 602/674-3618, offers humble motel rooms that might serve in a pinch (depending on how sleepy you are).

Holiday Inn, PO Box 307, Kayenta, AZ 86033 602/697-3221, features 160 rooms, a gift shop, and the **Wagon Wheel Restaurant,** serving three meals a day, including Navajo specials, frybread with honey, steaks, salmon and vegetable lasagna, and sandwiches.

Wetherill Inn, PO Box 175, Kayenta, AZ 86033, 602/697-3231 or 602/697-3232, fax 602/697-3233, offers 50 air-conditioned rooms a block north of midtown Kayenta.

Golden Sands Cafe, 602/697-3684, next to the Wetherill Inn, serves Navajo and American specials and possibly the only Oriental food on the reservation. The cafe's open for three meals a day.

Goulding's Lodge, PO Box 1, Monument Valley, UT, 84536, 801/727-3231, is just north of the Arizona-Utah border on the west side of US 163, three miles west of Monument Valley Tribal Park.

Established in 1924 by Harry Goulding and his wife, Mike, Gouldings's has grown from a small trading post housed in a tent, into the only full-service, year-round motel in Monument Valley. The hillside property includes 62 rooms with balconies, an indoor heated pool, a gift shop open March through October, and a campground with RV hook-ups.

Goulding's Stagecoach Dining Room serves three meals daily, including traditional Navajo and American food, Mexican food made with blue corn meal, huevos rancheros, roast leg of lamb and salads.

Goulding's Museum & Trading Post, adjacent to the motel complex, is housed in the original trading post. It includes exhibits of Anasazi artifacts and historical photos. And it contains motion picture memorabilia from the Gouldings' long-time association with director John Ford, actor John Wayne and others who trekked out here to work among the sage and monumental stone backdrops on such classic films as *Stagecoach* and *Fort Apache.* A set from *She Wore A Yellow Ribbon* is on display. The museum is open April through October.

The lodge offers nightly showings of a 20-minute multi-media photo and sound production, *Earth Spirit,* describing the creation of Monument Valley. Monument Valley and Mystery Valley tours, escorted by Navajo guides, are available.

Anasazi Inn at Tsegi Canyon, Kayenta, AZ 86033, 602/697-3793, is situated 10 miles west of Kayenta on US 160 at the junction with AZ 564, nine miles south of Navajo National Monument. Fifty-two modest rooms overlook scenic red rocks and undulating, rugged cacti-studded terrain in Tsegi Canyon. A restaurant serves homemade soups, pies, breakfast all day, American food, and Navajo specialties. There is a gift shop.

Tuba City Accommodations & Restaurants

Tuba Motel & Trading Post, Main Street, PO Box 247, Tuba City, AZ, 86045, 602/283-4545 or 602/283-4546, is a modern motel decorated in Indian-style. It includes the Mexican-American **Pancho's Family Restaurant**.

The classic, old-time **Tuba Trading Post**, a two-story octagon made of native stone in the early 1900s, is next door. The store carries groceries, snacks, souvenirs, hand-made rugs, jewelry, and pottery.

Greyhills Inn, 60 Warrior Drive, Tuba City, AZ 86045, 602/283-6271, extension 36, is operated by Navajo hotel management students as a 32-room hostel with shared baths.

Tuba City Truckstop, 602/283-4975, on US 160, is open 24 hours a day, serving Navajo tacos and sandwiches, stews, burgers, and breakfast anytime.

Hopiland Accommodations & Restaurants

Hopi Cultural Center Restaurant and Motel, PO Box 67, Second Mesa, AZ 86043, 602/734-2401, is in the center of the Hopi universe at the Cultural Center. The motel contains 33 comfortable, standard rooms. A restaurant prepares, steaks, burgers, grilled cheese sandwiches and hot dogs, as well as traditional Hopi dishes such as blue corn pancakes, Chil-il ou gyava, a bean chile, or Nok Qui Vi, a stew of lamb and corn, hominy soup, Hopi tacos, and tostadas.

Keams Canyon Motel, PO Box 545, Keams Canyon, AZ 86043, 602/738-2297, has 20 modest rooms. You might want to look at one before you check-in.

Keams Canyon Cafe, 602/738-2296, on AZ 264 in Keams Canyon, is open till 9 PM week nights, but only until 6 PM on weekends, serving Navajo sandwiches, such as hot beef on frybread with onions and green chiles, barbecue beef ribs, Mexican and Oriental foods.

Camping

Fires are permitted only in grills, fireplaces or similar control devices. No open ground fires are permitted in campgrounds. Campers must provide their own firewood or charcoal. Please observe quiet hours from 11 PM to 6 AM at all camping areas.

Bring water and everything else you'll need. Most of the camping areas provide few facilities, although many do offer picnic tables and shaded sites.

Antelope Lake, located eight miles north of Pine Springs, AZ, 24 miles southwest of Window Rock via some rugged dirt roads, offers primitive camping but RVs are not recommended.

Summit Campground, eight miles west of Window Rock, is open year-round and can accommodate RVs, but has no facilities.

Ganado Lake, three miles northeast of Ganado, on Tribal Route 27, allows camping, but there are no facilities at the fishing lake.

Red Lake, 15 miles north of Window Rock on Tribal Route 12, allows primitive camping at the fishing lake.

Camp Asaayi Lake Campground is 11 miles northeast of Navajo, NM, and 35 miles north of Gallup off US 666 on a convoluted series of rough dirt roads, deep in the Chuska Mountains. Open year-round. RVs are not recommended due to the poor roads.

Washington Pass Campground is six miles northeast of Crystal, NM, on NM 134. The site is generally open year-round, depending on the road conditions in the winter. RVs can be accommodated.

Berland Lake Campground is a few miles north of Crystal, NM, and is usually open year-round depending on road conditions. No facilities are available and RVs are not advised to attempt the rugged dirt road to the campground.

Wheatfields Campground is 44 miles north of Window Rock, AZ and two miles south of Tsaile, AZ, off Tribal Route 12 and usually open year-round. RVs can be accommodated.

Tsaile Lake Campground is a half-mile west of Navajo Community College in Tsaile, AZ, on the northeastern edge of Canyon del Muerto at Canyon de Chelly National Monument.

Canyon de Chelly National Monument has a large campground with water and bathrooms. However, disconcerting posted signs are plastered all over Canyon de Chelly warning visitors not to leave valuables in sight in their car or at the campsite.

Many Farms Lake Campground is a mile south of Many Farms, AZ, 15 miles north of Chinle off US 191.

Morgan Lake, next to the Four Corners Power Plant in Fruitland, NM, 10 miles west of Farmington, allows camping, but there are no facilities available and the road is bad, so RVs are not recommended.

Mitten View Campground-Monument Valley, Monument Valley Tribal Park, PO Box 93, Monument Valley, UT 84536-0289, 801/727-3287. Located a half-mile from the Visitor Center, the 100-site campground generally fills up by late afternoon in the summer and reservations are accepted only for groups of 10 or more. Plan to check in early for a choice campsite.

The camping area offers little privacy. It is on a sloping promontory overlooking the spacious valley, Sentinel Mesa, West Mitten Butte, Merrick Butte, and East Mitten Butte. For an easily accessed vista, the panorama from the campground ranks highly among choice scenes to see from your tent in the soft, desert morning light. Showers and RV hook-ups available.

Navajo National Monument has a small, tree-shaded campground close to the Visitor Center with restrooms and water. Several spots are large enough to park an RV, though there are no hook-ups.

For additional information regarding campgrounds or backcountry camping on the Navajo Reservation contact **Navajo Parks & Recreation Department**, PO Box 308, Window Rock, AZ 86515, 602/871-6645, 602/871-6646 or 602/871-6647.

Camping is permitted anywhere on the Hopi Reservation, but there are no camping facilities. There are free campgrounds, essentially worn spots in the sagebrush, at **Oraibi Hill**, **Oraibi Wash**, and **Second Mesa**, adjacent to the parking lot at the Hopi Cultural Center. You can use the bathrooms at the Cultural Center if you camp at Second Mesa. Another possible camp site is **Keams Canyon Community Park**, which is the only one of these spots with water.

INDEX